Global Animation Theory

Global Animation Theory

International Perspectives at Animafest Zagreb

Edited by
Franziska Bruckner, Nikica Gilić, Holger Lang, Daniel Šuljić and Hrvoje Turković

BLOOMSBURY
NEW DELHI • LONDON • OXFORD • NEW YORK • SYDNEY

BLOOMSBURY INDIA
Bloomsbury Publishing India Pvt. Ltd
Second Floor, LSC Building No. 4, DDA Complex, Pocket C-6&7,
Vasant Kunj, New Delhi 110070

BLOOMSBURY, BLOOMSBURY ACADEMIC INDIA and the Diana logo are trademarks of Bloomsbury Publishing Plc

First published in India 2025
First published in the United States of America 2019
Paperback edition published 2020

A catalogue record for this book is available from the British Library.
A catalog record for this book is available from the Library of Congress.

ISBN: 978-93-61319-11-2

Typeset by RefineCatch Limited, Bungay, Suffolk
Printed in India by Manipal Technologies Limited, Manipal

To find out more about our authors and books visit www.bloomsbury.com and sign up for our newsletters

CONTENTS

Foreword ix
Giannalberto Bendazzi

Introduction xi
Franziska Bruckner, Nikica Gilić, Holger Lang, Daniel Šuljić and Hrvoje Turković

Section 1 Historical and Theoretical Approaches from International Animation Studies

1 Animation since 1980: A Personal Journey 3
Marcin Giżycki

2 Animation in the Gallery and the Gestalt: György Kovásznai and William Kentridge 11
Paul Wells

3 On Analogical Thinking: Jan Švankmajer's *Jabberwocky* and *Alice* 29
Mareike Sera

4 The Successful Chorus of 'The Second Wave': An Examination of Feminism's 'Manifesto' of Digital Art 51
Chunning Guo (Maggie)

5 Seeking Truth in Facts: Historicizing Chinese Animation 61
Olga Bobrowska

6 Austria Unlimited – Chances, Spirits and Limitations of a Small Production Environment 83
Holger Lang

7 Beyond Self-images: The Context and Development of Animated Documentaries, the Cornerstones of Modern Animation in Sweden 99
Midhat Ajanović-Ajan

Section 2 Case Studies from Around the World

8 Short Circuits: On the Impact of the Flipbook in the Work of Robert Breer 117
Edwin Carels

9 '. . . The Film Is Not About That': Notes on (Re)Reading *Tale of Tales* 143
Mikhail Gurevich

10 The Importance of Ranko Munitić's Work on the Zagreb School of Animation 163
Andrijana Ružić

11 Animation Experienced through Music: Tomislav Simović and the Zagreb School of Animation 177
Irena Paulus

12 The Puppet as Not-Puppet: The Notion of Puppet as 'Human in Theatrical Performance' in the Works of Barry Purves (the Case of *Screen Play*) 197
Fatemeh Hosseini-Shakib

13 Subversive Machinery: DIY Method in the Work of Julian Antonisz 213
Michał Bobrowski

14 Lynsey Martin: A Case Study of 1970s Australian Experimental Animation 233
Dirk de Bruyn

List of Contributors 253
Index 259

FOREWORD

Giannalberto Bendazzi

'But what does that all *mean*?', asked Samantha, after having examined a Joan Miró painting. The professor had answered that same question a thousand times. She was a patient person.

> You see the contrasts of the colours, and the balance of the structure, don't you? This is the painting's language. Relax and let it speak to you. Imagine you are watching a tropical sunset. You instinctively let the sunset speak to you. You recall many beautiful things you have experienced; you would like to have your boyfriend next to you. You are giving your meaning to the sunset. Other people give their own meanings, which are possibly the opposite of yours.

Moral: Samantha still lacked an art theory, while the professor had one.

What, then, is an art (in our case, an animation) theory?

Pragmatically – not philosophically – we could say that it is any intellectual structure that helps us to better appreciate and understand art (in our case, animation).

An art theory may be a recipe. Although you will barely find examples of a successful work of art created by abiding a written or unwritten law, artists have often obeyed precepts that they share among themselves: a religion, a political party's ideology, or a moral cause.

An art theory may be a viewers' guide, too. Barocco, Art Nouveau, Pop Art, are labels attached to some practitioners' common stylistic approaches.

An art theory may have a lot to do with market and marketing, audiences' tastes, or audiences' understanding. Mass communication is full of dos and don'ts, of rules and manuals that practitioners are supposed to learn by heart and follow through.

An art theory should not be mistaken with the aesthetics of a philosopher's system. The latter is consequential to a major mindset that contains ethics, metaphysics and so on, while a good art theory is a generalization based on the actual works. Italian *Neorealismo* is a good example for what I mean.

Few people have written about animation theory, or have written essays that posterity would later consider to be of theoretical interest for animation; the best ones are probably Ranko Munitić and Ülo Pikkov.

The one I most like – and the only prophetic one – was Élie Faure, who stated:

> You know, these animated drawings, still so barren, so stiff, so meagre, that are projected on the screen are like, if you will, the forms I imagine a child's graffiti drawn on a blackboard compared to Tintoretto's frescoes or Rembrandt's canvasses. Suppose that three or four generations of people are harnessed to the problem of animating these images in depth, not by surfaces nor lines, but by thicknesses and volumes; of modelling, by values and half-tones, a series of successive movements that by long practice would gradually become habit, almost a reflex, so that the artist comes to using it at his pleasure for drama or idyll, comedy or poetry, light or shade, forest, city, desert. Suppose an artist is so armed with the heart of Delacroix, the passion of Goya and the strength of Michelangelo; he will throw on the screen a cineplastic tragedy entirely his own, a kind of visual symphony so rich and so complex, opening, by its rush through time, perspectives of infinity and the absolute, which are both exalting by their mystery and more moving by their tangible reality than the sound in the symphonies of the greatest musicians. There, that is the distant future, which I believe in but which I do not know can be achieved.
>
> FAURE 1920: 36[1]

It actually did not take three or four generations, but eleven years. Alexandre Alexeieff and Claire Parker's *Night on Bald Mountain* was screened in 1933.

Until now the theoreticians have not been numerous, so I welcome this rank-strengthening book. The essays contained within not only scan historical and current trends from different academic and artistic perspectives, but also present the newest findings by the global animation studies community. The minds that have produced it are brilliant, the subject matter is ripe, and every year animation studies grow and expand.

I wish you all an enjoyable reading.

Reference

Faure, E. (1920). 'De la cinéplastique', *La Grande Revue*, CIV 1920 (11): 52–72.

[1] Translated by G. Bendazzi.

INTRODUCTION

Franziska Bruckner, Nikica Gilić, Holger Lang, Daniel Šuljić and Hrvoje Turković

What is *Global Animation Theory*? In the Foreword, Giannalberto Bendazzi defines an art theory as 'any intellectual structure that helps us to better appreciate and understand art (in our case, animation)'. This structure is an evolving interdisciplinary field. It includes different theories, methods and perspectives from research areas such as film, media and cultural studies or art history, but also technical and artistic approaches.

Worldwide animation studies have been rapidly expanding and progressing in recent years, catching up with the increasing spectrum of animated films. By giving space to this international discourse, *Global Animation Theory* is at the vanguard of an interaction involving historical and theoretical positions on animation.

This anthology is based on a selection of the most relevant and interesting presentations from the first three editions of the Symposium for Contemporary Animation Studies, Animafest Scanner. It offers detailed and diverse insights into the methodologies of contemporary animation studies, as well as topics relevant for today's study of animation. *Global Animation Theory* has given way to academic writing that is very open to the practical aspects of animation, with several contributors not only being established as animation scholars, but also as artists. This contact between practical and theoretical approaches to animation is closely connected to the host of Animafest Scanner, the World Festival of Animated Film Animafest Zagreb. The latter was established in 1972 and is the second-oldest animation festival in the world.

Global Animation Theory highlights various significant aspects of international animation studies by introducing the newest developments from different cultural backgrounds – some of them still unknown to the English-speaking community – to the international, academic and artistic audience. Expanded and put into a new context, this anthology allows a more reflective and thoughtful review of the presentations that support a substantial and lasting contribution to an international dialogue.

The book features two different sections: The first section includes 'Historical and Theoretical Approaches from International Animation Studies', beginning with the changing role of animation and animation studies over the course of the last forty years. The following essays present new theoretical approaches on of well-known filmmakers such as Jan Švankmajer or William Kentridge, as well as feminist positions on digital art. Additionally, the section gives an overview about less-known animation habitats in China, Austria and Sweden.

The second section, 'Case Studies from Around the World', consists of re-readings on famous artists, such as Robert Breer, Yuri Norstein and Barry Purves. Essays on the film historian and theorist Ranko Munitić as well as musician Tomislav Simović give an interesting insight into the vicinity of the famous Zagreb School of Animation. Finally, some experimental aspects of animation are investigated within the work of Polish filmmaker Julian Antonisz and Australian-based artist Lynsey Martin.

Historical and theoretical approaches from international animation studies

The first chapter of this section traces Marcin Giżycki's personal animation journey since 1980. As editor-in-chief of the ASIFA quarterly *Animafilm*, he published the now infamous definition on animation, which was agreed to at the Board's meeting, taking place at the Animafest Zagreb in the same year: 'The art of animation is the creation of moving images through the manipulation of all varieties of techniques apart from live action methods.' The author recounts the relevance of that definition today, as well as the way animated film has proceeded since that time.

Paul Wells explores the work of recently rediscovered Cold War Hungarian animator, György Kovásznai in comparison with the famous South African artist William Kentridge. The discussion addresses the individual works of both artists, and how this is understood as directly affiliated to art and art's culture, and animation's presence in the gallery context. Further, it will seek to situate both works within a broader understanding of the gestalt of 'The Animation Spectrum', and with the presence of animation both in the academic and the public sphere.

Mareike Sera's chapter addresses two films by renowned Czech animator Jan Švankmajer, by applying the philosophical technique of analogical reasoning. First, the phenomenon of analogy is discussed from an academic perspective, as well as its role for Czech Surrealism. The second part discusses analogical thinking in different contexts, by relating *Jabberwocky* (1971) to

George Bataille's *Story of the Eye* (Analogy I) and *Alice* (1988) to the philosophical work of Franco 'Bifo' Berardi (Analogy II).

Chunning Guo focuses on a study conducted by a group of women artists in the digital field during the 1970s and 1980s. Their leader was Lillian Schwartz and her 'manifesto' could be regarded as the beginning of cross-field (and cross-gender) cooperation in digital art. In the chapter this movement of women artists in digital art is called 'The Second Wave of Digital Art', and it includes cross-field cooperation, software explorations and deconstructions of classic artworks.

The correspondence of the film canon built by international festivals' recognition and top-down established cultural policies is discussed by Olga Bobrowska in Chapter 5. Using the example of the history of mainland Chinese animation between 1955 and 1989, a particular pattern in the festival circulation of Chinese films is observed: international successes with awards in Annecy, Zagreb, Cannes, Locarno, etc. of films like *Where Is Mama?* (1960) and Wan Laiming's *Havoc in Heaven* (1961–64) confirmed their appreciation that had been received on a national level.

Holger Lang gives an overview about the animation scene in Austria, which had long been overshadowed by the broad recognition of Austrian avant-garde films. In the early 1980s a new generation of independent artistic animators started to build the basis for today's very diverse, multi-faceted and versatile environment. The originally strong focus on experimental and non-commercial animation has expanded during the last fifteen years, and producers, authors and filmmakers now embrace a wide spectrum of work, reaching from traditional to commercial to artistic expressions. The chapter presents the most relevant and influential protagonists as well as the key characteristics of their work.

The last chapter of this section features animated documentaries, prominently featured on the Swedish animation scene and eminently represented by Jonas Odell, Hanna Heilborn and David Aronowitsch. In Chapter 7, Midhat Ajanović-Ajan not only presents those specific cases, but also seeks to address the systems for Swedish production and financing animation, the film tradition in general, technology, distribution, audience and cultural context. The focus of this chapter is on Swedish filmmaker Birgitta Jansson, her seminal work and her unique method of combining documentary sound with claymation, which she introduced in *Semesterhemmet* (1980).

Case studies from around the world

In the first chapter of the case studies section, Edwin Carels features the impact of the flipbook within the work of well-known artist Robert Carlton Breer. Pursuing a highly personal and surprisingly consistent course, the painter, filmmaker and sculptor was driven by a persistent interest in visual perception. Through the (re-)discovery of the flipbook, he found his initial means to problematize the relationship between viewer and artwork. With this methodological breakthrough, the decomposition and reconstruction of movement became the centre of focus in all the strands of his work.

Tale of Tales (1979) has been repeatedly recognized as one of the greatest animated films of all time, and remains an enigmatic masterpiece, though its inner message is not fully deciphered. The film's charm and power are indisputable and irresistible; and yet, a complete and concrete understanding escapes us somehow. In his chapter, Mikhail Gurevich presents a re-reading of the film through analysing its poetic structure and interpreting its not so obvious symbolism.

In Chapter 10 Andrijana Ružić presents the chronology of film critic, theorist and historian Ranko Munitić's work in the history of the development of animation literature in former Yugoslavia, focusing primarily on his critical thought regarding the 'golden years' of the Zagreb School of Animation. The chapter underlines Munitić's pioneering work in the development of film theory and film criticism in the early years of animation studies in the former Yugoslavia. The author also describes why it is important to give Ranko Munitić credit for his outstanding contribution in the popularization of the animated films of the Zagreb School of Animation, both in the former Yugoslavia and abroad.

The role of music in animated films is only partly similar to its role in feature films: its task of illustration and its ability to create continuity and dynamism, as well as its emotional suggestiveness is used in both genres. But only in animated films does the role of music expand to the humanization of artificial imagery. Irena Paulus summarizes her research on the music in Zagreb film animated shorts scored by the 'good spirit' of Zagreb Film, Tomislav Simović.

Fatemeh Hosseini-Shakib's chapter explores the very diverse and innovative notion of puppets in the Barry Purves animation *Screen Play* (1993) in relation to the idea of 'puppet realism'. In this context the term 'realism' and 'puppet realism' do not describe a precise copying of life, or a filmic record of it. Puppets are used in place of human actors acting out different methods of live performances, mainly including theatre and opera. This goes beyond any straightforward notion of the puppet film, as represented and experienced by Purves' predecessors.

In Chapter 13 Michał Bobrowski discusses Julian 'Antonisz' Antoniszczak, a filmmaker from the Polish School of Animation who is remembered mostly as the author of oddball 'non-camera' films, drawn, painted, scratched, burned or woodcut-printed directly onto a 35 mm tape. The chapter focuses on Antonisz's pursuit for artistic independence in times of ideological hegemony. His work is treated as an exemplification of the wider context of Polish dissident art, which over the last two decades of communism employed guerrilla methods for sending subversive messages.

In the final chapter of *Global Animation Theory*, Dirk de Bruyn focuses on Lynsey Martin's short experimental animations, which are largely unknown internationally. His graphic 16-mm films *Approximately Water* (1972), *Whitewash* (1973), *Interview* (1973) and *Leading Ladies* (1975) are analysed for their technique and cultural positions, artefacts of a productive, but also marginalized, period of artist made films. Martin's films stand as historic aesthetic traces of an immediate hands-on approach to image making that came into crisis in Australia through the disappearance of technical education in the 1980s.

Acknowledgements

The editors would like to thank many great collaborators and contributors, but particularly Katie Gallof, Stefan Stratil, ASIFA Austria and the entire Animafest Zagreb team – Ornela Čop, Nino Kovačić, Matea Milić and Paola Orlić most of all.

SECTION 1

Historical and Theoretical Approaches from International Animation Studies

1

Animation since 1980

A Personal Journey

Marcin Giżycki

In 1980, I participated in the World Festival of Animated Film in Zagreb as an editor-in chief of the ASIFA quarterly *Animafilm*. I was twenty-eight years old then. It was a very special moment in Polish history. The economic crisis had caused growing social tensions, which were to explode in a series of strikes almost exactly two months later. Solidarność, the first independent workers' union in the Soviet Block, was just about to establish itself as a powerful force challenging Communist rule.

I got my appointment as the editor of *Animafilm* in 1979 by a grim chance. My predecessor, Mr Mieczysław Walasek, a journalist and Communist Party member, had died unexpectedly and some well-known Polish animators, among them Witold Giersz and Mirosław Kijowicz, suggested to the authorities that a young film critic interested in animation named Marcin Giżycki would be a good replacement. I was not a Party member, which was almost a requirement for a position of this kind, but apparently the decision-makers had other problems to take care of, so they agreed.[1] This is how I started attending animation festivals abroad: in Annecy, Varna and Zagreb.

So, there I was in Zagreb in June of 1980. It soon became clear that it was not only an important time in Polish history but also in the history of the ASIFA and animated film theory. During the ASIFA Board meeting that took place at the festival, after a few hours of deliberation, a new definition

---

[1] Officially, I was appointed acting editor-in-chief.

of animation was produced. Let me quote it now, although I do not doubt that every animator knows it by heart: 'The art of animation is the creation of moving images through the manipulation of all varieties of techniques apart from live action methods' (*Animafest* 1980: 8).

This definition appeared in the next issue of *Animafilm* after the festival ended. For many reasons, it was a groundbreaking but curious definition. First of all, it did not even mention 'animated film'. Instead it talked about 'the art of animation', as if the authors wanted to acknowledge that animated film was just one of several ways of putting images or objects into motion. What followed was even more puzzling. As the text stated next, 'the art of animation' is a way of creating moving images by all means 'apart from live action'. What is revolutionary here is the lack of the previously obligatory component of every previous definition of the subject: frame-by-frame photography. This approach certainly anticipated the advent of the computer as a future animation tool. The most questionable part of the Zagreb definition, however, was its rejection of live action. It raised several questions that are still relevant today: Was Norman McLaren's *Neighbors* an animation or live action film? Were Jan Švankmajer's *The Last Trick* and *Punch and Judy* animated films or not? And what about rotoscoping? Where actually is the border between animation and live action?

It seems that the ASIFA definition did not really solve existing problems as much as it opened the door to new possibilities. So, let's see what has changed in animation since this historic festival took place in Zagreb in 1980.

First of all, in 1980 all films submitted to the competition were recorded on 16 or 35 mm film. Today, most of the festivals do not even accept films on light sensitive media, and those that still do will stop doing so soon. Although we can mourn the good old film stock for . . . let's see . . . actually for what? Eight to ten years ago the answer would have been simple: for its continuous tone and lack of pixels. But that hardly counts anymore. The number of possible shades is in the millions now, pixels have become so tiny that they are almost invisible, and the quality of the image is still improving. But what I enjoy the most while watching a digital print in a cinema theatre is its sharpness. Let's face it: in 1980, most of the films screened in cinemas were partially or entirely out of focus. I cannot even recall how many times I was forced to go to the projection booth to wake up the projectionist and make him pay attention to the quality of projection. I do not want to say that this problem has entirely vanished, but without doubt it has improved significantly. Now another issue is plaguing film screenings, not as bad as focusing but still bad: the wrong aspect ratio.

I remember a festival that took place a few years ago in Poland. Almost half of the films screened were stretched way beyond their actual format. I had a film in the competition that was made in the old 4:3 ratio. Before the screening, I went to the projection booth and asked the projectionist to adjust the player accordingly. When the film started, I noticed to my horror that it was squeezed to approximately square proportions. I did not want to become a dubious hero of the festival and stop the projection, but I felt so devastated that I left for home right after the screening, being convinced that this disaster had ruined my chances. Two days later I got a call from the festival informing me that the film had won an honourable mention. My good humour was soon spoiled, though, by the thought that I had received this distinction because the jurors had found this square format very original.

Speaking of festivals, back in 1980 there was just a handful of animation festivals around and a few other festivals that accepted animated films. One could more or less follow all of them, and stay well informed. Even in a Communist country like Poland, film magazines published reports from most of these events. Today, the number of festivals, animation festivals included, has exploded to enormous proportions. There is no way to keep track of even a fraction of them. At the time of this writing the most comprehensive festival database on the Internet, Film Festivals Deadlines, proudly lists over 10,000 festivals from all over the world, at least half of them, probably more, accept animated films (and this amount is far from conclusive).[2] It seems like an enormous devaluation of this kind of event.[3]

There are upsides and downsides to all of this. The good one is that more and more people get exposed to art house animations and other kinds of films. The bad side is that many of these festivals simply exploit filmmakers, asking for submission fees that often exceed their budgets, especially if one wants to send his or her work to several events. I am especially speaking of those competitions that call themselves 'underground', 'independent' or 'no-budget' but charge $50 or $80 per film. Of course, there are some long established festivals like DOK Leipzig, Rotterdam International Film Festival, or Ann Arbor Film Festival worth paying the submission fee because of their reputation, but I believe that in the ideal world the authors should be paid for the privilege to screen their films rather than vice versa.

Putting this matter aside, there must be a reason for this proliferation of festivals other than greed. The explanation is simple: the festivals bloom because the number of films produced every year has grown proportionally as well. This has been propelled in turn by the technological revolution that has changed the whole film industry since 1980 and also enabled independent filmmakers to make films at home on a shoestring budget.

This digital imaging revolution coincided, as Tom Sito reminds us in *Moving Innovation: A History of Computer Animation*, with the larger information revolution. 'Until the late 1980s television [in the US] was seven

---

[2] http://www.filmfestivalsdeadlines.com.

[3] More about the variety of animated film festivals in my essay: 'Just What Is It That Makes Today's Animation Festivals So Different, So Appealing' (Ruoff 2012: 61).

channels – three networks, CBS, NBC, and ABC; three Metromedia or regional stations and one PBS public station on the UHF frequency' (Sito 2013: 7). Other well-developed countries did not have even this. In Communist Poland, just before the collapse of the regime, we had three channels, all of them owned by the state, and that was it. Today an average household in America, Europe, Australia and many parts of Asia or Africa has at its disposal hundreds, if not thousands, of cable or satellite channels plus countless websites on the Internet. This comparison shows perfectly the scale of changes in every aspect of human life that have been triggered by the information revolution since 1980.

In the animation world it means lower costs, faster results and much broader possibilities for exposure for independent artists. How this revolution has changed the industry is apparent in the example of animation units at big Hollywood studios. With the advent of television, they started to shrink steadily. As Sito puts it: 'The film and advertising industries' conventional wisdom in the 1970s was that classic animation was good in its time (the 1930s and 1940s), but it had become too expensive and was too labor-intensive to ever again prove profitable' (Sito 2013: 220). The animation staff at Disney was reduced from 2,000 employees in the 1940s to 175 in 1966. In 1977 Dave Wolf, a computer engineer quoted by Sito, attended a screening of *Sleeping Beauty* at the University of Southern California's cinema school. 'When the old Disney guys asked for questions, I asked if they could see a role for computers. Immediately, I got a lot of ugly looks from everyone' – he recalled (Sito 2013: 222). This attitude started to change in the 1980s. Today, as we all know, feature animated films turn enormous profits, and one of the reasons for this is that computers have taken over the whole production process. The numbers are impressive. According to Bruno Edera in between the beginning of cinema and 1974 approximately 180 feature-length films were made (Edera 1977). Nowadays, it takes two years or less to reach the same figure.

There is no doubt that the process of making an animated movie has become much less elitist than it used to be twenty years ago. One does not need a costly camera, featuring frame-by-frame possibilities, and financial resources to cover the costs of lab processing, in order to make an animated film. In fact, a contemporary animator does not need a camera at all. Everything can be done on a laptop computer equipped with free or reasonably priced software. The lack of economic barriers preventing amateurs from invading the field of artistic activity once reserved for the pros is not a bad thing. It finally makes animation a truly democratic art as accessible to anyone as writing, drawing, or painting . . . Or at least almost as approachable, since animation software, even the simplest one, is still more difficult for some to operate than a pen or brush. Anyway, this easy access to the means of production creates an environment in which real talent, inventiveness, creativity, etc. is not restrained by the high costs of the tools anymore. This situation has created a challenge to artists whose reputations were established in the pre-digital era. Today, they have to compete with an influx of student films at film festivals, and often they lose to young, up-coming filmmakers.

Of course, there are still projects that require significant financial input and here also new technologies come in handy. But an amazing thing is that even relatively costly undertakings can be realized without the backing of the big studios, thanks to the concept of crowdfunding. The newest film by Jan Švankmajer, *Insects*, which according to the filmmaker is his last feature, is being partially funded in this way. A Kickstarter-funded Japanese anime, *Under the Dog*, directed by Masahiro Andō (2016), proves that even in the field of commercial feature movies the big producers are losing their monopoly. Anybody with a good idea has a chance to secure enough funding to indulge in his or her fantasies. That might change the whole industry radically in the near future.

So, what could be the future of animated film? Animation is already present everywhere: on billboards, the little screens of our cell phones when we turn them on, not to mention the animated gifs populating websites. Animated special effects have invisibly invaded feature action, sci-fi and fantasy films. Stereoscopic movies stopped being experimental a long time ago. Interactive animation has already been here for a while under the disguise of computer games. What is left? Computer-made films. I mean exactly this: films made by computers. There are already programs, like EMI (Experiments in Musical Intelligence) developed by David Cope at Stanford University, that generate musical pieces in the style of a chosen composer, Rachmaninoff for example. Harold Cohen's AARON can produce drawings 'which are hard to distinguish from those of skilled artists' (Lopes 2010: 12). Some of them were shown in very respectful institutions like the Tate Gallery in London or the Stedejlijk Museum in Amsterdam. According to Dominic McIver Lopes, the author of *A Philosophy of Computer Art*: 'When one of these (drawings) was labeled "digital print by Harold Cohen," Coen objected, and the label was changed to attribute the work to "AARON, a computer program written by Harold Cohen"' (Lopes 2010: 12).

So why not have films made exclusively by computers? It is certainly possible with abstract films. Most of them already look like they are made exclusively by machines with all those fractals, codes and glitches (this is why I appreciate more those abstract movies which still display a human touch). But with the further development of artificial intelligence combined with CGI technologies, I can easily imagine computer generated non-narrative representational movies in the style of, let's say, Georges Schwizgebel or Jerzy Kucia. Pushing this idea a step further, why not imagine an ideal animated fable concocted by a computer fed with thousands of fairytale cartoons? Should I expect one of those 'ugly' looks now?

Ok, sooner or later computers will rule the world, but still at the beginning there were the men and women who invented them and fed them with our human experience, knowledge and art. Definitely computers can mimic us, but can they come up with something original? Can they surpass the vision of their inventors? I do not think there is an answer to this question. Certainly, I do not know it. But at least I know what we need right now: films as a political weapon. I do not want to give the impression that there is an obligation to create politically and socially charged films. Actually, I fully support the kind of film that many years ago the great Polish author and critic Karol Irzykowski described as 'cinema of pure motion', by which he meant works governed by their own poetic rules based on the conviction that the visual is the most important component of movies, either narrative or abstract (Irzykowski 1924: 7–16). On the other hand, I believe that in the world of animation there is a historically justified space for statements from the other end of the spectrum – that is for all kinds of politically informed works in which the message plays the most important part. And today, in the time of unprecedented peoples' migrations, terrorist attacks, growing fundamentalisms and the popularity of far right-wing demagogues, we need this kind of movie more than ever.

Since its birth, animated film has been used as a vehicle for propaganda and political satire. The oldest surviving animation recorded on light sensitive material ('films' drawn on paper strips had existed even before) is a work by the Englishman Arthur Melbourn-Cooper from 1899 *Matches: An Appeal*. Other artists soon followed: Quirino Cristiani with a feature-length *El Apóstol* in Argentina (1917), Winsor McCay with *The Sinking of the Lusitania* in the US (1918),[4] to mention just a few of the most prominent examples from the pioneering days of animated film.

Such were the beginnings of animated political cinema that later gave birth to countless propaganda films from the times of the building of Socialism in the USSR, World War II and the Cold War. But this is a theme for another paper. Here it is important to stress that besides all kinds of propaganda films serving the official policies of each of their respective governments or political groups, relatively early art-house animated films carrying important social messages also started to emerge. The best-known example of them is *The Idea* by Berthold Bartosch from 1932, based on Frans Masereel's graphic novel of the same title.

So, it appears that political animations have always been around. But today, thanks to the accessibility of the medium and the ease of its use, they

[4] The film depicted the fatal German submarine's attack on the British liner in 1915 that took nearly 1,200 lives and convinced the United States to join World War I. It is not widely known, though, that this was not the first animation on the subject. Immediately after the tragedy took place, a very similar British short film (although made with much less talent) was released as part of *John Bull's Animated Sketchbook*.

can respond to political events with a speed never possible before and be seen immediately by millions on the Internet.

An interesting phenomenon of this kind developed in Russia at the beginning of this century: flash animated *anekdots* – known also as *mults* – proliferated, often containing political messages. Produced by established studios as well as anonymous artists, they used the Internet to spread satirical comments on many aspects of everyday life. Vlad Strukov compared them to luboks – a popular printed art form from the eighteenth and nineteenth centuries on topics ranging from the religious to the historical – and to Russian poster designs of the 1920s (Strukov 2007). They also remind me of slogans and graffiti painted on the walls in Paris during the students' protests of 1968.

But this is not the only form of political animation that would be helpful now. More complex and thoughtful works exposing the hypocrisy of politicians, the manipulations of corporations, demagogy of all kinds, racism, etc. – these are areas where animated film can make a difference. Animation + the Internet = Power.

References

Animafilm. (1980). (3): 5 8.

Edera, B. (1977). *Full Length Animated Feature Films*. New York: Hasting House.

Irzykowski, K. (1924). *Dziesiąta Muza*. Kraków: Krakowska Spółka Wydawmicza.

Lopes, D. M. (2010). *A Philosophy of Computer Art*. New York: Routledge.

Ruoff, J. (2012). *Coming Soon to a Festival Near You*. St. Andrews: St. Andrews Film Studies.

Sito, T. (2013). *Moving Innovation: A History of Computer Animation*. Cambridge: MIT.

Strukov, V. (2007). 'Video Anekdot: Auteurs and Voyeurs of Russian Flash Animation'. *Animation: An Interdisciplinary Journal*, 2(2): 129–151.

2

Animation in the Gallery and the Gestalt

György Kovásznai and William Kentridge

Paul Wells

> The practice of drawing – professional knowledge – can be derived from two sources: either from universal faith, i.e. on the basis of the idea conception, which implies a collective ideal, or on the basis of a non-collective, individual–sensualistic, positivistically–individualistically solitary venture of discovery
>
> KOVÁSZNAI in IVÁNYI-BITTER 2016: 35

> We, however, who intend to do something for the people's sake as well as for our own glory, have to concern ourselves a great deal with politics, and in a proper manner
>
> KOVÁSZNAI in IVÁNYI-BITTER 2016: 41

This chapter explores the work of recently rediscovered Cold War Hungarian animator, György Kovásznai, and the contemporary artist to whom he has been most compared and affiliated, South African William Kentridge. Both were part of a co-exhibition in Budapest in 2015, and recently in London in 2016. Kentridge also appeared on a panel looking at 'Animation and the Avant Garde outside the Western Canon', talking about Kovásznai's work in 2016, in which I took part, too. This discussion will address the individual works of both artists, looking at their approaches and outlooks, and how this is understood as directly affiliated to art and arts culture, and animation's presence in the gallery context.

Further, the analysis will seek to use Kentridge's ethos and approach to mediate an address of Kovásznai's perspectives, summarized in his statements above, to situate works within a broader understanding of the *gestalt* of the 'Animation Spectrum', and the presence of animation both in the academic and the public sphere. It should be stressed that this version of the *gestalt* moves beyond the established and orthodox notions of animation as a cinematic and broadcast practice, into contexts where it is present and observable, but less recognized and acknowledged. This concept insists that animation is present in a range of moving images – for example, visual effects, virtual reality, data visualization and real-time interaction – and that these contexts are imbued with animation aesthetics. As such they represent an omnipresence of animation – the *gestalt* – that speaks to social and cultural processes and practices, which are in turn informed by cultural and political knowledge. This begins to suggest an 'animification' of human experience that has emerged throughout the history of animation as it has been re-configured through new technologies but, more importantly, the techniques applied by leading authorial sensibilities.

Writing in 2005, filmmaker and artist, Lewis Klahr (2005: 234), sought to distance himself from the idea that he was 'an animator', insisting 'the expectations of *collage* can help the viewer more deeply engage in and follow the formal decisions contained in my films. The expectations of "animation" will not'. Klahr is not alone in such preferences, of course, merely signalling that the sources and influences in his work are much more attuned to the Fine Arts. Interestingly, South African William Kentridge (Wells 2016) also resists the idea that his work should be associated with 'animation', but only because when he first considered using the form, at least, he felt his efforts did not have the competence and technical specificity of classical animation, exemplified at the Disney studio. When artists resist the view that they are 'animators', then, they are for the most part denying that they are animators not merely because 'Disney' might represent mass entertainment, global dissemination, serial characters and a cast of animals (Krauss 2005: 102), but because of the regulation in the Disney classical animation style, for a long time the dominant approach to the form. It is a style, of course, privileging the role of drawing within the process of making 'cinema', and not the singular drawing within 'art-making'.

There is some irony in this, of course, in the sense that the animators at the Disney Studios in the Golden era were inventing and refining an 'art form'. The newly emergent 'Eighth Art' of animation was in essence the theorization of the 'Twelve Principles' that govern the execution of effective drawn animation in the early shorts and features that emerged from studios as it established itself in Hollywood in the 1920s and 1930s (Johnson and

Thomas 1981: 47–69). The classical animation style that the Disney animators perfected, though, was soon perceived less as art than as an industrial process that serviced mere entertainment. Though the Disney model was understood as 'state of the art' worldwide in the pre-World War II period and after, and much copied by independent artists and major studios in, for example, the UK, Japan and Russia, the quasi-Taylorist model used to create shorts and features frame-by-frame at the Disney studio in essence diminished the idea that it had the imprimatur of Fine Art. Disney's animation nevertheless retained its primary and distinctive aesthetic and, as such, its long shadow of influence in defining 'animation' *per se*. It is this history and orthodoxy that other artists using animation are explicitly aligning themselves with – even if they are working in a different style or technique – or deliberately distancing themselves from. As a consequence, Disney's pop(ulist) art sat in direct opposition to the experimental tradition that emerged in Europe and elsewhere in the figures of Len Lye, Norman McLaren and Lotte Reiniger.

This schism has characterized the field of animation until comparatively recently when gallery shows like 'Momentary Momentum' at Parosol Unit, London in 2007 and 'Watch Me Move: The Animation Show' at The Barbican, London in 2012, sought to place animation – popular and experimental alike – into the gallery space. Lawrence Dreyfuss reminds us, though:

> Contemporary art is constantly generating new mediums, the study of which implies a radical revision of our habitual artistic categories. Animation is one of the least known of these forms because of its traditional production process, which places such importance on drawing, a discipline that has long been ignored to the advantage of painting and sculpture.
>
> DREYFUSS 2007: 30

This observation both recovers the significance of 'drawing' within industrially produced animation, but also of 'drawing' as a particular form of expression that might be ultimately animated. I would further suggest here, too, that 'drawing' might be understood to also stand alongside, and engage with painting and sculpture, in the broader context of specific kinds of mark-making. This seeks to locate 'animation' beyond its traditional boundaries as a drawn form, to embrace different formal properties and techniques as part of its vocabulary, and to promote a revision of production history that re-situates animation in the artist's 'studio' rather than in the 'quasi-factory' that now defines the production identity of major studios. It follows, thereafter, that animation may be placed within parameters by which it might be viewed and evaluated as 'art', measured by the codes and conventions of established arts practices and art historical idioms and, crucially, within an intellectual framework that properly and unselfconsciously acknowledges the relationship between animation, philosophy and politics.

In the modern era, and with the post-digital shift, the schisms and categorizations that separate different kinds of animation seem increasingly unhelpful in addressing the form, and serve only to distance particular kinds of more personal or authorial work from 'the (American Animated) cartoon'. This kind of positioning now seems intellectually as well as practically redundant when artists like Mathias Poledna make *Imitation of Life* (2013) – to all intents and purposes a Golden era, Disney-style, fully animated and orchestrated cartoon, but made within the context of art culture. As such, upon its premiere at the Venice Biennale, the catalogue could make two significant claims.

First:

> *Imitation of Life* appropriates and reassembles this language as it revisits the contradictions and ambiguities that accompanied the medium's development. Advanced methods of production and visual ingenuity – indebted to the syntax of European modernism in its handling of surface, depth and color, and lauded by the avant garde and critic intelligence of the time – coexisted with sentimental characterization and storytelling based on age-old fables and fairy tales.

And second:

> Beyond its engagement with animation, *Imitation of Life* incorporates into its fleeting narrative a number of other elements from the early history of entertainment, such as Vaudeville, silent comedy and film musicals, and diverse artistic forms including film, music, painting and literature. But even while it subscribes to the synergistic logic of its medium, the film deliberately eschews a seamless whole, remaining at once alien and utterly recognizable.
>
> PADIGLIONE AUSTRIACO 2013

These comments serve to remind contemporary audiences of the place of European Modernism in the development of classical animation, and the critical recognition that attended the films, especially at the Disney studio. Equally, Podema's work prompts the necessary recognition that animation is an inherently cross- and inter-disciplinary synergistic form. This is important because these synergies are at the heart of animation as a distinctive art form. Consequently, Dreyfuss talks about the ways in which the varying forms of animation production suggest 'indefinable modalities uniting drawing and movement' (Dreyfuss 2007: 30), and it is clear that by understanding all animation practice in this way, it is possible to see how technical and aesthetic innovation, prompted by varying sources, speaks to wider discourses. In the first instance, I wish to explore this idea by defining the contemporary 'Animation Spectrum', and why it then becomes helpful in determining a *gestalt*, that might be understood through the ideas and practices of Kentridge, and evidenced in the work of Hungarian Cold War Artist, Kovásznai.

The 'Animation Spectrum', in the first instance, acknowledges the presence of the form in different contexts and, as such, views it as a marker of applied practices, using a variety of technologies and disciplines within a range of moving image taxonomies. Crucial in this formation is what makes animation *identifiable*, rather than its particular methods of production, and how, thereafter, it becomes *situated*. The schemata[1] in Figure 2.1 will help to explain this idea further.

Moving from left to right, animation is first recognized as a form of moving image practice in cinema and television (taking in features, shorts, public information films, series, commercials, credit sequences, interstitials,

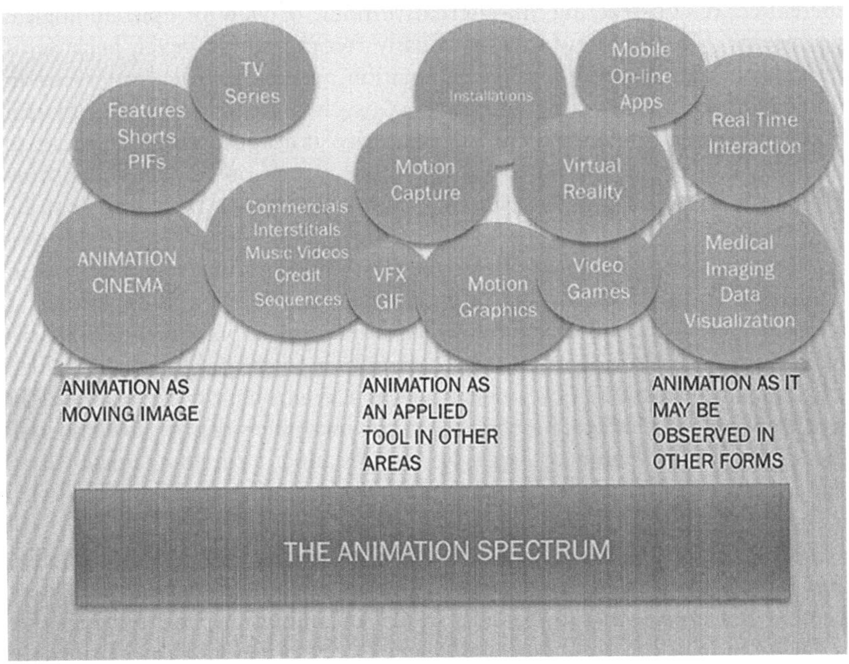

FIGURE 2.1 *The Animation Spectrum by Paul Wells.*

[1] The schemata was first posited and explored in the author's forthcoming book *Screenwriting for Animation.*

music videos, etc.). Thereafter, as it becomes an applied tool, it becomes less recognized in its traditional forms but is identifiable in a range of applications (these include visual effects, gifs, motion capture, motion graphics, video games, virtual reality and a variety of mobile and on-line operations). Once it reaches the far right, it becomes present and observed in other *normally non-artistic* forms (for example, medical imagining, data visualization, real time interaction, etc.). Many people do not perceive the presence of animation in many of the contexts noted as the 'Spectrum' moves from the middle to the right, mainly because these practices do not readily foreground the obvious, or even implied, presence of an artist or creative practitioner. For animation theorists (and probably for this group alone) the artist or practitioner is always present in animation, following Crafton's concept of the 'self-figurative' (1993: 11), which suggests that the overt artifice in the material manipulation and construction of the animated image necessarily reveals its maker. Such image-making resists the classical sutures and closure of traditional cinema (that normally hides its creator) and privileges the presence of the artist or creative practitioner as a figure that in essence is 'deconstructing' received knowledge of material culture and representations of reality, and thereafter, 're-constructing' an alternative point of view or epistemological perspective. The 'self-figurative' is usually recognized, however, because of the broader 'enunciative' identity of animation, and its 'rhetorical' intervention in the representation of different modes of psychological, emotional, physical and material reality. As such, the 'self-figurative' is not just about the presence of an artist or creative practitioner, but about animation being 'identified' as a mode of visualization and 'situated' in a context that thereafter may be defined as playing out new iterations of social and cultural knowledge and aesthetic innovation. Instead, then, of reiterating the normal schisms between animation and live action film, or commercial animation and experimental animation, or drawing for animation and drawing as pure authorial mark-making, it is necessary to resist 'differentiation' in form, and privilege the idea that animation must be best understood as a 'continuation' in form; one in which the embrace of other technologies and disciplines defines its distinctive *gestalt* as the mediator of ideas and issues, and ultimately leads to an 'animification' of human experience in its representation, and interfaces with culture and society.

The 'Spectrum' thus seeks to move considerably beyond the limits implied and imposed by Klahr, for example, and to show that rather than there being a schism between a classical model of animation, and the Fine-Art model of animation, these typologies have a continuum in their relationship to materials, resources and processes. In essence, when making animation, any artist is part of a 'Spectrum' that is deploying, revising or reacting to other kinds of application and approach. This, of and in itself, provides the platform by which animation sustains its identity as a Modernist practice, because at any one time it might simultaneously create a new medium for expression, as well as refine the means by which to express compelling and radical 'content' that emerges from fresh sources and contexts. At one and the same time, then, the 'Spectrum' provides the means to a stable model that might organize an approach, but also permit spontaneity and innovation. As such, the 'Spectrum' can accommodate the pioneering work of Disney animators, Kentridge's erasure technique, Kovásznai's drawing with paint, and a myriad of other approaches, by placing them in a proper relationship technically, aesthetically and conceptually. Perhaps, most significantly, the very choice of an 'animated' application by these figures implies that there is the need to represent the human condition in a way that defines the vision of the artist but also their perception of experience. One of the most often cited metaphoric structuring devices for such an experience employed in recent years has been 'gamification' – a view which suggests that in an age of video games and simulated virtual practices life echoes games structures and outcomes. This begs the question of how animation informs the representation of this 'gamification' process and, thus, I wish to suggest that the *gestalt* that embodies human experience is actually best represented and revealed by the 'animification' of culture, perceived across 'the Spectrum', and prompted by the numerous applications of animators, among them artists like Kentridge and Kovásznai.

Where this becomes most clear as a principle and a point of execution and contemplation is in the 'installation' – the placing of animation in the gallery. On the 'Spectrum', the installation is not (necessarily) part of a linear continuity in the exhibition of animation but rather a lateral continuity in representing a deliberate 'curation' of materials in the service of a concept or idea, taking into account all the cross-disciplinary and inter-disciplinary aspects that place art and artifacts into a presentational environment. The works themselves, therefore, not merely become a product of their own technical, aesthetic and cultural evolution, but of their architectural and infrastructural identity. In reducing difference and schism, and prioritizing continuity, the *gestalt* of animation becomes much more 'visible' because it does not resist its relationship to other forms of art, culture and society, but rather demonstrates and illustrates them. Kentridge's outlook and model of engagement proves invaluable at this juncture in illustrating this point, and enabling a helpful point of critical access to Kovásznai's work.

In his exhibition, 'Thick Time', which took place at the Whitechapel gallery in London from 2016 to 2017, Kentridge once more embraced his key themes in privileging the significance of the studio as a place to review and reorganize private and public worlds through some model of performative enactment – a creative strategy that includes animation. His pre-occupation with the deeper roots of Modernism was also to the fore, stressing the continuity of arts and cultural practices, rather than any sudden or unforeseen radicalism, and further how manifestations of the absurd or the satiric effectively offers up a context in which epistemological enquiry takes place, and ultimately generates new knowledge. In works as varied as *Tide Table* (2003), *I Am Not Me, The Horse is Not Mine* (2008) to *Film Flip Books* (2012), Kentridge has explored the ways in which narratives are generated in the spaces between plausible facts and materiality and promoted an ambivalent fictional turn that is made available by denying veracity and embracing the perceived, the surreal, or the seemingly illogical as the harboring agency of truth and insight. In challenging the falsehoods of received knowledge, and focusing on reconsidering and restructuring the 'fragments' of experience, Kentridge both reconfigures accepted (grand) narratives and engages with making sense of moral and political order. Animation and its 'Spectrum' of both technique and discourse offers him the mutability of expression that apprehends a continuous movement through the world that constantly prompts metonymic suggestion. In making images within images; books within books; moving parts within fluid mechanisms; and making process central to the outcomes of the works, Kentridge points up interiority/exteriority; inside/outside; and the execution of mark-making as the evidence of the physical and philosophic urgency to express.

Krauss has addressed Kentridge's technique of making 'drawings for projection' (a term that immediately re-defines 'animation' yet specifically relates to it) and his focus on 'stalking the drawing' by walking backwards and forwards between camera and canvas as he accumulates and erases his charcoal images. She notes:

> The automatism he has discovered – 'drawings for projection' – works itself out in a continuing series. Whatever else that series focuses on – apartheid, capitalist greed, eros, memory – the automatism of his process places procedure before meaning, or rather trusts to the fact that his new medium – his new automatism – will induce meaning. 'The hope is that without directly plunging the surgeon's knife, the arcane process of obsessively walking between the camera and the drawing board will pull to the surface, intimations of the interior' [Kentridge].
>
> KRAUSS 2005: 105

Kentridge's technique seeks to use the interval between frames as a space in which his unconscious, intuitive thoughts emerge to prompt the new intervention in the image. This is closely related to the approach of animators – all working in different techniques – from Norman McLaren to Nick Park to Chris Landreth, and many others, in which the palimpsest is evoked by the recognition that what has been erased remains in some sense present as something new is engraved, drawn, manipulated or layered upon it. Yet, Kentridge remains distinctive. His particular approach to apprehending the *gestalt* and insisting upon 'animification' is achieved by the synergistic aspects of his skill, background and consciousness in relation to the diverse disciplines of, and beyond, the medium, and permit him his individual voice.

This is the case for all the 'animators' across the 'Spectrum'. It was this kind of 'affordance' or 'correspondence' that was noticed by The Kovásznai Research Centre Foundation, however, when they approached Kentridge to engage with the rediscovered work of György Kovásznai.

The Kovásznai Research Centre Foundation felt that Kovásznai needed an introduction, both in relation to his role in Cold War Hungary and to contemporary arts culture in the modern era, so identified Kentridge as a figure with a parallel and related model of practice. Kentridge was always aware that any work by a South African artist in the period before the end of apartheid would be read in the light of the country's segregational politics, and this both inspired but partly compromised the artwork. Kentridge noted:

> These two elements – our history and the moral imperative arising from that – are the factors for making that personal beacon rise into the immovable rock of apartheid. To escape this rock is the job of the artist. These two constitute the tyranny of our history. And escape is necessary, for as I stated, the rock is possessive, and inimical to good work. I am not saying that apartheid, or indeed, redemption, are not worthy of representation, describing, or exploration. I am saying that the scale and weight with which this rock presents itself is inimical to that task.
>
> KENTRIDGE in KRAUSS 2005: 97

Kentridge presents the edifice of apartheid ideology as insurmountable in the same way as Kovásznai sees the authoritarianism of Soviet Russia in the governance of Hungary, but both see an imperative to let the art itself inform resistance, even if it is only implicitly political. The sheer imperative to express and individuate is to challenge orthodoxies and expectations. To do this in animation is to also thwart anticipated norms of creative practice, especially when it is used to embrace the *gestalt* in the context of installation; to insist upon an 'animification' that presents its own condition as a model of difference and resistance.

The sheer directness of mark-making in the work of Kentridge and Kovásznai signals an immediacy of intent and purpose and, as Kentridge remarked of Kovásznai's work, 'the urgency, the need to produce, the compulsion to create is evident in the painting and the animation. This in itself has something to say, because it is not bound up by any particular thing it feels it should say, or must say' (Kentridge 2016). Even when both do have something particular to communicate, neither betrays its complexity by propagandistic message-making, but rather by using the freedom of expression to represent the expression of freedom, while fully knowing the constraints against which such art needs to push.

This is where the rediscovered art and animation of György Kovásznai becomes especially important because the cache of material, in the first instance, simply existed as a 'body of work', and as such demanded categorization, contextualization and criticism. More significantly, from the point of view of this analysis, it is vital that the work is not explored and rendered as part of old schisms and categories but revealed through the *gestalt*; through an 'animification' of a previously limited material reality. Usefully, the first engagement with the material by the Kovásznai Foundation Research Centre took on the broad principle that Kovásznai's paintings and animation were equally significant, each relating directly to the other, and that Kovásznai's own writing would be pertinent in helping to offer both a historiography of, and commentary upon, the pieces. This also pointed to the idea that the work was primarily pertinent for installation, and the gallery context, but, crucially, that it was important to identify and situate the various aspects of the work, historically, technically and contextually. The Kovásznai Research Centre Foundation and the cultural bodies in Hungary essentially invested in the extent and variation of the work to explore the relationship between an artist and the State in Hungary during the Cold War, principally during the period of the 1960s and 1970s. Perhaps even more significantly, though, their work was prompted by the fact that Kovásznai was strangely absent from any prominent discourses in art history, animation history and cultural history, and thus offered up a curiously 'blank canvas' by which his achievement needed to be recovered, evaluated and explained. It was not the fact that Kovásznai was not known, but the confluence of his own contempt for, and distance from, such discourses, and the State's essential wish not to properly verify and acknowledge his work, that led to its marginalization and loss; all except for those who knew of it in his family and among his working cognoscenti. Kovásznai's own insularity and his commitment to the Hungarian context limited his presence on an international stage. Crucially, Kovásznai was also afforded the rare opportunity to both work as an individual and commercial artist within the Pannonia studio, thus rendering it as both a Kentridge-style context for private philosophical and political practice, and a place in which he worked on studio outputs to secure his living. These factors led to what Iványi-Bitter has noted was Kovásznai's absence from the canon even at the national level, but with the rediscovery of the work in a store outside Budapest in the mid-2000s, she suggests:

> [T]wo decades after the end of the Cold War, in the era of asynchronicity, of parallel modernities, of global assemblages, we must seize the special historical opportunity that artistic products of either the East or the West side of the Cold War period can be compared on the basis of their common domain of reference, on the common ground of modernism [. . .] Kovásznai should not remain an isolated phenomenon. It is time for his work to receive its due place in the art history of the Cold War Europe.
>
> IVÁNYI-BITTER 2016: 306–307

There is a pertinent confluence in the idea of the 'Animation Spectrum', Dreyfuss' 'Indefinable Modalities', Kentridge's 'Modernist Absurdism' and Iványi-Bitter's notions of asynchronicity and assemblage, in helping to define a *gestalt* that usefully conflates animation practice with its philosophic and political imperatives, without those imperatives being especially explicit or polemical, again helping to further identify the 'animification' of experience. Iványi-Bitter's relocation of Kovásznai's work, both in its period, but, more importantly, in the here and now of an uncertain and fluid 'Modernity', relates readily to the idea that while such a body of work can be retrospectively situated, the absence of a significant critical discourse around it permits its further relocation in contemporary debates. Equally, the work is inherently ideologically charged, and historically specific in some core respects, so it resists postmodern claims to mere aesthetic surfaces and glib intertextuality. Rather, it becomes readily located in the Modernist paradigm I first explored when looking at the emergence of the American animated cartoon (Wells 2002: 19–37). Frederick Kael insists that '[the] sense of Modern and Modernism in any era is always of "becoming". It may be new and different; it may be subverting the old, becoming an agent of disorder and even destruction' (Kael 1985: 3–4) Kovásznai's working context was one of resistance and challenge, not merely to the oppressive politics of the regime, but perhaps, even more pressingly, the limits of the arts establishment. It is in this that I also wish to point to 'animation' as *the* key creative vehicle in modernizing both art and political expression (then and now) and reconciling high and popular culture, and evidenced through the 'animification' of visual culture. Further, to take up Kael's model of 'radical', 'moderate' and 'conservative' Modernism (Kael 1985: 14), Kovásznai's work oscillated between opposition and difference (radicalism), critical revisionism (moderation) and satirical dismissal of known but less harmful aspects of culture (conservatism), and this brought him into varying degrees of contact and conflict with the authorities. Kovásznai obviously viewed this as being in dialogue with the figures and institutions that determined Hungarian culture, and though there was evident risk in both having his opinions and in producing his work, he nevertheless pursued his discourse through his art. He clearly possessed a compulsion to express, to essentially 'become' a citizen as his work traced the process of 'becoming' in its vivid colours, fluid metamorphoses and playful mixed-media interrogations of symbolically charged people, places and texts. Like Kentridge, the sheer imperative to make art, and to contribute to the understanding of the *gestalt* through 'animification', embraced its fragmented sources and fractured idioms in a re-combinative, re-constituted way that spoke its own language. Yet, it also achieved a universal level of expression drawn from the *gestalt*, while yet working to evolve it.

The discovery of the whole oeuvre of an artist, animator and polemicist, in a neglected farm building near Budapest, provided a dynamic, colourful and profound insight into Hungarian art and culture in the shadow of Soviet oppression. Recently exhibited at 'Kovásznai: A Cold War Artist, Animation, Painting, Freedom', in Somerset House, London in 2016, his work represents a relentless creative response to the Totalitarian regime and the emergence of 'Pop art'. Most importantly, though, it is a prolific response to his own conflicted passions, pains and philosophical principles – an inchoate outlook that constantly sought to express itself in the diversity of his vivid paintings, experimental animation and philosophical essays. These works ultimately insist upon a reappraisal of the relationship between Eastern European art sensibilities and the Western avant garde, as it has found a confluence in the animation *gestalt*, and found expression in the gallery, and in a culture of 'animification'.

Kovásznai evidenced his unique take on Hungarian art and authority early in his career. As a student, enamoured by the giants of Western Modernism – Picasso, Cézanne, Matisse – and frustrated by the academy's oppressive arts education, he left his studies to work as a miner in Komló, Dorog, Tata and Tokodaltáró. Fascinated by Marxist ideas but resistant to their authoritarian application, he wanted to reacquaint *Socialist Realism* with socialist reality. His experience with the real proletariat, and not the one imagined by the government, ultimately led to his film, *Joy of Light* (1965), a collage animation reminiscent of Len Lye's *Trade Tattoo* (1937). It combined photographs of the miners, painted backgrounds and Gerald Scarfe-like drawings of the sensual energies of the miners' excavations. If Klahr insists Kovásznai's art is best understood through a knowledge of collage, it is actually the animation that reveals its purpose and identity. The sheer diversity in the 'indefinable modalities' Kovásznai employs in his composition and editing repositions the implied narratives as a set of feeling states and emotive improvisations. This eclectic set of transitions both challenges the limits of State-approved art and draws upon the tension between documentary evidence and interpretive graphics to suggest a new mode of 'realism' that respects and admires the miners and their work, while exposing the challenges of Socialist 'work'.

Kovásznai's early films, part-collaborations with established Modernist painter and designer, Dezsö Korniss, fell foul of the regime. *Monologue* (1963), though permitted to screen for one week at the Corvin Cinema, Budapest, was thereafter banned for pointing a far too satirical finger at governance. Drawing upon the montage theories of Eisenstein, the influence of Polish animation iconoclasts, Jan Lenica and Walerian Borowczyk, and even the zany antics of Bob Godfrey and Terry Gilliam in the UK, the film was a clear statement of a free spirit. Told from the point of view of a young girl in her mid-twenties, Kovásznai portrays the girl's grandparents during the era of World War I, and her parents during the 1930s, as avatars for a critique of the State. The grandfather's moustache becomes a character of its own – 'it came, it saw, it conquered. A big moustache pleased women' – and operates as a direct reference to the Emperor of Austria and King of Hungary, Franz Joseph I. The lies and infidelities of the grandparents beneath the moral and ethical veneer they publically uphold becomes a thinly veiled critique of his regime. The decadence of her parents in the 1930s – embodied in carefree dancing – is also cast as a complicit engagement with the rise of Fascism, and both eras are characterized in Kovásznai's crossover photo-montage pop-art style by images of ordinary people lost to war and political oppression; a widowed nation lost to its authoritarian elites. The images speak to Kentridge's ideas about Modernist Absurdism; fragments and fractures recomposed to recast and animate Hungarian culture in a light that shows Kovásznai's distaste and disdain for the consensual practices that allowed authoritarian powers to prevail unopposed.

Young Man Playing the Old Masters' Gallery (1964) was to infuriate further. A young man playing a guitar in a gallery is visibly aroused at a female nude, a sensual experience so palpable that the nude also begins to dance under his gaze. Again, Kovásznai's recombinant style employs collage, photographic effects and cut-out animation allied to a rock 'n' roll and jazz score to play up the phallic play of the young man and the elusive distance of the nude. The film's offence essentially lies in its critique of Hungarian arts culture. Kovásznai essentially saw such a culture as complicit in its political conservatism and, as such, showed a flagrant disregard for the sobriety and canonical weight of past works. Both Kentridge and Kovásznai use the implied resonance of their own moral and ethical position as it is embedded in the work to reveal the unacceptable practices of the regimes they live within. By essentially co-opting the iconography of artistic and social bodies as they become politically entwined, evidencing their authoritarian agenda, Kentridge and Kovásznai use their animation process to re-configure the meaning and affect of culturally familiar signs and symbols – this is a crucial aspect of the ways in which 'animification' occurs, and such work contributes to an ongoing 'animification' of a changing *gestalt* in its historic period. If Kentridge craves reform, though, Kovásznai desires and prefers the progressive music, art and open sexuality of the West.

Metamorphoses (1964) was Kovásznai's clearest declaration of his intention to reinvent the animated film. 'This film is but a painting brought into a single movement,' he states at the beginning of the film, before embarking on a motion painting in which male and female 'portraits' in various styles and representations mutate. Such liminal flux draws attention to both form and content, simultaneously citing Modernist arts idioms and the constant uncertainties of relationships. The physical and material collapse of a man and woman into one another anticipates similar imagery in Czech experimental filmmaker, Jan Švankmajer's later clay animation, *Dimensions of Dialogue* (1982). If Kentridge's milieu is mark-making with charcoal, then Kovásznai's is paint, but both effectively 'draw' spontaneously in their chosen medium, privileging erasure and mutability in the image as the most vibrant embodiment of feeling and experience. Unknowingly, Kovásznai also echoed the desire of the first great Hungarian to impact upon the field of animation. John Halas, who established Halas & Batchelor Cartoons in the UK in 1940 and made the similarly innovative *The Magic Canvas* (1948) with fellow Hungarians, designer Peter Foldes and composer Mátyás Seiber. At the beginning, *The Magic Canvas* declares: 'Here is something different from the ordinary cartoon film.' Sadly, Kovásznai, even after one of his films was shown at the Annecy Animation Festival, was unaware of Halas' efforts in ASIFA – the global organization representing animation artists – to promote the form worldwide as the embodiment of a utopian outlook in an ever-darkening world. Kovásznai, it seems, was only dedicated to bringing utopia to Hungary, and carried out his work in a way that sought to use animation – however personal and seemingly abstract – as a documentary encounter with his own country. Crucially, this kind of documentary encounter is yet another instance of 'animification', in that such visualizations become the most significant evidence of a changing *gestalt*, and not one managed or authorized by more conventional representational means.

Employed by day at the Pannonia animation studio as one of its directors, he continued his prolific personal production at night, embracing numerous approaches and techniques, and drawing upon the *gestalt* in animation to play out his aesthetic experimentation as political intervention. Kovásznai, remained constantly monitored by the State, a fact established when it was discovered that he was regularly reported upon to the counterintelligence agency by his best friend László Végh, who described his colleague as a 'dangerous literary hooligan'. This dangerous literacy not merely manifested itself in his animation and huge, urgent, dynamic canvases, but in theoretical essays on cinema and art in the periodical, *Nagyvilàg*, and in theatre scripts. Kovásznai worked with illegal theatre groups, and often performed his plays to private gatherings. It is perhaps no surprise, then, that it is his ten-minute adaptation of *Hamlet* (1967), executed in simple watercolors and felt-tip drawings in the style of children's illustrated books, that reveals the most about his views on spying, betrayal and the decay of the State as a place without dignified human values – something he called 'the Danish Stench'. Undaunted, Kovásznai made the most of Budapest café life and the new sensualities of popular culture as the post-Ràkosi era encouraged 'thaw' and reduced 'terror'. Kovásznai's 'anima-vérité' combined personal experience with the depiction of material culture in Budapest, and anticipates the rise of animated documentary in the contemporary era as a way in which the subjective is readily imbued in the indexical and verifiably realist codes of conventional non-fiction texts (Kriger 2012, Honess Roe 2013). *Blossoming No 3369* (1971), featuring the contentious subject of a young woman advertising in the personal column of the newspaper, was Kovásznai's first explicit experiment in the form, which he describes as an attempt 'to depict the sociographic nature of the matter, within a subjective, artistic sphere' (Iványi-Bitter 2016: 76). It was also a vindication of his view that 'Total Cinema', defined in one of his essays, combined actuality and animation; the most persuasive moving image combination in using aesthetics to resist the received knowledge about the State in its 'realist' texts. Again, this becomes part of a cultural process in which verification of the *gestalt* emerges as a mode of 'animification'. Kovásznai produced many studies and prototypes to represent the woman in *Blossoming No 3369*, but the project did not turn out as Kovásznai originally intended, since he wanted to make seven vignettes addressing the topic, and only one was made. It is nevertheless an important step in the emergence of a signature style, and in once more privileging a woman's point of view as the mediator of difference in Socialist culture.

As in Kentridge's later works, Kovásznai also seeks to draw upon radical or formative modes of image making and performance to articulate subjective interventions into social processes and inchoate urban spaces. *The City Through My Eyes* (1971) and *Nights in the Boulevard* (1972) are essentially Kovásznai's 'city symphonies', animated hybrids of Dziga Vertov and Jean Rouch, each seeking to capture the atmosphere of his beloved birthplace. *Memory of the Summer of '74* (1974) aestheticizes the sunshine and sexuality of the new pop freedoms in Budapest, but only to use this veneer of openness and individual excess to invoke the memories of the suppressed uprisings in Hungary in 1956, and, for him, the more recent Soviet intervention in the former Czechoslovakia in 1968. For all his intellectual resistance, and contrived dandyism – itself a mockery of State elitism – Kovásznai could never fully reconcile his desire to replace the concrete limits of an oppressive ideology with the liberation of a more personalized yet universal consciousness. His one-man counterculture, using the synergistic opportunities in animation, could never succeed for all his efforts. There is some relationship here to the *gestalt* model developed by fellow Hungarian, film critic, theorist and screenwriter, Béla Balàzs, and his inherent challenge to Eisensteinian montage and a commitment to affective expression. It is *Ça-ira: Song of the French Revolution* (1973), with its vivid glutinous metamorphoses of the key figures of the Revolution – Robespierre, Marat, Danton and Saint Just – mixed with the pictorial suggestion of ordinary people that best represents Kovásznai's outlook at this time. Paris, symbolized in the mutating presence of Notre-Dame cathedral, itself signifies the impact and affect of the French enlightenment on Hungarian art in general, but also the tensions between individual faith and State hierarchy. The film's fluid manipulations of paint not merely suggest Cezanne or Van Gogh, but the very flux of existence, and the deep ambivalence, contradiction and brutality in the execution of State power. The film offers a perfect metaphor for Kovásznai's own talent and turmoil in the midst of the Totalitarian, while also speaking to the *gestalt* of both animation techniques as mediators of aesthetic and social discourse, and the 'animification' of culture.

Though little known, Kovásznai later made an animated feature called *Bubble Bath: A Musical Special Effects Film to the Rhythm of a Heartbeat* (1979), part of the Pannonia studio's plan to win back Hungarian audiences from their engagement with imported live action films. This may be seen as an important achievement in an era when classical animation in the Disney model was at a particular nadir, and feature animation was only saved by the efforts of Ralph Bakshi in more controversial adult fare like *Fritz the Cat* (1972) and *Coonskin* (1975). Inevitably, Kovásznai's intentions were more political than lurid, and though the jazz scored narrative revolves around a love triangle, his real theme is the everyday implications of 'fridge socialism', as the small-scale enterprise and consumerism informing the New Economic policies in Hungary began to characterize the János Kádár era of government.

Kovásznai died tragically early of leukemia in 1983, at the age of forty-nine, his late canvasses imbued with the colour of blood, and the self-conscious knowledge that the vivid colours that characterized both his painting and animation offered an enduring sense of 'life' beyond his own corporeal existence. This embrace of human experience and the fundamental sense of 'being' that his work embodied uses the synergies of arts practices and social engagement to create art that finds a ready place in the gallery, but moves beyond its confines to speak to a wider 'Spectrum' in animation, and interfaces with historically situated societal concerns to define the emergence of 'animification' in general. As such, his work extends the idea of the *gestalt* to properly evidence the synergistic nature not merely of animation as a form, or social infrastructures as intricate mechanisms of complex behaviour, but as the clear representation of consciousness engaging with its perception, reception and sensual absorption of his world.

References

Crafton, D. (1993). *Before Mickey: The Animated Film 1898–1928*. Chicago: University of Chicago Press.

Dreyfuss, L. (2007). *Momentary Momentum Catalogue*. London: Parasol Unit.

Honess Roe, B. (2013). *Animated Documentary*. Basingstoke/New York: Palgrave Macmillan.

Iványi-Bitter, B. (2016). *Kovásznai: A Cold War Artist, Animation, Painting, Freedom*. Budapest: Kovásznai Research Centre Foundation.

Johnson, O. and F. Thomas (1981). *Disney Animation: The Illusion of Life*. New York: Abbeville Press.

Kael, F. (1985). *Modern and Modernism: The Sovereignty of the Artist 1885–1925*. New York: Atheneum.

Klahr, L. (2005). 'A Clarification', in C. Gehman and S. Reinke (eds), *The Sharpest Point: Animation at the End of Cinema*, 96–125. Ottawa: XXY Press.

Krauss, R. (2005). '"The Rock": William Kentridge and Drawing for Projection', in C. Gehman and S. Reinke (eds), *The Sharpest Point: Animation at the End of Cinema*, 234–235. Ottawa: XXY Press.
Kriger, J. (2012). *Animated Realism: A Behind-the-Scenes Look at the Animated Documentary Genre*. Waltham, MA/Oxford: Focal Press/Elsevier.
Padiglione Austriaco, La Biennale di Venezia 2013 Catalogue.
Wells, P. (2002). *Animation and America*. Edinburgh: Edinburgh University Press.
Wells, P. (2016). 'Personal Interview with William Kentridge', February 2016.

3

On Analogical Thinking

Jan Švankmajer's *Jabberwocky* and *Alice*

Mareike Sera

Introduction

An 'intense and emotionally exhausting slice of life' (Cinephilia and Beyond n.d.). Is film able to cut a slice of life? On the basis of an intense and emotionally exhaustive experience? Is it able to change life? One might think so. Understanding film as a slice of life is a common film critical analogy. Similar to the analogy of film as philosophy (Rushton 2011, Read and Goodenough 2005, Wartenberg 2007, Vaughan 2013, Herzogenrath 2017). These analogies touch upon mimetic issues. How are representational and real world intertwined, the actual and the virtual? How do we understand each in relation to the other? A dialectical understanding sets both in dramatic tension to each other, expecting the non-identical 'essence' of fictional and real worlds to reveal the other, in the process of 'becoming Other'. This understanding accentuates the force of imagination, as Surrealist writing and art makes quite aware. Actual and virtual worlds meet on eye level, transform each other in the elements acted upon, but also in the intimate transmutation of the actor and her/his perception of the world. As André Breton (1969: 174) writes in *The Second Manifesto of Surrealism* 'the philosopher's stone is nothing more or less than that which was to enable man's imagination to take a stunning revenge on all things'.

In a similar vein, Richard Rushton (2011: 2) asks: 'Why should the creative aspects of the world be deemed secondary, as ornaments, as products devoid of being, a being which is reserved solely for natural or physical objects?' Rushton refers in this context to Cornelius Castoriadis' 'The Imaginary: Creation in the Socio-Historical Domain'. Castoriadis calls on 'the philosophers to reverse their approach and begin with humanity's creative acts – dreams, poems, music – as the basis of ontological enquiry' (Rushton 2011: 2). Rushton continues: 'Let the imaginary aspects of human life be those that determine the reality of things' (ibid.).

These passages indicate where one might break with the analogy of 'film as a slice of life'. The intention is not to place fictional over actual realities. The dialectical tension evolving around non-identity, mediation, negation and contradiction remains intact (Kautzer 2015: 34). As this paper would like to suggest, turning to imagination rather aims to understand the transmutations taking place between real and fictional worlds on a different level – the plane of analogical reasoning. The force of imagination – as means of knowledge and practice able to act on reality and transform it (Schmitt 2016: 232) – holds real and fictional worlds together, weaving them indistinguishably into one another. Dialectics designate the processes of dramatic confrontation and transformation, while analogy points towards hidden aspects of intimate initiation and revelation. At the moment of inspiration, of working through, of passion and devotion, real and fictional worlds are at their very nearest – indistinguishably close. The principle of analogy emphasizes how the imaginative experience transforms the acted upon and the actor in due process. It liberates the experience as a form of reflection that invites multiple perspectives, but dispenses of an ultimate end. It takes the form of an introspection, but turns its reflective mechanisms inward out – much like an inverted imagination.

As it will be put forward, analogy's relation to its 'object of imagination' is marked by an open and integrative attitude, but also by an irritating absence of intentionality. The lack of a specific 'object of imagination' does not only apply to 'how' but also to 'what' one imagines. This is crucial to surrealist understandings of imagination and its social role, particularly in the context of Czech Surrealism. This chapter will focus on two films by renowned Czech animator Jan Švankmajer: *Jabberwocky* (*Žvahlav aneb šatičky Slaměného Huberta*, 1971) and *Alice* (*Něco z Alenky*, 1988).

First, the phenomenon of analogy will be discussed from a broader academic perspective, while introducing in the second part Švankmajer's work and the role of analogy to Czech Surrealism. Parts three and four, then, will explore analogical thinking by applying it to different contexts: *Jabberwocky* is discussed in relation to George Bataille's *Story of the Eye* (Analogy I) and, in the following, *Alice* with reference to the philosophical work of Franco 'Bifo' Berardi (Analogy II). The result is a collage technique, which is vulnerable as analogical reasoning, especially if brought in resonance with dialectics, as will become clear. Different sets are to unfold and enrich each other. Accordingly, the argument might appear to jump occasionally, with explanatory bridges missing; however, this inconvenience appears worthwhile, as it stimulates and foments the hermeneutic passion of the palimpsest, a page of text written, erased and written over anew again.

Analogical thinking: the missing premise

Analogical reasoning allows us to stretch the possibilities of describing the world and the experience of it. By comparison, one explores the conjectures between distinct realms and learns new things about them in due course. As Julian S. Weitzenfeld (1984: 137) observes: 'One of the attractions of analogical reasoning has been that it is commonly taken to be a form of ampliative reasoning, reasoning that leads to knowledge about the target that is not contained in its premises.' Describing a film, thus, as a 'slice of life' – to return to this example – might evoke a series of spontaneous as well as highly developed concepts that link fiction and reality. 'And' is important in this respect. Analogical reasoning and feeling explores associations in a most open manner.

Cognitive sciences have conducted extensive research on the role of analogy in human perception over the past thirty years (Hesse 1966, Holyoak and Thagard 1995, Bartha 2010, Hofstadter and Sander 2013). Models explore, for example, mechanisms such as the retrieval of relevant source domains, analogical mapping across domains, the transfer of information and the learning of new categories (Hummel and Holyoak 1997). With the philosophical interest, the focus shifts towards the value of connecting and conjoining realms. Berardi's philosophy is a clear example in this respect, as will be elaborated. If analogy pertains to a central mechanism in human cognition, which criteria set 'good' from 'bad' analogies apart? This question is difficult to answer, as what is to be found, the premise, is and is not (yet) existent. Do you want to judge analogies from the promise of the result? Or the openness of the process?

The merit of analogical thinking emerges, once you embrace its uncertainty. This is where it fully develops its creative potential. The outcome is unknown and leans philosophically towards radical suspicion. The lack of certainty does not result from insufficient background knowledge. There are ways to methodologically work around it, such as enumeration, surveillance and inference (Weitzenfeld 1984: 146). These operations can substantiate arguments based on analogy. Nonetheless, suspicion works like a corrosive force on the underlying idea of sameness that draws different realms together. The shadow of a doubt accompanies the emerging 'new' and turns it inside out. Therein, analogical reasoning represents something like an 'inverse' imagination, as it does not work towards an expected outcome (premise). Analogy as inverse imagination leaves the imagined object open and susceptible to injury and failure. It opens an intimate void in a concatenation of references and objects, which is not indefinitely undetermined, but bare and susceptible to radical suspicion.

Czech Surrealism, dialectics and analogy

Analogy and dialectics are usually perceived as different types of reasoning, as incompatible or even opposed ways of thinking. The idea to perceive analogy as 'inverse imagination', which the next part of the chapter intends to root in surrealist understandings, draws a correlation between analogy and dialectics. According to Krzysztof Fijalkowski and Michael Richardson (2016: 11), Gérard Legrand (1971: 154) has spoken of analogy as the '"clasp" of the dialectical necklace', noting how '[t]he supreme relation of reconciled being does not cease to be dialectical, but it proves to be (or becomes) equally analogical'.

Correlating analogy and dialectics is important as it describes a specific way to approach the world and with this imagination. Analogy is thought to relate equivocally distinct but mutually participatory terms, while dialectics are meant to relate opposed and annulled propositions. Analogates (meaning the things, terms or concepts analogised) 'participate' in a congregation bound together by an uncertain but unifying analogon (meaning analogical principle), where the propositions of dialectics are meant to be annulled and resolved into a higher and richer synthetic unity of opposites. Analogy and dialectics describe different and even conflicting traditions of thought – with analogy associated with thinkers such as Aristotle and Aquinas and dialectics advanced by philosophers such as Plato, Hegel and Marx. Surrealist approaches submerge these traditions. A phenomenology of imagination, such as the surrealist's, explores 'ways of understanding' in their capacity to percolate the world and reproach social and political ills. Exploring the means of imagination means to understand and feel its force of transformation on reality. Opening dialectics towards analogical modes of reasoning allows us to integrate diagnostic and imperative ends. Social ills are analysed (diagnostic function) and acted upon (imperative function), but in a mode that embraces passivity, fragility and failure. The 'end' remains fractured and diverted towards 'and'.

The convergence of analogy and dialectics is particularly important to Czech Surrealism. Declarations by the group support this claim, inspired by the theoretical work of Vratislav Effenberger (Fijalkowski and Richardson 2001: 58–93, Dryje 2012). Effenberger was a key figure in promoting and understanding a surrealist phenomenology of imagination. He advocated a cycle of interpretation games that linked intimately to analogical models of thought ('The Platform of Prague Twenty Years On' 2001: 84). The idea was to support phenomenological understandings of imagination in ludic and experimental activities of the group. Švankmajer, who joined the surrealist group with his wife Eva Švankmajerová in the early 1970s, engaged intensely in these activities.[1] Švankmajer started making films in the mid-1960s. Before that, he worked in Black Theatre and was trained in puppetry at the Prague Theatre Academy (DAMU).[2] However, it was only with *The Garden* (*Zahrada*, 1968), *The Ossuary* (*Kostnice*, 1970) and *Jabberwocky* that Švankmajer 'developed the form of the Surrealist imagination [. . .] in the full light of a consciously Surrealist response to the world and a critical reflection on his own endeavours' (Dryje 2012: 263). An intense professional and personal relationship between Švankmajer, Effenberger and others in the group, such as Ludvík Šváb, Andrew Lass, Martin Stejskal and Albert Marenčin, formed. It was accompanied by a self-imposed marginalization of the group, a 'double isolation' that demonstrated the group's distance

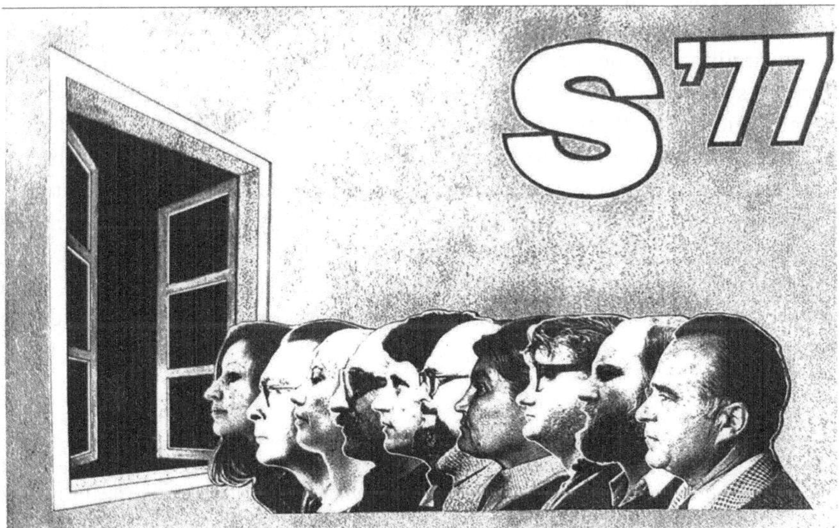

FIGURE 3.1 *Eva Švankmajerová, Vratislav Effenberger, Alena Nádvorníková, Karol Baron, Martin Stejskal, Juraj Mojžíš, Emilia Medková, Ludvík Šváb, Jan Švankmajer, Albert Marenčin, 1977, collage, 38 × 42 cm. Image copyright of and reprinted courtesy of ATHANOR, Film Production Company Ltd. Jaromir Kallista & Jan Švankmajer.*

[1] Ludic experimentation leans with Švankmajer strongly towards tactilism Švankmajer (1994, 2014) and Dryje (2012: 273–285).

[2] On Švankmajer's background in theatre and puppetry see Hames (1995) and Schmitt (2012 a, b and c).

towards both bourgeois and Stalinist ideology.[3] Related to this, the group signed *Charter '77* in 1977.

The declaration attests to the first public reclamation of resistance against uncontrolled Stalinist power. Among the first signatories was Effenberger, who reserved the right, though, to 'consider the need for differentiation in the forces forming the opposition later' ('The Platform of Prague Twenty Years On' 2001: 85).

The group's decision to enter a state of 'double isolation' relates inherently to the desire to develop the perspective submerging analogical and dialectical reasoning. Analogy allows to shield the 'noetic and integrating aspects' of imagination ('The Platform of Prague Twenty Years On' 2001: 87) from an idealist and positivist orientation as radical doubt works against ideological frameworks. Dialectics address the critical function of art, its diagnostic interest and ties it to socio-political realities. Analogy is able to breathe within these tight confounds, as 'the septic kernels of life' ('The Platform of Prague Twenty Years On' 2001: 89) find themselves implanted at the very heart of analogy (radical doubt), but simultaneously worked around and short-circuited in unexpected moments of spontaneous revelation. As these moments are non-intentional, they possess autonomy and the ability of self-organization. 'The Platform of Prague Twenty Years On' (2001: 89–90) cites Effenberger, who understood the 'imaginary object' as characterized by the tendency of the imagination to objectify and organize reality, and continues to explain how imagination creates: 'retroactively [. . .] reality itself, or rather clears a way of access by creating the new imaginary object [. . .] through the faculty of dynamising thought in the sense of the most consequent objectification and materialisation of this thought – towards the act'.

[3] The years between 1969 and 1977 were marked by public silence and repression by the authorities. In the brief period between 1968 and 1969, the group was able to publish some articles, among them the first issue of the group's journal *Analogon: Surrealism, Psychoanalysis, Anthropology, Diagonal Science*. The group managed to issue it despite the brutal end of the Prague Spring: '[The Surrealists were able] to take advantage of autonomous possibilities for publication only during the brief period of 1968–69 when the liberalisers had already retreated but the restoration of Stalinism had not yet put down roots. During this short period, the surrealists were able to publish several books which, for the first time in many years and for a long time thereafter, would be the only expression of their point of view: two works by Vratislav Effenberger, part of the complete works of Karel Teige, the *Surrealist Departure Point* collection and finally the first and also last issue of the review *Analogon*. Once more the great silence of official death followed, decreed from on high, forbidding all publications, exhibitions and other public activities [. . .] (the only attempt to organise a collective exhibition, *The Sphere of Dream*, in a small provincial gallery in Sovinec in 1983 was finally banned, although this was only announced on the very evening the exhibition, which had already been mounted, should have opened)' ('The Platform of Prague Twenty Years On' 2001: 85).

The 'new imaginary object', thus, represents an extrapolation of dialectic reasoning, intensified and liberated in analogy. Imagination's pretence to objectify and organize reality is cut lose in analogy, as the dialectic desire to form a synthesis is diverted towards analogy. A 'new source of motor energy' ('The Possible Against the Current' 2001: 67) rests in analogy as creative principle: processes of inventive short-circuiting take place, fleshing out imagination's drive to objectify and organize, materializing it and therein making it tangible and thinkable – before the fact. It paves the way for the impulse to act, contemplates the desire to act as it emerges and moves forward. The means are adopted, probed and adapted towards finding an attitude to action rather than describing an end of action. Analogy frees the means of creative invention and intuition by turning dialectics inside out.

This approach aims to strengthen what Teige terms the spiritual function of art, the auto-intentionality of the artwork. Teige (1971 [1924] in Vojvodík 2015: 28) writes: 'The work of art is complete and represents itself alone. [. . .] it has its own order, its own language, independent and autonomous and a full and specific form of expression. [. . .] It does not try to change the world or influence practical life.' The autonomous function of art has a quite specific meaning in this context. Rather than negation, it links to inversion: 'the negative grounds the positivity of a totalisation which is always essentially conserved. [. . .] the negative is a conservative principle which describes a situation in which nothing is lost' (Libertson 1982: 15). It is important to understand that the missing premise in analogical reasoning does not represent a 'straight' ontological negation of reasoning or the force of imagination in the senses of 'not possible' and 'not existent'. Analogy's premise is missing in a fragmented, discontinuous manner that relates to time rather than space. Ontological frameworks need to be adapted dynamically to fully understand this idea.[4]

Analogy I: Georges Bataille's *Story of the Eye* and Jan Švankmajer's *Jabberwocky*

Georges Bataille's *Story of the Eye* (*Histoire de l'oeil* 1987 [1928]), renowned for its excessive description of sexual obsessions and violence, takes an

[4] One way to adapt and adopt ontological understandings in a dynamic way is to allow the possibility of multiple and joined ontologies in the sense of a multiverse (Henare, Holbraad and Wastell 2006, Halbmayer 2012). The strong interest in animism as an ontological framework that Švankmajer takes in his work points in this direction. See the author's publication 'Intermedial Densities in the Work of Jan Švankmajer: A Media-anthropological Case Study' in Pethő (forthcoming).

unexpected turn on the last few pages. The story switches to a meta-narrative level that relates important motives of the story – for example, that of eyes, peeing and soaking through – (auto) biographically to a (fictive) author figure. As these details are part of the story and not, it is impossible to decide, how they relate to the 'real' author of the story. Meta-narrative turns tend to serve this function, implanting a sting of doubt into the heart of the narrative. As if to highlight this fact, the story ends (preliminary) with the following lines: 'I never linger over such memories, for they have long since lost any emotional significance for me. There was no way I could restore them to life except by transforming them and making them unrecognisable, at first glance, to my eyes, solely because during that deformation they acquired the lewdest of meanings' (Bataille 1987 [1928]: 96).

Any phenomenology of imagination is aligned to a phenomenology of remembering. The preliminary ending of Bataille's *Story of the Eye* attests to this. Imagined and memorized facts/motives blur into one another, sharing an unsecure ontological 'state' between reality and fiction. Within this state of ecstatic displacement, they cut themselves loose, gain autonomy and the ability to self-organize. The motive of 'eyes' is important in this respect. As it says in the above lines, the memorized facts/motives lose their emotional significance as they become unrecognizable to the eyes of the speaker/author. In the bizarre culmination of the story, the two main characters – Simone and an unnamed narrator – aggressively seduce and murder a Catholic priest, at the end of which one of their companions, Lord Edmund, cuts out his eyes. The Lord keeps one of them as a trophy and Simone pushes the other into her vagina, while having sex with the narrator.

The disturbing imagery works strongly towards transgression and emancipation. It objectifies and self-organizes the motives in an astonishingly liberated manner. The emancipatory process of the characters and objects/motives does not take place *for* the eyes, meaning in a transparent manner, but is implemented in the imaginative transformation of the objects/motives that culminates in literally divorcing them from the viewing subject and altering/expanding the perspective of perception – as the eye inserted into Simone's vagina describes a radically altered perspective of experience. The young adolescents cut themselves loose from bourgeois morals by pursuing sexual adventures. They rebel against the moral obligations that their parents expect them to follow and emancipate themselves in this respect. However, the revolt does not follow a surrogate idea of a better world.

The idea hides well 'beyond recognition' in the force of the images to transgress and self-organize. It becomes unrecognizable and uninteresting to the eyes of the writer and the reader. It no longer addresses and concerns them directly, but indirectly. As Roland Barthes (1972 [1963]: 239) writes: 'Although Georges Bataille's *Historie de l'oeil* includes several named characters and the narrative of their erotic adventures, he certainly does not give us the story of Simone, Marcelle, or the narrator [. . .]. *Histoire de l'oeil* is actually the story of an object.'

This object, the eye, enters, according to Barthes, a cycle of migration that places it 'essentially in an image system' (Barthes 1972 [1963]: 240) that turns its objects less into products but, rather, the substance of imagination. The system is based on analogy, for eyes as a motive become interchangeable with eggs, bulls' testicles and other ovular objects within the narrative.[5] These systems weave into another on the grounds of analogy, lacking the certainty of a common premise. As Barthes (1972 [1963]: 242) points out in relation to the biographical meta-narrative at the end of the story:

> doubtless the Eye, since this is its story, seems to predominate – the Eye which we know to be that of the blind father himself whose whitish globe rolled up when he urinated in front of the child; but in this case, it is the very equivalence of ocular and genital which is original, not one of its terms: the paradigm begins nowhere.

The biographical referent stands outside the imaginary system that relates eyes to testicles, to eggs, etc. without being able to break the chain of signification and flow of transformation between them. The cycle emancipates from its biographical source just as Simone and the narrator gain autonomy of their biological parents and their moral values by having each other. It/they concern[s] them no longer. This 'leap' describes a shift in focus from 'diagnostics' to 'imperative' values. The force of imagination requires a certain degree of distance to the biographic and biological experience in order to unfold. The immersive experience needs to be cut open in order to transgress and expand in order to be able to adapt and adopt 'new' perspectives (hermeneutic passion).

Jabberwocky: phenomenology of imagination and remembering

Jabberwocky shares this imaginative experience: interrelated, self-pertained objects of imagination that gain autonomy from biographical and biological sources and still remain true to them. They do not cease to attest to the ills and lesions molesting the background that they stem from (diagnostic function). Švankmajer's work is known for engaging intensely with personal obsessions and fears. Childhood is a central theme of his films, closely intertwining a phenomenology of imagination and remembering. Švankmajer's fascination for marionettes, for example, goes back to a puppet theatre that he received

[5] A second imaginary system uses liquid metaphors, relating tears to cats' milk, to egg yolks, to frequent urination scenes, to blood and to semen.

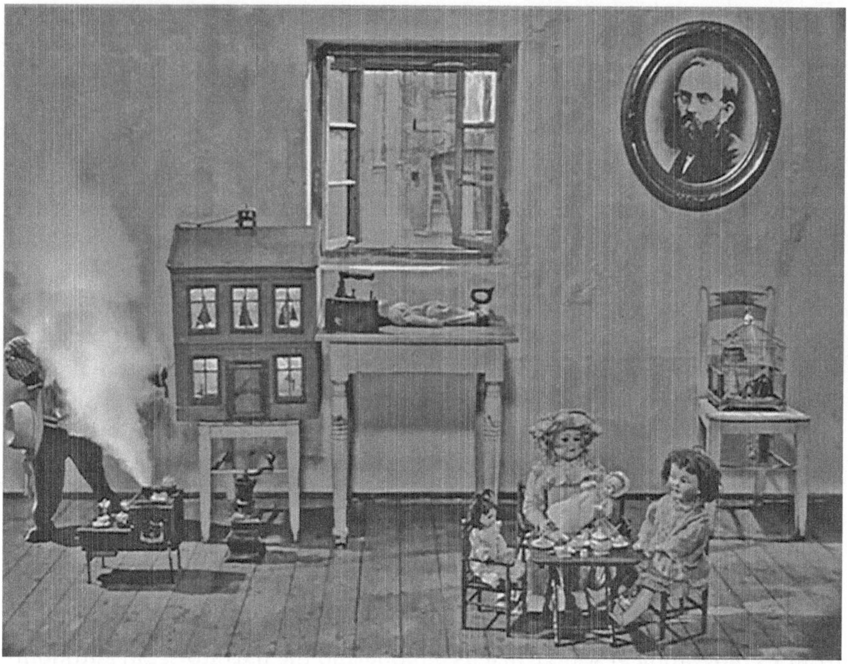

FIGURE 3.2 *Still from Jan Švankmajer's* Jabberwocky *(1971): The child's playroom.*

as a present in his childhood. The obsession with food relates to the experience that he was forced to eat and sent to camps especially designed for children with eating disorders. *Jabberwocky* like *Alice* focuses strongly on the imaginary world of children, drawing on the filmmaker's experiences.[6] The narrative layering is complex. The still reproduced in Figure 3.2 demonstrates this.

In five episodes, the film evokes a child's perspective in which the objects develop a spirit of their own, unveiling their innermost desires. Next to the dolls' house stands the main character, a boy's sailor suit, cranking frenetically a mechanism inside the house that moves little puppets until they fall into the mill to be ground. The overspill of energy is already evident in the still. A number of changeovers at different speeds (cranking, grinding, boiling, flattening, etc.) are taking place, filling the film dynamically and exhaustively. The excitement is concerted and counterbalanced in the overall impression of control and isolation seizing the scene. The room, the child's

[6] The third film in this concatenation is *Down to the Cellar* (*Do pivnice*, 1982), which deals with the filmmaker's experience of fear when he was sent down to the cellar as a child for potatoes.

playroom, has a window, but it opens only towards a courtyard surrounded by high buildings. The view offered by the camera is mostly up-front. Moreover, the idea of the painstaking manipulation of the objects before the camera in the process of object-animation speaks of control and isolation.

This impression reads in different directions. On the diagnostic level, the imagery overtly suggests children being gradually and unrelentingly formed to fit social roles and norms. The ending of the film strongly supports this idea: the boy's sailor suit is replaced by a black adolescent suit hanging stiff in the wardrobe. The child's creative energy is stifled by authoritarian structures. Alienation supplants the child's force of imagination.

However, the sheer transformative energy emancipates the imagery of 'strict' diagnostic readings and makes a 'leap' towards imaginary autonomy, just as the boy's sailor suit is divorced of the boy's body *and* remains true to it. Motives gather around objects of imagination and form autonomous referential systems or, rather, analogical constellation, as this paper would like to suggest. One evolves around boiling liquids. The boy's suit literally 'leaps' out of a bowl with boiling water. The steam 'gives birth' to the suit, just like the larger puppet with the smaller ones crawling out of it. Similarly, the oven rattles with steam cooking the puppet's parts for dinner for the puppet family, bigger in size. Water also boils in large test tubes filled with stones, chestnuts and shells. Another prominent example in the film involves blood. The fourth episode begins with a knife landing on a table. It starts to dance in the most wonderful manner, jumps and turns pirouettes with growing enthusiasm. Suddenly, however, it loses its passion and falls stiffly on the table. The blade snaps and blood runs from the knife's body. The blood of this delicate imaginary object has been brought to boil by sheer passion.

Thus, the imagery might protest against social alienation, cultural oppression and Stalinist/bourgeois ideology. The larger puppet family, for example, is dressed in Victorian dress, while eating the cooked parts of smaller puppets of supposedly lower class and therefore of 'less value'. On top of this, a milieu is set up where creative energy unleashes and breaks free. The same applies to the (auto) biographical and biological details, which inspire the imagery, but do not exhaust it. The filmmaker's memory of his childhood most certainly informs the design of the setting and the emerging imagery. It serves as a source of reference. The emotional, bodily and material experience, which adds up to create the biological milieu, adds to this. The motives remain in contact with these sources. They also enter a cycle of exchange and change, which detaches them from the milieu they grow in. They begin to aspire.

At the heart of the creative force of analogical reasoning, objects distance themselves from their utilitarian and descriptive function (directed at an end) and turn into sovereign imaginary objects – part of a constellation – exploring the relations emerging respectively. Imaginary objects aspire at a distance of their utilitarian and descriptive function, a remoteness that is created in ecstatic moments of displacement and transgression. Any phenomenology of imagination relates not only to a phenomenology of remembering, but also a phenomenology of aspiration. *Jabberwocky* intimates this in the affluent images of boiling objects, pertaining to different milieus to remember and to aspire: objects of everyday life, objects steeped in childhood memories, cultural artefacts, objects from natural origin, etc. They relate and do not relate, as the sting of doubt gnaws on their desire to conspire.[7] They do nonetheless.

Much more could be said about possible relations between Bataille's *Story of the Eye* and *Jabberwocky*, drawing out a field of rich analogies. The argument intends to shift to a new setting at this point, though, in order to gather a participatory view from 'inside' analogical reasoning. The shift to Berardi and his philosophy aims to divert the argument towards a different perspective on socio-political realities and how they might be analysed (diagnostic function) and dealt with (imperative function) in conjunctive and connective modes of understanding, in Berardi's terms. The first part of Analogy II will explore the conjunctive and the connective mode with analogy as a theoretical model in mind, while the second and the third part will look at autonomous structures in the imaginary and practical sense related to Carroll's *Alice in Wonderland*. The shift from Švankmajer's *Alice* to *Radio Alice* corresponds to and performs an 'imaginary leap', submerging the practical and the imaginary realm.

Analogy II: Franco 'Bifo' Berardi and Jan Švankmajer's *Alice*

Italian activist and philosopher Franco 'Bifo' Berardi focuses in his writing on the experience of living in the digital and post-capitalist age. Švankmajer, aged 83 and still active as a filmmaker, stays with analogue techniques of filmmaking, making the new films – again – unique in this respect. One might expect both positions to go astray, but a deep fascination with analogical reasoning draws them together. Berardi's work engages extensively with the question of how relational modes might differ and converge.

In *And. Phenomenology of the End* (2014), Berardi argues for a shift from 'conjunction' to 'connection' as the dominant mode of social interaction. The shift affects the experience of sensibility and sensitivity. From a diagnostic point of view, it results in a state of despair and a genuine mutation of social relations. Important, again, is the relation of 'and' and

[7] *Conspirators of Pleasure* (*Spiklenci slasti*, 1996), Švankmajer's third feature film after *Faust* (*Lekce Faust*, 1994) and *Alice*, highlights the creative principle of analogy in its title.

'end', as it is already intimated in the title of the book. Berardi (2014: 18) explains:

> I call conjunction a concatenation of bodies and machines that can generate meaning without following a pre-ordained design, nor obeying any inner law or finality. Connection, on the other hand, is a concatenation of bodies and machines that can generate meaning only following a human-made intrinsic design, only obeying precise rules of behaviour and functioning. Connection is not singular, not intentional, not vibrational. It is rather an operative concatenation between previously formatted agents of meaning (bodies, or machines) which have been codified, or formatted according to a code.

How these systems or constellations emerge, thus, differs fundamentally in various instances. Berardi distinguishes between directed/intentional modes of connection and those lacking a pre-conceived pattern or embedded design. Due to the lacking premise, conjunction is able to create an infinite number of constellations, each of which roots in singularity: 'Conjunctive concatenation [. . .] is event, not structure, and it is unrepeatable because it happens in a unique point in the net of space and time' (Berardi 2014: 12).

There is no design to fulfill and no code to comply with, in contrast to the connective mode. The conjunctive mode is quite reminiscent of analogical reasoning. It requires the vibrant state of sensibility, the immersive ability to 'process signs and semiotic stimulations that cannot be verbalised or verbally coded' (Berardi 2014: 30). It implies the regression to an emphatic state, which lacks the determination of a pre-existing design and is nonetheless able to establish links in between things and signs, revealing points of convergence from an altered perspective.

Indicators of psycho-physical fragility relate to and reveal the dire consequences of the shift towards the connective mode of social relations in the digital and post-capitalist age. Competitive pressure, acceleration of stimuli and constant attentive stress have a genuine deforming, psycho-pathogenic effect:

> The universe of receivers – the ensemble of human brains, of real people made of flesh and fragile and sensual organs – is not formatted according to the same standards as the system of digital transmitters. The functional paradigm of the universe of Transmitters does not correspond to that of the universe of Receivers. This asymmetry manifests itself in various pathological effects: permanent electrocution, panic, overexcitement, hypermobility, attention disorders, dyslexia, information overload, the saturation of reception circuits.
>
> BERARDI 2007: 81

However, strategies to escape this semiotic and productive over-agility (or over-kill) are not easily pinpointed. The intention to decelerate and reduce complexity runs counter to the human drive to produce and exhaust potentiality. Another possibility that Berardi refers to is to accelerate the 'post-human' condition and adapt the human cognitive and bodily system to the exigencies of the info-sphere. Finally, Berardi (2007: 85) suggests that 'a strategy of subtraction is possible, a strategy of distancing oneself from the vortex – but only small communities will be able to follow it, constituting spheres of existential, economic, and informational autonomy from the world economy'.

Alice's empowerment: phenomenology of aspiration

The use of masochistic imagery in Švankmajer's *Alice* points to the vibrant but vulnerable state of analogical reasoning and with this to the conjunctive mode in Beradi's terminology. Alice's fall down the rabbit hole (pictured in Švankmajer's version as a trip downwards in an elevator passing all kind of strange objects) reads as immersive and schizophrenic 'atmospheric thickening', while the end of the film signals a strong empowerment in the sense of a ritualist rebirth (phenomenology of aspiration). In between stands the Mad Tea Party, in Švankmajer's version an intensely performed masochistic ritual: The Mad Hatter, a wooden marionette, and The March Hare move around the table and perform the same acts over and over again, like spreading butter on a clockwork watch (see Figure 3.3), rewinding The March Hare's mechanical drive, pouring tea down the puppet's body, etc. At the end of each cycle, a fur in the shape of a woman's collar licks the tea cups clean.

In Gilles Deleuze's reading of Carroll's *Alice in Wonderland* in *Logic of Sense*, the story runs along a fine, but intractable line. One side describes the world of depth, of actions and passions with restlessly intermingling, edible and penetrable bodies, beings, objects and creatures – while the other side articulates the world of height, of impenetrable transcendence, of the metaphysical surface of the event. Thus, when The March Hare spreads butter onto the watch or the film shows tea running down the wooden body of the Hatter, Švankmajer highlights these incompatible, yet interdependent worlds of height and depth. Deleuze argues that Carroll's story can be divided into three parts, as he writes in relation to the first part:

> The first part [. . .] starting with Alice's interminable fall, is completely immersed in the schizoid element of depth. Everything is food, excrement, simulacrum, partial internal object, and poisonous mixture. Alice herself is one of these objects when she is little; when she is large, she is identified

> with their receptacle. The oral, anal, urethral character of this part has often been stressed.
>
> DELEUZE 1990 [1969]: 234

In contrast to the first part's relation to regression, the second part represents a phase of transition, in which Alice gradually realizes her power to choose between the world of regression and the world of abstraction. In relation to the Mad Tea Party, Alice seems inclined to decide between the artist who deals with heads – represented by the Hatter – and the animal that lives in burrows – pictured by The March Hare. The butter on the watch exemplifies this remarkably. Time emblematically represents metaphysical, disembodied abstraction, while butter intimates the very essence of nutrition, namely fat. The same seems true for the tea running down the puppet's body, as the puppet is unable to digest it. The edible and the inedible do not intermingle, but forge marvellous instances of poetic imagery. They highlight the insurmountable tension involved in the grotesque interplay between the worlds of height and depth.

Gaston Bachelard's reading of the trope of miniature and the notion of patience in *The Poetics of Space* is telling in relation to the imaginative processes involved in devising poetic/masochistic imagery. He (1994 [1958]: 159) writes: 'Indeed, we have only to imagine it [this peace] for our souls to

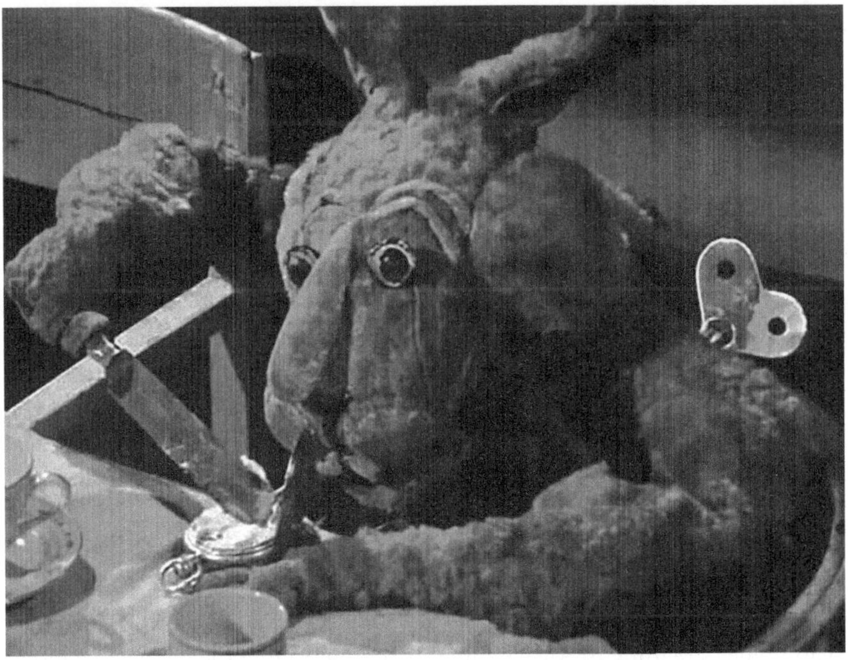

FIGURE 3.3 *Still from Jan Švankmajer's* Alice *(1988): The March Hare.*

be bathed in peace. All small things must evolve slowly, and certainly a long period of leisure, in a quiet room, was needed to miniaturise the world.' Bachelard (1994 [1958]: 174) goes on: 'the causality of smallness stirs all our senses, and an interesting study could be undertaken of the "miniatures" that appeal to each sense. [. . .] a whiff of perfume, or even the slightest odour can create an entire environment in the world of the imagination'.

Bachelard's observations on patience and heightened sensibility in relation to the trope of 'miniature' powerfully point in the direction of masochism. The masochistic world distinguishes itself by an enriched, saturated atmosphere that is to be bodily and structurally absorbed. It creates a phantasm that expiates the authoritative order. The point of subversion is the ritualistic death, forestalling the utopian event of rebirth; in *Alice*, we witness this in the sequence of superimpositions with Alice's head being replaced by the heads of the creatures of Wonderland. After this, Alice awakes out of her dream, while the things surrounding her appear to have returned to a state of 'dull' reality, as well unaffected and unimpressed by the enhanced, enriched world of the masochistic phantasm. This preliminary perception, however, overturns, when she realizes that the White Rabbit is missing. She draws out a pair of scissors and says, just like the Queen: 'He is late as usual, I think I'll cut his head off!'

The radical empowerment of Alice after she has had to endure an endless series of demeaning and cruel actions and passions clearly evokes the association of a mythic or ritualistic rebirth that re-adjusts the world to the maternal order. By devising a contract, the patriarchal order ends and is subdued to the law of the mother – that kind of ritualistic behaviour that we encounter in Švankmajer's version of the Mad Tea Party or the Queen's despotic call: 'Off with their heads!'

In this sense, Švankmajer's *Alice* suggests that change in terms of a revolutionary potential/actualization requires not only the bodily, fleshly and intentional side of action and passion, but also the insubstantial, abstract agency of the event. Moreover, on the level of the metaphysical event, poetic imagery exhibits a double-edged nature of being both diagnostic and imperative. The mimetic relation of the imagery to bodily experience *and* being both diagnostic and imperative stands in direct correlation to the artistic function of poesis. In poetic/masochistic imagery, one not only perceives the ontological possibility of revolution. One finds encapsulated the metaphysical surface unfolding and enfolding the facilitated sensory, fleshly and intelligible expansion towards the world of actions and passions.

Radio Alice

Švankmajer's reading of Alice highlights that betraying the connective mode of social relations (and therein escaping its pathologies) is closely linked to entering a survival mode of autonomous structures. The search for alternative routes of communication is intimately linked to the 'escape into reality'. To 'unleash' autonomous cycles of images, ecstatically and erratically transgressing descriptive and utilitarian functions, creates and draws on alternative modes, as famously epitomized in Lewis Carroll's nonsense literature. Švankmajer's *Jabberwocky* as much as *Alice*, engages intensely with Carroll's texts on this ground. Berardi's political engagement, too, exhibits strong ties to Carroll's work. Berardi is a prominent participant of Bologna's first free pirate radio station, *Radio Alice*, that started broadcasting in the late 1970s and derived its name directly from Carroll's *Alice in Wonderland* (1865).

While Švankmajer issued *Charter '77* together with his fellow surrealists from Prague, the first open call of resistance after years of repression and silence, as it has been intimated above, Berardi pursued a different form of open protest related to Bologna's creative autonomy movement of 1977. As Michael Goddard (2011: 1) points out:

> the naming was no mere accident; in part a reference to Gilles Deleuze's reading of Lewis Carroll and nonsense in *The Logic of Sense*, the name Alice announced this radio's desire to go beyond the rational limits of communication and politics in the directions of a surrealistic play with sense and nonsense, to produce a desiring form of political communication in which poetic delirium would have as much place as political events, or further a space in which false information could produce real events.

The radio station's name, thus, expressed the wish to communicate 'more' than rationally informed political trajectories. Just as the channel of communication intends to break free and self-organize in a subversive way, the broadcasting material wishes to do the same thing by drawing on 'the historical artistic avant-garde, Deleuzian philosophy, situationist practice and of course *Alice in Wonderland* itself' (Goddard 2011: 1). *Radio Alice* is an extraordinary example of a media-ecological reorganization that submerges the fictional and real desire to perform a 'leap' towards autonomous structures, breaking free of utilitarian and descriptive principles.[8]

This motion towards autonomy relates to the station's engagement with Alice as a literary figure and its schizoanalytic interpretations by Deleuze and Antonin Artaud. Goddard (2011: 6) explains that *Radio Alice* performed:

[8] An outlash of violence hindered the experiment to develop further, though the venture had, according to Goddard, the 'technical and social capacity to redefine what was meant by expressions like "autonomy" and "self-valorization"' (Goddard 2011: 3).

> a type of translation of Carroll's Alice, but one that like Artaud's schizophrenic reading was also transforming its meaning; one could say that despite or maybe because of the proximity to a schizoanalytic reading of Alice, a new Alice emerged, Alice as a subversive, a revolutionary Alice, whose play with sense and nonsense was directly articulated to challenge the official, dominant semiosis of the state, capitalism and conventional modes of political representation.

Drawing a mimetic relation between expression and experience means to draw an actual effect-relation between the event and the action/passion, which opens the possibility of actual change.

Conclusion

The sovereign function of art does not fulfill itself and does not withdraw from the world. It rather has a quite specific understanding of its relation to reality, as it is not directed in a specific manner towards some meaning and understating of the world, but arrives at this understanding by way of an inverse logic. It stimulates the hermeneutic passion to understand the imaginative experience through a variety of philosophical lenses (e.g. ontological, ethical, etc.). However, this exploring and understanding is *and* is not specifically directed at the same time. The former directs unrelentingly at the ills of social-political realities. The latter is quite clear in the respect that 'better worlds' are not simply 'imagined'. The ideal or utopian 'core' is deliberately voided, safe-guarded by radical suspicion.

The explorations aligned to analogical thinking do not work towards some imagined, utopian 'substitute reality'. Quite the opposite is the case. František Dryje (2012: 225) explains: 'Surrealism was indeed concerned not with an artificial, imaginary reality, or some kind of autonomous artistic world, but with the empirically given world, existent, but to be expressed in a new qualitatively enlarged spectrum of subject-object relations.' In relation to this, analogy creates on a cosmic scale, but the underlying principles of this creation remain hidden. The missing premise re-routes the desire to express and to understand 'other' structures of knowledge and communication, correlations that evade und subvert positivist identity principles. Engaging with these principles, conjoined to the desire to 'take a different path', results in empowerment – an imperative empowerment related to the diagnostic force to understand the source of inspiration.

Describing analogy as 'inverse' imagination, thus, means to understand it as a mechanism that directs diagnostically at political realities, but withdraws from the imperative to 'mean' and 'describe' in relation to imagining 'better' worlds. The diagnostic and the imperative function have different relations to the paradox of imagination, being intentional *and* not intentional at the same time. One does not easily translate to the other. The diagnostic sense observes and contemplates. It informs the desire to act (imperative function), to act in a socially and ethically agreeable way, but it is not able to provide exhaustive answers to 'what' this way might look like and which means are needed to achieve it ('how'). Finding answers to these questions requires adjustment to the way of imagining them, to contemplate and adapt possible ways. The imperative function forms a radical intensification of the diagnostic function with regard to adjusting the creative and critical means of imagination. It gives rise to an unknown autonomy of the means in the relation between the real and the fictional by obliterating the means' intentionality. Analogy as a creative principle takes a decisive role in this.

References

Bachelard, G. (1994 [1958]). *The Poetics of Space*, trans. M. Jolas. Boston: Beacon Press.

Bartha, P. (2010). *By Parallel Reasoning: The Construction and Evaluation of Analogical Arguments*. New York: Oxford University Press.

Barthes, R. (1972 [1963]). 'The Metaphor of the Eye', in R. Barthes, *Critical Essays*, trans. R. Howard, 239–247. Evanston: Northwestern University Press.

Bataille, G. (1987 [1928]). *Story of the Eye*, trans. J. Neugroschel. San Francisco: City Lights Books.

Berardi, F. (2007). 'Schizo-Economy', *SubStance #112*, 36 (1): 76–85.

Berardi, F. (2014). *And. Phenomenology of the End: Cognition and Sensibility in the Transition from Conjunctive to Connective Mode of Social Communication*. Espoo: Aalto University publication.

Breton, A. (1969). *Manifestoes of Surrealism*, trans. R. Seaver and H. Lane. Ann Arbor: University of Michigan Press.

Castoriadis, C. (1997). 'The Imaginary: Creation in the Socio-historical Domain', in D. A. Curtis (ed.), *World in Fragments: Writings on Politics, Society, Psychoanalysis, and the Imagination*, 3–18. Stanford: Stanford University Press.

Cinephilia and Beyond, *A Woman under the Influence: Cassavetes' Intense and Emotionally Exhausting Slice of Life*. Available online: http://cinephiliabeyond.org/a-woman-under-the-influence-cassavetes-intense-and-emotionally-exhausting-slice-of-life/ (accessed 16 September 2017).

Deleuze, G. (1990 [1969]). *The Logic of Sense*, ed. C. V. Boundas, trans. M. Lester and C. Strivale. London: Athlone Press.

Dryje, F. (2012). 'Jan Švankmajer, Surrealist', in F. Dryje and Schmitt (eds), *Jan Švankmajer: Dimensions of Dialogue/Between Film and Fine Art*, 219–322. Prague: Arbor Vitae.

Fijalkowski, K. and M. Richardson, eds and trans. (2001). *Surrealism against the Current: Tracts and Declarations*. London: Pluto Press.

Fijalkowski, K. and M. Richardson (2016). 'Introduction', in K. Fijalkowski and M. Richardson (eds), *Surrealism: Key Concepts*, 1–16. New York: Routledge.

Goddard, M. (2011). *Alice in Radioland: Radio Alice and the Movement of 77 Through the Looking Glass*, conference presentation at *Afterlife of Alice*, Hic Dragones, 2. December 2011. Available online: http://www.academia.edu/1709077/Alice_in_Radioland (accessed 16 September 2017).

Halbmayer, E. (2012). 'Amerindian Mereology: Animism, Analogy, and the Multiverse', *Indiana*, 29: 103–125.

Hames, P. (1995). 'Interview with Jan Švankmajer', in P. Hames (ed.), *Dark Alchemy: The Films of Jan Švankmajer*, 96–118. Westport: Praeger.

Henare, A., M. Holbraad and S. Wastell, eds (2006), *Thinking Through Things: Theorising Artifacts Ethnographically*. London: Routledge.

Herzogenrath, B., ed. (2017). *Film as Philosophy*. Minneapolis: University of Minnesota Press.

Hesse, M. B. (1966). *Models and Analogies in Science*. Notre Dame: University of Notre Dame Press.

Hofstadter, D. and E. Sander (2013). *Surfaces and Essences: Analogy as the Fuel and Fire of Thinking*. New York: Basic Books.

Holyoak, K. and P. Thagard (1995). *Mental Leaps: Analogy in Creative Thought*. Cambridge: MIT Press.

Hummel, J. E. and K. J. Holyoak (1997). 'Distributed Representations of Structure: A Theory of Analogical Access and Mapping', *Psychological Review*, 104 (3): 427–466.

Kautzer, C. (2015). *Radical Philosophy: An Introduction*. Boulder: Paradigm Publishers.

Legrand, G. (1971). *Préface au système de l'éternité*. Paris: Le Terrain Vague.

Libertson, J. (1982). *Proximity: Levinas, Blanchot, Bataille and Communication*. The Hague: Martinus Nijhoff Publishers.

Read, R. and J. Goodenough, eds (2005). *Film as Philosophy: Essays in Cinema After Wittgenstein and Cavell*. Basingstoke: Palgrave Macmillan.

Rushton, R. (2011). *The Reality of Film: Theories of Filmic Reality*. Manchester: Manchester University Press.

Schmitt, B. (2012a). 'Return to Origins: The Setting of King Stag', in F. Dryje and B. Schmitt (eds), *Jan Švankmajer: Dimensions of Dialogue/Between Film and Fine Art*, 23–42. Prague: Arbor Vitae.

Schmitt, B. (2012b). 'Jan Švankmajer and Johanes Doktor Faust by Emil Radok: From Primitive Myth to the Crisis of Civilisation', in F. Dryje and B. Schmitt (eds), *Jan Švankmajer: Dimensions of Dialogue/Between Film and Fine Art*, 43–60. Prague: Arbor Vitae.

Schmitt, B. (2012c). 'Detailed Bibliography with Commentary (I) 1934–1970', in F. Dryje and B. Schmitt (eds), *Jan Švankmajer: Dimensions of Dialogue/Between Film and Fine Art*, 61–94. Prague: Arbor Vitae.

Schmitt, B. (2016). 'Magic Art', in K. Fijalkowski and M. Richardson (eds), *Surrealism: Key Concepts*, 228–238. New York: Routledge.

Sera, M. (forthcoming). 'Intermedial Densities in the Work of Jan Švankmajer: A Media-anthropological Case Study', in A. Pethő (ed.), *Intermediality in Contemporary Eastern European and Russian Cinema*. Edinburgh: Edinburgh University Press.

Švankmajer, J. (1994). *Transmutace smyslů: Transmutation of the Senses*. Prague: Středoevropská galerie a nakladatelství.

Švankmajer, J. (2014). *Touching and Imagining: An Introduction to Tactile Art*. London: Tauris.

Teige, K. (1971 [1924]). 'Moderní umění a společnost', in Š. Vlašín (ed.), *Avantgarda známá a neznámá*, vol. I, 505–513. Prague: Svoboda.

'The Possible Against the Current' (2001) in K. Fijalkowski and M. Richardson (eds and trans.), *Surrealism against the Current: Tracts and Declarations*, 66–75. London: Pluto Press.

'The Platform of Prague Twenty Years On' (2001) in K. Fijalkowski and M. Richardson (eds and trans.), *Surrealism against the Current: Tracts and Declarations*, 81–92. London: Pluto Press.

Vaughan, H. (2013). *Where Film Meets Philosophy: Godard, Resnais, and Experiments in Cinematic Thinking*. New York: Columbia University Press.

Vojvodík, J. (2015). 'World of "Purely Artistic Conception" and a "Universal Art of the Spirit": Max Dvořák and Karel Teige between Phenomenology and Surrealism', *Slovo a smysl – Word & Sense*, 12 (24): 25–41.

Wartenberg, T. E. (2007). *Thinking on Screen: Film as Philosophy*. New York: Routledge.

Weitzenfeld, J. S. (1984). 'Valid Reasoning by Analogy', *Philosophy of Science*, 51: 137–149.

Films

Alice (*Něco z Alenky*, 1988), [Film], Dir. Jan Švankmajer, CH, DE, GB: Condor Film, Hessischer Rundfunk, Film Four International.

Conspirators of Pleasure (*Spiklenci slasti*, 1996), [Film], Dir. Jan Švankmajer, GB, CH, CZ: Athanor Film, Koninck International, Delfilm.

Down to the Cellar (*Do pivnice*, 1982), [Film], Dir. Jan Švankmajer, CZ: Slovenská filmová tvorba.

The Garden (*Zahrada*, 1968), [Film], Dir. Jan Švankmajer, CZ: Krátký film Praha.

Jabberwocky (*Žvahlav aneb šatičky Slaměného Huberta*, 1971), [Film], Dir. Jan Švankmajer, CZ, USA: Krátký film Praha, Wester Wood Studio.

Lekce Faust (1994), [Film], Dir. Jan Švankmajer, GB, FR, DE, CZ: BBC, Lumen Films, Pandora Film, Heart of Europe, Athanor Film, Koninck International.

The Ossuary (*Kostnice*, 1970), [Film], Dir. Jan Švankmajer, CZ: Krátký film Praha.

4

The Successful Chorus of 'The Second Wave'

An Examination of Feminism's 'Manifesto' of Digital Art[1]

Chunning Guo (Maggie)

Preface: the images of 'Father Power' and the voices of women artists

When talking about computers or digital technology, most people will not connect this terminology with the image of women. There are several male figures that serve as representatives of the computer, such as John von Neumann,[2] Alan Turing,[3] Thomas Watson[4] and Steve Jobs.[5] Even the

---

[1] The paper was originally presented at the 7th annual Under the Radar conference (Vienna; http://under-radar.com/2017/).

[2] A Hungarian-American mathematician, and computer scientist. The foremost mathematician of his time, he was a pioneer of the application of operator theory to quantum mechanics in the development of functional analysis, and a key figure in the development of game theory and the concepts of cellular automata, the universal constructor and the digital computer.

[3] He provided a formalized concept of the algorithms and computations that would be used to create the Turing machine, which can be considered a model of a general-purpose computer.

[4] A US businessman, the chairman and CEO of International Business Machines (IBM). He oversaw the company's growth (1914–1956), turning it into a highly effective organization.

[5] Co-founder and CEO of Apple (also served as CEO of Pixar), a pioneer of the personal computer revolution of 1970s and 1980s, together with Steve Wozniak.

pioneers of digital art seem to be nothing more than a group of men working in labs for NASA or Bell. However, with careful examination through the archives and research of digital art, a group of women artists during the 1970s and 1980s must standout. In the 'forest' of 'Fathers' images', their voices become even more meaningful and important.

The leaders of this group were Lillian Schwartz (1927–) and Katherine Nash (1910–1982), their 'manifesto' calling on collaboration among artists, scientists and engineers could be regarded as a beginning of cross-field (and cross-gender) cooperation in digital art. This manifesto and artistic practice offered a new perspective with which to rethink the movements of feminism as well as digital art. This chapter will demonstrate how 'The Second Wave of Digital Art' and 'The Second Wave of Feminism' clashed and developed into a chorus. And we will have a chance to review how this successful chorus offered the dialogue of gender equality (in the work 'Leo/Lisa' by Schwartz) through a digital collage combining 'Mona Lisa' and the self-portrait of Leonardo Da Vinci.

'Cold' computer and 'Father Power'

In 1982, 'The Computer' was selected as The Man of the Year by the very influential *Time* magazine (who called it The Machine of the Year). Most people only remember a man sitting in front of the computer in this *Time* cover, the image of the computer seemingly related only with the figure of a man. Even when people had a chance to see the whole front and back cover of this issue the computer was largely seen as a tool for business when it came to men, but for entertainment with regards to women users.

Though there were debates about the first inventor of the computer, we see in the following list that it is all about who is the real 'father' of the computing machine. In 1973, there was a court announcement regarding the first official inventor of the computer in America; it was Atanasoff and his student Berry. In 1942, Atanasoff shared his idea about the ABC machine with Mauchly, then Mauchly and P. Eckert invented ENIAC in 1946.[6]

When we look back at the history of the development of the computer, we find that behind the fatherly images, there are also a lot of nameless women. In the photos recording the process of inventing and operating ENIAC, there were females behind and beside the male scientists. Even though some women played an important role during the whole

[6] The name *ABC* machine is an initialism; A comes from Atanasoff, B comes from Berry and C means computer.

TABLE 4.1 The 'Fathers' of the Computer

Inventor	Timeline	Main contributions
John von Neumann	1903–1957	Stored-program computer
Alan M. Turing	1912–1954	Turing machine
J. Mauchly	1907–1980	ENIAC
P. Eckert	1919–1995	ENIAC
John V. Atanasoff	1903–1995	ABC machine
Clifford E. Berry	1918–1963	ABC machine

process, in the writing of history prior to the 1980s, little attention was paid to them.

One notable example was Joan Clarke (1917–1996),[7] who contributed to the development of the Turing machine. In recent years, people who watched the feature film *The Imitation Game* (M. Tyldum, 2014) learned about Clarke's contributions for the first time. The film, based on the eponymous novel, told us how the Turing machine was invented in order to beat the German enigma machine during World War II and how a woman set up the kind and warm collaboration required for this team effort to succeed. This film presents a feminine image within the fathers' forest, and this woman was Joan Clarke.

Even though Clarke was excellent in the field of mathematics, she was denied a full mathematics degree, which Cambridge University only awarded to men until 1948. Clarke became deputy head of Hut 8 in 1944, while still paid less than her male colleagues. Additionally, she needed to ask her parents' permission to work as at that time women were thought to be incapable of making decisions for themselves. In fact, there were more excellent women scientists like Clarke who remain unknown due to the continuing secrecy among cryptanalysts, and the systematic neglect of women's contributions. In the history of computing there has been a hidden forest of women, but the 'Father Power' has cast shadows over the presence of womanly images and voices. This is a time to re-evaluate the roles and contributions of these women.

[7] Also known as Joan Murray. She was an English cryptanalyst and numismatist best known for her work as a code-breaker at Bletchley Park during World War II.

The computer as an artistic medium: absence of women artists

Initially, the computer was invented as a weapon. *The Imitation Game* told us how the Turing machine was invented to beat the German enigma machine during World War II. The computer was especially developed as a new competitive technology during the arms race from the late 1950s to the 1970s. The early computers were inaccessible to the public and their most popular impressions from the medium were expensive, large-scale and kept in secrecy.

However, some of the scientists and professionals who worked in the big labs were not satisfied with computers, these expensive devices that were only being treated as weapons, so they also indulged in the aesthetics of the world of computing. From the late 1940s, computers began to be experimented with as an artistic tool.[8] Most researchers regarded the solo show named 'Electronic Abstraction' (1952) by Ben Laposky[9] as presenting the new stage of digital art. These works were actually not digitally drawn, but were captured using still photography to record the electrical vibrations as seen on the screen of the oscilloscope.

The position of digital art in the beginning is like the position of women artists/scientists, mostly neglected by the public. This is comparable to John Whitney's rarely mentioned contributions to the film industry. Most people acknowledge the collaboration between Saul Bass and Hitchcock for their famous title, *Vertigo*. While not many people know that for the title sequence of *Vertigo*, Hitchcock had an additional, often unmentioned, collaborator: the distinguished animator and pioneer in several technological fields, John Whitney.

In 1958, Whitney was hired to complete the seemingly impossible task of turning Bass's complicated designs for *Vertigo* into moving pictures. In order to complete the task, Whitney needed to shape the graphs of parametric equations from nineteenth-century mathematician Jules Antoine Lissajous, as well as make them move. Whitney finally fulfilled this daunting task by modifying an abandoned weapon as a kind of computer for use in making animation. And Whitney's work on the opening sequence for *Vertigo* could be considered an early example of computer graphics in film.

---

[8] For example, in 1946, Laposky began working with photographic pendulum tracings and harmonograph machine patterns.

[9] A mathematician, artist and draftsman in Cherokee, Iowa. He has been credited with making the first computer graphics, utilizing an oscilloscope as the creative medium for abstract art.

Whitney made use of an enormous, obsolete military computer called the M5 gun director,[10] plotting the beautiful and elegant graphs of parametric equations. To be precisely shaped, as opposed to being drawn by freehand, it was required that the motion of a pendulum be linked to the motion of an animation stand. However, no animation stand at the time could modulate such continuous motion without its interior wiring becoming tangled.

Whitney realized that the gun director could rotate endlessly, and in perfect synchronization with the swinging of a pendulum. He placed his animation cells on the platform that held the gun director, and above it suspended a pendulum from the ceiling which held a pen that was connected to a 24-foot high pressurized paint reservoir. The movement of the pendulum in relation to the rotation of the gun director generated the spiral drawings used in *Vertigo*'s opening sequence.

Based on the experiences of solving problems for new visual expressions, Whitney founded Motion Graphics Incorporated in 1960, which used a mechanical analogue computer of his own invention to create motion pictures and television title sequences, as well as commercials. The following year, he assembled a record of the visual effects he had perfected using his device, titled simply *Catalog*. In the first stage of digital art, the symbol is that of the male artists with their invented machine. In addition to the repackaging machines by Whitney, Desmond Paul Henry[11] and his drawing machines were another highlight in the period of the 1960s to 1970s in the field of digital art.

It seems that computers as heavy, fatherly tools excluded the contributions and efforts from women artists and scientists. Though women's images were presented in the pioneering digital artwork, they are shown either as fragments, such as cut images of eyes and mouth in the title *Vertigo*, or as silhouette female images 'imprisoned' in the monitors, as seen on the cover of the first book about digital art history, *Art of the Electronic Age*.

The real voice from females in digital art would have to wait to be heard until the 1970s, as a group of women digital artists led by Lillian Schwartz[12] and Katherine Nash not only paved a new way in digital art practices, but also called on a cross-field collaboration, and a new direction of software development.

---

[10] The M5 was used during World War II to aim anti-aircraft cannons at moving targets. It took five men to operate it on the battlefield, each inputting one variable, such as the altitude of the incoming plane, its velocity, etc. The M5 weighed 850 lbs and comprised 11,000 components, but its movement was dictated by the execution of mathematical equations.

[11] A Manchester University lecturer and reader in Philosophy, he was one of the first British artists to experiment with machine-generated visual effects at the time of the emerging global computer art movement of the 1960s.

[12] A twentieth-century American artist considered a pioneer of computer-mediated art and one of the first women artists notable for basing almost her entire oeuvre on computational media.

'Manifesto' of women artists in digital art

When the voices of women were finally heard in digital art, it changed everything. Since the late 1970s, a group of women digital artists, led by Schwartz and Nash, made their own voices heard to the public. Besides calling on the collaboration among artists and scientists, they experimented with new genres of digital artwork. They also demonstrated their art practices and new theory, broadcast by documentaries, exhibitions and websites.

Lillian Schwartz's work with computers at Bell Labs was shown in the documentary *The Artist and the Computer* (J. K. Ball, 1976). In an interview in the film, Schwartz says, 'I am always fascinated by the new materials and tools for art creation.' Through this film, the process of Lillian's exploration in digital art was revealed to the public. She experimented in avant-garde installation, and visualized the interactive power among colours and liquids with the pressure.

Actually, many of Schwartz's groundbreaking projects were completed during the 1960s and the 1970s, well before the documentary was filmed, and well ahead of the desktop computer revolution, which made computer hardware and software widely available to artists. Schwartz demonstrated the wonderful result of cooperation with filmmakers (such as Stan Vanderbeek) and engineers (such as Ken Knowlton). As a non-scientist, Schwartz often served in the role of 'friendly conversational sounding board' for AT&T researchers and Bell Lab scientists looking for feedback on their ideas. As an artist, she created a massive body of technology-based work over the course of thirty-four years. She became a bridge for scientists, engineers and artists and her calls for cross-field cooperation became a milestone in the second stage of digital art.

So, the 'manifesto' of Lillian Schwartz came from her own successful experiences and vision for the future of digital art:

> I expect art to come from artists or artists working closely with programmers – I do not expect much art to come from programmers alone, solely by virtue of their clever gimmicks for doing cute things. What this means in practical terms, then, is that we need to develop a great deal of collaboration between artists and programmers in order to develop meaningful, understandable, and useful sets of tools and ways of using them.[13]

[13] Ken Knowlton, 'Computer Films', *Filmmakers Newsletter* 4 (2) (1970). [As reprinted in Knowlton (1976)]

With the contributions of the series of documentaries, the photos of Schwartz are much more accessible online, while most other women artists are not so easily found, such as the other important pioneer female artist, Katherine Nash.

Different from the first wave of digital art's focus on devices and hardware, Nash realized software would be the key to break the 'bottleneck' for the computer as an artistic medium; if they paid more attention to software, artists would be more involved into the cooperation and requirements for computers as a new collaborative platform working for art.

In 1970, Nash, then at the University of Minnesota, and Richard H. Williams of the University of New Mexico, published a computer program for artists: ART 1. The authors described three approaches an artist might take to use computers in art:

> 1 The artist can become a programmer or software engineer
> 2 Artists and software engineers can cooperate, or
> 3 The artist can use existing software.
>
> NASH and WILLIAMS 1970

At that time, ART 1 already existed so Nash actually encouraged artists to choose the third path. It is interesting to see that this manifesto was not only a call for cooperation among artists and programmers, but also a unique 'advertisement' for her own art software.

There was also a statement as a unique manifesto from women artists. Though she made a series of important digital artworks, Vera Molnár (1924–) did not really regard herself as a digital artist. She believed the computer, after all, was merely a tool in the hand of the painter. For Molnár, her manifesto would call on people to rethink the position and function of computers: 'I use the computer to combine forms, hoping that this tool will enable me to distance myself from what I have learned, from my cultural heritage and everything else that surrounds me; in brief, from the influences of civilisation that define us.'[14]

Women artists like Molnár will pay more attention to how to set up computers as a platform for dialogue; their aim is still for communication through painting themselves, offering more chances for visual dialogue between the painter and what has been painted. She hoped the public would appreciate her artworks, not thinking about if they were made by a computer or a physical painter.

From cross-field cooperation to software exploration, as well as rethinking the computer as a dialogue platform, creative women artists offered a variety of artworks based on their manifestoes; their efforts gathered up the power

[14] http://dam.org/artists/phase-one/vera-molnar/artist-s-statement (accessed 31 October 2017).

of 'The Second Wave of Digital Art', which would flow into the historical trend of second-wave feminism, calling attention to a successful chorus of women to be heard.

The chorus of 'The Second Wave'

'The Second Wave of Digital Art', which includes the cross-field cooperation, software exploration and deconstruction of classic artworks, should be regarded on a bigger scale of changes in a broader social context. 'The Second Wave of Feminism' was led by Simone de Beauvoir and Betty Friedan from the 1960s until the 1980s, in other words, the digital art movements and Feminist movement were contemporaries, spreading more public consciousness of gender equality in business and the arts.

Second-wave feminism is a period of feminist activity that first began in the early 1960s in the United States, and eventually spread throughout the Western world and beyond. Different from the first wave of feminism evoked by Marsha Lear from the nineteenth century, which focused mainly on suffrage and overturning legal obstacles to gender equality (such as voting rights and property rights), 'The Second Wave' of feminism broadened the debate to a wide range of issues: sexuality, family, the workplace, reproductive rights, de facto inequalities and official legal inequalities.

The shift to second-wave feminism came about when many legal and institutional rights were extended to women. This offers context to a deeper understanding of Schwartz' and Nash's 'manifesto', which broke through barriers at large-scale labs and called for collaboration, as well as making these works of art accessible via the computer medium to the public. Additionally, women artists pushed digital art into 'The Second Wave', focusing more on software instead of hardware and drawing machines in the first wave of digital art.

Led by Lillian Schwartz, pioneering women artists realized software development would also attract more women artists into computer-based creation. Coupled with morphing algorithms, reflectography, ultrasonic imaging, holography, digital radiography and traditional x-ray, Schwartz and Nash invented their own image software, which offered more platforms to other artists who were interested in computers as a new artistic medium, but felt afraid of the new uncontrolled technology.

Schwartz also developed a new art archeological theory based on her digital art practices. She identified surprising similarities between the Mona Lisa and the self-portrait of Leonardo Da Vinci using digitally transparent means and created a collage using a computer. This newborn artwork entitled 'Leo/Lisa', could be regarded as a symbol of the chorus of 'The Second Wave' both from digital art and feminism.

On the one hand, Schwartz created a digital juxtaposition (before the invention of Photoshop software) to demonstrate Mona Lisa as a reflection of Leonardo Da Vinci himself, who was also deeply influenced by the studies of art theory and morphing[15] algorithms. On the other hand, Schwartz offered the dialogue platform, the self-portrait of Da Vinci as a symbol of 'Father Power' was faced with the equally beautiful female symbol of the Mona Lisa.

In fact, Schwartz would regard 'Leo/Lisa' not as an artwork, but as a methodology to re-examine Renaissance master works. By revealing a 'hidden' Mona Lisa in her new artwork. Schwartz demonstrated how morphing fulfills the creative decision-making steps Leonardo made starting with Isabella, Duchess of Aragon, the first model, and the changes he made using his own features to finally realize the celebrated face we know today. Schwartz still took advantage of a documentary film to present to the public and fans of digital art a step-by-step unravelling of the Da Vinci mystery.

Artworks such as 'Leo/Lisa' offered a pioneering example of how computers can serve as a detective, solving mysteries like of the identity of the 'real' Mona Lisa, which went on to influence the development of morphing techniques in police systems. By the 1990s, digital morphing techniques were commonly used by law-enforcement agencies to age or alter the facial structure of missing persons or suspects.

Inspired from computers working to find criminals, women artists developed more methods using faces in computers. By overlaying and blending visuals, American artist Nancy Burson (1948–)[16] made a major contribution to the method of 'morphing'. She regarded computers as a medium to composite portraits, especially the portraits of beautiful women. Burson provoked the public with an interesting question, 'Head Shot or Mug Shot?', by morphing the attractive faces of female movie stars.

The game of morphing faces, just like second-wave feminism, quickly spread through the world, also evoking cross-culture reactions and more experiments. The Berlin-based artist Andreas Müller-Pohle opened the images as ASCII text files, processing Western and Asian sign systems, creating a series of works entitled 'Face Codes'. These are selections from several hundred video portraits recorded in Kyoto and Tokyo in 1998. The portraits were digitally manipulated by first creating a standardized template and then adjusting the position of the heads, eyes, lips and chins.

---

[15] Morphing is a visual effect in motion pictures and animation that changes (or morphs) one image or shape into another through a seamless transition. Most often it is used to depict one person turning into another through technological means or as part of a fantasy or surreal sequence. Traditionally, such a depiction would be achieved through cross-fading techniques on film. Since the early 1990s, this has been widely replaced by computer to create more realistic transitions.

[16] An American artist known for creating photographs using computer morphing technology, including the Age Machine, Human Race Machine and Anomaly Machine.

'Face Codes' experienced a successful adventure from physical cities into the digital world. These videos, including faces of people in Kyoto and Tokyo, are digital video stills that were later reworked and typified using identical parameters. The text running along the lower edge of the image, similar to subtitles in a non-synchronized film, represents the alphanumeric code of the respective image, which has been translated 'back' into the Japanese code.

This work was seemingly a salute to Sergei Eisenstein and his theory and practices of 'Montage'. Eisenstein was also inspired from the structure of the Japanese haiku (a Japanese form of light and short poems) to the structure of film editing. The Berlin-based artist reconstructed the faces in digital moving images/codes according to the structure of written characters.

In 1983, the example work 'Adventures in Success' by digital artist Rebecca Allen (1954–) is not only an award-winning animation in the context of the chorus of 'The Second Wave', but also offers a unique critical concept about success and the images of women shaped by mainstream broadcast. Modern symbols of success, beauty blended in this music video, turned into something ridiculous. Rebecca Allen represented women artists calling for establishing a new image of women, as successful and beautiful should not only be defined by fatherly power.

Through the efforts and contributions of women artists led by Schwartz and Nash, their influential 'manifesto' fulfilled their own success, which brought more success from a wider range of cooperation. These women forerunners successfully forecasted a social trend, people need to communicate, interact and connect from cross-field (and cross-gender), with the new power from computers.

References

Baby, V. (2001). *Vera Molnár*. Grenoble: Réunion des Musées Nationaux.

Knowlton, K. (1976). 'Computer Films', in Robert Russett and Cecille Starr (eds), *Experimental Animation: An Illustrated Anthology*, 194–195. New York: Van Nostrand Reinhold Company.

LaFarge, A. (1996). 'The Bearded Lady & the Shaven Man: Mona Lisa, Meet Mona/Leo', *Leonardo*, 29(5): 379–383..

Leavitt, R. (1976). *Artist and Computer*. New York: Harmony Books.

Nash, K. and R. H. Williams (1970). 'Computer Program for Artists: ART 1', *Leonardo*, 3(4): 439–442.

Paul, C. (2015). *Digital Art*. London: Thames & Hudson; 3rd edition.

Popper, F. (1997). *Art of the Electronic Age*. London: Thames & Hudson.

Rush, M. (2005). *New Media in Art*. London: Thames & Hudson; 2nd edition.

Schwartz, Lillian F. and L. R. Schwartz (1992). *The Computer Artist's Handbook: Concepts, Techniques, and Applications*. New York: W. W. Norton.

Sporre, Dennis J. (2012). *Reality through the Arts*. New York: Pearson; 8th edition.

Wands, B. (2007). *Art of the Digital Age*. London: Thames & Hudson.

5

Seeking Truth in Facts

Historicizing Chinese Animation

Olga Bobrowska

Introduction

In the course of my research the initial approach based on the contextual analysis of historical development of animation in the People's Republic of China (PRC) had to be complemented with an attempt to reconstruct the entanglement of particular, ideologically determined cultural narratives (e.g. festival programming, academic discourse) and the specific apparatus of artistic production. This paper attempts to critically review the established narration on Chinese animation canon as mirrored in the West.[1] As early as 1971 the influential French scholar Marc Ferro talked about film's status as history and acknowledged sources deriving from the field of popular culture and non-material culture as a historical evidence that mirrors transformations occurring within the ideologically conditioned apparatus of culture production (cf. Ferro 2008). The contemporary Estonian scholar and artist, Ülo Pikkov (2010) in fact argues for similar analytical strategy. His term *animasophy* describes an approach focused on the interconnection of animated forms and human collective practices. The strength of Pikkov's writings lies in a capacity to demonstrate theoretical thinking through consequent case study analysis.

[1] Thanks to the support of many academics, experts and filmmakers, as well as visits to China in 2015 and 2016, I have collected much of the necessary material (primarily films from the Shanghai Animation Film Studio, SAFS; 1955–1989). I am thankful to many academics and artists for their support and encouragement, among them Alicja Helman, Guo Chunning, Li Yi, Georges Schwizgebel and Daniel Šuljić.

This scholar provides the audiences of artistic shorts with a set of conceptual tools enabling them to decipher the concatenation of authorial subjectivity, cultural practices and particular industry specificities, in other words to simultaneously perceive an animated film as an individual work of art, and a certain anthropological record of historically and culturally determined momentum. Considering and respecting the necessity of comprehending the formal aspects of animation art, the researcher should nevertheless stay committed to locating the phenomenon of the creation of illusionary movement in the net structure of experiences, recollections, myths and ideas that construct and explain humanity's activities and interactions.

The archives of film festivals and film studios' records, distributors' promotional materials and film magazines filled with audience surveys and report sections, along with interviews with the widest possible group of contributors, might shed a unique light on the process of the crystallization of the canon as these sources do not interpret the texts of culture (film works themselves), but historically explain the specific event of the text's conception and collective interpretation (Staiger 2008 [1992]). Film Festival Studies is a sub-field of cinema studies that provides complex and inspiring tools for the intellectual practice of analysing the phenomenon of the festival as an integral element of canon establishment and dissemination. This chapter outlines several problems of Chinese animated classics' ideological status and their position in the historical reception as recapitulated in the English language source literature, yet it is equally important to confront academic sources with the evidence found in the archives ('the evidence of the momentum'). This chapter will also attempt to examine and revise the notion of 'the 1980s Chinese animation crisis' with the aid of the printed materials produced by Animafest Zagreb, one of the chief meeting points between different traditions and schools of animation, between 1980 and 1988.

Animation and cultural nationalism, or the origins of *minzu* style

An outline of the historical development of Chinese animation reconstructed in reference to the source literature indicates five major phases: the pioneering experiments of the Wan brothers[2] and the establishment of the SAFS

[2] The brothers, born in Nanjing, worked in Shanghai. Twins Laiming and Guchan (万籁鸣, 万古蟾), Chaochen (万超尘) and Dihuan (万涤寰) worked together on commercials and experimented with artistic animation. *Havoc in Heaven* (*Da nao tian gong*/大闹天宫, 1961–64), an adaptation of the first part of the literary classic, *Journey to the West* (*Xiyou ji*/西游记), was a lifetime achievement of Laiming. Guchan was a pioneer of cut-out animation, while Chaochen worked with puppets. Dihuan collaborated with them in the early period, but later worked in the field of photography.

(Shanghai Animation Film Studio) structures (1922–1957); development of the *minzu* style period commonly referred to as the 'golden age' (1955–1966); the dreadful gap caused by the turmoil of the Cultural Revolution (1966–1976); the 'second golden age' (from 1976 until the 1980s or early 1990s); and 'the crisis of the 1980s' with the climax in 1987 that marks disintegration of the SAFS. Naturally such periodization is interconnected with the upheavals and historical turning points experienced by Chinese society during the overlapping time formations that can be described as the period of the Republic (1912–1949), the Japanese occupation (1931/37–1945), civil war (two stages: 1927–1937 and 1945–1949), Mao Zedong's rule (1949–1976) and the opening up and reform period (1976/78–mid 1990s). In an inspiring study, *Animation in China: History, Aesthetics, Media*, Sean Macdonald declares an attempt of historicizing animation history (Macdonald 2016: 3). The structure of this publication and films chosen for analysis and interpretation suggest a non-orthodox approach towards the accepted historical narrative.

Macdonald acknowledges: 'The Wan Brothers were the first animators in China, but the story of animation in the PRC is the story of the SAFS (Macdonald 2016: 3) and, like other scholars and admirers of the Chinese classic animation, he recognizes the utmost significance of the *minzu* style. Macdonald's meticulous research itself could be described as *animasophic*. SAFS mass artistic production mirrors and exemplifies ideological turns that have been influencing all aspects of social, political and cultural practices of everyday life throughout each historical stage, so Macdonald attempts to unveil the shifts of the doctrine through the analysis of films and the film critique discourse of the period. In addition to this, he reflects on the modes of the comprehension of these films in the fields of Sinology and Chinese Studies.

It is necessary to briefly explain the liaisons between animation artists and the Communist Party of China (CPC) before we ponder over the fascinating phenomenon of *minzu* style and its ideological inclinations. The history of Chinese animation starts with experiments of the Wan brothers but the history of animation's ideological engagement has even earlier origins. The figure of Te Wei (特伟, 1915–2010), a doyen of Chinese animation and most widely recognized SAFS artist, stands as a representative as his life and work directly connect animated film with its significant and ideologically engaged ancestor, the art of *manhua* (漫画, graphic cartoons). Te Wei was born in the year that marks a crucial moment for the emergence of the New Culture Movement, i.e. the release of the first issue of *New Youth* (*Xin qingnian*/新青年). Progressive, patriotic and educated youth gathered around Chen Duxiu (陈独秀, 1879–1942), an early leader of the CPC and editor-in-chief of *New Youth*, who postulated anti-imperialist struggle and cultural modernization, the implementation of necessary social conduct that would embrace both revolutionary intellectuals and peasant masses. The press, theatre and caricature served as a tool of communication inside the highly stratified society. Historians point out the strong polarization of Chinese public discourse and the radicalization of social and political life since 1928 when the Guomindang (GMD) government was installed in Nanjing.

Te Wei was born in Shanghai, a cosmopolitan metropolis pulsating to the beats of international business and popular culture; importantly, it was also a centre of *manhua* publishing houses. He worked as a graphic artist and, along with many other creators, Te Wei engaged his talent into initially the political, and eventually the military, fight for leftist ideals, the rise of class awareness and combat with the Japanese occupation. In 1937 the artists of the so-called National Salvation Cartoons group proclaimed a propagandistic military division under the auspices of The Third Bureau of the Political Department of the National Military Council (collaborative body of CPC and GMD). In 1938 the group was divided into two sections, one of them led by Te Wei (cf. Andrews and Shen 2012; Hung 1994).

Revolutionary *manhua* greatly differs from contemporary, popular comic books and cartoons. Sharp and concise messages are transmitted through exaggeration, deformation and analogies. Since the dawn of the Republic, visual artists have been discovering and reworking Western traditions of painting and illustration; some acknowledged inspiration from the art of Francisco Goya, Miguel Covarrubias, Georg Grosz or, as in the case of Te Wei, David Low, the master of typified caricatured representations of political actors. Initially satirical, *manhua* started conveying symbols essential for the model of military engaged patriotism, i.e. images of a united and strong nation, and visions of humiliated enemies. The artistic brigades operated in the big cities as well as on the frontlines of Sino-Japanese and domestic war. They organized plenty of specific performances that combined graphic exhibitions, stage plays and indoctrination talks. The leadership of CPC noticed the powerful impact of *manhua* representations on the masses, and in this regard the 1949 decision of appointing Te Wei, instead of any other more experienced animator, as a head of a newly formed animation film studio does not seem surprising.

Naturally, the Chinese Communists perceived animation mainly as a medium for the education and entertainment of children. Maoist doctrine assumed that knowledge and ideology are equated, and aimed at establishing a new understanding of the nation and citizenship. However, it would be wrong to regard Maoist thought as deprived of deep and conscious historical foundations. The problems of understanding and commemorating the past in Chinese Communist thought is widely elaborated in Political and Chinese Studies discourse. Animation scholars should primarily refer to the issue of the cultural nationalism model that found its expression in top-down proclaimed effort of developing essentially Chinese animated film stylistics.

Minzu (民族), generally understood as an artistic method of the transmission of the essential features of Chinese culture into a medium of foreign provenance, has dominated the popular and academic reception of Chinese animation. This seems only natural since the films realized as an expression of *minzu* have had an undeniable impact on worldwide animated film culture – the Chinese artists invented and mastered new forms of animation, most notably wash-and-ink painting and Chinese silhouettes cut-out animation. At the same time, the *minzu* style challenged propaganda modes accepted in the Communist world by replacing the socialist realism paradigm since an aesthetic and intellectual tissue of Chinese animation can be found in either *literati* or folk tradition situated genuinely far from the industrial landscapes inhabited by modern workers, soldiers and imperialist spies.

The issue of the artistic reinterpretation of tradition remains fundamental for the discussions between Chinese artists and intellectuals, which was formulated already in the 1870s by the imperial dignitary Zhang Zhidong (张之洞): 'Chinese Learning as Substance, Western Learning for Application' (*Zhongxue wei ti, xixue wei yong* 中学为体，西学为用)' (Pohl 2016 [1993]: 1). In fact, the authors of *manhua*, and consequently of animation, had to deal with the conflict of the aesthetic and ideological function of art, and develop a position that would effectively absorb foreign influences and inspiration into the realm of Chinese cultural production. The country's philosophical heritage, the leftists and Communists claimed, required profound revision: 'I don't attack Confucius as a person but as a figure that has been presented throughout the centuries, a figure that personifies tyranny; I attack the essence of despotism,' wrote Li Dazhao (李大钊, 1888–1927),[3] one of the most influential Chinese Marxists and co-founder of the CPC.

A common consensus among the early doctrinaires assumed that the folk tradition, though developed within feudal structures, was the only means of cultural communication easily accepted by the peasant masses,[4] therefore traditional culture was cultivated in a way that would emphasize its progressive elements and rigidly exclude its regressive ones. The absorption of Western innovations, be it Marxism or the cinema, would require consideration for *guoqing* (a specific national condition). This approach answered the dilemma raised by the New Culture Movement's participants

[3] See Li Dazhao (1962), cited in Pawłowski (2013: 67). Pawłowski discusses ideologically determined mechanisms of remembrance and construction of collective memory within the CPC doctrine. The Polish scholar presents large reference section listing Polish, English and Chinese language publications on the subject.

[4] In the 1920s and 1930s when CPC formulated its doctrine, the peasantry formed the overwhelming majority of Chinese society (ca 90 per cent), see: Pawłowski (2013: 73).

and their followers: new China did not have to choose between Western progressive models and Chinese traditional ones, instead the revolutionary aspects of folk culture could be enriched with adequate foreign contributions. Such method was supposed to allow for new, progressive and national paradigms of cultural production and historical memory to appear. Eventually, the inclusion of certain aspects of tradition into the revolutionary mindset and artistic expression would maintain a lineage of power between the communist leadership and the rulers of the oldest continuously existing civilization, a necessary and natural operation in the society subjected for centuries to the Confucian principles, hierarchy and rituals.

The term *minzu* notably entered the history of Chinese animation in 1957 when Te Wei came up with a slogan, 'The road to *minzu* style', hence the subsequent efforts of the workers became subordinated to the goal of adjusting the animated medium to the cultural specifics of the new Chinese national model. John A. Lent and Xu Ying (2010), Giannalberto Bendazzi (2015), and David Ehrlich and Jin Tianyi (2011) apply this term to Shanghai productions focused on the development of recognizably Chinese techniques (ink and wash painting animation, unfolded paper and cut-out collage) as well as works that use traditional techniques (cell and stop motion animation) but directly refer to the discursive and performative Chinese heritage (Beijing opera, literary classics, proverbs). Wu Weihua (2009) reflects upon *minzu* in relation to *meishu* (美术, fine arts). The term that appeared in the early twentieth century as Japanese neologism connotes institutional modernization tendencies in the Chinese arts and evokes the *zhongti, xiyong* dilemma. The Chinese scholar argues that 'the *meishu* film-related catachresis is a discourse-based cultural subversion rather than a linguistic revision' (Wu 2009: 32), while *minzu* can be considered as 'a collective political practice as opposed to aesthetic practice, and as ethnographic rather than artistic imagery' (Wu 2009: 52).

Macdonald on the other hand acknowledges the risk of cognitive reduction, i.e. limitations imprinted in comprehending *minzu* as a universal key unlocking the whole era. Additionally, he points out the interpretative redundancy of Wu's approach: 'National style is very much a process, but the cultural production that emerged alongside national style discourse cannot be simply viewed within the frame of national style' (Macdonald 2016: 82). The scholar argues that the national style of distinctive poetics, immersed in traditional culture, becomes most vividly displayed in a production that not only borrows cultural conventions and discursive motives, but also remains a variation of traditional artistic expression, providing an intersection of heritage and the newly adopted models of its understanding.

Though Macdonald examines painting animation to a lesser extent than cell and stop motion forms, it seems that films such as *Where Is Mama?* (*Xiao kedou zhao mama*/小蝌蚪找妈妈, dir. Te Wei, Qian Jiajun/钱家俊,

1960) or *Cowherd and His Flute* (*Mu di*/牧笛, dir. Te Wei, Qian Jiajun, 1963) bear great potential for such analysis. Especially as the production of *Where Is Mama?* crowns a rapid and intense development phase of *minzu*. Let us take a closer look on the liminal moments of this phase and the dominant features of the narratives applied to the so-called 'golden age' history.

The year 1956 appears as a turning point in the history of Chinese animation for the frequently reported fact,[5] inspired by Chinese film historiography, of an award at the Venice International Film Festival granted to the film *Why Is the Crow Black?* (*Wuya weishenme shi heide*/乌鸦为什么是黑的, dir. Qian Jiajun, Li Keruo/李克弱, 1955). This first Chinese colour animation was supposedly mistaken by the jurors as a Soviet production. The verdict interpreted by SAFS as a depreciation of Chinese art, instigated the studio's pursuits for autonomous national expression. This interpretation, however, cannot be sustained in the light of Macdonald's findings at the Venice festival's archives, which will be discussed in the next section.

The historiography rather marginalizes the role of *The Magic Brush* (*Shen bi*/神笔, dir. Jin Xi/靳夕, 1955) in the process of establishing *minzu* style. This skilful puppet film tells a folk story of a boy who breaks class divisions and learns the art of painting, moreover the magical power of his brush helps him to conduct revolutionary acts such as overthrowing the feudal ruler and modernizing the peasants' work. Jin Xi, a student of Jiří Trnka and an animation theoretician, saturated the tale with symbols and meaningful artefacts from the past feudal culture, and dynamic dramaturgy, accelerating the film's revolutionary content, as well as common language (the dialogue even includes vulgarisms). Macdonald (2016: 38) and Wu (2009: 38), after the writings of Zhang Songlin (张松林; another notable SAFS artist and theoretician), acknowledge *The Magic Brush* as the first actual attempt of *minzu* style. However, most sources locate the prelude of *minzu* in the production of *The Arrogant General* (*Jiao'ao de jiangjun*/骄傲的将军, dir. Te Wei, 1957), a cell animation that evokes characteristics of Beijing opera.

The wash-and-ink painting animation achieved the highest position among the essentially Chinese techniques of animation, as Te Wei said: '[The film *Where Is Mama?*] showed that this imported form of art had been completely absorbed' (Alder 1994: 5). '*Guohua* [国画, traditional painting] turn', the turn towards traditional art style, evokes a whole spectrum of a fascinating research problems. Above all, this contemplative and immersive animated form points the viewer's attention to one of the fundamental questions of Animation Studies, i.e. 'how was the scene/the sequence/the film made?' Since for decades SAFS has been keeping the technological

[5] See Lent and Xu (2010: 116); Wu (2009: 40); Giesen (2015: 26).

procedures applied in *shuimo donghua* (水墨动画, wash-and-ink painting animation technique) secret, few pieces of information are stated in the literature as definite.[6] Certainly, a leading role in achieving the visuals of blurred boundaries between characters and backgrounds should be credited to a true master of animated film cinematography, Duan Xiaoxuan (段孝萱, born 1934), a female filmmaker who has played a significant role in the SAFS production system. The work of Duan Xiaoxuan does form inspiring material for the gender-oriented researchers dedicated to unveiling *her*story of various cinemas.

A well-known narrative recapitulates the conception of the *shuimo donghua* idea as a chain-reaction of political challenges and pledges. In front of SAFS officials, Marshall Chen Yi (陈毅, 1901–1972) expressed a hope to see paintings of the master Qi Bashi (齐白石, 1864–1957) in motion. A dark and disturbing painting, 'The Sound of Frogs Issues Forth from the Mountain Spring for Ten Miles Around'[7] was transposed by the artists into the cheerful *Where Is Mama?*, a unique children's propaganda piece that interweaves slogans from the Great Leap Forward with the traditional, refined imagery of frogs, fish, crabs and water flowers. The second *shuimo donghua* production demonstrated the maturity and gentleness of the new animated art. *The Cowherd and His Flute* is inspired by the rural motives of Li Keran's (李可染, 1907–1989) paintings, thus directly referring to the concept of reworking feudal traditions according to the needs and expectations of the new socialist society.

Incidentally, the year 1956 was marked by the infamous political struggle between Mao Zedong and revisionists of his doctrine, i.e. the Hundred Flowers Campaign, a brief thaw and liberation inside the CPC and working units, and following the hardship of 'the anti-rightists' campaign of the same year. Instigated immediately after these campaigns, the Great Leap Forward brought about an economic catastrophe in Chinese society as well as a change in Mao's point of references in regard to historical and cultural policies. Mao's acknowledgement of the First Emperor Qin's totalitarianism was interconnected with the new social models prompted by the Great Helmsman, such as full collectivism and non-stop efforts in radical and rapid change of national conditions, symbolized most vividly by the commune kitchens and domestic steel production. The year of the first screenings of *Where Is Mama?*, 1960, correlates with the emergence of the drastic symptoms of the economic failure of Mao's policies, tragically marked by the mass starvation and illegal migration that led to the temporary

---

[6] Kiu-wai Chu's (2015) article 'Animating *shanshui*: Chinese Landscape in Animated Film, Art and Performance' stands for a highly interesting study on the subject.

[7] 'Washeng shili chu shanquan' (蛙声十里出山泉), painting from 1951, ink and colour on paper, 127.5 cm × 33 cm. Qi Baishi was inspired by the poetry of Lao She (老舍, 1899–1966).

exclusion of Mao from direct leadership in 1962. At that time, the national art of animation had already adapted foreign invention into ideological goals and representational strategies.

The intellectual fervour of 1956, as well as the totalitarian order of the Great Leap Forward, corresponded with the rigid criticism of the already existing means and methods of artistic expression, a criticism that eventually inspired daring undertakings realized through collective efforts. The policy of 'regulations', meant to uplift the society and national economy after the Great Leap Forward, was postulated by the opponents of Mao Zedong (among them Liu Shaoqi, Peng Denhui, Deng Xiaoping) and welcomed by Zhou Enlai (周恩来, 1898–1976), a loyal prime minister and a great admirer of SAFS productions,[8] who advocated the cultivation of traditional artistic forms in accordance with the dominant doctrine. Under such conditions, *minzu* style in its all multifaceted possible approaches and techniques, matured, flourished and eventually won the hearts of domestic and foreign audiences, prompting future nostalgia for somewhat old-fashioned imagery designed and composed in the most mysterious and elaborated manner.

How the canon was tempered

Film Festival Studies provides a wide spectrum for analytical frameworks, most significantly conceptualizing a festival as an element of historical, sociological or economical reflection.[9] The cultural phenomena of competition and celebration are imprinted in the very nature of the festival itself. A fundamental assumption about festivals' influence on the establishment of the canon and conventions in film history has been argued by de Valck and Loist (2009), who classified five axes indicating directions for film festival studies: film as a work of art; an economic *continuum*; the festival as institution; audiences and exhibition; the politics of place. The first axis, especially, triggers a reflection on the programming policies and canon-building inclinations of the festivals. The scholars have also emphasized the political non-neutrality of a festival as an event created upon ideological presumptions shared by the group of the organizers, and

[8] Lent and Xu recall the words of Te Wei: 'Zhou gave his attention, spiritual support and suggestions to animation. [. . .] On one occasion, when he visited Southeast Asian countries, Zhou took Chinese animation with him to show his hosts' (Lent and Xu 2010: 118).

[9] Film Festival Research Network (FFRN), founded by Marijke de Valck and Skadi Loist, stimulates academic work and provides an insightful academic database in the form of a website (http://www.filmfestivalresearch.org) that lists FFRN bibliographical references and further recommended readings. Among significant contributors to the emergence and development of the discipline were also scholars such as Dina Iordanova, Daniel Dayan, Brendan Kredell and Thomas Elsaesser.

developed in relation to the various systems of financial support distribution as designed in individual countries or within transnational structures (cf. de Valck 2007; Iordanova 2015; Jelenković 2016).

An emblematic example of the ideological functions of a film festival may be found in the history of the Asian-African Film Festival, an event established as a celebration of the Non-Aligned Movement. At its third incarnation, held in 1964 in Jakarta, a film *Golden Conch* (*Jinse de hailuo*/金色的海螺, dir. Wan Guchan, Qian Yunda/钱运达, 1963) was successfully presented and won the Lumumba Prize. Choirotun Chisaan (2012) reconstructs the dramaturgy of a power play between Islamic and Communist political parties over the organization committee of the festival. Eventually the Communists took over the committee and formally proclaimed the festival's agenda as anti-colonialist, anti-imperialist and anti-Hollywood. The festival, limited solely to its propagandistic function, was deprived of cultural significance and canon-building potential. Chisaan recalls the statement of Roshihan Anwar (1922–2011), a renowned Indonesian journalist, who claimed: 'I was surprised that Communists made no effort to mobilise their mass organisations to flood cinemas [. . .] The cinemas showing the festival films were quiet and empty. Even so, the Antara news agency reported that there was a gratifying level of interest from the viewing public' (Chisaan 2012: 292). Following the failed *coup d'état* of 1965, this festival, originating from the Bandung conference's agreements, was overtaken by the Soviet Union and the first edition of this 'new-old' event took place in October 1968 in Tashkent, Uzbekistan (former USSR).[10]

A series of screenings of Chinese live-action films in Paris and Pesaro in 1978 demonstrates another aspect of the politicized nature of the festivals and their audiences. In Paris, a short programme was presented in six small theatre halls, while the wider programme accompanied the Pesaro Festival of New Cinema. Both events marked a crucial step in building cultural relations between the Western world and China on the eve of transformation. The Paris programme, curated by Danielle Waserman, was collated with direct collaboration with the Chinese authorities. The curator pointed out periods of her interest (yet the selection included five films made during 1961–1965 and one from 1974) while the officials of the cinematography apparatus provided the body of films up for consideration. The French and Italian press[11] recalled the disappointment of the mostly young audiences – recently Maoist, currently confused, the revolted youth of Western Europe

[10] The history of the Asian-African festival is even more complex. The inaugural edition was held in 1958 in Tashkent (see Chisaan 2012: 292, British Pathé 1958). Yet the organizers of the 1968 event decided to erase this heritage (see Djagolov and Salazkina 2016). In 1974 the festival additionally embraced cinemas of Latin America.

[11] See Scianna, Henebelle and Bergeron, cited in Reprinted materials (1978) and Książek-Konicka (1978).

found neither an uplifting philosophy, nor truthful representations, in an idealized PRC cinematic model.

The programmers of Western animation festivals situated Chinese animation on the periphery of their interests, which might be connected with China's politics of isolation from the 1950s to the 1970s (decades crucial for the development of animated festival culture) and an intrinsic feature of Euro-Atlantic cultural reflection, a variant of eurocentrism and orientalism. Nonetheless several influential festivals placed Chinese films on their programmes during the 'golden era', providing SAFS with meaningful tokens of appreciation for wash-and-ink painting animations in Annecy, Locarno or Odense. The already mentioned presentations of Chinese cinema in 1978 in France and Italy suggest a Western interest in Chinese cinematic perspectives. Festival screenings of two feature-length films (*Havoc in Heaven* and *Nezha Conquers the Dragon the King*[12]) in 1978 in London and 1980 in Cannes elevated Chinese animation's recognition outside of the PRC. Animafest in Zagreb was at the forefront in recognition of the late/post-Maoist era (a retrospective of six Chinese films from 1962–1976 was hosted by the Yugoslav festival in 1978), along with the festival in Annecy that presented China as a country of honour in 1985 and again in 2017. Bruno Edera (1980) recalls the presentations of several productions made during 1973–1979 held at various European events as well as the interest of foreign film magazines in Chinese animation. Edera concludes, 'It seems now that the Chinese animated film is regaining its former good shape' (Edera 1980: 39).

John A. Lent and Xu Ying (2010: 119) argue for the categorization of the 'second golden age' (1976–1980) in terms of the return to the poetics and philosophical assumptions of the pre-Cultural Revolution period and generous state support for the animation industry. Macdonald suggests the interpretation of *Nezha Conquers . . .* is an example of 'scar animation' and thus emphasizes the appearance of new forms of expression. The scholar refers to a brief, but powerful literary tendency that attempted to rework the traumatizing experience of the period from 1966–1976. *Nezha Conquers . . .* along with *One Night in an Art Gallery* (*Hualang yiye*/画廊一夜, dir. A Da/阿达, Lin Wenxiao/林文肖, 1978) use means and stylistics developed in the *minzu*-dominated period, but directly envision dreadful symbols of the Cultural Revolution (four dragons as a figure of the Gang of Four in the first film, symptomatic slogans such as *zouzipai*[13] in the latter), and incorporate motives of revenge, resurrection and reunion. If the previous animated decade attempted to represent ideologically reshaped models of

[12] *Nezha nao hai*/哪吒闹海, dir. Wang Shuchen (王树忱), Yan Dingxian (严定宪), 1979.

[13] *Zouzipai* (走资派) means 'capitalist-roader' and connotes the political opponents of Mao Zedong and Jiang Qing during the Cultural Revolution.

unity, memory and heritage, animation of the early reforms and opening up period aimed at the sublimation of trauma. In this context, it is worth acknowledging the awakening of revisionist tendencies across Chinese artistic expression, including animation.[14]

The 'Venice incident', crucial for historical development of Chinese animation, has been examined by Sean Macdonald who came up with a ground-breaking finding: 'The official program of the Venice International Film Festival lists two films from China, accurately indicating the place of origin and the directors, *The Magic Brush* and *Why Is the Crow Black?* [. . .] A Czech film won the first prize for animation that year, while *The Magic Brush* won an award for Best Entertainment for Children 8–12. [. . .] Very possibly something did happen at Venice, but there is no textual evidence for this' (Macdonald 2016: 90–91). The historiographical mistakes regarding the awards received by the Chinese films in international circulation seem quite common and provide a fascinating area of archive-based research. As an example of such tendencies, one can refer to the information about the Certificate of Merit for *The Magic Brush* at the 1957 Stratford International Film Festival (Giesen 2015: 26), which has similarly left no textual evidence[15] or the more significant issue of an award for *Havoc in Heaven* at the 1978 London festival (Quiquimelle 1993: 186), which also finds no evidences in the archives,[16] nor festival reports from the period.[17]

Rolf Giesen's filmography of Chinese animation (2015) attempts to list festival success, though it should be noted that this undoubtedly valuable reference at some points lacks consistency in the presentation of collected data. Factual revision may fascinate film historians, but it certainly will not create an impact on an established canon, especially if the discussed works

---

[14] Similarly to Macdonald, Ehrlich and Jin Tianyi also notice the ground-breaking role of two discussed titles and the commencement of a new chapter in Chinese animation history. Ehrlich quotes Lin Wenxiao's recollections: 'When the Gang of Four fell in 1976, there was dancing again in the Shanghai Animation Film Studio and a tremendous release of artistic energy that had been repressed for ten long years' (Ehrlich and Jin 2001: 17). Ehrlich and Jin use the term 'the second golden age' but present the diversity of post-Maoist production without delineating its definite end (the authors refer to the 1980s as well as productions from the early 1990s).

[15] '*The Magic Brush* was included in the 1957 Stratford International Film Festival as part of the Children's Program. I have gone through our holdings and have not found any mention of *The Magic Brush* winning an award or receiving a Certificate of Merit' (an email from the Stratford Festival Archives Coordinator, Ms Christiane Schindler, May 2016).

[16] 'Checking through the 1978 London Film Festival Catalogue *Havoc in Heaven* (大闹 天宫, Da nao tian gong, 1961–1964, dir. Wan Laiming) was presented in the Animation Section. It doesn't record any awards it was nominated for at the festival, and that year the BFI Sutherland Trophy was won by a film called *The scenic route*' (an email from BFI Reuben Library, August 2017).

[17] 'Last but not least in the curio section was *Havoc in Heaven* by Wan Laiming. Made in 1965, this animated feature length cartoon . . . was not exported due to political intrigues as complex as chop suey', writes Kennedy (1978).

belong to the realm of exquisite filmmaking and hold a special position in collective cultural memory. Referring to 'festival data' (printed and ephemera materials) though might unveil the mechanisms of canon-building processes. In the case of Chinese animation, the decade of the 1980s seems the most interesting from this perspective.

The 1980s are also of essential significance in Chinese cultural history. In the course of only thirteen years (1976 – the death of Mao Zedong; 1989 – Tiananmen Square protests) China changed radically in terms of politics, art and economics. It is impossible to single out one major direction that brought a major impact on the society or dominated the rhythms of these changes with its inner dynamics. The Great Cultural Discussion, a debate on the methodology in academia, should be recalled as its conclusions remain highly significant for the development of cinema culture. Mirroring problems and features of the Cultural Fever, this influential academic dispute focused on the fields of ideology and philosophy, theory of culture and artistic practice. Three meaningful events have contributed to the debate: the reopening of the Beijing Film Academy in 1978 (followed by the premieres of ground-breaking live-action films such as *Yellow Earth*,[18] *The Horse Thief*,[19] *Red Sorghum*[20]); the first exhibition of non-political foreign art in Beijing in 1977 (Romanian paintings from the nineteenth and twentieth centuries) as well as Pablo Picasso's exhibition in 1982 (Helman 2010: 20). Naturally the discussion touched upon the *zhongti, xiyong* dilemma and attempted an examination of the Marxist and modernist principles as they appeared at the end of the twentieth century, fractured, crumbled and deprived of dogmatic integrity.

Alicja Helman defines the so-called rudimentary modernism as 'a contemporaneity attacking its myths; it is a need for work of demystification' (Helman 2010: 17). In this brief period, the representatives of the Chinese rudimentary modernism absorbed the significant corpus of Western twentieth-century philosophical problems, and reworked them accordingly to their experiences, social and artistic expectations determined by the intrinsic nation-state world-outlook (conglomerate of Chinese heritage, communist identity and ongoing modernization). Such intellectual efforts resulted in an outburst of liberated creativity, leading to the reinvigoration of artistic practice in all its sectors and possible cross-cuts, reaching a dramatic finale between 27 April and 4 June, 1989. Animation art, depending on the Shanghai studio (an institution strongly attached to the country's power structures), and witnessing a revival of visual and performing arts, found its own valve that enabled modernized expression.

[18] *Huang tudi*/黄土地, dir. Chen Kaige/陈凯歌, 1984.

[19] *Dao mazei*/盗马贼, dir. Tian Zhuangzhuang/田壮壮, 1986.

[20] *Hong gaoliang*/红高粱, dir. Zhang Yimou/张艺谋, 1987.

Undoubtedly, the structural crisis of SAFS that led to its division and disintegration around 1987 (a process directly connected with the emergence of free market elements within centralized, Communist economics), decisively transformed the means and conditions of mass animated production. New times required new models of representation and narration that would be able to compete with foreign (mostly Japanese) television production. Time and labour-consuming forms of traditional animation would additionally require from a viewer a certain aesthetic sensitivity and readiness for contemplation of its temporality. Such films inevitably lost the attention of the newly emerging consumerist audiences, which is the most important fact for the producers who could no longer rely on the state for financing. The artists of SAFS struggled to improve technological aspects and enrich traditional imagery and narrative forms with new intellectual inclinations such as ethnic diversity (*Effendi/Afanti*, 阿凡提, TV series, dir. Jin Xi, 1979–88) or religious spirituality (*The Nine-Color Deer/Jinse lu*, 九色鹿, dir. Qian Jiajun, Dai Tielang/戴铁郎, 1981). As SAFS entered the path of capitalist filmmaking and production, the authors regained access to an international circulation of films, i.e. a festival chain of communication and exhibition.

The 1980 edition of Animafest epitomizes the significant shift that occurred in the relations between Chinese and Western animators. Festival jurors (Vasco Granja, Roswitha Fischer, Attila Dargay, Laurentiu Sibiu, Zdenko Gašparović) acknowledged with a Special Mention the animation in the film *The Fox and the Hunter* (*Huli dalieren*/狐狸打猎人, dir. Hu Xionghua/胡雄华, 1978). The impressive cut-out collage may be read as a highly subversive story about the hunter, deprived of power, masculinity and authority by the loss of his rifle. The cunning forest animals (a fox and a wolf) begin to hunt the humiliated would-be torturer. A man who lives in poverty and disdain fears the animals who put on demonic masks. Hu Xionghua's film continues the line of 'scar animation', even if this tendency was not officially proclaimed. It is a children's film that develops one of the most famous *minzu* techniques of animation, but whose traditional surface (beautifully executed animation) hides strong tensions, grief, remorse and desire for revenge. The 1980 Animafest bulletin points out another significant cultural turn in the history of SAFS transformation and its inclusion in the global independent art circuit.

An article under the telling title 'The People's Republic of China to Join ASIFA?' recalls the discussion between John Halas, Bruno Edera, Jin Xi (at that time a deputy director of SAFS) and Hu Xionghua. An unknown festival journalist writes: 'Mr Halas pointed out as always, Yugoslavia was acting as a friendly catalyst in the relationships of the various countries in the world' (Animafest 1980: 8). The recapitulation of the discussion brings to light a lot of pieces of information about the state of the Chinese industry. According to the delegates, SAFS employed 500 workers, produced 200–300 minutes of animated films a year; annually trained twenty students at special courses held at the studio; produced films mainly for television, and successfully broadcast them on Sunday mornings. Interestingly, the delegates claimed that the inner structure of SAFS assumes a division into three sections: directing, animating and scriptwriting. Testimonies given in the following years and the source literature do not sustain this notion, instead they speak of the division into cell, stop motion and collage sections. Jin Xi stated: 'But there are cases where one person rolls all this into one, writing, designing, animating and directing films on his own' (Animafest 1980: 10). During the same festival, the Chinese delegation attended the extraordinary General Assembly of ASIFA as observers. The records of the 1980 Animafest seem to emphasize a value of tight international cooperation; introducing the structure of the Chinese animation studio system, but at the same time demonstrating the fact that Chinese artists were self-aware as *auteur* figures in the filmmaking process.

Two years later the festival in Zagreb was attended by arguably the most fascinating classic Chinese animation author. A Da (1934–1987) reported his experience in Yugoslavia in an extended article (A Da 1983) where he deliberates on the nature of the festival, its organization and programming, but above all presents analyses of cinematic language and animation means of expression. At the 1984 Animafest, SAFS was represented by three distinctively different films: A Da's *Three Monks* (*Sang ge he shang*/猴子捞月, 1980), Zhou Keqin's (钱家骅) *Monkeys Fishing for Moon* (*Houzi lao yue*/南郭先生, 1981) and Qian Jiaxing's (钱家骍) *Mr. Nan Guo* (*Nanguo xiansheng*/南郭先生, 1981). A Da, Zhou Keqin and Zhong Songlin (present in Zagreb as a deputy director of SAFS) answered the questions of Animafest's journalists and participated in a press conference. SAFS delegates left Yugoslavia without any award,[21] but they managed to establish an artistic exchange with Western filmmakers, mostly thanks to A Da's friendship with artists such as David Ehrlich and Georges Schwizgebel.

A Da, who had already worked in the studio for thirty years and experienced each stage of production (as a background artist, chief designer, animator, eventually director), strongly emphasized the role of the festival as a powerful learning experience. While referring to his art, he focused on the efforts in modernizing an animated film language and noted features differentiating his work from various animation traditions: 'We have seen some of Disney's older films. . . . We have also seen films from socialist

---

[21] The artists participating in the competition were probably not satisfied that the 5th Animafest jury (Bob Balser, Saul Bass, Miloš Macourek, Yuri Norstein and Borislav Šajtinac) decided not to give the Grand Prix. In a released statement the jury encouraged the filmmakers 'to aspire to deeper commitment to the marriage of meaningful content and new forms, and to the recognition of the importance of appropriate pacing and conciseness of expression' (Animafest 1982: 2).

countries. It is all very inspiring, but it is inspiration from other countries. We want to make films in a certain national style. The idea expressed in my film *Three Monks* is both national and international. It is a Chinese story, but the film has been made, so to speak, in an international way. There is no dialogue and it can be understood by all' (Animafest 1982: 16). Descriptive and refined voice-over narrative was common in Chinese production and its rejection emphasized a radically new approach. *Three Monks* stems from a proverb that speaks about an impossibility of cooperation between contradictory agents, but A Da consciously changed its meaning, allowing the caricatured monks eventually to work together in harmony. However this somewhat propagandistic happy ending extends a simplified ideological cliché. A Da's film is dictated by the poetics of an anecdote, and absurd, dynamic editing plays a primal role among the cinematic means of expression, while the character and background design become reduced to symptomatic outlines and attributes. Such aspects of filmmaking became more visible and dynamic in his following short *Super Soap* (*Chaoji feizao*/超级肥皂, 1986).

The 1984 Animafest jurors (Osvaldo Cavandoli, Paul Driessen, Adrienne Mancia, Anatoliy Petrov, Nedeljko Dragić) awarded the film *Snipe-Clam Grapple* (*Yu bang xiang zhang*/鹬蚌相争, dir. Hu Jinqing/胡进庆, 1983) with a Mention for special sensibility, charm and atmosphere. A collage of cotton paper cut-out and painting animation techniques revealed a new approach of SAFS towards the most impressive and immersive animated achievement of the past. Hu Jinqing had been conceptualizing the film for four years, the filmmaker's crew had been trained in the technique for almost five years (the actual work took eight months, the usual production timeline of SAFS). The contemplation of the water landscape is related to the humans' experience: 'While two people are fighting, the third takes advantage of the situation. It has often happened during the course of Chinese history that two small states have been in conflict while a third would benefit' (Animafest 1984: 7). This film anticipates *Feelings from Mountains and Water* (*Shanshui qing*/山水情, co-dir. Wang Shuchen, Ma Kexuan/马克宣), a 1988 masterpiece made entirely in the wash-and-ink painting animation technique that gently reflects on the inevitable transformation of cultural values and rites.

A Da arrived in Zagreb again in 1986 with a film *36 Characters* (*Sanshiliu gezi*/三十六个子, 1984) that won an award in an educational film section (coincidently, this was yet another festival edition without the Grand Prix). This time A Da represented the Chinese Animators' Association as its vice-president and an ASIFA board member. He also announced preparations for an animation festival in Shanghai, the first international undertaking of such a kind in the PRC.[22] While interviewed he focused on the overview of

[22] National festivals had already been organized in PRC (most notably the 'Hundred Flowers' Festival), yet A Da's and other delegates' festival experiences in the West contributed to establishment of the new festival model in China.

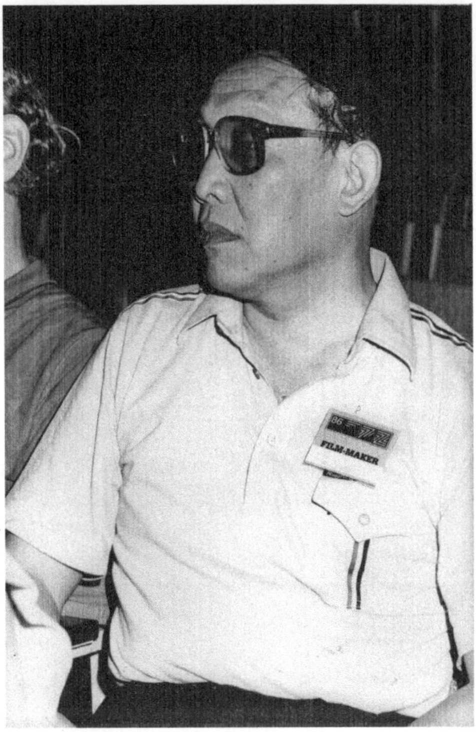

FIGURE 5.1 *A Da in Zagreb (1986). World Festival of Animated Film – Animafest Zagreb.*

production conditions in the Chinese animation industry, listing the numbers of films and awards appearing in the history of SAFS, but he also stated directly: 'They are over 500 people working there . . . 200 of them are auteur in their own right' (Animafest 1986: 13). The possibility of directly interacting and mutually influencing artists from various cultural and cinematographic contexts appears as something very significant for A Da. Asked about the origins of his unique film (a certain kind of Chinese handwriting instructions for beginners), he says: 'I got the idea at the Zagreb Festival four years ago, from my friend David Ehrlich. He knows how to write some of the Chinese characters as it is a drawn script. Instead of talking about it, I'll draw it for you. There, now you can learn new Chinese characters' (Animafest 1986: 14).

The eagerness of the Chinese authors to learn and rework Western influences and to develop modern representative and narrative modes of national animation was welcomed in Zagreb by the artists from Switzerland,

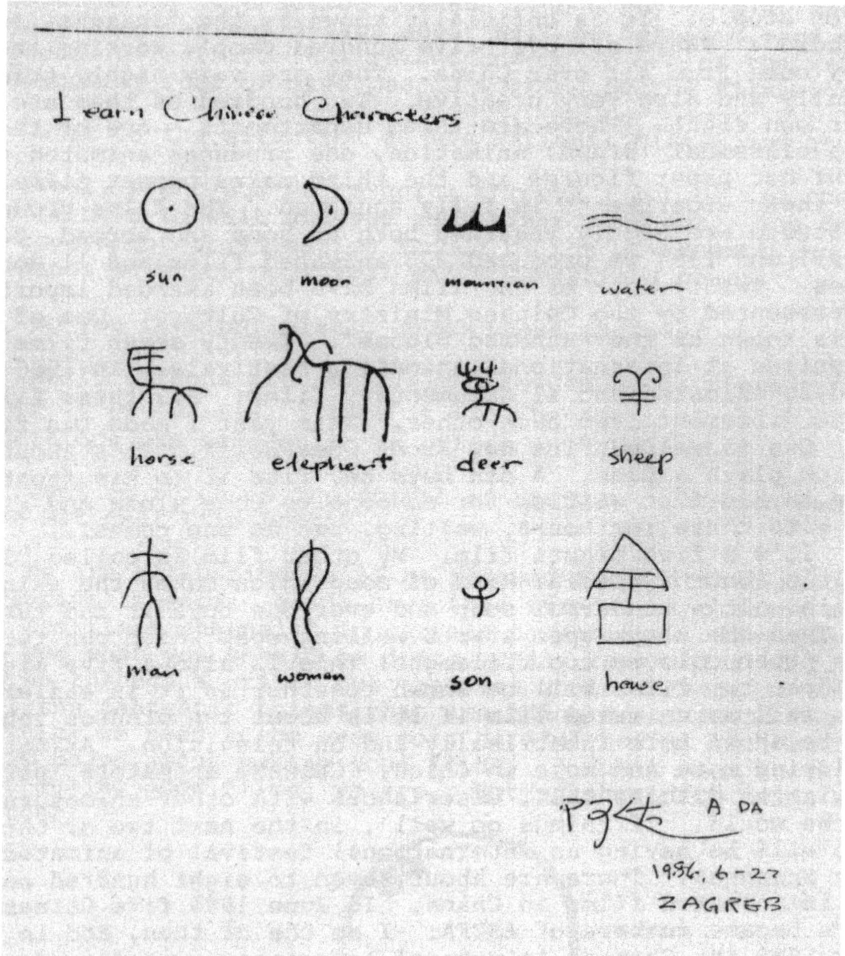

FIGURE 5.2 36 Characters *(1986). World Festival of Animated Film – Animafest Zagreb.*

the United States and Poland. A group of experimentalists and *auteurs*[23] created a unique collective work, *Academy Leaders Variations* (1987, awarded at the Cannes animation competition). Referring to the primal and universal film material, i.e. a film leader, the artists presented variations of a countdown imprinted on a film tape. They changed the standard numeration

[23] Georges Schwizgebel, Claude Luyet, Daniel Sutez, Martial Wannaz (Switzerland); David Ehrlich, Skip Battaglia, Paul Glabicki, George Griffin, Al Jarnow (USA); Jerzy Kucia, Piotr Dumała, Stanisław Lenartowicz, Krzysztof Kiwerski, Mieczysław Janik (Poland); Yan Dingxian, A Da, Chang Guangxi, He Yumen, Hu Jiqing and Lin Wenxiao (China).

(from eleven to three) into a new one (from eight to two), each number evoking new atmospheric and absurd or surreal imagery. A Da did not live to see the final result of the collective work realized in this transnational mode (all the artists worked separately from each other while David Ehrlich coordinated the editing of the material). A Da died in the winter of 1987, as Ehrlich recalled:

> On the train to Beijing to begin the new animation department at the Beijing Film Institute, A Da complained of a severe headache and when he arrived in Beijing, he was taken to the hospital. When the Doctor was told his name, he exclaimed, 'Oh, you're the director of the famous *Three Monks Carrying the Water*!' A Da, who has been working tirelessly for years in creating ground-breaking films, teaching a new generation of animators, and in bringing Shanghai animation and its artists out into the world, answered with a sigh: 'Yes, but I can no longer carry the water'. He then collapsed and never again regained consciousness, passing away the following day from a cerebral haemorrhage. He was 53 years old, as he used to say with a laugh, 'the same age as Donald Duck'.
>
> EHRLICH 2001: 20

The 1988 Animafest edition commemorated A Da with a presentation of his last film *The New Doorbell* (*Xinzhuang de menling*/新装的门铃, co-dir. Ma Kexuan, 1986). In the same year the festival in Shanghai was inaugurated. ASIFA China fully entered the international scene delegating artists not only to represent their works but also to discuss and judge the achievements of other cinematographies. Yan Dingxian, a close collaborator of A Da in the past, joined the 1988 Animafest jury along with Richard Evans, Jim Henson, Karel Zeman and Zlatko Bourek.

Conclusion

Reflection on distant cultural context derives from the need to embrace the Other, i.e. to understand the cultural components applied in the creation of the model of the Other, and the cognitive patterns that enable its deconstruction; in so doing, one reveals one's own intrinsic philosophical assumptions. An outsider may come close to the inherent meanings of cinematic art examined as a complex and dynamic record of specific cultural practices, but never close enough to provide a fully satisfactory explication of the discussed phenomena.

It is worth recalling Werner Herzog's statement expressed while interviewed about *Where the Green Ants Dream* (*Wo die grünen Ameisen träumen*, 1984):

> Absolutely no one, no anthropologist, missionary or anyone else may be capable of comprehending their myths with all their consequences. We are too far from both their religious concepts and their dreams. And so the border exists, it is impossible to cross it and it would not be wise to disregard that. I have stopped on the border of my own understanding. The fact that beyond this border I have been still thinking is, as I believe, a specific feature of my occupation.
>
> HERZOG 1994 [1985]: 34

A Chinese animation researcher's border of understanding is delineated with a highly diverse body of classic films of alluring stylistics, works that in general might be treated as compounds of strong ideological charge, artistically sophisticated references, and innocent, even naive, narratives. Existing writings on the subject, limited in number in the case of English language studies, may be regarded as 'check points'. Publications by authors such as Sean Macdonald, David Ehrlich and Jin Tianyi, John A. Lent and Xu Ying, Wu Weihua, Rolf Giesen and the earlier articles of Bruno Edera or Marie-Claire Quiquemelle, serve as guidelines into *terra incognita*, present a timeline and a filmography, trace industry characteristics, suggest directions for further investigations and interpretations, and sometimes provide intimate insight into individual stories. Beyond the metaphorical border of understanding, one seeks clarification of the seemingly neutral, yet potentially ambiguous facts from film history; awaits confrontation of the established canon with the means and acts that led to its crystallization. The aim of such a mapping might seem ephemeral and in this regard appears as a perfect match for Animation Studies that put the intangible aspect of cinematic art centre stage. However, the method must be grounded in a sceptical research based on fact-checking and pursuit for evidence. Such an approach bears resemblance to one of the most significant Chinese Communist leaders' slogans of 'seeking truth in facts'.

The presented brief overview of the bulletins and catalogues of Animafest Zagreb serves merely as an initial step in archive-based, festival research that would support historical deliberations. I fully realize the necessity of researching other archive materials and applying a comparative perspective (Animafest is a case study). Such work should be eventually complemented with an examination of similar initiatives held in China. I have decided to focus on Animafest for its fundamental role as a 'meeting point' between West and East throughout the period of the Cold War, the direct influences of such meetings on the artistic development and sensitivity of A Da, as well as for the accessibility of Animafest archive that seems quite rare on the wider background of significant European animation festivals. The analyses of such source material contribute to the comprehension of an issue of the canon-building process, an act of political, anthropological and discursive nature.

Paradoxically the principle of 'seeking truth in facts' comprises a thought that seems highly relevant for the studies on Chinese animated film, an area that still requires further critical recognition. Chinese animation history is a history of the studio, artistic collectivism, and the creation of ideologically determined national identity and memory. At the same time, it is a story of ambitious artistic undertakings, subversive modernisation, and eventually of the liberation of individual, *auteur* subjectivity.

References

A Da (1983). 'Z xing manji – yi canjia segele di wu jie shije meishu dianying jie' ['Notes on Visit to Zagreb – Participating in the Zagreb Fifth World Artistic Animation Festival'], *China Academic Journal Electronic Publishing House*, 214–230.

Alder, O. (1994). 'Te Wei. Chinese Doyen of Animation', *Plateau*, 15 (2): 4–8.

Andrews, J. F. and K. Shen (2012). *The Art of Modern China*. Berkeley, Los Angeles, London: University of California Press.

Animafest 1978 Bulletin, Zagreb: Zagreb Film, Executive City Council of Zagreb.

Animafest 1980 Bulletin, Zagreb: Zagreb Film, Executive City Council of Zagreb.

Animafest 1982 Bulletin, Zagreb: Zagreb Film, Executive City Council of Zagreb.

Animafest 1984 Bulletin, Zagreb: Zagreb Film, Executive City Council of Zagreb.

Animafest 1986 Bulletin, Zagreb: Zagreb Film, Executive City Council of Zagreb.

Animafest 1988 Bulletin, Zagreb: Zagreb Film, Executive City Council of Zagreb.

Asian and African Film Festival in Tashkent (1958). [Newsreel] British Pathé. Available online: https://www.britishpathe.com/video/asian-and-african-film-festival-in-tashkent/query/tashkent reel (accessed 20 April 2017).

Bendazzi, G. (2015). *Animation: A World History, Vol. 1–3*. Boca Raton: CRC Press, Taylor & Francis Group.

Chisaan, C. (2012). 'In Search of an Indonesian Islamic Culture Identity 1956–1965', in J. Lindsay and M. H. T. Liam (eds), *Heirs to World Culture: Being Indonesian, 1950–1965*, 283–314. Leiden: KITLV Press.

Chu, K.-W. (2015). 'Animating *Shanshui*: Chinese Landscape in Animated Film, Art and Performance', in C. Pallant (ed.), *Animated Landscapes: History, Form and Function*, 109–124. New York, London: Bloomsbury.

de Valck, M. (2007). *Film Festivals: From European Geopolitics to Global Cinephilia*. Amsterdam: Amsterdam University Press.

de Valck, M. and S. Loist (2009). 'Film Festival Studies: An Overview of a Burgeoning Field', in D. Iordanova and R. Rhyne (eds), *Film Festival Yearbook 1: The Festival Circuit*, 179–215. St. Andrews: St. Andrews Film Studies.

Djagalov, R. and M. Salazkina (2016). 'Tashkent '68: A Cinematic Contact Zone', *Slavic Review*, 75 (2): 279–298.

Edera, B. (1980). 'The Animated Film in the People's Republic of China', *Animafilm*, Spring: 35–39.

Ehrlich, D. and T. Jin (2001). 'Animation in China', in J. A. Lent (ed.), *Animation in Asia and Pacific*, 7–32, London, Paris, Rome, Sydney: John Libbey.

Ferro, M. (2008 [1971]). 'Film. Kontranaliza społeczeństwa?' ['Le film. Une contre-analyse de la société?'] ['Film, a Counteranalysis of Society?'], in I. Kurz (ed.), *Film i Historia. Antologia [Film and History. Anthology]*, 67–92. Warszawa: Wydawnictwa Uniwersytetu Warszawskiego.

Giesen, R. (2015). *Chinese Animation: A History and Filmography, 1922–2012*. Jefferson, NC: McFarland and Co.

Helman, A. (2010). *Odcienie czerwieni. Twórczość filmowa Zhanga Yimou [Shades of Red. Cinema of Zhang Yimou]*. Gdańsk: słowo/obraz terytoria.

Herzog, W. (1994 [1985]). 'In Conversation with Jean Roy', in B. Zmudziński and P. C. Seel (eds), *Werner Herzog*. Kraków: 'Secesja'.

Hung, C.-T. (1994). *War and Popular Culture: Resistance in Modern China 1937–1945*. Berkeley, Los Angeles, Oxford: University of California Press.

Iordanova, D. (2015). 'The Film Festival as an Industry Node', *Media Industries*, 1 (3): 7–11.

Jelenković, D. (2016). 'Politics, Ideology, and Programming Practices: How the Yugoslav Documentary and Short Film Festival Abandoned the Idea of Yugoslavia', *New Review of Film and Television Studies*, 14 (1): 76–92.

Kennedy, H. (1978). 'London Film Festival – 1978. A Heady Brew', *American Cinema Papers*, online: http://www.americancinemapapers.com/files/LONDON_1978.htm (accessed 15 May 2016).

Książek-Konicka, H. (1978). 'Pesaro 1978: Chinese Film', *Kino*, 9: 46–47.

Lent, J. A. and Y. Xu (2010). 'Chinese Animation Film: From Experimentation to Digitalization', in S. Rosen and Y. Zhu (eds), *Art, Politics and Commerce in Chinese Cinema*, 111–126. Hong Kong: Hong Kong University Press.

Macdonald, S. (2016). *Animation in China: History, Aesthetics, Media*. London, New York: Routledge.

Pawłowski, J. (2013). *Przeszłość w ideologii Komunistycznej Partii Chin [Past in the Ideology of the Communist Party of China]*. Warszawa: Wydawnictwa Uniwersytetu Warszawskiego.

Pikkov, Ü. (2010). *Animasophy: Theoretical Writings on Animated Film*. Tallinn: Estonian Academy of Arts.

Pohl, K.-H. (2016 [1993]). 'Zu Beiträgen Li Zehous in der Debatte um Tradition und Identität in den 80er Jahren in der Volksrepublik China' ['On Li Zehou's Contributions to the 1980s Debate on Tradition and Identity in the People's Republic of China']), 41–56, in Ralf Moritz (ed.), *Sinologische Traditionen im Spiegel neuer Forschung*. Leipzig: Universitäsverlag.

Quiquemelle, M.-C. (1991). 'The Wan Brothers and Sixty Years of Animated Film in China', trans. C. Béliard, in C. Berry (ed.), *Perspectives on Chinese Cinema*, 175–186. London: British Film Institute.

Reprinted materials (1978). 'Chinese Films in Paris and Pesaro', *Kino*, 9: 41–46.

Staiger, J. (2008 [1992]). 'W stronę historyczno-materialistycznych badań nad recepcją filmu' ['Toward a Historical Materialist Approach to Reception Studies'], in I. Kurz (ed.), *Film i Historia. Antologia [Film and History. Anthology]*, 131–138. Warszawa: Wydawnictwa Uniwersytetu Warszawskiego.

Wu, W. (2009). 'In Memory of Meishu Film: Catachresis and Metaphor in Theorizing Chinese Animation', *Animation*, 4 (1): 31–54.

6

Austria Unlimited – Chances, Spirits and Limitations of a Small Production Environment

Holger Lang

Introduction

When two special programmes of Austrian animation were introduced at Animafest Zagreb in June 2015 (Kožul 2015: 192–211), festival staff asked the curators from ASIFA Austria onto the stage. However, the initial conversation started with an extended moment of silence. With a puzzled expression on his face, the presenter said: 'I don't know what to say, I have not seen anything like this before.' The following lively discussion made it clear that the knowledge of and the experience with Austrian animation may benefit from a recapitulating overview that allows some more insight into conditions and dynamics of the local scene.

The following text does not attempt to approach animation in Austria from a strictly functional or factual angle, and it does not attempt to create a complete picture of it. But, while compressing the historical evolution by using a broad-brush strategy and by applying a fragmented focus on partially disengaged elements in its discussion, the main intention of this proposition is to look beneath the surface and thus to recognize underlying streams and tendencies. By doing this the situation in Austria should get recognized as a special case to demonstrate elements that can also contribute to the reflection on global developments in animation theory.

On the one hand, animation cannot be the only relevant area to include in this discussion to understand its specific qualities in Austria and on the other hand it is not necessary to go into excessive detail with its historical appearances to follow the rationale of the claim. In its particular manifestation and development animation in Austria reflects a cultural environment that has as many individual qualities as it most likely will also have in many other countries in the world. Here the purpose is to sketch out an integrative and interdisciplinary prospect that wants to raise some more questions than it wants to answer. This begins with the proposal to not describe an environment by listing individual work or through a rough outline of a period or even a specific example that would represent the situation. The idea is to step back and to get a sense for a general direction of the cultural development including the specific relationship to animation.

The investigation of animation in Austria should also not get started without referring to the overshadowing domain of Austrian avant-garde cinema. For an extended time, the artistic work with film in this country had been discussed with a focus on this conceptually and historically recognized frame. Through acknowledging this academically widely examined field, while opening up the debate to consecutives and overlaps with animation, one may propose to adjust and modulate the external view on the conditions in this country based on many of the well-established approaches in avant-garde cinema. By doing this the relationship between both domains will then also be up for analysis and exploration.

The statement presented here suggests an extensive intersection of experimental, avant-garde and underground filmmaking in Austria, so that a significant part of local artistic animation could get supported and underpinned by comparing individual examples of work from both sides. However, such a process comes from a position that would require a balancing act, necessary to maintain the integrity of consolidated research in established fields, while involving a much broader, expository process in the negotiation of animation. Such a case-study based approach is not the agenda of this text, but it suggests an even more distant view of the overall environment. In other terms, the underlying intention of this hypothetical review is the opening of boundaries between areas that enjoyed very different amounts of attention, investigation, and recognition. Animation in Austria is the related vehicle to explain why this may be useful also in a global context.[1]

[1] Coming from inside this environment, also as an artistic participant, preoccupation and potential bias are a comprehensible obstacle to a scholarly discourse. This is kept in mind during the discussion, but a subjective element cannot be excluded from the overall picture and a consciously considered aspect of the here proposed strategy as a possible way to reorganize the view on animation in Austria from a much more associative angle. This approach is only reasonable by applying an expanded understanding of animation, as a technique, and also as an open conceptual method to work with audio-visual media. Based on the complexity of the intention it is only possible to sketch out some of the underlying conditions that endorse the hypothesis, without claiming to provide a full-scale and in-depth examination.

There are two interconnected approaches to the proposal: The specific working conditions in the field of animation in the country and the related theoretical exploration of the more fundamental question: 'Are there any boundaries to animation?' In both directions, plenty of space for more thorough research is available, but the primary ambition of this text is the promotion of an argument that can get traced through historical developments in Austria. Today it also contains significant potential for the consideration of animation at large. Even in the confined circumstances of this relatively small nation the complexity of conditions allows only a sketchy and incomplete depiction of artistic evolution and progress, but it should be dense enough to stand up to the claims of the hypothesis. Comparable or similar environments – namely other countries – may well show analogies in their local circumstances, but this will not be a focus of attention in this synoptic proposition.

From a distance – an outline of origins and backgrounds

Countries are communities that carry and promote ideas and ideals that occupy the people living within them. These subtle, subjacent social conditions differ even between very closely related environments, but they do influence the cultural microclimate profoundly. To cast some light on the current situation in Austria one has to look back on the most defining historical events that reverberate even up to present days. In this context, one has to start with the Austro-Hungarian Empire during a period that is undeniably considered the golden age of cultural and social sophistication. What is still seen as the classical image of Austria and even more so of its capital Vienna derives mainly from a few decades around the turn of the nineteenth to the twentieth century. This period also marks the beginning era of film and animation and is, therefore, an appropriate starting point for the attempt to contextualize the development of Austrian animation.

The roots into the pre-cinematic realm do reach much further back, and for this country it is justifiable to point out Simon von Stampfer, a professor at the Imperial Polytechnic Institute in Vienna, as an innovator and precursor. His *stroboscopic discs* represent an invention that stands equally in significance next to the work of Joseph Plateau in Belgium. Extensive discussion and documentation of Stampfer and his work is included in Thomas Renoldner's (2010: 42–54) contribution to the German language publication *Die Kunst des Einzelbilds*. Unfortunately, no English translation of the book is available at this point. This collected edition currently represents the most extensive effort to portray Austrian animation also in its historical context. The title, translated as *The Art of the Single Frame*, indeed already casts a clear direction for the understanding of later developments and this publication is used as one of the prominent sources for information on the most relevant individuals and examples mentioned here.

In 1914 the oldest remaining and therefore undoubtedly confirmed Austrian animation was presented. This silent movie was produced in stop-motion technique and showed precisely what the title expressed: *Ideale Filmerzeugung* (*Ideal Filmmaking*). The animation depicts all technical steps necessary for the production of a film up to the delivery of the first copy. In German language, animated films have long been called 'Trick-Films', using 'film-tricks' like stop-motion, as methods to create scenes and events that otherwise could not have been displayed in cinematic environments. Produced by Sascha-Film in Vienna and shot by Ludwig Schaschek, this approximately seven-minute long clip is an early example of the self-reflective potential of filmmaking and its interdisciplinary nature. The medium was used to not only contain and transmit a message about itself, but it was also already used as a device to represent the message within its own manifestation (Renoldner 2010: 55). Introspection and self-observation are not exclusive to Austria, but the contributions of Josef Breuer, Sigmund Freud and Alfred Adler to the development of the new discipline of psychoanalysis in Vienna should not be seen without the specific relationship to the environment that they originated from. The coincidence of an animated film that picked up this methodology in its essence is indicatory and for sure more than merely anecdotal.

The historical period between 1914 and 1918 includes a rough transition in Austria, from a large, thriving and dominating empire to a small, worn out and almost destroyed torso of itself. The size and volume of the country had been reduced to nearly a tenth of its previous dimensions, and it brought the very sudden disappearance of structures, ideas and ideals that had functioned as focal points for national and personal identification for a very long time-span.

Of course, this situation had been experienced in various parts of the former 'Danube Monarchy' in many different ways, but the experience of radical diminishment and reduction would not be seen to the same extent in other parts of Europe. Countries like Croatia and Slovakia, the Czech Republic and Bosnia, all had their own, individual way out of a once-connected history to their own independent history. What remained a lot more specific in the country that today is called Austria is a massive downsizing on all social, economic, cultural and political levels. The long-lasting legacy of this dramatic change had its effect also on work with film and animation and should be seen as an important element, subsequently influencing self-conception, identity and introspection, specifically in Vienna. This claim requires some crude simplification and generalization as it is recognized as a superordinate influence, a vague, but also a prominent force that may not be dealt with consciously on a daily basis. It can still be traced as a real factor, even in a diluted form, up to current times. Under such influences the development of animation as a part of the cultural and artistic climate can also be seen as an indicator for more general changes in this country and some of these relationships will be discussed here.

After a very short early blossoming of animation in Austria between 1920 and 1925 the success of American producers like Walt Disney and Max Fleischer in the 1930s, and the drying out of virtually all financial resources, led to a situation where copying the style and aesthetics of these dominant studios turned into the main objective of local production (Walkensteiner-Preschl 2010: 185–194; Renoldner 2010: 79–85). The complex changes in Austria, the fact that many hundreds of thousands of people had left the country for good, in particular, the capital Vienna, the overall consistently worsening economic situation and the cultural down-spiralling created an environment that was not supporting any social progress. The brain-drain and the elimination of production environments during this time had been distinct and widespread.

Der Filmbote (1918–1926), an Austrian cinema-journal owned by the Association of the Austrian Cinematic Industries, described the situation in 1924 as this: 'Already in 1922, the fate of the Austrian film industry was sealed. This means: In its blossoming, it already found its end. Now it's all about stabilization and the maintenance of those companies that had a chance to survive capitalistically and to produce on a large scale' (Renoldner 2010: 58). Despite the turmoil and suffering that the shattering of the Austro-Hungarian Empire created in the remaining country, significant parts of everyday life had remained in its pre-World War I style – well up to the 1930s and 1940s. In particular in Vienna many aspects of society had been paralyzed and one could almost describe the situation in many areas as virtually 'frozen' in its development after the year 1918. To understand the slow and laborious 'rebirth' of film and animation in Austria one must see the restrictions created by the overall cultural, social and political situation in this suddenly tiny country. For Austrian animation, the decades of decline after 1918 can therefore not be described as a very significant period; thus we jump ahead in time – through the next war and post-war period – to the 1950s.

A new start – slow ascent to progressive thinking

From today's perspective, a distinctive quality and characteristic of animation produced in Austria is its independent, exploratory, and relatively self-contained complexion. The roots of this virtue should be seen in connection with artistic responses to the general social and political developments following the second 're-boot' of the national identity. On 27 July 1955 the

'Austrian State Treaty' finally re-established Austria as a sovereign state after ten years of occupation following World War II. In the decade leading up to this the majority of industrial complexes in the country, especially in the eastern parts, had been removed, either destroyed or demolished by occupying forces. Still, on 1 August 1955 the first test-broadcasting of Austrian Television took place – it was fully rolled out from 1957 onwards – originally only in the major cities, until in the late 1960s television was finally reaching all areas of the country (Dassanowsky 2005: 166). On 26 October 1955 Austria declared itself 'permanently neutral' and a politically stable environment had been established.

The period between 1955 and the 1970s was predominantly characterized by a widespread avoidance of the past and the necessary reprocessing of it. It showed a strong conservative and reactionary tendency in many social and cultural areas and a wish for an idealized, simple and happy life. On the surface, this seemed to have worked for a while as even Pope Paul VI, during a visit in 1971, still called Austria the 'Isola Felice' or 'the island of the happy', which Austrians were truly appreciative to hear. People even started to modify the meaning of this quote by shifting the emphasis towards the more enthusiastic self-definition of being an 'Insel der Seligen' – an 'island of the blessed'. Such an attitude could not pass unnoticed by the cultural avant-garde, and this is the domain where a robust intellectual resistance started to rise.

One must also mention that, similar to the rest of Europe, this was also the time of rebuilding countries, dominated by massively growing consumption, by commercialization, by the pursuit of undisturbed happiness, and by a focus on the present instead of the past or the tomorrow. At the same time, traditional role models still influenced the lives of most people in Austria and cultural progress, including modernization and emancipation, had a steep ascent. Despite the recovery from the pressures of the previous decades much of the society remained stuck in its slow and hesitant internal social development.

In animation, only small manufacturing structures had remained actively working. The broad disappearance of an industrial economy was a prominent factor in the working conditions. Promotional work was one of the few areas in Austria that provided the necessary financial resources for production. Small production companies tried to find ways to survive between the market demands, created by the dominating styles of international corporations, and a local identity with specific forms of expression. One remarkable individual who started his career during this time and remained almost isolated in his domain was Hans O. Sindelar, who worked with puppet-animation, creating programmes for television (Renoldner 2010: 127–130).

Despite all structural, logistical and financial limitations artists saw chances to explore new ways to work and started to develop innovative approaches. Getting involved with advertising on TV and even more so for the cinemas had an unexpected side-effect. Promotion was an area where some production money was available. Several cases of early artistic films were therefore also connected to a commercial application already by the middle of the twentieth century. This most likely contributed in an understated form to the origins of some of the Austrian avant-garde, underground films and experimental animation.

Two examples demonstrate very well how advertising played a part during the early years of experimental film and animation in Austria. Both already included aspects of subsequent and long-lasting developments that shifted the focus from a narrative and concrete style to a format that embraces fragmented, abstracted, formal and non-narrative sequencing: *Schwechater* (1958) by Peter Kubelka, originally projected as a promotional film for a beer brand, and *Humanic Varese* (1959) by Hans Albala, advertising a local shoe manufacturing company.

Schwechater is a one-minute long film with a complex internal structure that alternates and interweaves blocks of individual frames. Peter Tscherkassky cites a conversation between Peter Kubelka and Jonas Mekas about the conceptual direction of this work: 'Cinema is not movement. This is the first thing. Cinema is not movement. Cinema is the projection of stills.' Continuing with the conclusion that 'In *Schwechater* his (Kubelka's) aesthetic creed is the core of the entire formal construction. The visual impression that this film leaves on the viewer is deeply saturated by the ephemeral properties of each individual frame' (Tscherkassky 1995: 118).

Humanic Varese, also about one minute long, includes a catchy, drum-driven song that provides the basis for an animation. It also uses patterns, stylized photos of characters – women wearing shoes and 'showing their legs' – and letters of the company logo. Aesthetically this clip created a convincing bridge between the concepts of visual music and the captivating qualities of Pop Art. Thomas Renoldner (2010: 110) qualifies this film as Hans Albala's 'masterpiece' and sees it as 'the first commissioned experimental film to fine artists'.

These examples already demonstrate the connection between alternative sources of funding, the radical focus on a formal and conceptual approach to filmmaking, and the embrace of artistic freedom and independence. This must be recognized as a benchmark for much of the later following further developments in Austria.

As Robert von Dassanowsky (2005: 195–196) writes in *Austrian Cinema: A History* about conditions of the creative environment that nurtured such independent and groundbreaking work:

> Over one hundred films were created between the early 1950s and 1968 by the members of the Art Club movement by such artists as Peter Weibel, Kurt Krenn, Mark Adrian, Ernst Schmidt Jr., Peter Kubelka, Otmar Bauer,

> Hans Scheugl, Günter Brus and Gottfried Schlemmer. Yet for all their startling new visions and even new performance art tactics in the showing of these films, the lack of government and media industry disallowed any showcasing as was available in Western Germany, where theatres and television attempted to offer at least a taste of the avant-garde experience.

While Hans Albala continued to produce a variety of abstract animations for different companies, Peter Kubelka moved into a prominent position in the global art-scene that allows us today to see him as one of the defining protagonists of an international film avant-garde. His iconic work *Arnulf Rainer* – the title corresponds to the name of the Austrian artist – is a radical and consequent continuation of his artistic search for the essence of the cinematic experience.

'The film that Rainer had commissioned and financed as a documentation of his own art of painting, consists of black and white frames, silence and white noise, covering the entire audible frequency spectrum' (Tscherkassky 1995: 120). The cinematic composition consists of a structure of combinations of various sequential patterns that Kubelka strung together in a complex array. Independent of the elimination of the camera as the device to create a frame, and also independent of questions related to the actual content within a frame, the focus on the fundamental visual units that define and represent film as a medium let such work have a very conclusive impact also on animation. At the level of Kubelka's work, the separation between areas like film, art and animation loses all relevance.

As much as this bold achievement must be acknowledged for both anticipating and overshadowing a vital part of the later developments also in artistic animation in Austria, it should likewise be seen as a reason for the more isolated community that it created. Robert von Dassanowsky describes the radical style as a 'factor that made Austrian alternative filmmaking less accessible to the audiences than their European counterparts'. Continuing, 'The intellectual/artistic core of this film movement that totally opposed dominant or commercial motion pictures (rather than influence them or replace them, as was the case in France, Italy and to some extent, England), found its ideology in modern painting and the Austrian performance art known as Viennese Actionism. [. . .] The iconoclastic aim was to angrily protest against what was seen as calcified, even fascistic, socio-politics and retrograde cultural elitism of the nation' (Dassanowsky 2005: 196).

The 1968 performance *Kunst und Revolution* (*Art and Revolution*) finally brought to the surface in the broad public the group of people that is in retrospect now called '*Wiener Aktionismus*' or '*Viennese Actionism*'. These 'actionists' used violence, nudity and many then (and still now) socially unacceptable activities to express their ideas and attitudes. Kurt Kren, whose work is often referred to as 'underground films', is a paradigmatic example for an artist moving between nowadays artificially separated fields – performance, filmmaking, documentation, animation and fine arts. The connecting attitude and artistic identity that allowed such a free flow between genres and disciplines was identified by Austrian filmmaker and writer Hans Scheugl by quoting theoretician Michael Siegert (1996: 12–13): 'The Actionists confronted the system with their sovereign ridicule, they just let their pants down, and the authorities lost their breath. Our powerless loathing turned into triumphant laughter' (Siegert in Scheugl 1996: 12–13).

Kurt Kren worked as experimental filmmaker, collaborated in and documented performances, and also explored aspects of experimental animation. A part of his filmmaking demonstrates how the deconstruction of recorded events, and the following reconstruction in ways that create new mediate experiences, is playing with foundations of free exploration in cinema and conceptual animation. In his film *48 Köpfe aus dem Szondi-Test (48 Heads from the Szondi-Test)* Kren was using a single-frame recording process to create a montage from forty-eight examples of faces, printed for use in a psychological test. By using these small cards as source material for his experimental film/animation, he is expanding their original purpose to create an exploration of perception. Kren says: 'Yes, what does one see and what not. In Vienna, someone wanted to bet with me for 100 Schilling after watching the film a second and a third time, that it had actually not been the same films. To be fair, I did not accept the bet' (Kren in Scheugl 1996: 12–13).

To portray a historical social situation in a very brief manner, it is helpful and efficient to use significant figures and contributors. Up to the 1970s, the role of women in the Austrian society had been governed by a legal situation that still had not granted them equal rights and no equal position in society. Without question, women had also been very active as artists during this time. However, the public appearance and even more so the recognition had still been heavily dominated by men. Much of the extensively engaged and influential work by women had been documented a lot less; it had been less presented, less promoted and – which is historically even more dramatic – less archived. It is not possible to make up for such negligence and ignorance in this compressed review, but it is necessary to point out that also the contribution of women to animation as part of a more complex artistic and cultural scene in Austria during this period has never been accredited accordingly.

VALIE EXPORT, Maria Lassnig

Artists have often performed their role in society in a consciously political manner. On the other hand, artists' work has repeatedly been politicized by others, to influence or comment on a specific period or situation. The discussion of artists' work, their attitudes, intentions and their effects, can and shall not get separated from the political potential that is connected to such a process.

It is necessary to emphasize that women were able to slowly gain public recognition in Austria in the 1970s because this effectively contributed also to the animation scene in a very direct way. The rise of prominent female protagonists is an indicator of the cultural development that started to take place. However, one can still not say that today, almost 50 years later, the society in Austria can provide fully equal rights and conditions for both genders. Nevertheless, the effects of positive role models have a slow, but long-lasting impact. Out of a much larger group, two women stand out as important representatives.

VALIE EXPORT achieved international recognition with her performances and media-related work. As a principal protagonist in the artistic field of 'expanded cinema', her focus on feminism and the position, role and significance of women in art and society represents a small, but still significant stream of artists, contributing to the redefinition of the Austrian identity. EXPORT did not primarily challenge traditional and established artistic and cultural strategies and methods, although this has commonly been seen as one effect of her work, she predominantly expressed a strong, autonomous and self-conscious position as an artist. This unbound attitude is an internationally acknowledged expression of creative independence in communication with the surrounding social context. Also, EXPORT had previously collaborated in parts with the 'Viennese Actionists', but her work needs consideration in a much broader scope. Gabriele Jutz writes, in her extensive investigation of avant-garde film in *Cinema Brut*, that EXPORT successfully opened up the cinematic experience from a collective experience in a movie theatre to the much more intense, personalized and reflective experience of her 'expanded-cinema' performances.

What matters in connection to animation is the conceptual premise that artists have all the rights to define a medium and its use, according primarily to their own will. EXPORT aggressively displayed her views related to the treatment and perception of women in Western society and on gender issues in general. Her work was communicated frequently through recording media – like film, photography and television and it reverberates up to the present day. Although her oeuvre seemingly had no direct impact on practical work in animation, her radical attitude, multi-disciplinary approach, and her autonomous standpoint make her a clear identification figure for later-born artists. 'It's interesting that the most "radical" protagonists of expanded-cinema often have no desire to "enlighten" or to "liberate" their audience', writes Jutz (2010: 170), 'the audience does not need to get won and resolved, but combatted'.

Maria Lassnig was an Austrian painter who is considered one of the most renowned artists of her generation. By the 1950s she had left Austria together with Arnulf Rainer to live in Paris for some time, returned to Vienna to complete her studies with Albert Paris Gütersloh and then had left the city again during the 1960s, first back to Paris and finally to New York. Between 1970 and 1972 she studied animated films and produced several short pieces of which *Selfportrait* from 1971 and *Art Education* from 1976 can be seen as indicators for her own future path. Her engagement with the depiction of the female body and its perception in society had been a central theme in her paintings. Also, the very personal interaction with her mother got woven deeply into her self-reflective work.

In 1980 Maria Lassnig was asked to head the painting class at the University of Applied Arts Vienna, and by this she was appointed as first female professor for painting at any Austrian university. The relevance of the political decision to invite Lassnig can be recognized in response to a coincidentally almost simultaneously occurring circumstance that intersects the careers of her and VALIE EXPORT. In 1980 both women represented Austria at the Biennale in Venice. Fritz Billeter describes their contribution: 'Both women don't whitewash the situation, they present (mainly related to bodies and their person) the oppressed situation of their gender: poses and situations of submission, violation, moment and revolt' (Billeter 1980: 4).

Lassnig brought to Vienna a unique combination of resistance against stiff social frameworks, her experience of the art-scenes of metropolitan cities, the openness to experiments and explorations and no desire to work for commercial, but rather for artistic goals. She even went one step further and created a mark in the history of Austrian animation that must be recognized as a defining turning point, which still echoes within many active animation artists of today. In 1982, she initiated the 'Studio for Experimental Animation', the first formal education for animation in Austria, being offered as an optional element during the studies in the painting programme.

Her basic thoughts and foundations behind this were, as described by one of her students, ideas to 'develop films – out of the visual – or – from a visual position (Filme aus dem Optischen heraus zu entwickeln)' (Stratil 2017). This class, her initial approaches, the spirit that she brought to Austria, embedding animation mainly in an artistic context and the connection to a broader field of visual communication are defining ingredients that affirmed the further development of local animation. Franziska Bruckner writes in her 2011 published work on the history and impact of the 'Studio for Experimental Animation' about Lassnig's role:

> In general the stylistic and contentual diversity of Maria Lassnig's own animated films stands exemplary for the diversity of student-films created at the studio. Also, the independent film scene in the USA can be considered as an inspiring influence for the establishment of the animation studio at the University of Applied Arts Vienna and thus also for the emergence of an experimental animation scene in Austria.
>
> BRUCKNER 2011: 93

There was no intention at her studio to educate animators for a commercial environment, particularly as there was no large scale or even industrial type of animation-production happening in this country anyway. The work was a vital part of a painting class, where students were now also enabled to learn about and to work with animation as a time-based medium. Nowhere else in Austria did training or education in this field exist. Lassnig taught at the university for about ten years, and the studio that she had installed was continued successfully after she retired and returned solely to painting.

A long-lasting effect of the 'artist as auteur' approach that Lassnig had introduced was the self-understanding of the filmmaker as the primary and often single creator of an artwork. In an international context, this conception can be regarded as containing a double-edged quality. It may emphasize the independent voice of the artist and may also encourage a confident and sincere expression of one's ideas and attitudes. However, it can also isolate from a broader creative environment and potentially inhibit a more collaborative and interactive production appreciation. Nevertheless, it contributed to the generalized notion that animation in Austria had developed in a semi-detached, relatively 'wild' and artistically charged atmosphere. For quite some time the involved players did not mind such an external perception too much.

Exponential expansion – prospects and expectations in an opening world

The final two decades of the last millennium entailed several events that also had an impact on the 'happy island' of Austria. Inconceivable, but often imagined incidents suddenly actually took place and had a discreet effect on all of us. The Chernobyl nuclear power plant disaster exposed most of Europe to high levels of radiation in 1986, the Berlin Wall crumbled to dust in 1989 and Austria gave up its Perpetual Neutrality to join the European Union in 1996. All this pushed Austrians to a necessary new attitude about their general role in a global environment. Coming from a much more secluded position this then resulted in many further chances for the animation scene as well, but it was still a laborious path.

In 1980 the first exhibition on 'Österreichischer (Austrian) Avantgarde und Undergroundfilm 1950–1980' took place. It celebrated a new Austrian position related to the creation of art films and was organized by Ernst Schmidt Jr., who also initiated the reconstitution of the 'Austrian Filmmakers Cooperative' in 1982. Schmidt, a protagonist of the internationally recognized group of Austrian avant-garde filmmakers, also participated in organizing a screening of films by this association's members at the University of Applied Arts Vienna during the same year. Film-technologies became affordable, and Super 8 film was at its peak, inspiring young filmmakers. In 1983 the exhibition 'Geschichte des Österreichischen Animationsfilmes (History of Austrian Animation)' reflected for the very first time upon this field in Austria, and soon students from Maria Lassnig's class travelled to Annecy to attended their first animation-film festival (Stratil 2017).

While the 1980s and 1990s showed the consistent growth of what Lassnig had initiated, one has to keep in mind that substantial financial support for animation production never existed – and still does not as of today, in 2018. Various projects were initiated to facilitate the work of animation artists in Austria. Hubert Sielecki played a crucial role in starting the Austrian chapter of 'ASIFA' (Association Internationale du Film d'Animation) in 1985. It was created in collaboration with students from Lassnig's class, inspired by their previous trip to Annecy. In 1987 the introduction of the Prix Ars Electronica for international digital animation brought significant international attention to Austria. In 1990 'sixpackfilm' was created, first to organize screenings of Austrian experimental films but soon also to work as an organization to distribute artistic films from Austrian – and, subsequently, animation also gained some more space in their catalogue. In 1993 the 'Diagonale Filmfestival' for Austrian film-productions was organized the first time, originally in cooperation with the 'Salzburg Festival', and after a few years it was finally established as the primary festival for Austrian film.

All these individual activities encouraged animation artists in Austria, but next to the education at the University of Applied Arts Vienna, a central element to support production during this period turned out to be the group around ASIFA Austria. Animation had still been based on analogue technology and this organization provided the necessary facilities to former students and to interested independent artists. Besides Hubert Sielecki, who ran the university's animation studio for thirty years, people like Bady Minck, Renate Kordon, Mara Mattuschka, Stefan Stratil, Sabine Groschup, Thomas Renoldner, Moucle Blackout, Daniel Šuljić, Tone Fink and many others collaborated with and through this society.

During this time, virtually all members of this group had begun their work as students, as artists that often had to adopt the concept of 'low tech and low budget', as the available production environment remained economically very limited. What had to be created – almost as a counterweight to balance the lack of a reliable infrastructure – was an attitude, a mindset and a climate that would prove to be very accepting, free and open over a long period of time.

Even though some artists managed to gain small financial revenues from their work, the lack of a local market for animation in Austria and the continuing absence of a commercial production scene required the focus on artistic integrity and independence. This did not mean that the involved protagonists were not looking for the bigger picture, for 'the world to conquer', but for a sequence of approximately 15 to 20 years, the local development focused on the manifestation of the, today still solid, defining qualities of the animation scene in this country. However, change was gradually happening.

After being nominated for an Oscar with *Copy Shop* in 2002 (category 'live-action short'), Virgil Widrich's *Fast Film* was nominated for the Golden Palm in Cannes in 2003. While both his films still embraced analogue work, they also expanded the medium and demonstrated how the influence of electronic media and digital production began to spread in Austria. *Fast Film* not only bridged between traditional and new production means, but it also achieved market acclaim and broad critical recognition. Widrich is an example for artists who started to engage in productions that would also contain the potential for commercial success – his company and many other smaller companies began to shift towards digital output and extended into non-artistic work.

With the new millennium, many new initiatives widened the scene in Austria massively. The most significant and sometimes overlooked influence is similar in impact to what Maria Lassnig had done about twenty years earlier: the conscious creation of spaces to study and practice. After private universities were finally permitted for the first time in 2001, the possibilities for education in animation started to spread across Austria, especially outside Vienna. Several new universities, most notably Universities of Applied Sciences, included a focus on contemporary directions in animation, in particular digital production. They embraced more open possibilities to also work for an animation market, even if such a demand would still exist mainly outside Austria. New projects consolidated the consciousness and self-awareness within Austria. In 2001 the 'Tricky Women Filmfestival' started, the first Austrian event focusing only on animation and presenting films created predominantly by women.

In 2004 the 'VIS–ViennaShorts' festival was founded, and Thomas Renoldner from ASIFA Austria started the 'One Day Animation Festival' that evolved into a 'Two Day Animation Festival' in 2017. In 2007 the first 'Pixel Vienna' conference, focusing on computer graphics and animation, took place, and the ASIFAKEIL opened, a public exhibition space to display work at the intersection of fine-arts and animation, located prominently at the 'Museums Quartier', a highly recognized cluster of museums and cultural institutions. In 2009 the City of Vienna endowed the annual 'Content Award' for creative industries. In 2010 Thomas Renoldner began a collaboration between ASIFA Austria and the VIS-festival, represented by Wiktoria Pelzer and Daniel Ebner, to curate a series of programmes under the title 'Animation Avantgarde'. In 2011 the first 'Under-the-Radar' conference, targeting international networking, academic discourse and interdisciplinary research in animation and media theory was held in Vienna. Several of the main contributors to the organization of this event later also started a collaboration with ASIFA Austria and SCANNER at Animafest Zagreb.

The same year several former animation students from Austria set up a production company called 'Neuer Österreichischen Trickfilm (New Austrian Animation)' that expanded successfully into Germany and began producing TV programmes and animated films. In 2013 the 'University of Applied Sciences Hagenberg' started a cooperation with the 'Ars Electronica' festival to initiate the first symposium on digital arts and animation in Linz, titled 'Expanded Animation'. The summer of 2015 presented the first barrier-free short-film festival 'dotdotdot' in Vienna, and ASIFA Austria celebrated its thirty-year anniversary with screenings of historical and contemporary programmes of Austrian animation at festivals and academic institutions in Europe and the United States. Sponsored by the University of Applied Arts Vienna, the first 'RADAR AWARD' was presented during 'Under-the-Radar' in 2016, honouring outstanding work by students engaging in animation or new media at an Austrian educational institution.

Conclusion

The here mentioned list of festivals, conferences, activities and initiatives is not complete, has changed over time and will change even more in the future. Some people in Austria have already started to complain that 'too many small events' are taking place each year, fearing that they will begin to cannibalize each other and compete for the few available funds. Despite the ongoing growth and acceptance of animation in Austria, the stressed financial situation is still the main obstacle for all types of production – but that's not unique to Austria.

What is, however, unique and 'special' is the impression that the presenter from Animafest Zagreb expressed a few years ago, right after the screening of historical and contemporary animation from Austria. It is the unbound spirit that has carved out its niche in this small country. The community of artists matured, it embraced the open and interested global community and started to connect. People began to reflect upon the local traditions and idiosyncrasies that they worked with, often without recognizing them consciously. To remain surprising, to stay independent and to appreciate the voice of artists is a quality that Austria should hold on to.

Global networking, converging media, financial pressure, extensive competition and the assimilating restrictions of markets are pushing creative people more and more in the same direction. While filmmakers are looking for new ways to finance their work, to collaborate and to adapt to international tendencies and demands, it is necessary to remember questions about qualities and characteristics that are unique to this country and that are rooted in the local environment. Austria may be a small country, but it has a legacy that is worth remembering. Especially on a conceptual and theoretical level, the pioneering work of artists should remain recognized as a rich source of ideas and arguments that carry the potential for a very encompassing discussion of animation as a theoretical field.

Limitations had unintentionally provided fertile soil for the development of a robust artistic identity that strengthened and stabilized the Austrian animation scene. The focus on artistic and conceptual animation not only reinforced a local aesthetic character, but it also created a functioning model for productions driven by artists as creative authors. The exploratory force that occupies independent artistic minds in Austria always tended to accept the radical nature of resistance and revolt. Such attitudes continuously encourage adventurous new ideas and surprising proposals.

The refined mindset that the majority of individuals in Austria engaging in this field has, is still greatly influenced by the rich and encouraging cultural heritage. With an ideally limitless approach, they are balancing out a lot of the external conditions that we are all consistently attempting to overcome. This may also be a model to discuss animation on a global scale from a distinctively integrative, interdisciplinary and unbiased perspective, while simultaneously being bold and subtle in one's advance.

References

Billeter, F. (1980). 'Werk, Bauen + Wohnen', *Architektur und Landschaft*, 9(4).

Bruckner, F. (2011). *Malerei in Bewegung*. Vienna, New York: Springer.

Dassanowsky von, R. (2005). *Austrian Cinema: A History*. Jefferson, NC: McFarland.

Jutz, G. (2010), *Cinéma Brut*. Vienna, New York: Springer.

Kožul, M., ed. (2015). *Animafest Zagreb: 25th World Festival of Animated Film*. Zagreb: Hulahop.

Renoldner T. (2010). 'Animation in Österreich 1832 bis heute', in C. Dewald, S. Groschup, M. Mattuschka and T. Renoldner (eds), *Die Kunst des Einzelbilds – Animation in Österreich 1832 bis heute*, 41–152. Vienna: Verlag Film Archiv Austria.

Scheugl, H., ed. (1996). *Ex Underground – Kurt Kren – seine Filme*. Vienna: PVS Verleger.

Stratil S. (2017). 'In Conversation with Holger Lang', Vienna, July 2017 (unpublished).

Tscherkassky, P. (1995). 'Die rekonstruierte Kinematografie. Zur Filmavantgarde in Österreich', in A. Horwarth, L. Ponger and G. Schlemmer, *Avantgardefilm – Österreich 1950 bis heute Verlag*, 113–122. Vienna: Wespennest.

Walkensteiner-Preschl, C. (2010). 'Humoristisches in den Animationsfilmen der 1920er Jahre', in C. Dewald, S. Groschup, M. Mattuschka and T. Renoldner (eds), *Die Kunst des Einzelbilds – Animation in Österreich 1832 bis heute*, 185–194. Vienna: Verlag Film Archiv Austria.

7

Beyond Self-images

The Context and Development of Animated Documentaries, the Cornerstones of Modern Animation in Sweden

Midhat Ajanović-Ajan

It seems that the first decades of the new millennium have brought about a small renaissance of documentaries, especially those that combine live action and animated pictures and even those visualized totally by employment of various animation techniques. My concern in the following chapter is the conspicuous propensity in Swedish animation towards animated documentary. In my view Sweden is the country that, besides Canada and Great Britain, has developed the most prolific production of films that merge documentary purposes and animated imagery.

In this chapter I define animated documentary, as I understand it. I will also take a look into the history of Swedish animation and documentary, with an emphasis on the features that might be the base for the development of the animated documentary. The text will also focus on some factors in the production and social background that, at least partly, explain why the animated documentary is such a prominent feature on the Swedish animation scene and, lastly, it will point at some films and filmmakers that eminently represent the genre.

Non-photographic documentary

It is a fairly usual misconception that animation is a depoliticized art form indifferent to reality. Actually quite the opposite is the case: some of the strongest stories of our time have been told through the medium of animated pictures. Owing to the animation method, which I define elsewhere as an 'accelerated metamorphosis';[1] this art form is a unique means of dealing with some fundamental aspects of our existence and allows for the invisible to be seen. Animated films often successfully present a form of pictorial microanalysis of a certain society and time; precise and 'realistic', so that they are faithful witnesses of the time and space they were made in, just as somebody's caricature successfully presents the person's face. An example could be the spirit of pessimistic resistance in a great number of animated, particularly puppet, films made in Central Europe, a region forcefully drawn into the 'Communist' block during the Cold War era or the bizarre, nauseating political fantasies that questioned the social system and announced 'perestroika' made by Estonian artist Priit Pärn and by Russian artist Igor Kovalyov. Another example is the connection between British society during the so-called 'Thatcherism' and the socially critical films produced by Channel 4, etc. Most animated documentaries deal with the social and psychological condition of human existence in a wide socio-political context.

Although the so-called 'animated documentary'[2] is a somewhat problematic conceptual blending, this genre has been established in both film production and researches as well. Formerly an obscure sub-genre, animated documentaries have recently become a significant phenomenon that has gained a strong momentum thanks to modern technological progress. As film entered the digital age, animated documentaries have also grown in number from year to year.

Simply put, an animated documentary could be defined as an animated film made in accordance with the standards and conventions adopted in documentary filmmaking. In one of the very few comprehensive books on animated documentary, Annabelle Honess Roe, paraphrasing Bill Nichols, insists that we can characterize this type of animation as documentary because 'it's about *the* world rather than *a* world' (Honess Roe 2013: 4). She also proposed several categories like mimetic, substitution, mnemic, evocation and so on

The animated documentary occurred as a result of filmmakers' timeless desire to depict in a believable way events that have not been caught on

---

[1] For example in my book *Animation and Realism* (Ajanović-Ajan 2004).

[2] Of course, it is an unfortunate name just like 'film', 'comics' or 'video games' but the good news is that people easily get used to unusual names. What was unusual yesterday is the norm today.

camera because: (1) they happened before film was invented, (2) they are unfilmable at the time, like space, or germs, or (3) no camera was present at a certain, important event. The first case includes, for example, an entire sub-genre that might be dubbed 'dinocumentaries', stretching from Winsor McCay's *Gertie, the Trained Dinosaur* (1914) and *The Dinosaur and the Missing Link* (1915) by Willis O'Brien, to the BBC-produced mini-series *Walking with Dinosaurs* (1999) and onwards.

For the materialization of the world of religions, by depicting goddesses, angels, devils, fairies and other similar creatures, French filmmakers used cinematic tricks and animation to reach beyond the limitations of cinematography, with its optical and chemical restraints. This sort of animated film was further developed within educational films in which the animation was used to visualize various science experiments and theories or to reconstruct historical events. Thus, the impossibility of filming some invisible parts of physical reality was compensated entirely with the help of different animation techniques, so filmmakers 'showed' for instance microbes and viruses that were 'recorded' with their rostrum camera. During the 1920s and 1930s, the Fleischer brothers in the United States made animated educational films, which in the form of funny cartoons explained Einstein's theory of relativity and Darwin's theory of evolution.

Probably the most interesting is the third case, which is usually the recreation of events that occurred in reality, but were not recorded. With his film *The Sinking of the Lusitania* (1918), Winsor McCay made a great contribution to this type of animated film. The film is a 'documentary' consisting of hand-drawn, animated images that very dramatically and convincingly reconstruct an actual incident and thus create the illusion of an eye-witness report. In this case, animation compensates for the absence of a camera at a historic event where a German submarine sank the passenger ship *Lusitania*.

Actually, there have been quite a number of animated works that have reconstructed unfilmed events since *Lusitania* and even before it. The reconstruction of historic events such as the visualization of old battles had started already with Cohl, for instance in *The Battle of Austerlitz* (*La Bataille d' Austerlitz*, 1909), and even Frank Capra's crew incorporated animated parts in the documentary series *Why We Fight* (1942–1945), for instance for schematic presentation of *Blitzkrieg*. *The Romance of Transportation in Canada* (Collin Low, Wolf Koenig, Roman Kroiter and Tom Daly, 1953) as well as *The Mighty River* (Frédéric Back, 1993) are examples of Canadian history recounted in the form of animated film.

Such films are also *A Song for Hiroshima* (Renzo Kinoshita, 1978) an inside story on the Hiroshima inferno and *Peter Mansfeld* (Melocco Miklós, 2007), about a falsely accused and executed young boy in the aftermath of Soviet intervention in Hungary in 1956. This film is based on the court records, just like the feature length *Chicago 10* (Brett Morgen, 2007) that uses 3D CGI in order to believably re-enact testimonies during the 1968 trial against anti-war activists in the United States. The dark side of human nature is distinctly captured in *Silence* (Orly Yadin, Silvie Bringas, 1998) based on the testimonies by poet and Holocaust survivor Tana Ross.

We find a more recent example for that type of animated documentary in *Broken – The Women's Prison at Hoheneck* (*Kaputt*, Volker Schlecht and Alexander Lahl, 2016), a powerful film revealing the sordid conditions in a women's prison in former East Germany. Former inmates Gabriele Stötzer and Birgit Willschütz unsentimentally recount everyday life in the prison, where the female inmates worked like slaves to produce export goods. The film is evocative of the conditions humans lived in under a dictatorship now gone, while reminding us that such things occur even in this day and age.

Visual biographies

Another, very frequent subcategory of the animated documentary is the one in which narrative and historiographical perspectives are taken from the filmmaker's personal experience. Those films are usually distinguished by storytelling based on everyday realism and autobiographical narratives.

In addition to the pictures coming from the imperfect time machine called memory that we all have in our heads, the credibility of depictions strengthens by the employment of authentic material, such as a person's diary, testimonies, documents, photos and live-action footage. Such a film was *Drawn from Memory* (1995), a feature made by the brilliant animator and cartoonist Paul Fierlinger, who collected his memories of growing up in the country of refugees, America, after his Central European Jewish family had managed to escape from the Holocaust. A similar issue was dealt with by Belgian artist Jung in his *Approved for Adoption* (*Couleur de peau: miel*, Laurent Boile and Jung, 2012). As a child adopted during the Korean War, Jung, through a graphic novel and a film based on it, investigated his own identity. *Persepolis* (Marjane Satrapi and Vincent Paronnaud, 2007) is based on Satrapi's graphic novel in which she applied a drawing style of old Persian miniatures to depict her childhood-memories from the turbulent years of the Islamic Revolution in Iran. Another feature-long animated autobiography based on a graphic novel is *Tatsumi* (Eric Khoo) in which the cartoonist Yoshiro Tatsumi melancholically recounts his life and career in post-war Japan.

Anca Damian distinguished herself with two features: *Crulic: The Path to Beyond* (*Crulic – drumul spre dincolo*, 2011) and *The Magic Mountain* (*La montagne magique*, 2015), in which she aptly used harsh cut out-animation to reconstruct the extraordinary fate of the people portrayed.

However, *Jasmine* (Alain Ughetto, 2013), another work based on autobiographical material, might be the strongest artistic achievement in the field. On the first level this amazing piece of work that takes place in several time–space dimensions can be seen as a subtle criticism of Western regimes that actually helped clerical cliques gathered around Khomeini to take power in Iran. But the film is, above all, a story of passionate love, so strong and genuine that it proves that time does not cure everything. Time has passed, but deep wounds in the soul are still there. In the film, set during the 1970s, a young French animator falls in love with a drama student from Iran. The two of them are in Tehran when the Revolution launched by the young, burning hearts demanding democracy and justice is transformed into a cruel theocratic dictatorship. As an alien, he is forced to leave the country. She decides to stay in her homeland despite everything. The story is mostly told through pictures, shades and shapes created by the touches of Ughetto's fingers on plasticine under the camera. By using sophisticated visual language, symbolic figures and moving sculpture of the plasticine that continually pulsates on the screen, the whole film feels like a gentle message of love and affection to a beloved being. It is very rare that a movie in any form and genre reaches such lyrical heights.

Jasmine is a film about the world, which at the same time is *a world* in itself, just like every true work of art should be.

Animated interviews

The interview, one of the most frequent standard forms of documentary film, the one that might make the strongest impression of truthfulness, has also been applied in animation. Often one makes use of interviews with people who know the person the film is about, or interviews with the actual subject of the film. While most animated documentaries come across as a sort of simulacra – a reconstructed copy of a reality never filmed – the interview films rely on the specific individuals that share or shared the world with us. The fact that we are watching a person talking and at the same time hear his or her words lends a high degree of credibility. The interview film actually developed in the late 1920s when it became technically possible to copy the sound on the same film strip as the movie's pictures and in precise synchrony with them.[3] Films such as *Housing Problems* (E. Anstey and A. Elton, 1935), in which people talk about their lives on camera, strengthened the notion of moving images as a realistic reflection of life. This method was later adopted by television, becoming the dominant means of expression for TV journalism and documentary programmes. Alongside documentary films and interview films, the genre also evolved within the field of animation – at first as a

[3] Already in Warner Brother's film-news Introduction of Vitaphone Sound Picture from 6 August 1926 we can see rudimentary interview techniques. Will Hays announces a sound film addressing the viewer with the words 'Dear Friends'. In the second example from the same year, *The Voice from the Screen*, Edward B. Craft uses some editing techniques and we even see his collaborators who ask him questions.

comical parody wherein sound played a key part. For example, at WB's animation studio cartoonists combined caricatured imagery of a famous person with that person's recognizable voice – be it authentic or imitated.

The method of combining documentary sound with animation for parodic or satirical purpose was adopted in many films produced by Aardman, such as Nick Park's breakthrough mockery *Creature Comforts* (1990). Park interviewed several foreign students about their lives in student homes, and then gave their comments to various charming animated clay animals complaining about their living conditions at a London zoo. For yet another example of how animation can cut into 'the reality of fiction' by using the interview method, one can see *Abductees* (1995) by Paul Vester, which combines animation with authentic voices in order to visualize real people's alleged experiences of alien encounters. Sheila M. Sofian based her impressive film dealing with the war in Sarajevo in Bosnia and Herzegovina in *A Conversation with Haris* (2002) on an interview with a Bosnian boy Haris Alić whose family immigrated to the United States.

The next step in the evolution of the genre was a reworking of the actual photographic cinematic image in order to reach beyond its surface. It is usually agreed that animation's illusory movement has no precedent in a real-time movement, which is considered to be a fundamental difference between animated and live-action films. Animation is seen as a form of moving pictures that is unbound by reality or physical laws like gravity. However, we have a 're-animation' of previously filmed footage instead of animating new images, something that is more and more common thanks to technical innovations in digital media.

A crucial film in this context was *Ryan* (2004) by Canadian animator Chris Landreth. His starting material was a series of filmed conversations with the main character Ryan Larkin, who in the early 1960s made a swift career within the state-run film company National Film Board (NFB) in Canada. He gained international recognition with animated films where he used a harmonious series of moving 'stream of consciousness' images, colourized in a psychedelic hippie style and drawn by hand on paper instead of any of the prevalent techniques – such as cel, cut out or puppet animation. His film *Walking* (1968), a bold look at big city life, depicting the various ways in which people walk, based on their different gender, age and background, definitely established 26-year-old Larkin as one of the leading artists in animation. But then Larkin's life and career suddenly swerved off course. For no apparent reason, he started abusing drugs and alcohol. He spent the following thirty years in complete anonymity at a Montreal homeless shelter.

Landreth's idea was to make a short biographical film in precisely this genre – the animated documentary based on a filmed interview with Larkin. *Ryan* became a film about alcohol abuse, which, at the same time, on a deeper level, emphasized the artist's irreconcilable conflict with society. But what made the film extraordinary was the way in which Landreth processed the images. With the help of digital 3D animation, he chipped off large portions of Larkin's face, turning it into a stripped fragment of his appearance. The idea behind this, of course, was to show how alcohol had destroyed what was once a respected human being and artist. It won the 2005 Academy Award for Best Animated Short Film as well as more than sixty other international awards.

Another Academy Award winner and equally important film that contributed to further recognition of animated documentary is the feature-length *Waltz with Bashir* (2008), an autobiographical piece by Ari Folman. Known previously as a documentary filmmaker, Folman was serving as an Israeli soldier in Lebanon in 1982 at the time of the notorious massacre in Sabra and Shatila. The main hero of the movie, Folman's alter ego, is a man who has lost his memory and is tormented every night by nightmares. He searches for his lost memory by conducting interviews with the people who served in the same unit. The quest for truth and the nightmares are depicted in interviews transferred into animated drawings by rotoscope, which are connected to each other associatively until the remembrance of the main character in the fascinating final scene depicted by live-action documentary images of massacred bodies that cause physical pain and nausea in the spectator's body.

Save for a few exceptions, the use of interviews is the main method in Swedish animated documentaries. So, let us go to the second part of the chapter where I highlight some of the details from the Swedish film and animation history.

Bergdahl and the fact-based animation

Victor Bergdahl was a sailor, a painter, a cartoonist, a reporter, but above all he deserves his place in history as an animator. His first encounter with animation was in the early 1910s when he, by coincidence, had seen some early animated film made by Emile Cohl and Winsor McCay, which gave Bergdahl the impulse to try animation himself.[4] What is noteworthy in the

[4] A cinema owner 'explained' animation to him: 'The magic is brought about by letting the pictures joined together in the shape of a book dash past with the help of one's thumbs in front of the camera, to enable the optical illusion of motional pictures to be caught on the celluloid' (Jungstedt 1973: 43). Hearing this, Bergdahl's only choice was to develop a technique of his own. To avoid drawing the same backdrop over and over again, he had the backdrops printed in hundreds of copies on which he would drew his figures. He constructed his own version of an animation table with light from beneath (later he also created an innovative cut out method, with paper dolls and a movable scene from cut out parts). His first animated film *The Magic Potion* (*Trolldrycken*, 1915), also the first animation in Sweden, with its bizarre contents and abstract graphic elements, looks at least ten years ahead of its time. The 'leading character' is alcohol, which continued to play an important role in Bergdahl's films. He was soon to create 'the drawn pictorial joke' series about his alter ego Captain Grogg, a discarded sailor with a

framework of this discussion is Bergdahl's interest in fact-based animation. With his methods, he could produce commercials and educational films much faster, excelling in another area of animated filmmaking he pioneered. Actually, his last animation was a gynaecology educational film, about female sexual organs and foetus development.

With Bergdahl, but also his contemporary colleagues like Emil Åberg and M. R. Liljeqvist, Swedish animation received a striking start. Cartoonists Robert Högfeldt and Einar Norelius, who learned animation from Bergdahl, achieved another great success in this early period.[5]

The first factual animations

However, Bergdahl had an unusual successor in Arvid Olsson, who was Sweden's most prolific film animator from the 1930s up until the 1950s. Olsson became interested in animation as a young student in Paris in the 1930s. Back in Sweden he devoted his time to commercial animation. He created the first Swedish animated film with a soundtrack, a humorous commercial about Swedish monetary value, *The Lunar Eclipse of the Krona* (*Kronans Månförmörkälse*) in 1931. In 1934, Olsson became the first Swede to work with colour film in a professional way. Among hundreds of commercials he animated some election campaign films for the Centre and Social Democrat Party, and also did some educational and informative animation.

During the 1960s and 1970s many popular characters from children's literature became heroes of TV series and animated features. Alongside the former Czechoslovakia, Sweden was actually one of the European countries with, relatively speaking, the biggest production of animated feature films, which were almost exclusively made in the Disney-inspired cel animation technology. Thanks to such a considerable production Gunnar Karlsson,

---

pug-nose, armed with a pocket flask that often helps him out from difficult situations. This was one of the first true European animations with a recurring character – there are thirteen episodes with the liquor-loving hero. Rather frank erotic passages, jokes and innovative animation made Bergdahl famous internationally. The real masterpiece is *The Portrait of Captain Grogg* (*Kapten Grogg skulle porträtteras*, 1917), where both live and drawn pictures are used in complex double exposure, a technique developed in the studio of Julius Pinschewer around 1910.

[5] They produced a Disney-inspired film *Bam-Bam and Taming the Trolls* (*Bam-Bam, so toktas trollen*, 1934) with synchronized sound and smooth animation, which laid the foundation for the first dominant genre in Swedish animation – children's film. Norelius soon started his ambitious new project – a long animated film based on Selma Lagerlof's book *The Adventures of Nils Holgersson through Sweden*, but the war put an end to this plan. After the break due to World War II, animation production recovered in the mid-1950s when children's films bloomed so strongly that even today in the country there exists an idea of animation as 'something for children'.

Stig Lasseby, Olle Hallberg, Tor-Erik Flyght, Rune Andréasson, Jan Gissberg, and Per Åhlin as a leading figure, built the second-generation of professional animators.

Per Åhlin, who made a number of shorts and features as well as commercials is perhaps the most prolific European animator. He distinguished himself primarily as a cartoonist whose style has been characterized by carefully studied figures and an Åhlin-typical twisted and curvy line (as if he is sitting in a swivel chair as he draws). His animation and drawing style was totally in tune with the most modern trends in the contemporary world of animation, enriched with distinct Scandinavian traits and feelings. In the early 1960s he got the chance to make animated vignettes for various television programmes, where he began his collaboration with popular authors and stand-up comedians Hasse Alfredson and Tage Danielsson. They were the team behind *In the Head of an Old Man* (*I huvet på en gammal gubbe,* 1968), an animated feature not intended for children. It was a mild satire of the Swedish welfare state, produced with humour and kindness. The film is situated in a retirement home and deals with pictures from the memories of its inhabitant, the old age pensioner Johan.

After the 1980s many talented female animators came forward, fighting for gender equality in Swedish animation. Like in other animation cultures, female animators in Sweden showed a propensity to experiment and use other techniques than cel animation. A special place in that context belongs to Birgitta Jansson, one of the college trained artists, who began animating with Per Åhlin in the 1970s and then continued on her own. The enormously talented Jansson, who unfortunately passed away too early, was inspired by Will Vinton, so she used a clay technique in the late 1970s. She realized that clay allows dimensionality and great elasticity and flexibility of the characters' arms and legs and stronger expressiveness in the face than it was possible by using cel animation. Her biggest success was Sweden's first clay animation and the very first animated documentary, the thirteen-minute long award winning *Holiday Home* (*Semesterhemmet*, 1981). Jansson's documentary-like approach was probably encouraged by the enormous success and relevance of some contemporary Swedish live-action documentaries.

Animation in *Holiday Home* brings to life conversations recorded at a retirement home, where the tenants tell their life stories. The astonishing modelling, timing, and especially the film's finale, which can be viewed as a brilliant example of postmodernity's doubts concerning the concepts of reality and illusion, make the film fascinating even to this day. Jansson did not forget to pay respect to Per Åhlin by providing a cameo appearance of Dunderklumpen, a main character from Åhlin's successful feature.

Holiday Home is a film whose documentary qualities laid the groundwork for a whole genre that would become an important identifying feature of

Swedish animation – animated documentary. Moreover, the method of combining documentary recorded audio with animation has become common since this film.

People's Home and critical documentaries

The first question concerned with this subject matter is obvious: why are there so many animated documentaries produced in Sweden? One reason is practically prosaic – the Swedish Film Institute does not finance animated films as a separate category, neither is there a commissioner ('konsulent')[6] responsible for animation as there are for other forms and genres including documentary. That is why some animators apply with their projects simply called documentaries.

The other reason is, I believe, connected to the very essence of the nature of documentary film. Documentaries never serve for entertainment only; they are either educational or critical dealing with the oldest dogma of moving pictures, which is truth.

Right after film emerged, it was proclaimed the first media in history to reflect the true and accurate image of the world. But political power has always endeavoured to chisel the truth according to its own interest. Just as in the novel *Snow*, Orhan Pamuk describes a dictatorial power that has 'nourished' its people by meteorologists issuing an order to increase the daily temperature by five to six degrees each day, cinema was often used to beautify reality. Since talent and morality, unfortunately, do not always get along, some of the most fascinating documentaries were created in the service of propaganda. However, there have been more than enough gifted documentary filmmakers who actively observed and critically commented on the time and society in which they lived. Namely, unexpected and unpredictable thought processes, as well as the look of the camera in the artist's hand, proved to be impossible to control so that the history of documentary has been characterized by clashes between the 'truth' of the power and the truth of independent filmmakers.

Despite its strong democratic tradition Sweden is no exception whatsoever. What is specific in Swedish documentaries is perhaps the fact that the most critical documentaries question certain, generally accepted assumptions and self-images connected with the Swedish Social Democratic model, the

[6] When I expressed a criticism against that illogical system in an interview to the film critic Emma Engström, the reaction from the Swedish Film Institute was Monty-Python-like: 'No, we don't need a commissioner for animation. What we need is more money for the institute.' See more here: http://sverigesradio.se/sida/artikel.aspx?programid=478&artikel=6078748 (accessed 31 October 2017).

so-called People's Home ('Folkhemmet')[7] characterized by solidarity and equality, outside the country often labelled as democratic socialism. Many people, both in the country and abroad, are still convinced that nothing has changed since the time of Olof Palme despite abundant evidence that the country has fervently moved towards so-called 'liberal' capitalism since the 1990s. However, documentaries have provided a lot of evidence of the problems in Swedish society that mainstream media and politics seldom discuss, such as some hidden aspects of structural inequalities in society, political corruption, racism and segregation, Holocaust denial (an issue excellently elaborated in the 2008 mockumentary *Conspiracy 58* by Johan Löfstedt), domestic violence and similar things existing silently in 'the best country in the world'.

As a typical Swedish documentary, one can take *The Swedish Theory of Love* (2016) in which the recognized filmmaker Erik Gandini examined the idea of a society of independent individuals rooted in the 1970 political manifesto called *Family of the Future* (*Familjen i framtiden*). It is the system in which the people would be free from each other. After the years in which society had achieved a 'comfortable life and highest standard of living, progress, modern thinking', the 1970s were the time to take another step forwards and free the people from the 'old fashioned way of thinking'. Instead of households like in other developed countries, the welfare state focused on individuals, 'people working for themselves'. As the film suggests, the experiment resulted in alienation of gigantic proportion, with more than 40 per cent of the population living alone, the highest rate in the world.

Actually, the Swedish documentary has a long and rich tradition. Its founder was Arne Sucksdorf, who started his career in the 1930s. He was the first Swede to win an Oscar in 1949 for *Symphony of the City* (*Människor i stad*, 1947) and he also made the first Swedish feature-length documentary, *The Great Adventure* (*Det stora äventyret*, 1953). Thanks to Sucksdorf's commercial and international success, documentaries gained more favourable treatment within the Swedish film industry.

But arguably the most important Swedish documentary filmmaker became Stefan Jarl, who started his career as Suckdorf's assistant. Though Suckdorf's disciple, Jarl never assumed Suckdorf's aesthetic concept and Disney-like approach. In the wake of the British movement 'Free Cinema', he employed arranged or 'performative' documentary with some methods

[7] It is a big question whether we can talk about People's Home any longer. After losing two consequent elections to the right-wing coalition and the massive privatization of public properties as a consequence, the Social Democrat Party itself moved further to the right. Even the Swedish famous neutrality may be questioned now with American customs controlling passengers at Stockholm airport and the Swedish army being regularly a part of NATO missions and manoeuvres.

typical for live-action film as well as synchronized sound. Instead of dealing with individual characters he was mainly interested in social groups, especially the younger generation. Starting with enormous public success was the feature-length *They Call Us Misfits* (*De kallar oss mods*, 1968), in which Jarl confronted the lack of purpose, the futility and aimlessness of the younger generation with the spiritual decline and moral weakness of the older one. With this brutally unsentimental and pessimistic depiction of the generation gap caused by arrogance and a lack of understanding for the younger generation, Stefan Jarl set a standard for critical documentaries that would flourish in the years to come and also with him as the leading creative force.

In her comprehensive book about Swedish documentaries, *Fight for Reality* (*Kampen om verkligheten*), Ingrid Esping described the long history of clashes between researching documentaries and censorship (Esping 2001: 196) but nevertheless the documentary filmmaker continued to scrutinize the shadowy side of the People's Home.

When it comes to subject matter and the critical examination of society, there are actually no differences between live-action and animated documentaries except for the more humorous and satirical elements that are involved in the latter, due to the multi-coded quality of animation. So, let's conclude the text by giving a short overview of the most representative animated documentaries produced in Sweden.

Animated documentary foremost practitioner

Animated or not, documentaries, when they are good, are always an interpretation, i.e. a commentary, and not a copy of reality. This is the case with most Swedish animated documentaries that, as mentioned above, reveal some hidden aspects of the social and psychological condition of human existence in society, telling stories untold in public communication. These films are usually personal, polemical, sometimes dark and pessimistic, and even a class perspective is present.

During the 1990s Swedish animation in general was impacted by technological developments. It was a period when digital media replaced analogue film technology. Digitization meant democratization in both production and distribution. Although it did not reduce production costs, animation became accessible to more people and young people especially embraced this medium as a way to articulate their voice. Digitization also increased the possibilities for animated documentary, which definitely became the most prominent genre in the new millennium. Another important event occurred at the same time, when Konstfack, University College of Arts, Crafts and Design in Stockholm founded its department for training in animation. In addition to educational activities, the Department also managed to conduct serious research, organize conferences and seminars, start an animation festival and a regional resource centre for film and animation, and present the students' work at various places in the world. Most important of all was the fact that over 120 pupils and students have graduated from the College of Arts, Crafts and Design, which changed Swedish animation for all time. Many of those students from the first few generations of educated animators chose factual animation as their vocation.

As typical examples for the documentary approach in Swedish animation one can take *Blu-Karma-Tiger* (2006), subtitled 'a documentary about graffiti', by the filmmaker duo Mia Hulterstam and Cecilia Actis. In Birgitta Jansson's footsteps they used claymation combined with some real graffiti artists' authentic voices. Another successful tandem is Hanna Heilborn and David Aronowitsch, who made the film *Hidden* (*Gömd*, 2002). Through animated images and documentary sound, the story of 12-year-old Giancarlo is told. He is an undocumented immigrant, hiding in Sweden, who feels hunted by everyone. With their animated documentary *Slaves* (*Slavar*, 2008), which presents two children's tragic fates during the civil war in southern Sudan, they managed to win the Grand Prize in Annecy – the biggest international success of Swedish animation to date. Besides the aesthetic reasons, in all these cases animation was used in order to hide the real identities of the films' actors because live-action recording and discovery of their names would put them in real danger.

Maja Lindström made her reality-based films by using 3D CGI. Visually stunning, *The Gang of Lidingo* (*Lidingöligan*, 2009) is based on an autobiographical story about the filmmaker's childhood in the Stockholm suburb Lidingö. The film is a strong statement on the People's Home becoming a society sharply divided into one side supporting a strong welfare state and another of so-called 'liberals' insisting on privatization, globalization, low taxes and deregulation. The time when the modern political and social environment is characterized by intense ideological and class divisions is seen through children's eyes.

A very frequently discussed subject matter in animated documentaries is connected to people's sexual habits. In her film *Embryo* (2013), Emma Thorsander used interviews in order to examine the state of mind of young women who had had an abortion. Teresa Glad explored teenagers' approach to sexuality and love in *Ugly Feelings* (*Fulla känslor*, 2008), which is also based on pre-recorded interviews. Glad would also be the main creative force behind the animation series on sexual education, *Sex on the Map* (*Sex på kartan*, 2013), which caused strong controversy after being broadcasted on Public Service Television because it shows explicitly rendered sexual intercourse.

Jonas Odell, who undoubtedly appears as the genre's foremost practitioner – both in terms of the number of films, and artistic and cinematic quality, also had sexuality as a topic in probably his best movie so far, *Never Like the First Time!* (*Aldrig som första gången!*, 2005).

Together with Lars Ohlson, Stig Bergquist and Marti Ekstrand, Odell formed the Swedish animation studio Filmtecknarna ('Film cartoonists') in 1981. They started out producing independent films but have also made commercial and music videos. *Revolver* (1993) was their breakthrough work. This tragic comedy about the passing of time is constructed as several short animations combined into a kind of musical collage. A collage-like structure can also be found in the other films that Odell made on his own, all of them animated documentaries, a genre in which he became a specialist.

In all of Odell's films technical brilliance and visual richness are combined with clear storytelling. Odell employs a fragmented visual mode of storytelling, founded on either interviews or research in order to create 'micro physiognomic' pictures of modern Sweden. By applying an imaginative visual vocabulary he transfers the reality of the everyday into an artistic reality within which he sets light to some marginalized dimension of society, people and ways of life.

The most interesting one is, as mentioned above, *Never Like the First Time!*, based on recorded interviews with four people, all telling recollections of their respective sexual debuts. The film is not only a great artistic achievement based on interviews and research, but also a sensitive insight into the human condition in modern Sweden. In a personal manner, the film highlights the relationship between our ancient carnal desires and our lives in modern society as well as the incredible complexity of the term *love*. For the three young people, obviously from the generation of 'independent individuals', their sexual debut was something violent, awful or emotionless. At the end, their experience is confronted with the 80-year-old man's recollection, who clearly remember what was 'the best day in his life', describing it in beautiful poetic language. His memories are wonderfully visualized through the ingenious recreation of advertising pictures from a 1930s Stockholm newspaper and the use of shifting patterns that, in the fraction of a second, consolidate and concentrate their meaning, melting nuances together. In doing so, Odell, as conceivable as Ughetto did in *Jasmine*, shows us not only how animation can penetrate deep into the human psyche and but also that animation in some cases can reach lyrical areas unattainable by live-action film. The film was a major international hit and award winner at, for example, the Berlinale.

Even in his other projects, *Lies* (*Lögner*, 2008) and *Tusilago* (2010), Odell continued featuring real people's experiences. Particularly successful was *Tusilago*, a sad story inspired by the authentic biography of a woman 'A', which in the 1970s was the girlfriend of West German terrorist Norbert Kröcher. The film's starting point was a famous court case from the 1990s. The documentary quality emphasizes an innocent woman paying the highest price for something she has no responsibility for, besides her own naivety, while the animation and imagery penetrate deeper into 'A's inner world.

In his latest film, *I Was a Winner* (*Jag Var en Vinnare*, 2016), which is the first time he uses 3D CGI, Odell highlights another big problem that is downgraded in public discussions – game addiction. As in his previous films he uses metaphoric imagery, in this case three avatars that present real game addicts, to tell the story of the most alienated people in contemporary society.

As one of the most consistent creators of this extraordinary genre, Odell has proven that the animated documentary has come to stay in Swedish cinema.

References

Ajanović-Ajan, M. (2004). *Animation and Realism*. Zagreb: Hrvatski filmski savez/ Croatian Film Association.

Chunning, G. (2016). 'The Archeology of Memory: The Exploration of Animated Documentary', in Olga Bobrowska and Michał Bobrowski (eds), *Obsession, Perversion, Rebellion. Twisted Dreams of Central European Animation*, 42–63. Krakow: Bielsko-Biala.

Esping, I. (2001). *Kampen om verkligheten*. Stockholm: Hjalmarson & Högberg.

Honess Roe, A. (2013). *Animated Documentary*. Basingstoke: Palgrave, Macmillan.

Jungstedt, T. (1973). *Kapten Grogg och hans vänner*. Stockholm: Sveriges Radios förlag.

Lysander, E. (2015). 'Birgitta Jansson, en animationens stjärna'. *Filmrutan*, 3 (16): 38–43.

SECTION 2

Case Studies from Around the World

8

Short Circuits

On the Impact of the Flipbook in the Work of Robert Breer

Edwin Carels

Introduction

Pursuing a highly personal and surprisingly consistent course, painter, filmmaker and sculptor Robert Carlton Breer (1926–2011) was driven by a persistent interest in visual perception. No matter how diverse, Breer's works always make us aware to what extent human perception is both culturally conditioned and physiologically determined. The formats he developed to achieve this lead us back to optical toys and the technological origins of media-art. The interaction he provoked between such parameters as time, space and movement were aimed to short-circuit viewing habits. This chapter retraces how for Breer the fundamental decision to destabilize the visual regime within the context of modern art came about. Through the (re)discovery of the flipbook, Breer found his initial means to problematize the relationship between viewer and artwork. With this methodological breakthrough, the decomposition and reconstruction of movement became the centre of attention in all strands of his work.

With forty-three films in fifty years, Breer remains a household name in the world of animation and avant-garde film. And yet his career began as a painter, with still images. Upon his arrival in Paris in 1949, Breer adopted the radical modernist stance of abstract, neo-plastic painting. Inspired by Mondrian, he imposed the same types of restrictions on himself to come to the purest interplay of lines and solid colour surfaces on canvas. But in the same year that he could have started to exhibit in the reputed gallery Denise René in Paris, Breer had already begun to 'decompose' his major influences with his first film, *Form Phases* (1952). Translating his own rigourous, two-dimensional paintings into a time-based medium also led him to conceive three-dimensional objects, starting with flipbooks. In April 1955 Denise René placed him alongside such prominent, or then still promising, names as Duchamp, Calder, Tinguely, Bury and Vasarely in the groundbreaking group show *Le Mouvement*. And yet it would be Breer's final *act de présence* at the gallery.[1] His ultimate contribution consisted of a one-off film programme and the production of a multiple, in the form of a flipbook. Once he had experienced the sensation of the moving image, the absoluteness of painting was no longer an option.

The flickering, fluttering films Breer started to make are like moths heading towards a flame: his images appear only for the briefest of moments, always already at the brink of their disappearence. The rapid-fire animation technique Breer favoured in his filmworks, he contrasted with a second strand of works that evolved from the rupture with painting. Via the flipbook Breer not only found his way into film, but as objects they also steered him towards kinetic sculputures. Gradually these evolved into enigmatic shapes that move about at a nearly imperceptible pace. Over the last decade this spatial aspect of his work has been foregrounded and the radicality of his critical practice better understood.[2] The aesthetic questions raised by blurring the distinction between sculpture and pedestal, between object and background, between stasis and movement continue to reverberate.

Pivotal moments

After spending the first ten years of his career in Paris (with frequent return trips to visit his family in the United States), Breer felt the real debates about the developments in contemporary art were happening in New York. Upon his return in 1959, he quickly became acquainted with instigators of the Fluxus-movement, John Cage and Nam June Paik, as well as befriending prominent Pop artists such as Claes Oldenburg and Robert Rauschenberg.

[1] The gallery opened right after the liberation of Paris in November 1944 with a solo show by Vasarely. *Le Mouvement* ran from 8 April to 30 April 1955. Although the initiator passed away in 2012, the gallery still continues.

[2] A few examples of this reviving interest in his work: in March 2010 an article appeared in the magazine *Kaleidoscope*; in November 2010 an interview appeared in *Artforum*; in 2011 a retrospective in the Baltic (Gateshead, UK) and in the museum Tinguely (Basel, Switzerland) was organized, accompanied by a catalogue.

His filmworks were regularly featured in the programmes of Anthology Film Archives and Cinema 16, two hotspots of avant-garde film. Breer has been a fellow traveller and occasional participant to many of the modernist movements of the second half of the twentieth century, but he never really became Op, Pop or Rock. An eyewitness as much as an actor on all these scenes, Breer quietly, yet systematically, developed a separate category, a parallel movement of his own. There were many pivotal moments in his early career that led him to start questioning and expanding his field of vision. During his training as a painter, he discovered geometric abstraction through an exposition of Mondrian, which incited him to abandon figurative painting.[3] This implied a complete distantiation from his teachers and fellow students at Stanford University, but Breer persevered in isolation.

When he first arrived in Paris, from early on he befriended such visionaries as the Swiss orchestrator of sculptural machines, Jean Tinguely, and the Swedish art collector, Karl Gunnar Pontus Hultén, which led to several collaborations in the longer term. The former was then still developing his disruptive style that would make him world famous a decade later; the latter would in 1973 become the founding director of the new museum at the Centre Georges Pompidou, opening in 1977. Another decisive moment came when Breer stepped back from the ambition of absolute painting to focus on the transformational steps and thought processes that lead towards the composition of a painting. In 1952 Breer picked up the camera in order to register each step of the creative process in a sequence and soon started to explore the parameters of this new medium. During a visit to his parental home in Michigan he borrowed his father's Bolex movie camera and filmed the images from his flipbook one at a time with the camera clamped to a closet door. Breer came back to Paris with three short films, and in 1954 he made the fourth one in this series, *Form Phazes IV*.

Another step towards liberation from the abstract, geometric, post-Cubist orthodoxy came along with his friendship with Pontus Hultén, co-curator of the exhibition *Le Mouvement*. Together they set up a programme of historical avant-garde films, including their own works. Breer showed *Form Phazes IV* (1954) and, under a pseudonym, his first animated photocollage, the anti-clerical joke *Un Miracle* (1954).[4] Together with Pontus Hultén, Breer also documented the exhibition.[5] The first applause after a film screening

---

[3] This was in 1947 at the occasion of a field trip to San Francisco as a student. Breer's college years had been interrupted by a two-year service in the US army. Right after his graduation, he arrived in Paris in April 1949 at the age of twenty-two.

[4] At its first screening, *Un Miracle* was still called *Le Pape*, and Breer presented it under the pseudonyme of B. Dieu. Pontus Hultén's film was named 'X' (1955).

[5] The film is 14 min and simply called *Le Mouvement* (1955).

at the Brussels' Cinémathèque in 1956 was also a moment of epiphany.[6] Although he was primarily there with a solo show in a gallery, the discovery of an entirely different audience was another motivation to abandon painting. When Breer was back in Brussels for the 1958 EXPRMNTL festival, this was the first occasion for several avant-garde filmmakers to meet each other. In the company of Kenneth Anger, Stan Brakhage and Jonas Mekas, Breer discovered there actually was a whole different context for his filmwork. In particular, his meeting with Peter Kubelka, who also conceptualized film as a metric sequence of autonomous frames, would lead to a long-lasting and productive friendship.

Frame by frame

To the actual gallery show, Breer contributed the flipbook that he created as an alternative strategy for showing film in the bright-lit conditions of a white cube.

Although being part of a breakthrough show, for Breer it also brought a sense of departure. His name did not appear together with Agam, Bury, Calder, Duchamp, Jacobsen, Soto, Tinguely and Vasarely on the front of the 'Manifeste Jaune', which accompanied the exhibition and considerably

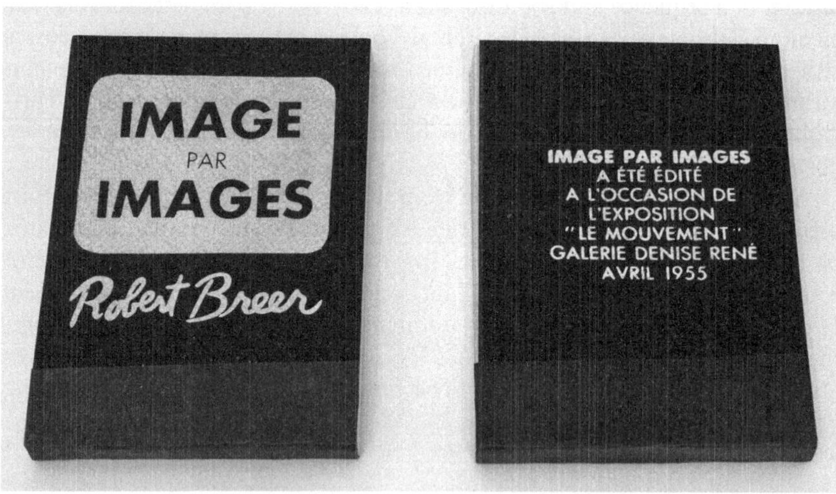

FIGURE 8.1 Image par Images, *flipbook (cardboard, paper, 1955). Courtesy: gallery gb agency, Paris.*

[6] On the initiative of the director of the Brussels' Cinémathèque, Breer's film was paired with *Sunrise* by Friedrich Murnau. Ledoux was also the director of the EXPRMNTL festival and invited Breer back in 1958.

helped to launch '*cinétisme*' as a new art movement.[7] As the youngest in the line up of the show, and the only American under the roof of the gallery Denise René, Breer increasingly felt that 'at times the elitism of Pure Art needs to be questioned too, and put in its place' (MacDonald 1992: 27). As he later confessed to his American collaborator Billy Klüver:

> I realized I was making a lot of absolute statements, paint on canvas, about one a week. I began to ponder how many absolutes there could be, and wondered if the process of getting there might be more interesting than the final resolved composition. I put together a flip book of successive stages in a composition – one shape/color giving rise to the next on their way to a perfect but not final resolution. I wanted to see if that could be of any use to me analytically in showing how I arrived at the final painting. At this time I had become aware of experimental films and I naturally slid into the idea of preserving a flip book on film.
>
> KLÜVER 1990: 20[8]

When Breer made his first official flipbook (*the* first avant-garde flipbook), the title *Image par Images* signalled the fundamental insight that no image can be totally absolute.[9] *Image par Images* reads like a statement: every image is the outcome of many different visual impressions, any image consists of a multitude of images. An image is never entirely autonomous, but is always the culmination of several images that preceded it. The French expression *Image par Images* can be read as image by image, like 'frame by frame' and thus 'one after the other', but also as 'an image mediated by images' or 'one image as the outcome of other images'. This preference for the composite could already be retraced in the compositions Breer elaborated on canvas in earlier stages of his career. All his abstract paintings consist of a dynamic interplay of different colour planes that deny the gaze any self-evident point to focus upon. In contrast with most of his fellow neo-plastic painters, Breer often left the centre of his canvas empty to suggest an

---

[7] The 'notes pour un manifeste' were written by Rogier Bordier. When the exhibition was reprised in New York in 1975, there was, again, no mention of Breer on the catalogue cover. He was included only by the film stills from his documentary on *Le Mouvement*. Even when the Tinguely museum restaged *Le Mouvement* in 2010, Breer was not listed as one of the participating artists. He did get a separate interview in the catalogue *Le Mouvement – vom Kino zur Kinetik*, but in the caption accompanying the only photograph that features his flipbook in the context of the exhibition (p. 31), again his name is not even mentioned.

[8] Klüver was the founder of Experiments in Art and Technology (E.A.T.) in 1966, together with Robert Rauschenberg, Fred Waldhauer and Robert Whitman. He also invited Breer to become part of their projects.

[9] Although claiming a 'first' is always a hazardous affair, we base ourselves on the thoroughly researched catalogue that accompanied the exhibition *Daumenkino – The Flip Book Show*, curated by Christoph Benjamin Schulz for the Kunsthalle Düsseldorf (Schulz 2005: 72).

expansion of the field of vision beyond the frame. As his friend Ponthus Hultén noted when Breer was at the peak of his painterly concentration: 'Breer's preferred tactic is to stretch the surface to the limit. He often places forms around the edges of the painting, thus giving them an important role in tightening the canvas like the head of a drum. This creates a constant, perfectly controlled tension, where the surface seems to vibrate in a kind of static dynamism' (Klüver 1990: 4).

Although after *Le Mouvement* Breer continued with painting for a few more years, the process of fragmentation, of analysis and synthesis was becoming an ever more prominent concern. When the feedback he received after the Brussels' screening of his film *Form Phazes IV* was far more encouraging than the response to his paintings he showed concurrently in a solo show, this also incited Breer to focus more on work for the silver screen, rather than the painter's canvas.

Doodle or spaghetti

But the move towards film did not mean Breer abandoned the flipbook (or in French 'folioscope').[10] *Image par Images* was produced by the gallery Denise René as his patroness paid for the production, which involved very simple black and white stencil on silkscreen and the extra labour of an artist friend to operate a stapler in Breer's studio.[11] The flipbook was an edition of 500, and has now become a real rarity. One way to catch a glimpse of this multiple is by watching out for the brief moment when Robert Breer himself flips the booklet in the documentary he shot of *Le Mouvement*. The drawings are in black and white and purely abstract. Over ninety-eight pages, a black line that is both sinuous and angular evolves, breaks open, multiplies and grows into more solid volumes, rounded squares, three black and one white, all in one continous choreography. As Jennifer Burford describes in her monography on Breer: "'Floating line" is one of the most frequent terms used to describe Breer's films. The straight line is pulled taut, whereas the doodle or spaghetti is the same elastic line allowed to fall into a random position. Breer confers to the line an autonomy charactersistic of modern art' (Burford 1999: 86). What would appear as a constant motif in his filmwork was already there in *Image par Images*, almost literally in a nutshell, a small book that fits the palm of a hand.

---

[10] Other terms for the same optical toy are: kineograph, feuilletoscope, cinéma de poche, flick book or flicker book, thumb book, thumb cinema, flip movie, fingertip movie, riffle book, living picture book, hand cinema, etc. (Fouché 2005: 10).

[11] The dimensions of the flipbook are 12.5 × 9.2 × 1.1 cm. On the back it bears the inscription: 'IMAGE PAR IMAGES a été édité à l'occasion de l'exposition "Le Mouvement" Galerie Denise René, April 1955'.

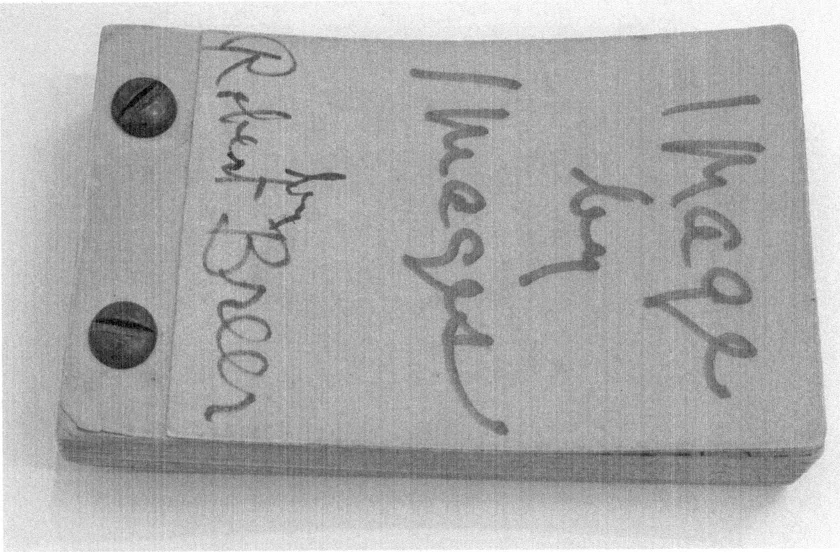

FIGURE 8.2 Image by Images, *flipbook (cardboard, screws, 1960). Courtesy: gallery gb agency, Paris.*

In 1960, shortly after his definite return to the United States, Breer created another flipbook, hand drawn and thus existing only as a single copy. Tellingly, the title is the same as the former flipbook, only now in English: *Image by Images*. The words are handwritten in red on somewhat yellowed paper, but the drawings inside are a close variation of his first flipbook, without literally copying the same shapes. Also, halfway, the black lines are replaced by red, followed by an alternation between the two colours. Large screws replace the staples from the French edition. In this period Breer produced two more (untitled) flipbooks, again single copies with big screws that hold them together.[12] What this ongoing flipbook activity demonstrates is minimally that the 'move' Breer made at the occasion of *Le Mouvement* was not simply a gimmick. For Breer, the flipbook had gradually evolved from an instrument of research to an end in itself. In fact, as a visual artist, Breer had already made his very first flipbook in 1950.[13] Having only recently converted to geometric, post-Cubist painting, the imagery of this flipbook is also entirely abstract, yet covering more surface than the more

[12] In the catalogue for the Baltic and Tinguely museum exhibition, the flipbooks are specified as follows: *Image by Images*, flipbook, ca 1960, Cardboard, screws, 12.6 × 7.6 × 2 cm; *Untitled* flipbook, 1960, Cardboard sheets, watercolour, screws, 12.7 × 10.2 × 1.5 cm; *Flip Book*, 1961, Paper, screws, 5 × 1 × 6.3 × 1.3 cm (Pardey 2011).

[13] Flip Book, Slidecraft, Screws, 10.1 × 8.2 × 3 cm (Pardey 2011: 38). Menegoi (2010: 46) mentions that Breer had already toyed with flipbooks during his youth.

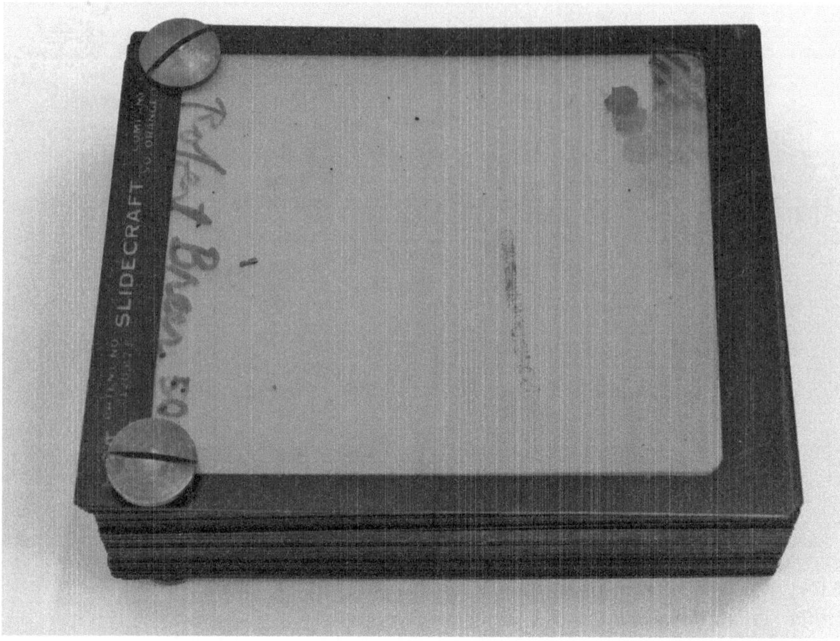

FIGURE 8.3 *Flipbook (slidecraft, screws, 1950). Courtesy: gallery gb agency, Paris.*

minimalist dance of single lines in his later flipbooks. From a combination of an even red square and a hatched black square, the imagery evolves towards a dance of blue lines interrupted by red dots. As Breer explained: 'Single images one after another in quick succession fusing into motion . . . this is cinema. For the 60 years of its existence it has been used mainly as a recording instrument, and as an abstract painter I first came to cinema looking for a way to record the myriad form-color relationships I had encountered in painting' (Breer 1963: 69).[14]

Looking at his very first flipbook it immediately becomes clear that Breer did not use the entire surface of the slides to draw on, but only the side farthest removed from the screws, just like in all his consecutive flipbooks. This implies that already in 1950 he understood how to make the best use of the format, which allows us to think he made this flipbook on purpose, not merely as an aid in the process of conceiving a film. When he proposed Denise René a flipbook as a multiple, Breer knew what he was aiming at. However brief the animation, the flipbook offered a cinematic experience without the need of a projection room.

---

[14] The text is dated April 1959.

Hand and eyeglasses

By the time Breer introduced this abstract flipbook in the gallery world, he had made six films, mostly experiments using ink drawing and cut-out animation that are wonderfully dense yet lyrical abstractions based on Breer's own geometric paintings (*Form Phases I-II-III-IV*, 1952–1954). In the same period leading up to the exhibition, he also made a very different, entirely figurative cut-animation film, *Un Miracle* (1954), as well as a film with the title *Image by Images* (1954). This again became the first of a series of four (*Image by Images II-III-IV*, 1955).

An important difference with *Form Phases* is that Breer started to photograph objects and incorporate actual images of reality, including his hand and his eyeglasses. Breer described it as follows: 'An endless loop of film composed entirely of disparate images. Through repetition, certain images isolate themselves from the flow reforming the original pattern.'[15] The loop wore out and is now lost, but it is clear that *Image by Images I* (1954) freed the path to his most radical title, *Recreation* (1956), which consists of nothing but three-dimensional objects photographed and filmed under the camera. *Recreation* is one of Breer's most reputed films, because it has the impact of a visual splinterbomb, attacking the viewer's retina with a radically different image on each frame. But as Lebrat observes, this provocative project did not come out of the blue: '*Recreation* breaks definitely with Robert Breer's earlier filmmaking style, abstract and "elegant" films which can still be considered to stem from a '20s avant-garde film tradition of decomposing pictorial forms. Nevertheless, *Recreation* is the result of slow maturation, for already in his earlier films, especially starting with *Images by Images I* (1954)' (Lebrat 1999: 74).

With this experiment, Breer decided to make every single frame unique, carrying to the extreme the idea that a film is composed of discrete still pictures visible for only a 1/24th of a second. And yet the title of the film was also applied a year later to this stylistically entirely different, purely graphic flipbook in 1955. The fact *Image by Images* could cover both hand drawn and more photorealistic work again suggests that the philosophy behind this persistent formulation reached further than a purely formalist interpretation. Film after

---

[15] Text drawn from a commented filmography, compiled by Breer himself. Further descriptions by Breer, from the same document: *Image by Images II* and *Image by Images III* (together seven minutes) were showing simplified abstract forms with special emphasis on change of pace, both in black and white, *Image by Images IV* (three minutes) was shot on Kodachrome and shows a 'further development of *Image by Images I* but in continuous band instead of a loop. A set of images is repeated several times but is arbitrarily modified'. Information courtesy from the Paris gallery gb agency, who runs the estate. Thanks are also due to Mark Toscano, currently working on the restoration of Breer's film works, and Andrew Lampert, who supervised the transferral of most of Breer's work onto 35mm for Anthology Film Archives.

film, flipbook after flipbook, Breer refuted the absoluteness of the single image by stressing over and over again that no image is singular, yet every visual impression is unique.[16] Breer: 'The next time you see the same thing it is different because it's the second time you've seen it' (Beauvais 2006: 166).

Loops and mutations

Recreation was the outcome of Breer's experiments with filmloops in his studio, and by 1957 he also became interested in adopting the format of the mutoscope to escape the linearity of the flipbooks.[17] Instead of a mere few seconds, he could now invite the viewer to endlessly crank the handle and watch the flickering pages for any length of time.

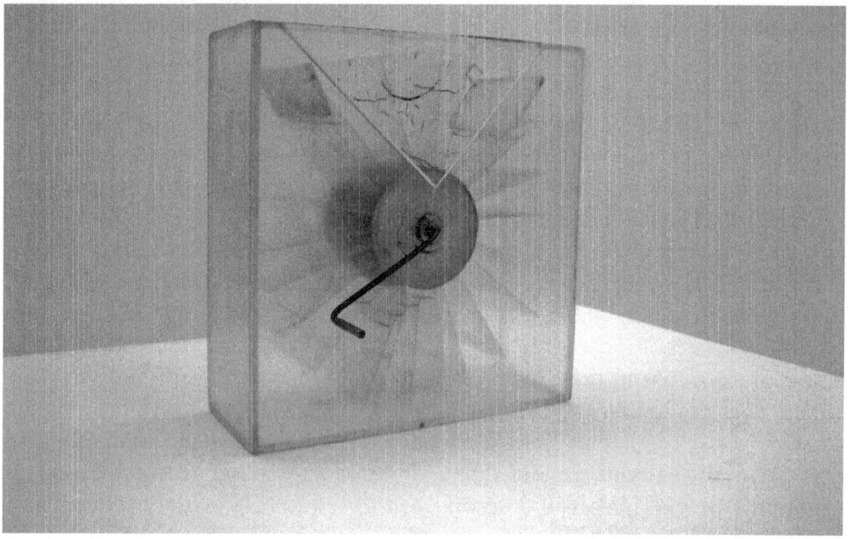

FIGURE 8.4 *Folioscope, mutoscope (plastic, metal, 1964). Courtesy: gallery gb agency, Paris.*

[16] Twice Breer made another flipbook as an edition: In 1967, he contributed with *Flix* to a series of flipbooks produced by the Cinémathèque québecquoise, Montréal and in 1988 he allowed a flipbook to be released as a Christmas card by the Factory record label: *Blue Monday Manual.* This was based on his work for the 1988 videoclip for Blue Monday by New Order, directed by Michael Shamberg and also involving William Wegman. Both can be viewed on the DVD accompanying the catalogue *Daumenkino* (Schulz 2005).

[17] The mutoscope worked on the same principle as the flipbook and was introduced in 1894 as an improvement of Edison's kinetoscope that used reels of film. In early 1896 the Lumières patented their kinora, a variation on the mutoscope in smaller format. Breer had contemplated, in 1957, buying a second-hand historical mutoscope but the Disney company bought up everything before Breer could act (MacDonald 1992: 29).

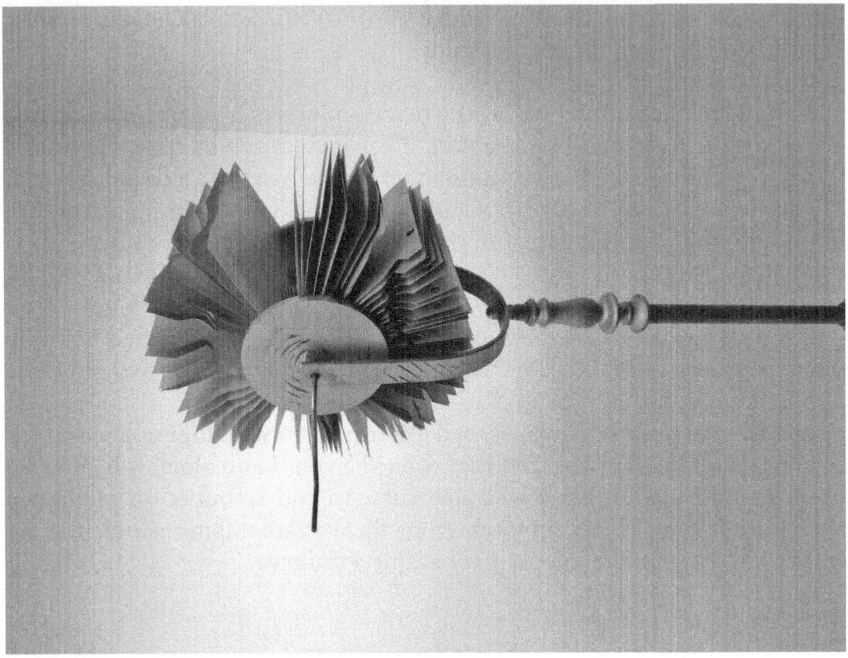

FIGURE 8.5 *Homage to John Cage, mutoscope (metal, plastic, acrylic paint, 1963). Courtesy: E. Carels.*

Apart from its more autonomous status as an object, a major difference with the folioscopes was that the mutoscopes allowed one to stop a frame and study it. Breer had a show planned in Paris at Iris Clert in 1959 where he would combine mutoscopes with a new film to be projected onto the gallery window (*Eyewash*, 1959). However, this show was postponed and never happened, as Breer had moved back to the United States.[18]

By the time he would have his first solo-exhibition in New York, Breer had already improved his 'french' mutoscopes and was no longer using paper, but plastic foil that did not wear out after so many rotations.[19] The logical elaboration from folioscope to mutoscope would affect his work in two directions: from handheld objects, he evolved towards free standing kinetic sculptures, and from the accumulation of drawings on small pieces

[18] In 1959, a show called 'Mutascopes and Films' was scheduled to open at Iris Clert's tiny gallery in St. Germain de Prés, between shows of Tinguely and Yves Klein. 'I had made the film *Eyewash*, expressedly to be shown on her front window. But Yves decided that he needed more time and I was put off till the next fall' (Mendelson 1981: 9).

[19] Robert Breer: *Constructions and Films*; Galeria Bonino, New York, 12 January to 6 February 1965.

of paper he went on to adopt index cards as an equivalent. As Jennifer Burford notes in a monographic study:

> Inspired by the mutoscope, he also made sculptures from ordinary objects such as the Rolodex. This standard office item, made by the millions and once found on every desk, consists of a base with an axle onto which address cards can be easily attached or removed, like in a mutascope, in order to find a particular card, the user turns a knob on the side.
>
> BURFORD 1999: 80

For his show *Constructions and Films* (1965), Breer presented not only the folioscopes and mutoscopes he had made in the past five years, but he also played out the principle of the thaumatrope, with its minimalist alternation between two images, and experimented with flipbook murals as a variation on the flipbook, but that you riffle your hand along.[20] By then he had also experienced that it was impossible to find an outlet for selling the remaining copies of his flipbook from the Paris exhibition and thus he stopped making unique pieces and became a sculptor.

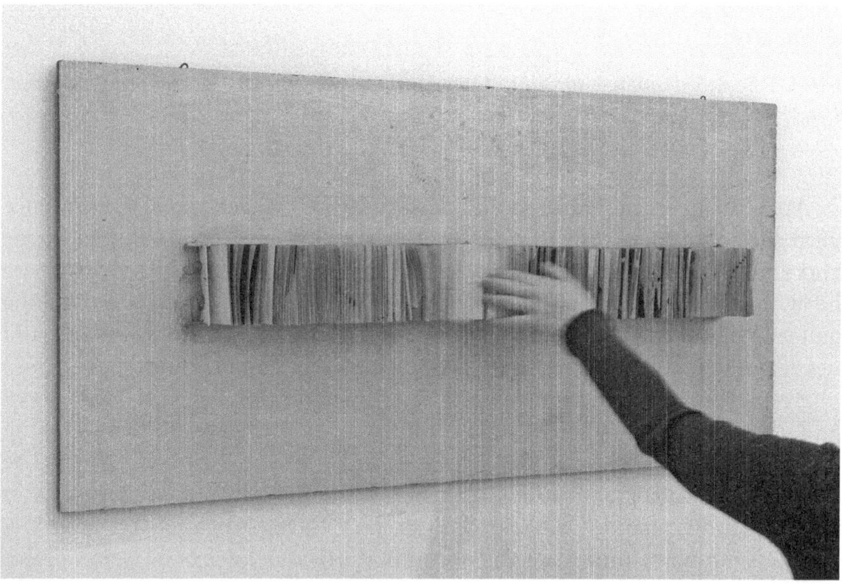

FIGURE 8.6 *Mural Flip Book (wood, metal, paper, 1964). Courtesy: gallery gb agency, Paris.*

[20] Breer made a first Mural Flip Book in 1964 (56 × 117 × 12.5 cm). He reprised the principle of having a viewer interact while moving along the work with the long panoramic peepboxes he introduced in 2006.

What Breer did retain from his period of neo-plastic orthodoxy was the notion that 'a painting is an object and its illusions have to acknowledge its surface as reality' (MacDonald, 1992: 18). In his earliest days in Paris, Breer already had an intention to study sculpture. He had signed up to study at Académie de la Grande Chaumière to satisfy the requirements of the US government scholarship, known as the G.I. Bill, but he actually took a sculpture class with Ossip Zadkine at the Académie Colarossi, down the street. However, as his later collaborator Klüver noted:

> After Breer had worked with Zadkine for a few days, Zadkine wanted him to study the plaster model in the afternoon. Breer told him he couldn't do that because he painted in the afternoon. . . . Zadkine replied that he couldn't paint and be a sculptor at the same time, he would have to decide. Breer decided. He quit the sculpture course.
>
> KLÜVER 1990: 6

But a decade later Breer's research led him back to sculpture, as he wanted to move away from an ersatz film experience of folioscopes and mutoscopes towards a more unique concept of kinetic objects.

Adding a motor to a mutscope made it resemble film too much, so he started to do away with the accumulation of pages. An important transition was the broomstick with an invisible motor on one end to make it rotate (*Rotating Broom Stick*, 1964). Breer:

> The only reason that you can see that it's rotating on its own base that hangs on the wall is because the broomstick is discolored here and there. If you pay attention, you see it's rotating very slowly, quietly, on the wall. It seems to me that that's full circle. It answers all the requirements of something that's formally composed, self-contained, and so forth.
>
> CUMMINGS 1973

As a mutoscope that has lost all its pages, the broomstick is painted brown and thus evokes a minimalist branch without any leaves. At this point Breer leaves the flipbook method with its flicker aesthetic behind and starts to focus on the imperceptible movement of what he has labelled as his 'floats'.

A similar transitional moment came when Breer decided to motorize a bent wire (*Untitled – Flower Pot*, 1962):

> It's just a long wire that undulates and not in any regular way, except it revolves around an invisible axis. When you revolve it slowly it does seem to undulate, although actually it's a wire that is turning. When you see it in profile it looks like a wavy line and this was the way of solving the problem of kinetic drawing.
>
> CUMMINGS 1973

From flashing before the eyes like a lightning sketch, the simplicity of a floating line is now slowed down to an absolute minimum.

Animated archives

In his early sculptures Breer moved away from the page by page aesthetic of the flipbook via a series of variations on the thaumatrope, consisting of merely two sides, two images. In his films, however, the methodology of the thumb cinema was implemented in an ever more consistent way. From 1960 onwards Breer made nearly all his films on the same material support, standard index cards of 4 by 6 inches. These became the key ingredient upon which he would draw, scratch, spray or collage his visual ideas. Again, the transition from canvas to cardboard happened when he first adopted uniform samples of heavy paper for his 1955 flipbook. It was very likely this bold move that showed Breer the way to a film practice based on a systematic use of the index card. Handheld like a flipbook, the cards allowed for instant testing of the illusion of motion. Easy to process and to store, they provided Breer with a convenient and consistent working method. Breer did not necessarily draw the cards in a predetermined order.

Depending on his mood, he produced one series of cards, then another idea generated another series. He did usually number them, but that did not prevent him from shuffling and reshuffling them, using sequences several times in different orders within the same film or even having drawings recur from film to film. The order of the cards and the editing of short moments in the film could be tested as easily as cutting a deck of playing cards.[21]

By using the most common index cards for his drawings and collages to be filmed, Breer evidently opposes himself to the conventional use of a pegbar ruler in animation. Breer never punched his file cards so that they could be kept in place like with card catalogues. Each drawing representing a single film frame, the ordering of so many file cards inevitably brings along the connotation of an animated archive. With his quizzical accumulation of doodles and randomly chosen magazine cut-outs, Breer radically parodies the use of the index card as a standard format for storing information, as these cards were for nearly two centuries used for making inventories and thus accumulating knowledge and rationalizing experience. Invented around 1760 by 'the father of modern taxonomy', Carl Linnaeus, cards cut to a standard size became the conventional medium for storing small

[21] Of all documentaries, *The Two Dime Animator* best documents the way Breer handled his index cards like instant flipbooks.

amounts of information or discrete data. Adopted by the Belgian lawyer and peace activist, Paul Otelet (who in 1904 also introduced the universal decimal classification system, still used by most libraries), the index card became the building brick of the *Mundaneum*, a visionary library conceived as a city of knowledge that would harbour the references to all books ever published.

At the height of his ambitions, Otelet's *Mundaneum* project comprised 15 million index cards, 100,000 files and millions of images. Until the breakthrough of the computer, the primary tool used to store and share information remained the card catalogue.[22] With his idiosyncratic use of index cards, Breer subverted conventions, sabotaging any form of existing categorization to create a hyper individual rather than a standardized order. As with the Rolodex, there was the connotation of subverting a typical component of the bureaucratic apparatus. 'Breer seems to have sensed, with grinning wit, that this quality of relentless and contingent movement would come to be our environment. Our response, he knew, would lie somewhere between awareness and reflex, science and spectacle' (Kuo 2010: 215).

Synaptic cinema

As with the handheld flipbook, the notion of scale was another aspect that also came into play with the index cards, only in a reverse way. Whereas the small dimension of his flipbook resulted in a nearly unnoticed presence at the gallery show, by blowing up index cards to fill a whole screen in a film theatre, Breer demanded full attention for his aberant enlargement of small cards. He recalls having a similar experience of warped dimensions in his years as a student: 'My art history course took place in a huge auditorium at the University at the end of which was a screen, and slides were shown. Mendelowitz was teaching. I saw Paul Klee on a screen the size of Lincoln Center, and I was completely floored when I saw the first Paul Klee the right size' (Cummings 1973). For his own films, Breer considered this alienating effect of enlargement as a welcome characteristic: 'because of the scale, the line is blown up, it's almost like a drawing on film' (Mekas 1973: 45). Back in his Paris years, Breer was lauded by Michel Seuphor notably for his sense of scale:

> Breer's paintings are full of silence and solitude. He excels in creating immense spaces in a small area. He punctuates them with a black line or

[22] The remnants of Otelet's utopian project are now kept in a *Mundaneum* museum in Mons, Belgium. Google built a data-centre in the direct neighbourhood of Mons in 2007, that became operational in 2010.

> a slight skewing of the geometry so that they seem not to take themselves too seriously. But nothing is more serious than this lightheartedness, nothing is more appropriate that this bit of humor. In fact, their lightness and discrete humor are what distinguish these paintings from all others in their genre.[23]

More explicit than ever was the case with his paintings, Breer's drawing gestures are highly present in every image. As Burford notes: 'He is the sole author of his images, whether they are iconic or indexical; in this sense, he does not contest the artist's status' (Burford 1999: 101).

On the small index cards, Breer never 'worked out' his drawings. He clearly wanted them to remain sketches, rough designs, preferring to hint at an idea, rather than to give away every detail. His aim was primarily to put the viewer's mind to work by representing the activity of his own brain. The

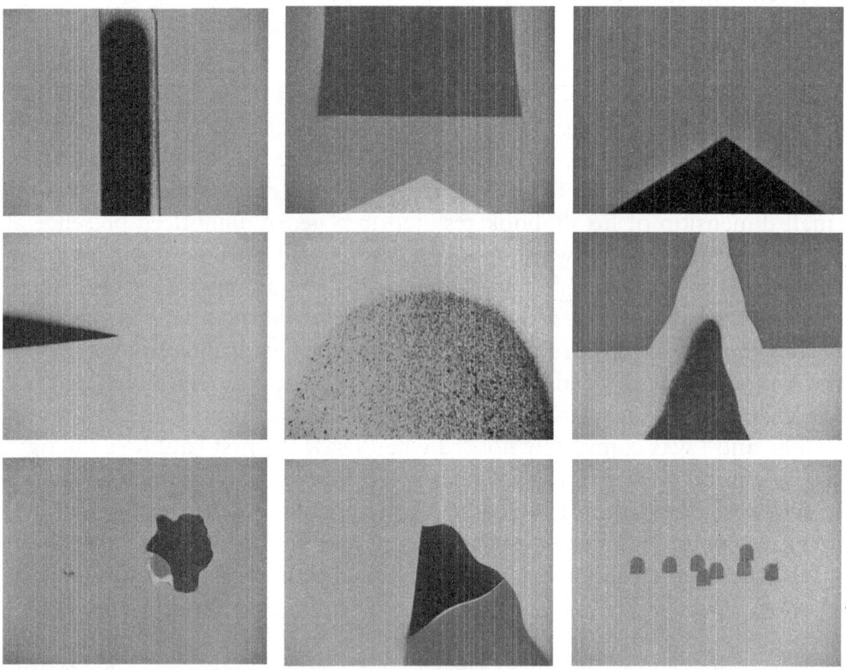

FIGURE 8.7 *Nine stills from* 1970 *(16mm film, colour, optical sound, 1970). Courtesy: Simon Preston Gallery, New York.*

[23] From a preface by Michel Seuphor for an invitation of an exhibiton, at the American Students and Artists' Center on Boulevard Raspail, 11 October to 31 October in 1956 (Klüver 1990: 4).

utterly fragmented flow of information becomes a stream of consciousness by the way the viewer's mind completes the allusive imagery. The drawings are showing us Breer's frames of mind, seismographic registrations of the most varied and minute motions in his awareness, the electroencephalography of a protean artist. Considered individually, the majority of these cards do not even contain any 'readable' information or representation. They merely show indirect indications of an action, like the scribbles in a traditional cartoon that indicate speed, but then with all figuration erased from them, or like exclamation marks without the surprised faces. Comparable to diagrams that do not signify anything without a reader's prior knowledge of the codes that form their basis, Breer's rapid-fire procession of index cards remains pointless if we are not willing to reflect on the functioning of our eyes and brain.

His scribbles often evoke purely abstract patterns, and do not represent any recognizable form or a conceptual scheme. They rather illustrate what the mind sees when looking inwards, what has been labelled a hypnagogic vision: random lines, patterns of speckles produced by phosphenes. Behind the radical abstraction on Breer's index cards lies the project of a synaptic cinema that has the phenomenon of visual thinking at its core. Any experience of an optical illusion is also a demonstration of how the brain works.

A semantic cinema

The company of the artists of the gallery Denise René may also have felt uncomfortable because Breer found it hard to take the same purist, elitist stance. He was rather a rebel and an iconoclast, as explicitely illustrated by the subversiveness of his early short film, *Un Miracle*. Breer was not only interested in Mondrian and Klee, but to the same degree in Kurt Schwitters and his Dadaist mix of typography, newspaper and all sorts of humble materials. As he explained in 1957: 'By jamming together and mixing both abstract and representative material, I find that I can satisfy my need to express both pure plastic sensation and ideas of ideational nature without compromising either. I believe that the fixed image is unable to serve this double purpose without the return to old and worn-out conventions' (Pardey 2011: 22).[24] Although he never really came close to the Situationist movement, Breer was in Paris at the same time and applying a similar liberating strategy. Films such as *Recreation* (1956–57), *Jamestown Baloos* (1957) and *Fist Fight* (1964) can be considered as equivalents to the *dérives*, the derailing guided tours the situationists undertook. When knowledge equals control, Breer propagates deregulation and chaos.

---

[24] A quote from Robert Breer is cited in Laurance Sillars' text, *Time Flies*.

Giving an apparent order to particles of life via a linear consecution of film frames, Breer has systematically refused to subject his viewers to any conventional narrative or logic. He prefers to incite an outburst of free association in each individual mind. To get rid of the diegetic impulse inherent in film, he always tried 'to counter one movement with another. A deliberately incoherent rhythm and the dispersal of vision into an allover field – with no single point of focus – was Breer's discovery upon his initiation into film circa 1952' (Kuo 2010: 215). In Breer's semantic cinema, the viewer is challenged to decode every instant, every index card on its individual characteristics and experience how the brain fails to work at such speed. Breer's cards do not represent a textual universe. They do not inventorize by means of words or numbers, but through different types of markings: tracings, blots and other forms of graphic signs. Most of the cards do not even offer drawings in the traditional sense, but rather show furtive annotations, elliptic representations of objects and figures.

If anything, Breer is rather heir of the French physiologist Étienne-Jules Marey than of his British contemporary Muybridge. Having discovered his avant-garde predecessors in the French Cinémathèque, Breer must have been aware of Marey, as the director of the Cinémathèque Henri Langlois had already organized a pioneering exposition on Marey in 1955, and then another one in 1963. In 1949, the year Breer arrived to spend a decade in Paris, the Cinémathèque had an exhibition on about the birth of cinema, focusing on Joseph Plateau, Émile Reynaud, the Lumière brothers and Marey.[25] Although the scientist Marey motivated his research with the optimization of human actions in mind, his mapping of the body and the translation of movement into purely graphic markings are quite akin to the poetic abstraction of the 'floating line' that Breer started to pursue, half a century later. On a purely formal level, the major difference between Muybridge and Marey is that the former lined up his image sequences in a disciplined, severely regimented order, whereas the latter preferred to condense multiple exposures onto one negative, with often quite a lyrical result. One can be considered a precursor to photorealistic cinema, the other to animation, which always involves a degree of abstraction.

Whereas Muybridge spent great care in giving his sequences a perfectly linear layout, Marey compressed his multiple exposures onto one photographic plate, to make a motion pattern instantly visible. Marey's graphic approach also required a plurality of exposures to obtain a single image. This also became the central principle that Robert Breer championed throughout his career and in all aspects of his work: it is always about the dynamic interrelation of things. There is nothing static in his universe. Breer:

---

[25] For documents on these early exhibitions by the French cinematheque (Païni 2014).

> I find myself combining freely very disparate images and finally using continuous motion simply as a means to connect up the various fixed images. This technique tends to destroy dramatic development in the usual sense and a new continuity emerges in the form of a very dense and compact texture. When pushed to extremes the resulting vibration brings about an almost static image on the screen.
>
> RUSSETT and STARR 1988: 135[26]

Multiple firsts

Although apparently reduced to merely a footnote during the 1955 exhibition of *Le Mouvement*, Robert Breer did eventually acquire equal billing in the international circuit that promoted Kinetic Art.[27] Particularly with his ultra slow moving 'floats', he gained notoriety among his contemporaries, culminating in the big outdoor installation for the Pepsi Pavilion at the world exhibition in Osaka 1970.[28] With his film works he gained recognition even sooner, promoted by such stakeholders as Jonas Mekas and his magazine *Film Culture*.[29] A selection committee that included kindred spirit Peter Kubelka canonized fifteen of Breer's films by making them part of a regularly rotating 'essential cinema' cycle at Anthology Film Archives in New York.[30]

---

[26] The quote is originally from Breer 1963.

[27] The exhibition *Vision in Motion/Motion in Vision* (Antwerp, 1959). Breer was part of a group show comprising Bury, Klein, Mack, Mari, Munari, Mecker, Rot, Soto, Spoerri, Tinguely and Van Hoeydonck, but again he was the only one without an entry in the catalogue. With *Bewogen Beweging* (Amsterdam, 1961, moving on to Stockholm the same year as *Movement in Art*), he was part of a massive show that included Kaprow, Calder, Gabo, Mack, Moholy-Nagy, Piene, Rauschenberg, Schlemmer, Tinguely, Duchamp and Vasarely. The catalogue (merely 25 pages) does not feature Breer. In 1968 Pontus Hultén included Breer in his exhibition for the MoMA New York: *The Machine as Seen at the End of the Mechanical Age*, with a separate entry in the exhibition catalogue on page 192. In 1970 Breer was included in the equally expansive show *Kinetics* in London where he did get equal billing in the publication. However, in the recent restaging of *Le Mouvement* (Basel, 2010) Breer was again not listed as part of the original line-up, but got a separate page with an interview at the end of the catalogue.

[28] For a longer reflection on how Breer aims to choreograph both the space and the viewer, see Carels (2013).

[29] At the occasion of his Independent Filmmakers award, extensive coverage of Breer was published in the issue #56–57 of *Film Culture* in 1973, but Breer had already been given serious attention in previous issues, namely in #26 (1962), #22–23 (1962–63) and #42 (1966).

[30] For an overview of the entire programme, see http://anthologyfilmarchives.org/about/essential-cinema (accessed 31 October 2017).

At the basis of these complementary strands in his work, the fast films and the slow sculptures, lies the flipbook, which had by 1955 already become an end in itself. In retrospect, it was perhaps in all its modesty the most unique and radical statement of the kinetic art show. *Le Mouvement* actually acknowledged, by the inclusion of Calder and Duchamp, that kinetic art was not a totally new manifestation, but rather an elaboration of these earlier practices. What makes Breer's *Image par Images* unique is paradoxically that it is an edition, not a unique piece of art. It is not only the first modernist flipbook to be included in an exhibition, it is also a multiple.[31] Only a decade later the publication of artists' books and ephemera would really take off, in the slipstream of the activities of Fluxus artists, the expanded cinema events and the conceptualization of para-cinema as a critical response to the ideology of the filmic dispositif.[32]

What distinguished Breer perhaps most from his colleagues at Denise René was his lack of instinct with regards to self-promotion, something that Vasarely mastered to the extreme. Breer was never interested in claiming 'firsts'. He realized very well that his film practice was influenced by Hans Richter, Fernand Léger and several other first generation avant-garde filmmakers he had discovered in Paris. Even for the revolutionary visual overload of *Recreation* there were at least partial precedents to be found, such as (at particular moments) the fast editing pace of Dziga Vertov or Abel Gance. But Breer was only secondarily inspired by film history. In the art world Duchamp had already subverted all sculptural conventions by presenting ready mades such as the *Bicycle Wheel* (1913), *In advance of a Broken Arm* (1915) and *Fountain* (1917). For *Recreation* Breer equally appropriated the most mundane objects to make a film that flickered as fast as possible. Of course, when put in motion, Duchamp's *Bicycle Wheel* offered a similar experience of rapid flicker, only more abstract. Breer had the opportunity to show Duchamp his *Recreation* when the godfather of conceptual, post-retinal art visited his studio.[33]

Duchamp was included in *Le Mouvement* with his *Rotary Demisphere (Precision Optics)* (1925).[34] Curiously, the film programme Pontus Hultén and Breer had compiled did not feature *Anémic Cinéma* (1926), the film

[31] A year later another artist's filmbook was made, but as a single copy only (Roth 2005: 112–113).

[32] The avant-garde filmmaker and live performer Ken Jacobs (born 1933) was the first to coin this concept during his film classes around 1974. The term has since been reintroduced by Walley (2003), Levi (2012) and others.

[33] Breer says about the meeting: 'I was able to invite Duchamp to my studio in Montparnasse one day – his comment: "Very nice, but don't you think they're a bit too fast?". That tickled me very much' (Breer 2010: 149).

[34] Painted *papier maché* demisphere fitted onto velvet-covered disk, copper collar with plexiglass dome, motor, pully and metal stand.

Duchamp had conceived on the basis of the same research on illusory depth.[35] Perhaps the insertion of verbal puns at regular intervals made the film not 'pure' enough for the largely abstract statement that *Le Mouvement* intended to make? With his spoken soundtrack for *Recreation*, however, Breer did demonstrate that he personally enjoyed verbal puns and nonsense poetry as well. Breer must have known that Duchamp also made an edition of Rotoreliefs, similar to the ones used for his film. In 1935 Duchamp issued what is regarded as the first multiple in the art world, a set of six cardboard discs, printed on both sides in colour offset.[36] For the New York reprisal of *Le Mouvement* in 1975, Denise René included these Rotoreliefs, rather than the *Rotary Demisphere*.

Subverting the aura

Son of an engineer, Breer may also have been aware of the several boxes with notes that Duchamp issued, the first one already in 1914.[37] In a commercial photographic supply box Duchamp offered facsimiles of sixteen manuscript notes and one drawing for sale. Refusing to bundle his conceptual notes in a linear bookform or give them any sense of systematic order, Duchamp accentuated the sudden manifestation of an idea, not unlike the furtive incoherence of Breer's filmed index cards that evoke a brain at work.[38] Duchamp's predeliction for loose scraps of paper does not exclude an interest in flipbooks. Although there is no actual proof that he occupied

[35] The playlist for '*Un Programme de Film Abstraits*' (21 April 1957) demonstrates Breer's awareness of the first wave of avant-garde cinema from the 1920s and 1930s (Eggeling, Chomette, Fischinger), but perhaps to avoid overlap with the regular programmes of the Cinémathèque, most titles in of *Le Mouvement* were from the 1940s and 1950s (including three films by McLaren, two by Mortensen, two by Breer) (Wetzel 2010: 80).

[36] Duchamp, Marcel: *12 Rotoreliefs*, Lithography, each 20 cm in diameter, designed to be rotated at $33\frac{1}{3}$ rpm in a circular plastic holder (25 cm in diameter). Text of the accompanying instruction leaflet:

'*12 Rotoreliefs. These discs, turning at an approximate speed of 33 revolutions per minute, will give an impression of deft hand, the optical illusion should be more intense with one eye than with two. The 12 drawings will be best seen kept in their black frame, the large ones through the larger side of the frame. In order to make use of the turnstile of the long-playing record machines, see drawing showing how to place the pack of discs, above the pin, on white cardboard. Marcel Duchamp.*'

[37] The title of Duchamp's first cardboard box with facsimiles was: *Box of 1914*, 1913–14; it is in the collection of the Philadelphia Museum of Art, Pennsylvania, PA, USA.

[38] 'Cornell's dossiers and Duchamp's fascimile projects are a testament to a school of note-making that found even the most rudimentary tablet unnecessary. Certainly, no leather-bound journals were in evidence. Instead, both artists wrote on any scrap of paper at hand. Cornell especially was fond of overwriting printed materials, squeezing words into every blank space, front and back, sideways or upside down' (Koch 1998: 249).

himself with them, there are many instants in his work that illustrate he enjoyed appropriating diverse forms of vernacular entertainment. And when for instance Guillaume Apollinaire already had a portrait of himself turned into a flipbook in 1914, this demonstrates that flipbooks were indeed around and not unpopular, even among avant-garde artists.[39] Duchamp also must have seen the various thaumatrope adaptations that his friend and fellow 'scrap' artist Joseph Cornell made in the 1930s.[40] It is clear then that optical toys had already surfaced in the context of modern art, long before 1955.

With or without such prior knowledge of other artists appropriating the format of the flipbook or film, Breer's trajectory in painting did culminate in a questioning of the value of painting itself: 'It was a kind of philosophical effort to pose the question of multiplicity versus the one original act. It was in the air and I thought, my god, film, here it is and the original is worthless' (Cummings 1973). Breer was attracted by the notion that filmprints as such don't have value (or 'aura' in the terms of Walter Benjamin) except when they are projected. From his 1955 flipbook onwards, Breer addressed the issue of the artwork in the age of mechanical reproduction, as he realized that 'uniqueness enhances the market value of art, but I didn't want to participate in that way of thinking. I had my democratic idealism to justify working in film – and I didn't even need that: film was just fun' (MacDonald 1992: 31).

Subverting the aura and authority of the single image through a multitude of cards and film frames did not mean that Breer altogether abandoned the hanging of frames against a wall. But to keep the eye restless and the mind active, he quite systematically persisted in applying his concept of generating one image through an accumulation of visual impressions. Although the original loop of *Recreation 1* got completely worn out, the work still exists as a photographic print that consists of dozens of photograms.[41] In the film version of *Recreation* (1956) Breer cut one print into strips of equal length to sandwich it between plexiglass.[42] Once as he started using index cards for his films, Breer also mounted some of the cards he had filmed into

[39] *Guillaume Apollinaire im Gespräch mit André Rouveryre* (1914) in Schulz (2005: 24–25). Apart from the artist's flipbooks documented in this catalogue, from its inception the flipbook (or Kineograph, as it was patented in 1868 by Barnes Linnett) was also used for scientific purpose, as for instance during the International Congress of Meteorology of 1900, to show meteorological maps in motion.

[40] Cornell, Joseph: *Jouet surréaliste* and *Le Voyageur dans les Glaces* (both thaumatropes, c. 1932); *Object (Hotel Theatricals by the Grandson of Monsieur Phot Sunday Afternoons)* (box with marbles, referencing Muybridge and Marey, 1940); *¾ Bird's-Eye View or 'A Watch-Case for Marcel Duchamp'* (bow with thaumatropes, 1944).

[41] *Untitled (Recreation 1)*, 1956–57 (190.5 × 76.2 cm) reproduced in Beauvais (2006: 17).

[42] According to the Paris gallery gb agency, coordinators of the estate, this version was made on the occasion of the opening exhibition of the Centre Georges Pompidou in 1977, at the request of Pontus Hultén.

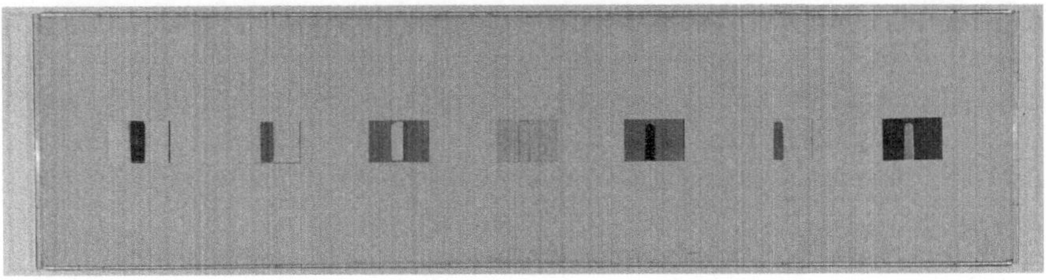

FIGURE 8.8 70 *(seven original drawings on wooden panel from the film* 1970, *1970). Courtesy: gallery gb agency, Paris.*

compositions he could exhibit. He thus frequently reprised selections of drawings on cards, actual components of his short films, like the series culled from the film *70* (1970) and mounted on several 244 cm long wooden panels, each presenting seven of the original, small cards.

On each panel, regular-broad intervals separate the abstract images that were used in the film. On other occasions, Breer joined together side by side four or even twenty-four images, selected from one film into a single frame, like in a grid. Once they had been recorded on camera, however, most his drawings on cards never left their storage space – a simple cardboard box. The drawings from *A Man and his Dog out for Air* (1957), the unique film for which Breer did use a pegbar and transparent paper, he exhibited by stacking a whole section of the film behind a piece of glass, so the viewer could clearly see through the first layers.

Although Breer did not want to return to showing 'ultimate' images in isolation, this nevertheless raises questions regarding the status of drawings originally made to be exposed under the camera, in order to appear in front of our eyes for only a flash of a second. Once it is permanently visible, hanging fixed behind glass, its impact is entirely different. How to approach in an exhibition a drawing identical to the one featured in a film projection? In general, film stills or photograms extracted from live action films are rarely considered to have the autonomy of a work of art. They remain documentation, a reference. Intermediary components like painted cells, paper with drawings or charcoal traces, or other graphic elements from animated films do sometimes end up as works in their own right, but then they lose their dynamism and promote a different quality instead.

Back and forth

After he quit painting, Breer never really upgraded a single image into a self-sufficient work of art again. Even within a single frame he preferred to confound and frustrate longer scrutiny of his graphic work by always bringing multiple elements together. When he did include drawings on a single sheet of paper in his exhibitions, they usually had the appearance of a study, a sketch that often combines a preliminary drawing of a project with some handwritten notes, not unlike the boxed notes Duchamp put in distribution. Some drawings contain a sequence that suggests a transformation, like the flower and the American flag in the drawing *Untitled* (1971), but most are working sketches and ideas put on paper without any aesthetic pretense.

On one such drawing from 1960, Breer says: 'I have contrived myself a funny problem; How to get back to the fixed image by way of cinema. I like to cross back and forth dragging elements from both worlds. I like to cross back and forth between cinema and fixed imagery. I like to have the belongings of one into the world of the other, and never get caught.'[43] As soon as Breer had mastered abstract composition on canvas, he started to deconstruct it again by foregrounding the preliminary steps of how a painting comes into being. Once Breer had discovered his working method to make films with index cards, he questioned himself how these intermediary steps could gain a significance of their own.

As he had already made clear in 1955 with his contributions to *Le Mouvement*, the multifarious Breer did not categorically distinguish a projection from an exhibition, or a sculpture from a flipbook. It was the interval that appealed to him. As he made clear with his title *Image par Images*: our impression of an image is always the outcome of an accumulation of a whole string of images. Even his seemingly monolithic sculptures (that he always presented in groupings) loosen their impact if they are considered in a static pose and from a single vantage point. Their specific aesthetic lies in the succession and combination of different viewing positions. Whatever medium Breer adopted, the central question always remained the movement of the beholder *vis-à-vis* the artwork, be it the movement of the eye scanning a selection of cards grouped in a frame, or the brain fusing the rapid-fire of frames during a projection, or of the entire body relating itself to a sculpture moving almost imperceptibly on the floor. The function of the work, even the graphic work, is there to choreograph the viewer, to activate both body and brain, and to short circuit all the viewing habits that traditionally come into play when we a approach a painting, a sculpture or a film.

References

Beauvais, Y. (2006). 'Interview with Robert Breer', in M. Denaës (ed.), *Robert Breer – Films, Floats & Panoramas*, 157–169. Freddy & Teicher, Gaël, Montreuil: Éditions de l'oeil.

Breer, R. (1963). 'A Statement', *Film Comment*, 29: 69.

[43] Robert Breer: *Untitled* (drawing on paper, 15.5 × 10 cm) 1960 (Beauvais 2006: 62).

Breer, R. (2010). 'Interview on the Occasion of the Exhibition *Le Mouvement*, from Cinema to Kinetics', in R. Wetzel (ed.), *Le Mouvement-Kino zur Kinetik*, 147–150. Heidelberg: Kreber Verlag.

Burford, J. L. (1999). *Robert Breer*. Paris: Éditions Paris Expérimental, RE: Voir Éditions.

Carels, E. (2013). 'Spaces of Wonder: Animation and Museology', in S. Buchan (ed.), *Pervasive Animation*, 292–316. London: AFI Film Readers, Routledge.

Cummings, P. (1973). 'Oral history interview with Robert Breer', 10 July, Archives of American Art, Smithsonian Institution. Available online: https://www.aaa.si.edu/collections/interviews/oral-history-interview-robert-breer–11951 (accessed 31 October 2017).

Fouché, P. (2005). 'Versuch einer Geschichte des Daumenkinos', in C. B. Schulz (ed.), *Daumenkino – The Flip Book Show*, 10–23. Düsseldorf: Kunsthalle Düsseldorf.

Hultén, P. (1968). *The Machine, as Seen at the End of the Mechanical Age*. New York: The Museum of Modern Art.

Klüver, B. (1990). *Robert Breer – a Painter in Paris*. Paris: Galerie 1900–2000.

Koch, P. (1998). *Joseph Cornell/Marcel Duchamp . . . in Resonance*. Ostfildern-Ruit: Cantz Verlag.

Kuo, M. (2010). 'Everything Goes – An Interview with Robert Breer', *Artforum*, November 2010: 214–221.

Lebrat, C, (1999). 'Robert Breer's RE-creation', in Jennifer Burford (ed.), *Robert Breer*. Paris: Éditions Paris Expérimental, RE:Voir Éditions.

Levi, P. (2012). *Cinema by Other Means*. New York: Oxford University Press.

MacDonald, S. (1992). *A Critical Cinema 2: Interviews with Independent Filmmakers*. Berkeley: University of California Press.

Mekas, J. (1973). 'An Interview with Robert Breer Conducted by Jonas Mekas and P. Adams Sitney on May 13, 1971 in New York City', *Film Culture*, 56/57 (Spring 1973): 39–55.

Mendelson, L. (1981). *Robert Breer, A Study of His Work in the Context of the Modernist Tradition*. Ann Arbor, Michigan: UMI Research Press.

Menegoi, S. (2010). 'Engineering Uncertainty', *Kaleidoscope Magazine*, 3: 42–47.

Païni, D. (2014). *Le musée imaginaire d'Henri Langlois*. Paris: Flammarion.

Pardey, A., ed. (2011). *Robert Breer*. Bielefeld: Kerber Verlag.

Roth, D. (2005). 'Entwurf zu Material 5', in C. B. Schulz (ed.), *Daumenkino – The Flip Book Show*, 112–113. Düsseldorf: Kunsthalle Düsseldorf.

Russett, R. and C. Starr (1988). *Experimental Animation*. New York: Da Capo Press.

Schulz, C. B., ed. (2005). *Daumenkino – The Flip Book Show*. Düsseldorf: Kunsthalle Düsseldorf.

Walley, J. (2003). 'The Material of Film and the Idea of Cinema', *October 103* (Spring 2003), 15–30.

Wetzel, R. (2010). *Le Mouvement-Kino zur Kinetik*. Heidelberg: Kreber Verlag.

9

'. . . The Film Is Not About That'[1]

Notes on (Re)Reading *Tale of Tales*

Mikhail Gurevich

Preface

My attempts at interpretative writing on *Tale of Tales* have a rather long history. The first lengthy essay on the film I wrote around 1987; it was published, in Russian, in a preprint-type collection of articles *Multiplicatsiya, Animatograph, Fantomatika* under the auspices of First All-Union Animation Festival Krok–89 (held in Kiev, not yet in floating-on-the-ship format). In the following years, I had a chance to discuss this topic in different forms at a couple of SAS conferences. In the 1990s, Jayne Pilling tried to prepare my text for publication in her *Reader in Animation Studies* and even commissioned a third-party translation to assist in my then uneasy English writing; those rather laborious efforts, however, did not result in publication in the end (I was using certain wording from that translation and joint editing in subsequent work). Much later, at Giannalberto Bendazzi's

[1] The recurrent phrase in proposal and script treatment for the film; published in English translation in Kitson (2005: 123–130) (though this particular phrase, as well as a few others, quoted further, are, in translation, different from mine). Unless indicated otherwise, all other translations of Russian-language sources are mine.

suggestion, I wrote a new and different version for his *Animation: A World History* (among numerous other contributions). While this book was underway and hanging in publishing limbo, I delivered the paper, in a sketchy abridged form, at the first Animafest Scanner conference in 2014.

The fuller version, thoroughly edited, was finally published in 2016 in Volume 2 of the *Animation: A World History*, under the title 'Dream of Eternity, Lullaby of Re-birth: Notes on Re-reading *Tale of Tales*'. Here I'm submitting yet another, largely expanded and reworked version, incorporating elements of the previous ones (also, at the special request of Animafest in 2014, I wrote for the festival programme book a short, more general essay, 'Breathing a Soul into the Things Existent: Animation According to Norstein' – from which I'm borrowing here a few formulations as well).

The text offered here presents a combination of different critical perspectives and styles; being aware of the risks involved, I nevertheless hope that this kind of deliberate inconsistency in method and take might still be of some merit, if it can possibly spark a light of understanding.

Of expectations and frustrations

When it was shown for the first time as a finished product at the 'artistic council' of Soyuzmultfilm studio, in the summer of 1979, the recorded reactions of sympathizing (and trying to help, no doubt) colleagues ranged from 'contemplation on a future of our country and of humanity as a whole' to 'a summation of the experience of Soviet poetry', and to 'a new form of animation expression' (Kitson 2005: 107). With all the considerations of place and time, and undercurrents involved, this range and tone of response remains, in retrospect, quite characteristic and telling – both in degree of recognition and in its vague generalized nature.

Giannalberto Bendazzi recalls the reaction at the Zagreb selection committee screening in March 1980: 'We viewed the film almost without breathing, hypnotised. From then on, we never referred to it by title, but only by the masterpiece.' And writing about that twenty-five years later, he still holds: '*Tale of Tales* is the ultimately enigmatic, cryptic film. You don't doubt its great art. You just hardly understand what it is all about' (Bendazzi 2005). Clare Kitson also testifies:

> What sort of animal was it, then, living in that abandoned house, and roasting potatoes, burning its fingers (paws?) as it ate them? And who was that old woman, suddenly popping up in the middle of the abandoned house to stoke the fire? What is all that about? These were the kinds of not very profound questions that exercised audiences at the 1980 Zagreb International Animation Festival, as they tried to get to grips with *Tale of*

> *Tales*. [. . .] Despite its mysteries, everyone sensed that this poetic, wistful work, full of idiosyncratic humour, was a masterpiece.
>
> KITSON 2005: 1–2

She goes on to note a quite unique overall effect and '*frisson* of expectations' at the award ceremony (Kitson 2005: 3). Years later, in the introduction to her book on this film she admits, once again, the sense of puzzlement as the major reception point. Kitson sympathetically refers to the film's scriptwriter, Lyudmila Petrushevskaya, who also confesses in a letter to Norstein: 'Only when you had finished shooting the film did I begin to grasp your idea. I have seen *Tale of Tales* no less than fifty times. But the mystery never goes away' (Kitson 2005: 4).

And that kind of admission-reservation would become common place in the entire discourse on and around the film, up to regular media journalism or the newest film buffs' blogs. For sure, that can also be seen outside Russia or the orbit of its native language. However, within the domestic cultural realm that would be noticeable too, if only being gradually substituted rather with some kind of shy matter-of-course acceptance and satisfaction with safe-to-apply vague generalities, which is probably the sign of the same perplexity.

Well, I myself can attest to more or less the same, recalling the moment, clear in memory, when I watched it for first time, around 1981, in the only place available – our first and the only multiplex of that time, the movie-house Rossiya in the very cultural centre of Moscow, and at a short strike from Soyuzmultfilm studio's main facility; there was apparently a special arrangement to screen some new releases here in the smallest theatre, with just a few dozen seats in capacity.

This purl of images was hard to decipher clearly; yet, the mere fact that they are 'pregnant' with (certain) meaning was tangibly obvious. The image ligature did not seem clear-cut, but still felt needful, bounden, which only pushed even more to the duty and labour of understanding – and at the same time not promising easy ways, if any at all. I suspect that today, almost forty years after its creation, *Tale of Tales*, having been repeatedly recognized as the greatest animated film of all time, still remains an enigmatic masterpiece, its 'cryptic' meaning or message not fully deciphered. The film's charm and power are (still, I believe) indisputable and irresistible; and yet, the sense of or hope for complete and concrete understanding still escapes us somehow.

When I first attempted a critical reading of this film back in the mid 1980s, not much of the (recorded) discourse around it had been yet generated. By now, however, it is probably one of the most reflected upon, or at least talked about, animated films in history. Especially, and mostly, through the self-reflection of the director himself, in his numerous lectures, talks, interviews (eventually collected/re-edited into several books). Virtually every move and image is described and attributed, in terms of origins and connotations, and put tightly within a film(making) context.

And yet, one would hardly find there anything close to a wholesome, explicit articulation of the message or meaning of the film. Partly, perhaps, due to the fact that practically the entire body of this most extensive self-commentary was recorded after Norstein, by different people and under different conditions, not actually written by him. And besides, while having extreme riches in creative practice and observations to share and being quite a deep artistic personality, capable of insights and paradoxes, and uncanny sensual memory, Norstein is not really a creature of reflection in a strictly intellectual sense, rather he is more for a meditation of sorts, which might provoke a lot on a receiving side – but might need yet another effort in deciphering and contextualizing.

That became, for the most part, a task in the book, which finally appeared in English, by Clare Kitson, to justified acclaim, inevitably becoming a primary reference source: a quite detailed, close to exhaustive, account of the work process, surrounding circumstances, real-life context and such, immersed in direct or indirect dialogue with the creator(s). With all due credit, Kitson does try along the way to give meaning to certain details, to trace motives, to hint at parallels; yet, the book culminated in merely a descriptive record of the film material in the final cut, presented in its entirety and attempting to include every minor move – but with no real inclination to an interpretive reading per se, it seems. That might be justified by the very genre chosen and, moreover, seen as a special merit – as Nick Park rightly indicates in the introduction: not to over-explain and thus spoil the magic . . . Nevertheless, this kind of persistent 'perception gap', manifested through times and methods, must have something to do with the artistic nature of the subject at hand, with its poetics and structure.

Of plot and verse

Getting back to my personal history of perception and reading – yes, again, I do remember all too well my first impression of *Tale of Tales* – it was stupefaction at the unknown quality of the 'cartoon': the density of this artistic text was just striking; and, also, the feeling/sensation of fluid continuity, wholeness, harmony. 'An uninterrupted discourse, a unified poem': this crossed my mind early, before any spoken or written conversations, in which the comparison to verses and poetry was quickly becoming a common reference.

And how do we deal with poetry in the first place, in the initial attempt of 'reading'? – of course, we *recite*, albeit in an inner voice, gradually learning by heart, thus appropriating the meaning in its only possible form-inclination; and simultaneously, or later and sometimes for years to come, we go through elements, look through rhymes and motives, and tropes, thus interiorizing the form and substance in sync. In that, we engage in retelling, inwardly, if or until we are not forced otherwise.

Perhaps that's the mechanism in play that drives practically everyone talking about *Tale of Tales* to do ultimately the same: to sort and list the stuff in the content and how it falls into memory – the visual impressions per se.

. . . The old house, the boarded-up windows, the stove, and the fire in the stove, and the old woman in its reflected light; the yard, the old tree. The fire from the burning leaves, which vanishes after a brief flash; and the sparse, ghostly little wood; and earlier, the old-fashioned, wretched street light over the tiny dance floor; and men, torn from the dance by the crackle as the gramophone needle is plucked off, and the rainproof marquee, extending into the sky, and the women's eerily solitary tango, the invalid accordion player, the tears on the glass; and then, throughout, the strange creature staring fixedly at everything . . .

And there are also other worlds: dimensions of existence, parallel ones, separate in style and storyline. Another house, by the sea, and a family, a bull (Minotaur?), a poet, and a traveller. And yet another family, on their Sunday walk; a woman with a high hat, a man with a bottle, a boy with an apple, and crows in the snow. Here and there, a day in life, in its simplest and main elements. And in both places, there is a child: a happy slip of a girl participating in the ritual flow of the everyday; and a poor little boy, held tightly by the hand, but deprived of anything worth participating in, a dreamer and a rebel, alone within and by himself.

Three worlds, three planes (and correspondingly, a stylistic collage – of clearly 'quoted' styles); three dimensions – of what? They are separated, but is it by space or time? Warmly mythologized, shabby and dear past; vulgar and itchy, and still deserving compassion, mask-wearing present; and mysteriously transparent, elemental and so close to eternity. Characteristically, we find the similar kind of 'preliminary' retelling of the motives and in sorting the imagery in the very beginning of this film's history, in Petrushevskaya's script texts, in different stages:[2] 'The washing on the lines, the bull with the ring through its nose, full of terrible, fatal passions, the little old man with one leg; our neighbour, who came back from the war like that . . . All this can be organised into a simple plot, but a particular plot, a concertina-plot, which moves apart, expands' (script proposal, in Norstein and Yarbusova 2005: 21). In her script proposal, Petrushevskaya seems to

[2] A genius author in her own turn and right, she was especially good at drafting scripts and sketches for the film; in my mind, even her earliest sketch, the 'proposal', in all its generalized vagueness, offers the true feeling and inspiration, and foresees the interplay of motives, which moreover justifies getting back to her and their joint formulations here (proposal and treatment are officially attributed to both Petrushevskaya and Norstein; the treatment as translated in Kitson (2005: 125–130); the proposal – rather in my version of translation from Russian text incorporated in more than one of Norstein's books, here as in Norstein and Yarbusova (2005: 20–21).

leave out just one obvious word: a *lyrical* plot. That is what the authors were striving for from early on – and this shift in genre is quite significant. It is no less of a turning point in animation (genre) history than the move towards the social parable, towards the conventional grotesque of two decades earlier.

This important distinction also brings up in a different light another persistent trait of common discourse around the film (and a facet of the 'perception gap'): laments on the lack of narrative clarity, if not the absence of narrative structure per se, suggesting that we deal with a non-narrative flow of images . . . – as if we just cannot assume the idea of a non-linear narrative as such, not action-based and determined, but rather within the logic of associations, sensations, thoughts, after all. Which is exactly the type of lyrical narration, plot-development – or, for that matter, of an essay, in its initial sense and shape, from Montaigne on, but also in certain film genre varieties, in fiction and documentary categories.

And what is also essential in this regard is, 'The great themes of lyric poetry are not always "eternal", but are always existential in the sense that they are concerned with the fundamental aspects of man's existence', says Lidiya Ginzburg (1981: 153), an outstanding Russian theorist and historian of literature; lyric poetry as such is 'a kind of exposition of values' (Ginzburg 1986: 95).

Tale of Tales is a poetic utterance par excellence, and it is shaped, basically, after the literary examples, verse per se (one more testament to the literary-centred nature of the Russian culture-mentality), as was noted years ago and not by this critic alone. What is worth clarifying, however, is a more precise reference(s) to literary sources and influences. Although, as Petrushevskaya testifies, in the work process Norstein would bring along many books of poetry: 'all the romantics, García Lorca, Pablo Neruda, Nazym Khikmet' (Encyclopedia of the National Cinema n.d.), and the film borrows its title from a short poem by Khikmet (a Turkish political émigré in the Soviet Union), the poetics traces its roots rather to different and sophisticated modernist lyrics of the twentieth century, not in a sense of cerebral construction, for *Tale of Tales* is not cold and cerebral at all, and on the surface its imagery seems ingenuously plain-hearted, but rather in terms of the interplay between the implicit motive-impulses and explicit moves and images that are to manifest them.

In a Russian tradition, that would be, maybe (though on the surface distant from Norstein's intuitive taste), the poetry of Osip Mandel'štam is, at first glance, often totally enigmatic, the free flight of seemingly unrelated, albeit strikingly precise, tropes, which, however, at close reading and analysis would reveal absolute coherence and cast-iron logic in the unwinding of metaphors into an ultimate narrative of meaning. A similar mechanism is at work in this narrative of visual poetry: the flow of free distant associations, visualized impressions, pregnant of metaphors, which are nevertheless solidly grounded and interlinked on a deeper level, beyond the frame and off the screen. Once in a film-school lecture, Norstein quoted Mandel'štam's lines: 'One feels the crackle of an apple // In the frosty sound of a sleigh', and goes on to hold this as an example of complex structuring when 'the line grows in different directions, in a single instant attracting the multiplicity of sensations. Upon the same principle, you build up a film shot' (Norstein 2005: 136).

With all the seeming dissociations, this 'purl of images' does build an integral world. There is indeed a common ground for all the things and beings here, in the world of the film itself, that is the whole of the author's utterance is sewn through with many reiterated and harsh threads, refrains, repetitions, momentary flashes: a dry leaf, gliding down to the ground, an echelon, marching past, violent tapping, and the table-cloth, flying down off the tables, covering the whole town, rolling itself into a ball in the sky, as if it were alive ... For that is how a poetic utterance is created, and that is how a lyrical plot (narrative) takes shape, and it is precisely in the 'lyrical induction' (Lidiya Ginzburg's term; see, for instance in Ginzburg 1981), as an attribute of the poetry of our age, from the specific to the general; from the concrete, the detailed, the material and perhaps the profane – to the existential.

In some of the general and most impressive sketches for *Tale of Tales*, the film's designer, and director's wife, Francheska Yarbusova, had on a single sheet, as if the whole storyboard was in loose order, images and scenes (plotlines, for that matter) juxtaposed in simultaneous existence. This principle of free composition feels to me quite essential, and in the film, it is, in one way or another, consistent on all levels, unrestrained, and that is exactly the point. A similar freedom is adequate to the composition of our consciousness, the structure of human memory. A lot was said about *Tale of Tales* regarding these kind of things, and, probably, not without reason. This is the freedom of deeply personal, even of autobiographical lyricism, and in that, not so much of memory per se, as of recollection, the sheer act of recalling from one's memory. This by definition is subjective and unique, and there is tact and precision in that. It ought to be somewhat out-of-focus, that is unpremeditated, not pre-organized into a structured system, but chaotically instinctive, with a vacillating weave of fragments, sparks of memory, lighting up something out of the darkness at will and through whimsy.

The blissful mumbling of a child's dream; the blissful self-sufficiency of poetic speech ...

Of dreams and visions

'It must be a film about memory. Do you remember how long the days were during childhood?' (Norstein and Yarbusova 2005: 21). It is hard to overlook, but even harder to unambiguously accept this animation piece as a confessional film. But what is this confession about? And what did it, deliberately or not, reveal?

In fact, the narrative structure proper of *Tale of Tales* is not exactly memory-like (as suggested first by Mikhail Iampolski[3]), and not simply that of recollection (as this critic had suggested earlier), but rather it is of an oneiric nature. A dream screen, where even the fleshly real images with straightforward connotations inevitably acquire a degree of conditionality. And yet what complicates things is the 'agent' of dream(s), the Little Wolf, who is himself an oneiric element, a chimera of dreams. Moreover he is a character of a lullaby, who at the end sings over the cradle the very song about himself . . . There are even signs formally indicating the dream in conventional cinematic language: luminous spatial openings, like doors, that can or must be treated as second-order screens inside a lager screen, the frame of the film as such. And the punctuated appearance of mirrors, of this or that kind, hints at the same framing technique. The 'reality' of this dream-world is doubling and reduplicating itself, blurring in the gallery of mirrors, but in a strange, paradoxical way it is also obtaining a new degree of substantive density.

It is the dream about a vision, a fantasy of insight, a dreamy state of awakening. It is indeed about awakening, after all, if it is not spiritual, in a narrow sacramental sense, then it is at least that of mind and soul. The previous iteration of my 'reading' was entitled 'Dream of Eternity, Lullaby of Re-birth' – now I'd rather reverse the logic: the film is in fact a lullaby of eternity and the dream of rebirth. At a certain point, the whole symbolism, at first so obscure and tempting, no longer calls for deciphering, it has become transparent and almost . . . unnecessary.

After all, *Tale of Tales* is really a very simple film. As Norstein himself says: 'Life consists of very simple moves of the soul, of very simple human conjunctions' (Norstein 2005: 138). The apple is an apple, the house is a house, and the Little Wolf is a Little Wolf, because he really does exist. Indeed, he alone exists as a certainty. His modality is indisputable. Only, it goes without saying, not in the material world of events, flowing biographies, changes in the weather, in governments, fashions, but in the inner world of personality, the intimate universe of a thinking and sensing, and reflecting being. In those geological deposits of inner biography, the Little Wolf from the lullaby is the first horizon, a reference point for the conscious memory.

Norstein provides, however, yet another marker or foundation, though this one belongs rather to the 'collective unconscious', than to the personal biographic memory. Its 'literariness' is evident: Madonna and Child, a

[3] See, for instance, his essay 'The Space of the Animated Film: Khrzhanovsky's *I Am With You Again* and Norstein's *The Tale of Tales*' (1987 [1982]: 104).

canonical subject, a cultural archetype. And not accidentally this shot/image serves as a headpiece, a lead-in, for it is not from this subjective-unique time-space, not from the history of a concrete conscience. It belongs, strictly speaking, to pre-memory. That's why it lies practically 'beyond the frame', outside the brackets of the lyrical plot. But in a different, grand sense, in the memory of his cultural, conscious self, it is of fundamental values, and that's why it turns up as a brief refrain in soaring culminations. And the Little Wolf that looks eye to eye at the baby suckling the breast, this is, perhaps, the sharpest juxtaposition of the worlds or planes here. A collision between the personal and the super-personal. In other words, between recollection and knowledge, and, correspondingly, between lyrical elements and the epic modality of the myth.

The guardian angel, or house-spirit of my childhood, that lives in and through the semi-delirium of my first sensations, suddenly takes a look at what had happened before he came about, in the very beginning, when no one had sung lullabies, when individual memory had not yet started. And it feels as though he, the angel-house-spirit, the chimera of babyhood dreams, has started an act of 'cultural introspection': he reaches out for the clean sheet, the empty page, coming to surmise that the word equals life, and beginning to understand the mystery of creation as the secret of man's birth. This point, this contraposition is probably the most profound accent in Norstein's work.

However, the true, essential problematics of his confession, of his lyrical message, lie elsewhere.

Of times and spaces

'Every day stood as it was, things of today became true today, and the happiness of tomorrow could wait till tomorrow . . . The film is not about that' (Norstein and Yarbusova 2005: 20).

Is the film about memory? The film is about what we are left with. It is about the axiological framework of existence, albeit hardly articulated by the creators in that sort of high-brow lingo. At the risk of losing the poetic nerve, let us nonetheless try to somehow ground this thorough vision in (historic) reality, both in space and time, starting just with plain topography. Maryina Roshcha (which the director constantly evokes as a 'holy land' of his childhood and a principal protoplast of the filmic space) is not really a suburb of Moscow, as some Western commentators would hold. Once, a long time ago, it was the town's woody edge (as the very name hints: 'roshcha' stands for 'grove'), then a shabby, sort of blue collar, tenement barracks, almost shantytown, outskirt, notorious for its low-life and hide-outs. It was also one of the areas where Jews, coming from the Pale, were traditionally settled, legally or not, back in tsarist times, and then later still going to this spot.[4] Now it lays practically within the city's central belt, a fifteen to twenty minute bus ride from the Red Square vicinity, halfway to the TV tower and broadcasting centre Ostankino (symbolically enough), while the real outskirts are about ten to fifteen kilometres further on.

Norstein left the neighbourhood around 1967. I moved in, maybe the same or following year, but already into a different environment. My family left communal dwelling in Moscow's central quarters for a separate, individual apartment here. The same reason drove Norstein from the area. The sign of changing times, the entire era in fact, that was taking place gradually, from the early 1960s onwards. Old tenement buildings, or 'barracks' in common lingo, were being demolished to give space for a new variety of more or less the same: pre-fabricated panel middle-rises, five-storied buildings.[5] But with that, the very basics of (co)existence were subject to change with certain, essential ideological shifts.

In one of her most remarkable and revealing sketch-drawings, Francheska Yarbusova shows the entire block of barrack houses, linked like train cars, being bent upwards into the sky, as if they were about to take off, to fly away. The entire way of life, a complete universe of sorts, was being pushed away by bulldozers, and Yuri Norstein was not the only one who felt a phantom limb pain. Actually, that was a common thread or theme in the literature, theatre, and film of the period: a meditation on the loss, nostalgia for the poor and pure past. Some authors would look deeper and sharper. Yuri Trifonov's then famous novella was entitled *Exchange*, with connotations not only to an apartment swap, but to betrayal, the selling out of moral values and ethical codes that come along with the process. It seems that Norstein shares, to an extent, this kind of sentiment.

This period marked, basically, the end of the 'classic' Soviet history and way of life, which was transforming itself into the late degenerative phase, essentially, neo-petit-bourgeois, in terms of real values of the everyday, which was quite a tangible departure from the (proclaimed and in some sense interiorized) austerity, sacrificial spirit and 'equality in the common misery' of the heroic and tragic era. And on a certain level *Tale of Tales* clearly, albeit in an oblique metaphorical way, documents the dubious nature of the emasculated ideological empire that tries to adjust somewhat to 'normal' human conditions at the price of a gradual decline in moral disrepair.

---

[4] I do not see much of meaningful manifestations of a 'Jewish theme' in his work. However, Kitson dwells somewhat on Norstein's personal reflections in this regard. And with a much stronger emphasis, given the sharpened focus, the issue is addressed by Maya Balakirsky Katz in *Drawing the Iron Curtain: Jews and the Golden Age of Soviet Animation* (2016); her loaded argument on this motif's weight in *Tale of Tales* (in a special chapter 2006: 204–225) calls for a separate discussion.

[5] Infamous 'khrushchobs', nicknamed after Stalin's successor on the Soviet throne, under whose rule these housing developments, as well as other steps on promoting a relative improvement in living standards, were initiated.

In the world(s) of *Tale of Tales*, those 'eras' and 'codes' are manifested by almost the direct juxtapositions of their material, object epitomes: a rusty old sewing machine of once reputable German brand Singer (that likely served the needs of the entire apartment block for generations) vs. a glossy-new Zhiguli, a compact car produced under Fiat license at turn-key purchased Italian plant. There are palpable, sensible signs of change. Remember how Little Wolf swings on the treadle of the Singer, and steps off to look into the car's wheel cap as if into a magic mirror.

In the film's virtual space and time, it is as if Little Wolf is a 'missing link' between the worlds, either a liaison or spy, who penetrates them all. Amazingly, he can go out of the old house through the luminous door, leading into the eternal one, and even come back. But, by some deeper reason, not into the snowy park of the present, that path is locked, and that boy is not under his wing. Strictly historically, however, Little Wolf, as an old dwelling's house-spirit, materializes, naturally, when the walls are falling, exactly on this crucial divide (and that's where the film's authors, along with this conditional alter ego, found themselves), somewhere perhaps in the late 1960s or early 1970s, rather than in exactly the (post)war time. Norstein himself, born in 1941, certainly carries war in his bones, not as an actual conscious experience, but rather as a family's or communal memory, and it is exactly through imagery and tone of impersonal or common recollection that this motif plays out in the film.

But there is more to that. This is a collectivist experience par excellence. And it is exactly the collectivist ethics, code of conduct, presumably, the core facet of ideology's 'human face', and the cornerstone in the communal survival that is being washed away by the flow of time. Houses with their backyards, and street corners under the lamp-post, and the tables put together cannot escape the bulldozers, cannot fly straight to heaven, only the village-long tablecloth will wind itself into a strange ball (an unborn child?) in mid-air. The very (ethical) foundation of existence (and of educating, bringing up the new generation) is gone, new times are marching in, and they are like a new Iron Age, deprived of bygone warmth and depth, and tragic clarity.

Another foundation is needed, but will it be this time an individualistic one? Not exactly or not necessarily so. The Little Wolf, a lyrical protagonist (and maybe the actual authors hidden behind him, too), is rather left striving for yet another community, if only of a different kind, and it seems that he had discovered a virtual one, in the (mythologized) depths of cultural tradition and artistic canon. The fisherman fishes, the mother feeds the child, the Bull swings the rope, the girl stamps her feet, and the poet twangs the lyre. Where they are all of equal rights and merits. Where, once again, they all have a place at the same table. A true golden age, this harmony of simple existence. And it is no longer a matter of generation, but of deeper kinship. More accurately, of belonging to humanity and to culture. And, besides, an escape from these dear contemporaries, away from the *mores* of the times, from this simplicity (worse than thieving, as the saying goes) in patent-leather boots, and cocked hats – the way out is also through here.

The artist-witness would take, nonetheless, full responsibility for all the dust and groans of a generation's common fate, of the flow of history. This moral obligation is not cast off. Just as it is not cast off for this poor, dear, tragic, zany, immortal baseness of the everyday; that's why there is so much concealed pain in the grotesque parable about the family walk in the wintry public garden. All the obligations are still valid. The artist does not renounce his participation in this world, his own past and present, nor memory. Simply, his true place, his ecological niche is there.

Of eras and escapes

The late William Moritz, one of the most keen and deep animation scholars, viewed *Tale of Tales* (along with the key films of Walerian Borowczyk/Jan Lenica, Jiří Trnka and Priit Pärn) as an example of 'narrative strategies for resistance and protest'. In some generalized sense this is true, especially with certain reservations Moritz allows: 'Rather than a specific protest against government policies, the message of *Tale of Tales* urges artists to accept the burden of keeping better times alive through Art' (Moritz 1997: 41). But the heart of the matter, I believe, lays elsewhere.

In my longstanding view, the principal undertaking of the Soviet 1970s generation (that is to say, the certain part of the 'progressive' intelligentsia, except for the thin layer of dissidents and much thicker layer of those who would choose hopeless conformity if not officialdom) was a (quasi) spiritual journey 'inside themselves'. In the wake of the reaction that followed Khrushchev's 'thaw', the turbulent 1960s, comes the quest for a (new) cultural identity, realized mainly through emersion, studies and quiet experimentation. In a sense, this dim time was perhaps the most fruitful period in the late Soviet era, in which major intellectual, if not spiritual, breakthroughs were taking place, the most influential ideas were being discovered and discussed, and artistic insights were occurring.

At forty, part of the (younger) 1960s generation, and the already (older) 1970s, Norstein looks back and, with a vague anxiety and lyrical excitement, attempts to understand who we are and where we are from. There is a parallel within the boundaries of one in particular of all the film's worlds, this world of there and then: the town's outskirts, the House. How is an individual biography linked to the path of a generation? The Little Wolf swings on the Singer sewing machine and gets scared by the Zhiguli car. He remembers the bread in the stove, and does not remember, does not know how to behave on the highway . . . He is from there, from the time of *primuses* (kerosene heaters), tables under a common table-cloth, of stoves and bread. And we, where are we from?

'The film *Tale of Tales* has begun for me with the lullaby and the sun-lit long corridor,' says Norstein (1983: 118). Just so, with the subjective, with a patch of light, drawn from what has been deeply embedded in the consciousness, with a sign of one's own memory. But it is exactly the common, historic experience and memory that Norstein grapples with, in other words, that of the generation. The house, the joined tables, the Singer machine and so on, are signs of the communal historic existence. And for this, consciousness (which equals memory) is almost like a primordial myth: the poor golden age. It seemed as if he were somehow under obligation to remember (which is – to record, to embody) all this, all the building blocks of the indispensable background behind an individual life. And later to provide a nostalgic respect for and memory of the war, echelons and dance floors, and the inherent tragedy of life, the inescapable and proud poverty, ascetic simplicity, all that would penetrate into a generation's moral code. And, needless to say, he holds those things sacred, and of course understands in full, and he is quite sincere, he is even convincing, but . . . But that is not the crux of the matter.

'If only we could go back now to that poor childhood, sustained by ration cards, to that long corridor, to the sunny Sunday yard – without grown-ups' (Kitson 2005: 125).

That corridor of childhood, suspended in the ray of sunlight, what did it promise and what did it mean? The boy drifted through it – what for? Where to? Is it in the realm of fantasy, of a poetic dream? No, not exactly there, it just stepped right into that mystic golden pillar of light, drawing closer to the smell of the rooms that would live in you forever on, to all the sensation of living that would spark in subsequent recollection. But, to be more precise, this is a path into his memory of himself. That is, of the future artist, whose very core grows out of this memory alone. And that is why this corridor morphs into a light-path beaming into eternity. Or into the primordial. It is all the same here. That is why that hand-drawn world 'beyond the screen' is something more than the world of 'poetry', or 'myth'; this is the realm of ideal existence. In other worlds, it is the world of an artist. And if it is also a myth, then only in the sense of the inner mythology of an individual creativity, isomorphic to the grand mythology of Culture.

This, if you like, is the escape into oneself, but also the way out. Let-out, a variation on the life-path, is a means of overcoming historic memory, the experience of a generation, which seems to have suddenly been discovered, but oh, how gradual and hard this revelation came to be for the generation born in 1940. From the old house, which is doomed, but still alive, from the lonely widows at a dance-floor, from the family stories of front-line death letters, and troop echelons, from the cobble-stone outskirts, which became a meadow of the child's play, to the timeless, eternal, existential. 'To the shores of deserted waves' (Pushkin 1977 [1827]: 23). On those shores, where everything is natural and essential, where everything has its proper and undistorted place.

Of gaps and subtexts

Liberation from the 'household chores' of historicity, no matter how dear to the heart, understanding that there is another, different realm of existence, with a different framework of reference, and yet a different sort of community, uncovering anew primary values: that is what was underway, in this or that fashion, through the 1970s, the emancipation from the imprisonment of the here and now, of the given, while finding a new/old foundation for self-reliance of free human spirit.

Not without limitations, though. Let us be honest, with all its insights and free spirit, *Tale of Tales* is, at a certain level, a deeply 'Soviet' creature, and lies exactly within this universe. As is *The Mirror* for that matter. And, similarly, it is vulnerable, exposed to possible doubts and concerns. First of all, one can question the lacunas, look at what's absent in this kind of (historical) memory, and the manifested experience. It may easily lend itself to descriptions of the work of 'soft memory' within the 'politics of mourning', belonging to a repressed, post-catastrophic socio-cultural mentality, in the words of Russian–British cultural historian, Alexander Etkind:

> In Russia, where millions remain unburied, the repressed return as the undead. They do so in novels, films and other forms of culture that reflect, shape, and possess people's memory. The ghostly visions of Russian writers and filmmakers extend the work of mourning into those spaces that defeat more rational ways of understanding the past. Embracing the confusion of present and past [. . .] the melancholic dialectic reenactment and defamiliarisation produces a rich but puzzling imagery.
>
> ETKIND 2013: 18–19

Petrushevskaya, upon recalling all the troubles and tribulations the project had to undergo, consoles the director: but now, look, they would show it on TV at each and every World War II Victory Day[6] celebration. A somewhat dubious consolation or compliment, on consideration. Does it not really mean that the film also lends itself to a rather easy appropriation by the (new) official-propagandistic myth-making, which appears to be somehow isomorphic to the film's inner mythology, in its very vocabulary and drawn boundaries?

The most gruesome, and in that the most crucial, parts and/or imagery of the deeply troubled history, and thus memory, seem as if by definition excluded from the narrative and/or the metaphoric field – or are they, really? And that is not just a matter of plain censorship, external or internal (self-

[6] A longstanding national holiday on 9 May, growing even more in official recognition in recent years with the demise of other milestones of Soviet history, like the October Revolution anniversary day.

imposed); at least, it's not that simple and clear-cut of a case. Among numerous things over which Norstein had to struggle with Goskino (State Cinema Committee) functionaries, was, reportedly, the episode where Little Wolf, alone in the deserted courtyard, cooks potatoes on the bonfire and eats them burning-hot, ping-ponging in his hands – and in this very scene, now a textbook reference to Norstein's signature 'poetic realism', the over-zealous, or overcautious, bureaucrat's eye sees a hint of a deserter from the fronts of the Great Patriotic War . . . Today's scholar brings it up as an example of the characteristic, the 'witch-hunt taken to absurd' (Krivoulia 2002: 74). Well, we can question instead: why would it not be, in fact, implied here? After all, the motives and characters of this knotty nature, and even worse, did manage to penetrate published and released war-themed novels and live-action films of the period, with difficulty, sure, but not being completely forbidden and cut-off. Here, of course, it is a reading-in on the censors' part; however, they had sensed something with the right intuition, I'd argue. The depth of life in Norstein's 'realistic' dimension appears multilayered, akin to his cut-outs, going to the very 'elemental' foundations, constant fixtures of existence on this land and within its history or tall stories. Therefore, a particular episode or character can indeed, even if obliquely or not quite deliberately, encompass different kinds of references, including, yes, that of an eternal figure of a lost soldier, or of any lost soul, for that matter.[7]

Of the plane and the amalgamated

On visiting his native land of Maryina Roshcha with his cameramen Aleksandr Zhukovsky right before its 'once-noisy life' would 'turn into humus' by bulldozers – and as field-trip preparation for the film, Norstein notes: 'Sasha took over a hundred photographs. The departing world was taking on a fine silver amalgam' (Norstein and Yarbusova [2005] in Kitson 2005: 63). For me, this brings to mind a parallel with Joseph Brodsky's line: 'Even thieves here steal apples by scratching the amalgam first.' His metaphor underlies the portraying of 'sorry quarters' with the 'sense of abundance supported by puddles' (Brodsky 2000: 38); but its ironic complex nature needs some deciphering: not real fruits, but those displayed in the store window are being stolen in this weird manner, destroying their display from inside out. And in a larger act of deconstruction the poet is involved here, in his rather topical-declarative poem of 1969, in a way summarizing his

[7] Compare also with an intuitive comprehension of today's animation blogger: 'there's a philosophy that creeps through: unmistakably Eastern European in its conviction that we are ultimately doomed to recreate past mistakes and lying stagnant in the present. [. . .] Memory, in this telling, is less what shapes our present and more the thing that haunts us, but it is not a hopeless film' (Brayton 2016).

pre(forced) emigration period, *The End of a Beautiful Era* – well known, even in early 'samizdat' circulation and certainly later in the official Nobel laureate's publications after perestroika.

Thus, Norstein might have known it too and then had that in mind as a reference point – or maybe not. But regardless, the contrast is telling, or at least this parallel is hinting to a principal difference in the very approach of preserving the vanishing past with photographs. Moreover, by reincarnating it in bits and pieces of cutouts on the animation stand, Norstein does exactly the opposite: he fills the amalgam in an order to re-construct, or rather to re-mythologize. And he reveals almost an opposite attitude in flying over the natural sarcastic scepticism of dissident-underground poet, both in terms of ideology and aesthetics.

Artistically, *Tale of Tales* encompasses, it may seem, too much of a territory. This is really a 'mill of styles',[8] from Picasso to Chagall to Russian folk primitivism of the fifteenth century and Soviet book illustration of the 1930s, including some pretty trite, trivial and overexploited pieces as propagandistic-kitschy cliché imagery, especially in the 'war' theme. The same goes for certain filmic devices that look like unabashed borrowings from Soviet cinema of a somewhat affectedly pathetic kind (along, for instance, with visual quotations from Tarkovsky's *Mirror*), and even so for the music score, where a sweet and stale tango intertwines with Bach and Mozart. Yet, we tend to happily accept these neo-eclectics and to perceive all the unevenness as strength, not as weakness. A true son of the land and completely a product of the larger era, a self-made artistic personality, remarkably self-educated through a laborious personal journey, absorbing various influences and with the help of co-workers and a friendly circle, this artist is luckily free of snobbish limitations of refinement. He does embrace the universe of the everyday and its historical-cultural context, and his own artistic quest – as a (stylistic) whole, equalizing all the elements and harmonizing them in the thin air of a higher purpose (isomorphic in a way, to ethical move – fidelity to all facets of historical experience).

In a word, he just manages to deeply interiorize the elements of dubious 'collective memory' – the root of rather vile mass-pop mythology – melting them ultimately in the mythology of the self, and a very specific one.

Of wolves and incarnations

. . . Still, there is yet another twist, and we recognize the main theme-overtone only close to the end, although it was somehow announced virtually from

[8] A familiar expression in our critical discourse of the time; first introduced by Mikhail Iampolsky.

the very beginning: 'The film is not about that. It must be a film with a poet in the leading part, although the poet does not necessarily have to appear on the screen' (Norstein and Yarbusova 2005: 20). This is what has taken us unawares: the expectation of direct personification!

Especially in this light, the Little Wolf is a brilliant find, a stroke of genius in all its inconsistency. A chimera of the subconscious, a character with a profound folkloric origin, he is at the same time a lyrical 'ego' (albeit of a quite unconventional nature), according to the law of 'substitution' that the director himself speaks of: that is what embodies the make-believe protagonist and incarnates, channels the inner voice of the true 'author'. A liaison between the worlds, he is indeed a link between layers of being; between memory and consciousness; between a man and an artist. This is, perhaps, what the film is more about. This might be its last (or first) horizon of meaning: its core existential theme. Herein lies his exposition of values.

> He runs, wild and stern,
> Full of sound and flurry,
> On the shores of deserted waves,
> Into the rustling of the leafy oak grove . . .
>
> PUSHKIN 1977 [1827]: 23

Classics of national poetry comes to mind, and into play, not without reason. From his work with Andrey Khrzhanovsky on films after/about Pushkin, Norstein took out not only the visual stylistics of the 'mythic' part of *Tale of Tales* arising, by his own admission, at the meeting point between Picasso's graphics and Pushkin's manuscript drawings, but also something more: 'We shall speak of Pushkin as the author of his own destiny . . . We shall show him "self-directing" his creative personality' – that's how Khrzhanovsky defines the thrust of his 'animated Pushkin studies' or, referring to Yuri Lotman's words: 'the carrying over into reality the freedom of poetry' (Khrzhanovsky 1986: 160). Playing as animator, a 'drawing actor', the role of Pushkin, animating self-portraits (and self-caricatures) from the manuscripts, Norstein couldn't help but learn, hands-on, some classical lessons in artistic self-reflection (that shapes the self-standing of creative personality).[9] And the mysterious sense of harmony that permeates *Tale of Tales*, dare one say it, is that of Pushkin's origin, emanating from this universe.

---

[9] Petrushevskaya's own plays are entirely 'of this world' and fundamentally tragic; if they are at all illuminated or harmonized, it is only through paradoxical catharsis of the hole-and-corner of sorts. In the script-proposal it's not just a slip of the tongue: this concertina-like plot 'finally boiling down to one simple sound: "we live" . . .' (Norstein and Yarbusova 2005: 21). This is her grand-theme and her 'exposition of values'. As to Norstein alone, he would seem to rather boil down his implicit plot into yet different sound: we create. . . (One phrase runs through their joint script like a refrain: 'yet all the same I am a poet . . .'.)

It seems that the glowing, luminous sheet of paper, as a recurring image, as a material sign of the Word and its eternal symbol, comes from the same work as Pushkin's manuscripts. And the boldest, contrapuntal metaphor in the film, the scroll that turns into a child, a newborn, who has entered the world, is a hint at the ultimate sameness, the identity of art and reality, of creation and life; and that, too, within the broad tradition of culture, essentially resonates as Pushkin's reference.

... All that would, at last, be quite essential in the film's final turn. Whether a new human being was born, or the same full circle completed, all the same he is 'from there', it just cannot be otherwise. That's where we descend from, after all, in that incarnation of primordial memory, dwell Madonna and Child, a quotation, the seed of tradition that builds and preserves the culture. He will grow up here, at the ashes of hearth and home; but he came from there. Where else from? And the light-radiating sheet of paper, which Little Wolf steals from the Poet (not accidentally, kind of a composite portrait of many poets, from Pushkin to Mandel'štam to Gumilev, with hints of others and more), is the deed of estate. Here is inscribed the word, the genetic code of culture, inherited by the newborn and the new artist. And the Little Wolf's job is still the same: to sing this old lullaby, so that it too would be memorized ...

As for the director himself, he would rather downplay that a bit. 'I wanted to use animation to make a documentary about life, as it had passed through me,' Norstein reportedly once said, addressing the screening audience.

Maybe, however, the film is not about that either.

References

Balakirsky Katz, M. (2016). *Drawing the Iron Curtain: Jews and the Golden Age of Soviet Animation*. New Brunswick: Rutgers University Press.

Bendazzi, G. (2005), 'Yuri Norstein and *Tale of Tales*: An Animator's Journey', Animation World Network, 19 September. Available online: https://www.awn.com/animationworld/book-review-yuri-norstein-and-tale-tales-animator-s-journey (accessed 4 December 2017).

Brayton, T. (2016). 'The Wolf at the Door', Alternate Ending, 10 October. Available online: http://www.alternateending.com/2016/10/the-wolf-at-the-door.html (accessed 4 December 2017).

Brodsky, J. (2000 [1969]). 'The End of a Beautiful Era', trans. D. Rigsbee, in A. Kjellberg (ed.), *Collected Poems in English, 1972–1999*, 38–40. New York: Farrar, Straus & Giroux. Available online: https://www.poetryfoundation.org/poems/57938/the-end-of-a-beautiful-era (accessed 4 December 2017).

Etkind E. (2013). *Warped Mourning: Stories of the Undead in the Land of the Unburied*. Stanford: Stanford University Press.

Encyclopedia of the National Cinema (n.d.). http://2011.russiancinema.ru/index.php?e_dept_id=2e_movie_id=5993 (accessed 4 December 2017).

Ginzburg L. (1981). 'The Particular and the General in a Lyrical Poem' ['Chastnoe i obshchee v liricheskom stikhotvorenii'], *Issues of Literature* [*Voprosy literatury*], 10: 152–175.

Ginzburg L. (1986). 'The Meaning of Life – in the Life Itself . . .' ['Smysl zhizni – v zhisni, v nei samoi'], *Youth* [*Yunost*], 12: 95–96.

Gurevich, M. (1987). 'Stones and Cathedral ['Sobor i kamni],' Interview with Yuri Norstein', *Soviet Screen* [*Sovetskiy ekran*], 7: 16.

Gurevich, M. (1989). 'This Is not the Film about That' ['Ne ob etom film'], *Animation, Animatograph, Fantomatics* [*Multiplikatsiia, animatograf, fantomatika*], First All-Union animation festival KROK–89: 122–149.

Gurevich, M. (2014). 'Breathing a Soul into the Things Existent: Animation According to Norstein', *Animafest Zagreb, 24th World Festival of Animated Film* (Program Book), 152–154.

Gurevich, M. (2016). 'Dream of Eternity, Lullaby of Re-birth: Notes on Re-reading *Tale of Tales*', in G. Bendazzi (ed.), *Animation: A World History,* vol. 2, 309–311. London: Focal Press, Taylor & Francis.

Iampolski, M. (1987 [1982]). 'The Space of the Animated Film: Khrzhanovsky's *I Am With You Again* and Norstein's *The Tale of Tales*' ['Prostranstvo multiplikatsii: *I s vami snova* A. Kharzhanovskogo i *Skazka skazok* Y. Norsteina'], *Film Art* [*Iskusstvo kino*], 1982 (3): 84–99; in English: trans. A. Braddel, *Afterimage*, 13: 93–117.

Khrzhanovsky, A. (1986). 'Journey to Arzrum during the Campaign of 1829 by A. S. Pushkin. Projection onto the Screen' ['A. S. Pushkin. Puteshestviie v Arzrum vo vremiq pokhoda 1829 g. Proektsiia na ekran'], in A. Prokhorov, B. Raushenbach and F. Khitruk (eds), *Problems of Synthesis in Artistic Culture* [*Problemy sinteza v khudozhestvennoy kulture*,] 157–205. Moscow: Nauka Publishing.

Kitson, C. (2005). *Yuri Norstein and Tale of Tales: An Animator's Journey.* Bloomington and Indianapolis: Indiana University Press.

Krivoulia, N. (2002). *Labyrinths of Animation* [*Labirinty animatsii*]. Moscow: Graal Publishing.

Moritz, W. (1997). 'Narrative Strategies for Resistance and Protest in Eastern European Animation', in J. Pilling (ed.), *A Reader in Animation Studies*, 38–47. London: John Libbey.

Norstein, Y. (1983). 'Reality Created by the Artist' ['Realnost, sozdannaya khudozhnikom'], in S. Asenin (ed.), *The Wisdom of Make-Believe: Masters of Animation on Themselves and their Art* [*Mudrost vymysla: mastera animatsii o sebe i o svoem iskusstve*], 116–120. Moscow: Iskusstvo Publishing.

Norstein, Y. (2005). *Snow on the Grass* [*Sneg na trave*]*: Fragments of a Book, Lectures on the Art of Animation*. Moscow: VGIK.

Norstein, Y. and F. Yarbusova (2005). *Tale of Tales* [*Skazka skazok*]. Moscow: Krasnaya Ploshchad.

Pushkin, A. (1977 [1827]), *Complete Works in 10 Volumes* [*Polnoe sobranie sochinenii v 10 tomakh*], 4th edn, Leningrad: Nauka Publishing.

10

The Importance of Ranko Munitić's Work on the Zagreb School of Animation

Andrijana Ružić

Art should be poked, no matter what. Then it gladly starts to dance, colorful and human. Like every abandoned human message that cannot fade away, even if nobody listens to it. Pronounced, no matter what.

DUŠAN MAKAVEJEV, film director and screenwriter (MUNITIĆ 2012: 49)

Introduction

Ranko Munitić (Zagreb, 1943–Belgrade, 2009) was one of the most esteemed, acute and controversial Yugoslav film critics, a film theorist and a film historian, scriptwriter and excellent connoisseur of film, animated film and comics. He published his first text in May 1961 in the high-school magazine *Polet*, and his first professional review in November 1962, in the art and culture magazine *Telegram*. Munitić collaborated on several scripts for live action films and wrote a number of scripts for animated films. In the 1970s and 1980s, as a member of the Board of Directors of the ASIFA, he took part in the popularization and promotion of the Zagreb School of Animated Film[1]

[1] Both the names – Zagreb School of Animation and Zagreb School of Animated Film – are widely used.

worldwide. He was a member of juries and selection committees at around twenty international festivals of short and animated films.

Munitić organized about a hundred retrospectives of Yugoslav short films at home and abroad, most notably of the works of the Zagreb School of Animation and the Belgrade School of Documentary Films. His versatile talents and his innate curiosity brought him to write about various film genres, animation, television, comics, actors and actresses. As of today, Munitić's seventy-eight books written in Serbo-Croatian have been published in various republics of the former Yugoslavia.[2]

In his continuous efforts to foster the animation medium and thus promote its high artistic value in the former Yugoslavia, Munitić wrote about a dozen books on cinematographic animation. Half of these books were dedicated to animated films born in the 'workshop' of the Zagreb School of Animation. One of his books is regarded as a milestone in the history of Yugoslav animation studies: *Zagrebački krug crtanog filma* (Zagreb Circle of Animated Film) in four volumes, edited by Zlatko Sudović, while his *Estetika animacije* (Aesthetics of Animation) is the first published book on the aesthetics of animation in the world. In order to enrich this official biography and better understand the personality of Ranko Munitić, I thought that this short autobiographical note, where he presented the most significant facts about himself in the third person, should be added. His particular, Dalmatian sense of humour[3] and the taste for ironical syntheses are evident in these light-hearted definitions:

> Lives his childhood in Trogir, receives education in Zagreb.
> Travels around the world. Settles down in Belgrade in 1972.
> His nationality: a man from the seaside.
> His political aspirations: a film fan.
> His vocation: criticus vulgaris.
> His conviction: a nonconformist person.
> His status: a freelancer that is a marginalized person.[4]
>
> From 1961 he publishes shorter or longer essays on live action film, animated film, comics, science fiction films, on television, on acting and actors. He believes in the right of his own choice and in life until death.[5]

Munitić was deeply fascinated with the professional figures of actors and animators. In one of his books of film memories he explained why he always felt deep admiration for animators:

---

[2] http://www.rankomunitic.org/en/books (accessed 25 May 2016).
[3] Dalmatia is the coastal region of Croatia in which he was born and spent his childhood.
[4] http://www.rankomunitic.org/en/ranko (accessed 25 May 2016).
[5] http://www.rankomunitic.org/en/ranko (accessed 25 May 2016).

> I have learned from them how much the process of art creation is a difficult, long and very expensive phenomenon. Expensive from the inside, of course, in the sense of that part you have to melt and shape into the material with which you work and give to that creation, that 'artistic being', the most important thing: a 'soul'. I have learned from animators the most important fact that the things you cannot comprehend by your rationality, analysis and written diagnosis, you shouldn't even try to discover. You simply just feel the presence of a miracle and that's it. And what remains is silence and gratitude.
>
> MUNITIĆ 1997: 101–102

In my opinion Munitić had two pioneering roles in the development of the history and theory of animation in the former Yugoslavia and in his critical opus he preferred a historical and theoretical approach to the subject matter.

His first pioneering role as an animation historian was his elaboration of the first systematized history of animated film production made in Zagreb. His work consisted of archival research, and he collected, prepared and co-edited (with Zlatko Sudović) all the reviews of Yugoslav film critics contained in the first (1978), the third (1978) and the fourth volume (1986) of the book *Zagrebački krug crtanog filma*. His incessant and argumentative criticism of animated film production in the former Yugoslavia was closely linked to his historical approach to the subject matter, although he has written several books on film theory and film criticism.[6] His most important critical essays of the Zagreb School of Animation's films are to be found in the third and the fourth volume of *Zagrebački krug crtanog filma*, among the texts of other critics and journalists. These reviews did not only contain Munitić's highly subjective, independent and argumentative evaluations of the animated films, but were at the same time severe critical observations of the superficial and amateurish way that some critics and journalists wrote about Yugoslav animated film in general.[7]

Munitić's second pioneering role as an animation theoretician concerns the invention and the development of a specific method of 'morphological and comparative analysis of animated films'[8] that had not existed before in Yugoslav film theory. This particular methodological approach, developed and perfected in his continuous reviews during the 1960s, 1970s and 1980s, led him to write the very first book on the aesthetic of animation in the world, published in Belgrade in 1982.

---

[6] Munitić also wrote film theory books: *O dokumentarnom filmu* (1975); *Filmske zvrsti in žanri* (1977); *Dokumentarni film – da ili ne?* (1982) and *Filmska slika i stvarnost* (2009).

[7] Munitić edited a historical collection of Belgrade film criticism, *Beogradski filmski kritičarski krug 1–3* (2002, 2005, 2007). See also Munitić (2012).

[8] This approach appears for the first time and is thoroughly explained in Munitić (1973).

Genesis of an almanac – *Zagrebački krug crtanog filma*

Zagrebački krug crtanog filma, a pioneering attempt of historiography, is an almanac that consists of four volumes, and I shall discuss the first, the third and the fourth, in which the chronology of the development of animated film production in Zagreb is laid out.

The idea to write an almanac on this topic was born in 1965 at the Film Makers Association of Croatia (*Društvo filmskih radnika Hrvatske*). Screenwriter, scriptwriter and film director, Zlatko Sudović (1929–2017) was an editor of this book and the almanac is usually listed under his name in bibliographies. He was the initiator of the idea to collect, systematize and publish the most important articles about the films from the Zagreb School of Animation. Many important facts about Munitić's contribution to the completion of the almanac are to be found in the short acknowledgement of the first volume written by Sudović:

> This publication is the result of enormous, collective efforts,[9] but we especially would like to mention the contribution of Ranko Munitić. He was extraordinarily accurate in the research of both known and unknown data, always taking into consideration even the insignificant details that seemed unimportant in the first place. Consequently, he was convinced that in every effort, even in the ones that seemed unsuccessful, there was an origin of this phenomenon we proudly call today the Zagreb School of Animated Film.
>
> SUDOVIĆ 1 1978: 12

In the first volume of *Zagrebački krug crtanog filma*, Munitić's archival research inspired him to come up with a new chronology of animation in Zagreb, revealing some unknown facts and names in its history (for example the origins of animation in Zagreb with the pioneers Sergije Tagatz, the Maar Brothers and Viktor Rybak; Kamilo Tompa's first experiments in puppet animation in the 1930s).

This volume presents the history of Zagreb animation from 1922 to 1978 through the collection of the most significant paragraphs of the articles and reviews about animated films published in international and Yugoslav newspapers and magazines as well as interviews with Croatian and foreign animators regarding the films of the Zagreb School. The list of festival participation, the list of Yugoslav and international achievements,

[9] Animation authors and their collaborators were the key contributors to this achievement since the 'film archive in Zagreb was almost nonexistent. The biggest part of the Croatian film historical fund was irreversibly lost, destroyed or dismembered' (Sudović 1 1978: 12).

acknowledgements and awards for the studio and a filmography were compiled by Munitić, except for the biographical chapter, 'Who is who in Croatian animation'.

For the second volume of *Zagrebački krug crtanog filma* (Sudović 2 1978), Munitić selected and prepared the scripts and storyboards of fifty-two of the most significant films produced in the history of animation in Croatia before 1972: from *How Kićo Was Born* (*Kako se rodio Kićo*), directed by Dušan Vukotić and Josip Sudar, produced by Duga Film in 1952, to *Tup-tup* directed by Nedeljko Dragić, produced by Zagreb Film in 1972.

The third volume of *Zagrebački krug crtanog filma* (Sudović 3 1978) consists of the bibliography and the collection of around eighty of the most significant texts about animated films of the Zagreb School published in Yugoslav newspapers and magazines from 1951 to 1972. Zlatko Sudović edited the book, while Munitić selected the texts, which were chosen for their own value and for their informative and polemic nature. In the acknowledgement, Munitić describes the Zagreb School of animation as 'the most valuable phenomenon of Croatian and Yugoslav cinema so far', and hopes that with the proposed critical analyses 'the mysterious freshness of the films of the Zagreb School of Animation' (ibid: 17) will be discovered, appreciated and understood better. Munitić's ten critical essays are to be found in this volume; the first one 'Suprotne obale' ('Opposite Shores') was written in 1962 and the conclusive one is 'Kritička retrospektiva: Zagrebačka škola crtanog filma' ('The Critical Retrospective: Zagreb School of Animation'), written in 1972, in which he chooses and analyses ten anthological films of the Zagreb School.

The fourth volume of the almanac, *Zagrebački krug crtanog filma*, comprises the period from 1979 to 1985; Munitić figures here, again, as the only author who had been systematically collecting the material (articles, essays, short critics) over the years and selected them for the occasion. In the foreword of the fourth almanac the animator Nikola Kostelac gives credit to Munitić:

> A great number of essays and articles (in this book) are signed by Ranko Munitić who has already published numerous critical notes, analysis and several books on animated film. He accurately follows the development of animation in Yugoslavia[10] and is the only author that does so continually and with constancy. In my opinion Munitić's article 'The Tamers of Wild Drawings' is one of the best analysis of the Zagreb School of Animated Film examined from the various aspects. I find also very interesting Ranko's observations in his analysis 'Off – Zagreb, Twenty

[10] Munitić wrote a chronological overview on Yugoslav animation, *Kinematografska animacija u Jugoslaviji*, Beograd, 1979 and *Pola veka filmske animacije u Srbiji*, Beograd, 1999.

> Years of Some Valuable Animating Experience', where he explains the importance of an organizational basis necessary for the development of animation art in any country.
>
> KOSTELAC 1986: 15

This volume contains the chronology of Zagreb animation (Zagreb Film, Filmoteka 16, Adria Film and Jadran Film companies) and a filmography of the animated films produced in Croatia between 1972 and 1982. It also includes the list of festival participation, the list of Yugoslav and international achievements and awards for Zagreb Film's studio, scripts and the storyboards of twenty-one of the most significant films. The selected bibliography, along with twenty-nine critical articles and essays on the films from the Zagreb School of Animation published in Yugoslavia from 1972 until 1982, close the story of an achievement called *Zagrebački krug crtanog filma.*

Theory of animation and animation aesthetics

Munitić wrote the first book on the aesthetics of animation in the international history of animation studies, and published it in Zagreb in 1982. The genesis of this pioneering work is described by the author himself in the prologue of the book *Estetika animacije (Animation Aesthetics).*

Munitić was discontented with the absence of arguments with which Yugoslav film critics reviewed the Zagreb animated films, and above all he himself was not satisfied with his own, early, critical articles published in 1962 and 1963 (please note that Munitić started publishing film criticism in the Yugoslav reviews when he was only nineteen). He thought that there was a strong necessity to invent a new approach to the methodology problem. Munitić set up a model of animated film criticism, inspired by the method his art history professor Vera Horvat Pintarić in her lectures on the 'morphology of style' developed and perfected at the faculty of Art History at the University of Zagreb (Munitić 1997: 56–57). This new critical approach to animated film was defined as a comparative morphological analysis.

'Animation is a specific morphological system of values whose sense and significance becomes legible by an analysis of its certain shapes and morphological characteristics. In this judgment value, we should use the comparative approach (a simultaneous analysis of two or more phenomena in order to comprehend its essence) based on evident similarities and differences that define their structure' (Munitić 1973: 5). Animation's specific aesthetics, its expressive and formal condition, required a division of the elements of animation into two constitutive parts: visual and kinaesthetic. The visual elements of animation are line, surface, volume, space and colour whereas the kinaesthetic ones are animation, film shooting, editing, sound effects and film music.

Munitić's five theoretical essays published in his book, *O animaciji (On Animation)*, illustrate the suggested five types of methodological and analytical possibilities of animation analysis: 1) the analysis of a single film, 2) a comparative analysis of several films within a unique, single author's opus, 3) a comparative analysis of two different authors' opuses, two independent concepts and models of animation, 4) a comparative analysis of several films that represent an evolution process of a specific phenomenon, current or school, 5) a comparative analysis of classical and modern system values within the global framework of animation.

This new methodology of analysis and its interpretation of animated film is fully represented for the first time in Munitić's article 'Suprotne obale' (ibid: 31), published in the magazine *Filmska kultura* in 1964, where the animated artistic worlds of Vatroslav Mimica and Dušan Vukotić were examined and compared. In this morphological approach to animation, Munitić tried to get rid of 'arguments' connected with the emotional experience and to decode the film structures in their formal significance. This text generated several negative reactions from his colleagues; most of them objected that a film critic could not possibly write about animation by analysing lines and stains of colours (Munitić 1997: 58). Nevertheless Munitić continued to use his new method, proclaiming that: 'The problems of aesthetic structures are to be resolved on the level that is superior to everyday qualifications of beautiful and ugly, positive and negative, useful and useless' (Munitić 1973: 37).

In his article 'A Critical Retrospective: The Zagreb School of Animated Film?' (ibid: 36), a comparative analytical expertise of the most influential creative period of the Zagreb School from 1958 until 1968, written in May 1972, in occasion of the Seventh Festival of Animated Film in Zagreb, Munitić used very severe criteria in order to present the best ten animated masterpieces born in Zagreb Film's studio for animation. The ten analysed films were listed in chronological order: *The Avenger* (*Osvetnik)* by Dušan Vukotić, *The Inspector is Back!* (*Inspektor se vratio kući!*) by Vatroslav Mimica, *The Piece of Chagreen Leather* (*Šagrenska koža)* and *Don Quixote* (*Don Kihot*) by Vlado Kristl, *The Substitute* (*Surogat*) by Vukotić, *A Little Story* (*Mala hronika*) by Mimica, *Bećarac* by Zlatko Bourek, *The Fly* (*Muha*) by Jutriša and Marks, *Curiosity* (*Znatiželja*) by Borivoj Dovniković and *Passing Days* (*Idu dani*) by Nedeljko Dragić. The criteria for this selection were:

I. The demonstration of personal variations on the common theme of reduced, stylized animation developed by the Zagreb authors in their films.
II. Selected films as morphological (formal) and revolutionary milestones in the evolution of the Zagreb School style and their further influence on future artists.

'Criteria are not invented by the theoreticians and aesthetic critics: art itself creates them. Each new triumph elevates previously reached value limits and imposes a new dimension. Our selection here is based on the division of the results that the School offered as the final ones and in which she overcame itself in a certain moment' (Sudović 3 1978: 284), concludes Munitić in this 1972 anthological selection of the ten best films produced in Zagreb.

In the meantime, Munitić wrote three books of animation theory (*O animaciji*, published in 1973, *Dežela animiranih čudes* in 1976 and *Teorija animacije* in 1981) in which he continued to improve and polish his new method. This new and improved methodology practised throughout the years led Munitić to write his aesthetics of animated film. The book was entitled *Uvod u estetiku kinematografske animacije* (*An Introduction into the Aesthetics of Animated Film)* and was published by a synergy of Zagreb and Belgrade publishers, in 1982.

In 2007 Munitić enriched and updated this book in which he treated all the essential problems on the animation medium. The new volume, published in Belgrade, called *Estetika animacije* (*The Aesthetics of Animation*), discusses the issues about the structure of the animation medium, the techniques of animation, the evolution of its development (from classical era to computer animation). The last chapter of the book contains a curious list of the 100 most important animated films of all time (from 1892 until 2004) selected by animation historian Giannalberto Bendazzi, animator Rastko Ćirić and Ranko Munitić. Another edition of this book was published under the same title in Zagreb in 2012.

The most important of Munitić's achievement in this particular morphological approach is condensed in the following passage:

> Animation, in our understanding, demands a special approach, a specific notion and categories, instruments of analysis, it demands discovery and interpretation of its specific material and shaping of distinct analytical apparatus. It is 'against' a subjective experience rephrasing as well as applications of notions and methods of another, different area of artistic morphology.
>
> MUNITIĆ 2007: 24

Critical reviews and theory of critics

In the 1960s, 1970s and 1980s, the animators of the Zagreb School of Animation were more appreciated and highly respected abroad than at home. Ranko Munitić's friend and 'teacher', influential Hungarian and British animator and theorist, John Hallas, once said:

> I've heard that some of your films are accused of being too intellectual and dedicated to highly cultured persons. However, I disagree with this. You have to give a certain amount of time to the public to get used to your very original style that is at the same time clear and close to the people. Disney's films that do not make you think spoil today's audience: in his films, everything is explained. The key value of your films is that they make you think.
>
> SUDOVIĆ 1 1978: 156

However, the Yugoslav critics were seldom full of doubts lamenting mainly the narrative and visual contents of Zagreb animated films and describing them as hermetic, abstract and uncommunicative. One can easily discover this negative attitude by browsing the bibliography of the third and the fourth volume of *Zagrebački krug crtanog filma*. It contains the most important articles published in the Yugoslav newspapers and film magazines in the period from 1951 until 1986. Munitić was constantly encouraging Zagreb animators to continue in the affirmation of their individual and personal animated shapes of content, criticizing at the same time the film critics who wrote the pessimistic, superficial and non-argued reviews of Zagreb Film's authors (Sudović 3 1978).[11]

With his critical essays on animation issues, written for several leading Yugoslav film and art magazines (*Filmska kultura*, *Umetnost*, *Oko*), Munitić's main intention was to urge Zagreb animators to continue with their experimental and innovative way of doing animation. Munitić was convinced of the idiosyncratic artistic values of their short films and was constantly defending these values in certain so-called 'periods of crisis' that the school faced around the first years of the 1960s, according to Yugoslav cultural public opinion. He was a fervent supporter of modernism in animation and often wrote about innovative, abstract, experimental films usually ignored by other critics.[12] In his critical look at Vladimir Kristl's film *Don Quixote* (Munitić 1986: 369), written in 1973 for the art review *Umetnost*, he concludes that Kristl, 'the poet of chaos and confusion', was the only author able 'to visualize the notion and to represent with a vivid sign not a person or an object, but idea, notion or essence, or if you wish, an ideal archetype of a certain person or an object'.

His predilection for Nedeljko Dragić's formally and narratively condensed films is crystallized in the following sentences from his article published in

---

[11] See Munitić's articles 'Mladi animatori' (p. 202) or 'Između filma i publike' (p. 222).

[12] Croatian scholar Hrvoje Turković emailed me on 26 June 2016: 'I give a credit to Munitić since he was the only one that valued positively Aleksandar Srnec's important contribution in Dragutin Vunak's film *Man and the Shadow* (*Čovjek i sjena).*' In 1960 Turković reviewed the same film in his article 'Neprepoznata avangardnost crtanog filma *čovjek i sjena* i neostvaren projekt apstraktnog animiranog filma'.

the magazine *Oko* in 1974: 'The meaning of *Diary* is the medium of drawn animation itself, or to be more precise, a visualized dialogue of the author's curiosity with constitutive potentials and constructive possibilities of this animation technique. The content of *Diary* is the fundamental *animation movement* understood as an autonomous, self-sufficient dialectical and poetical value.'[13] In the article 'Moralni pobednik' ('Moral Winner'), published in *Filmska kultura* in 1979, Munitić reviewed Zdenko Gašparović's film *Satiemania* defining it as: 'a step forward from the film *Diary* (directed by Nedeljko Dragić), a kind of renaissance of Kristl's untidy and uncleaned animation magma – realized without an illusion about the necessity of external uniformity and formal harmony' (Sudović 1986: 437).

In the article 'Off-Zagreb, Dvadeset godina dragocjenog animacijskog iskustva' ('Off-Zagreb, Twenty Years of Precious Animation Experience'), written in 1979 for *Filmska kultura*, Munitić indicates the principal features and results of two-dimensional animation production in the Yugoslav studios in Ljubljana, Sarajevo, Belgrade, Novi Sad and Skopje. This text is important because it emphasizes the importance of the experience of the Zagreb School's authors in the fields of animation production, organization and research and its indirect influence on other Yugoslav animation centres (Sudović 1986: 438).

There is also another important essay, particularly significant for Munitić's predilection for modernist authors, entitled 'Napad izvana i iznutra. Joško Marušić i njegov permanentni vizualni eksperiment' (Attack from Outside and Inside. J. Marušić and his Permanent Visual Experiment), written for *Filmska kultura* in 1982. Munitić defines Marušić's creative ascent as 'one of the most important and most complex events in the eighties' since this young animator from Split 'tried and succeeded to imply in his films the change, revaluation and enrichment of all dimensions of the complex cinematographic animation organism' (ibid: 459).

Conclusion

When I started to study Munitić's reviews about the world of animated film (in which he also wrote about the importance of the role of a film critic in the Yugoslav history of animated cinema), I was amazed by the elevated measure of zeal in Munitić's stubborn and continuous intentions to determine the most appropriate definition of the term 'film critic'. In some of his texts on the topic, it is clear that he did not feel very comfortable being defined as one. I had an impression that he felt the urgent need to justify and clarify the reason for the existence of such a profession.

---

[13] Ranko Munitić, 'Nedeljko Dragić i njegov *Dnevnik*' (Sudović 1986: 372).

Here are the two most pertinent examples of definitions of the term 'criticus vulgaris' he came up with. A Belgrade film critic and theoretician, Dušan Stojanović (1927–1994), wrote one: 'A critic is someone who gives his personal opinion in public in order to give a chance to other people (who are also critics, but so called the private ones) to compare their judgments with his. Only that, nothing else' (Munitić 2012: 20).

The other definition, a quite pretentious one, is provided by a philosopher and professor of aesthetics from Sarajevo, Ivan Focht (1927–1992): 'The art criticism could not be the criticism of art, but a criticism that is art in itself' (ibid: 20). American critic John Simon defined a good critic as a person who possesses four chief virtues: intelligence, good taste, capacity of good writing and moral integrity (ibid: 16). If we agree with such a definition of a film critic, we are in a position to conclude that Munitić definitely possessed all of the above-mentioned virtues in question.

I remember the conversation I had with the animator Pavao Štalter some years ago. When we mentioned his film *The Last Station* (*Poslednja stanica*), he confided in me that he was not satisfied with the way he ended it, and added, in a low voice: 'Ranko Munitić noted the same thing and told me so.' This significant example illustrates the fact of how much the artists from the Zagreb School appreciated, asked for and accepted Munitić's opinions about their films. It couldn't be otherwise since Munitić was often with them (he was their 'companion and not just a passive observer' (Munitić 1997: 58)), in the studio or visiting festivals together. Animators accepted him as one of them and trusted only this animation fan and theorist who analysed their films in an objective, profound and serious way.

Each year the animators from the Zagreb School (and this is a fact that few people are aware of) had to earn their place again from the very beginning within the Yugoslav cinema hierarchy in spite of the fact that they had had enormous success abroad, or maybe even precisely because of that fact. The dubious and discontented minds of the Yugoslav public cultural opinion rendered the animators suspicious and acerbic towards the film critics and journalists (Sudović 1 1978: 226–227).[14]

In the introduction of the first volume of the almanac *Zagrebački krug crtanog filma*, referring to every single author of the Zagreb School, Munitić writes:

> Each author has at his disposal the key to the sense and the meaning of animation, each one of them is in possession of the poetics derived from their intimate inclinations and the infinitive opportunities of the medium that challenges him with its possibilities.
>
> SUDOVÍC 1978: 17

[14] Testimonies of Borivoj Dovniković and Zlatko Grgić.

Allow me now to invert the subject and to rewrite this phrase as follows in order to conclude this chapter: The film critic and theoretician Ranko Munitić had at his disposal the key to the sense and the meaning of animation. His poetics derived from his intimate inclination and the infinitive opportunities of the medium that challenged him with its possibilities ... The conclusion seems even better when using Munitić's own words from a television interview, found on YouTube, but no longer available on that platform: 'I am a film fan and I love writing about film.'

References

Kostelac, N. (1986). 'Foreword', in Zlatko Sudović (ed.), *Zagrebački krug crtanog filma 4*, 13–16. Zagreb: Zavod za kulturu Hrvatske.

Munitić, R. (1973). *O animaciji (ogledi)*. Beograd: Jugoslovenska kinoteka.

Munitić, R. (1975). *O dokumentarnom filmu*. Beograd, Zagreb: Institut za film, Filmoteka 16.

Munitić, R. (1977). *Filmske zvrsti in žanri*. Ljubljana: Univerzum.

Munitić, R. (1982). *Dokumentarni film – da ili ne?* Beograd: Institut za film.

Munitić, R. (1986). 'Vladimir Kristl: krotitelj suprotnosti – pjesnik haosa', in Zlatko Sudović (ed.), *Zagrebački krug crtanog filma 4*, 367–370. Zagreb: Zavod za kulturu Hrvatske.

Munitić, R. (1997). *Filmski prijatelji, autobiografski putopis*. Novi Sad, Beograd: Prometej, Jugoslovenska kinoteka.

Munitić, R., ed. (2002, 2005, 2007). *Beogradski filmski kritičarski krug 1–3*. Niš: NKC Art Press.

Munitić, R. (2007). *Estetika animacije*. Beograd: Filmski centar Srbije, Fakultet primenjenih umetnosti.

Munitić, R. (2009). *Filmska slika i stvarnost*. Beograd: Filmski centar Srbije.

Munitić, R. (2012). *Pitanje filmske kritike*. Beograd: Filmski centar Srbije.

Sudović, Z. 1, ed. (1978). *Zagrebački krug crtanog filma 1*, Zagreb: Zavod za kulturu Hrvatske, Zagreb film.[15]

Sudović, Z. 2, ed. (1978). *Zagrebački krug crtanog filma 2*. Zagreb: Zavod za kulturu Hrvatske, Zagreb film.

Sudović, Z. 3, ed. (1978). *Zagrebački krug crtanog filma 3*. Zagreb: Zavod za kulturu Hrvatske, Zagreb film.

Sudović, Z., ed. (1986). *Zagrebački krug crtanog filma 4*. Zagreb: Zavod za kulturu Hrvatske.

[15] In spite of the great contribution of Munitić to *Zagrebački krug crtanog filma*, bibliographies and libraries list it under the editor's (Sudović's) name.

Bibliography of Munitić's books on animation

Animated film: Theory

O animaciji [On Animation], Beograd, 1973.
Dežela animiranih čudes [The Land of Animated Wonders], Ljubljana, 1976.
Teorija animacije [The Theory of Animation], Beograd, 1981.
Uvod u estetiku kinematografske animacije [An Introduction to the Esthetics of Animated Film], Zagreb–Beograd, 1982.
Kritička retrospektiva Zagrebačke škole [A Critical Retrospective of the Zagreb School], Zagreb, 1982.
Estetika animacije [The Esthetics of Animated Film], Beograd, 2007.
Zbornik o animaciji [A Collection of Texts on Animated Film], Beograd, 2009.
Estetika animacije [The Esthetics of Animation], Zagreb, 2012.

Animated Film: History

Zagrebački krug crtanog filma I [The Zagreb Circle of Animated Films I], Zagreb, 1978.[16]
Zagrebački krug crtanog filma II [The Zagreb Circle of Animated Films II], Zagreb, 1978.
Zagrebački krug crtanog filma III [The Zagreb Circle of Animated Films III], Zagreb, 1978.
Kinematografska animacija u Jugoslaviji [Animated Film in Yugoslavia], Beograd, 1979.
Pet svjetskih festivala u Zagrebu [Five International Festivals in Zagreb], Zagreb, 1984.
80 filmova zagrebačke škole [80 Films of the Zagreb School], Novi Sad, 1984.
Zagrebački krug crtanog filma IV [The Zagreb Circle of Animated Films IV], Zagreb, 1986.
Pola veka animiranog filma u Srbiji [A Half-century of Animated Film in Serbia], Beograd, 1999.

[16] See previous note.

11

Animation Experienced through Music

Tomislav Simović and the Zagreb School of Animation

Irena Paulus

To match visual modernism: music with its own imaginary space

Since cartoons can, by definition, do things that we can't (or shouldn't) do, the music exaggerates and celebrates that difference. Cartoon music does more than simply add life to cartoons – it makes cartoons bigger than life.

GOLDMARK and TAYLOR 2002: xiv

This may be said for American animated shorts made in the first half of the twentieth century (the 1930s and 1940s), but is even more valid for movies made within the so-called Zagreb school of animation.[1] The first animators

[1] The term Zagreb school of animated film was associated with the group of enthusiasts who, during the 1950s, gathered in Zagreb, Croatia, in the Federal Socialist Republic of Yugoslavia. Part of the 'team' were Borivoj Dovniković, Aleksandar Marks, Zlatko Bourek, Boris Kolar, Zlatko Grgić, Vlado Kristl and Dušan Vukotić, who, alongside Vatroslav Mimica, became a leading figure of the first phase of the school's development. They were primarily interested in animation as a way of artistic expression and they found their home in the Studio for Animated Film (est. 1956), within the newly formed Zagreb Film company (est. in 1953). During the 1960s, 1970s and the beginning of the 1980s others joined them, for instance Nedeljko Dragić,

in this group developed their skills through trial and error. Their reduced animation and tendency towards avant-garde graphics, reflecting contemporary tendencies in the visual arts of the 1960s and 1970s, led them to develop their stories around the 'common man', but also around his 'horrors of existence', the 'desperation of man caught in the web of modern civilization' and especially as a critique of the 'trivialities of popular (American) culture' (Bendazzi 2016: 70). These animated films were considered the summit of world animation of the twentieth century; they

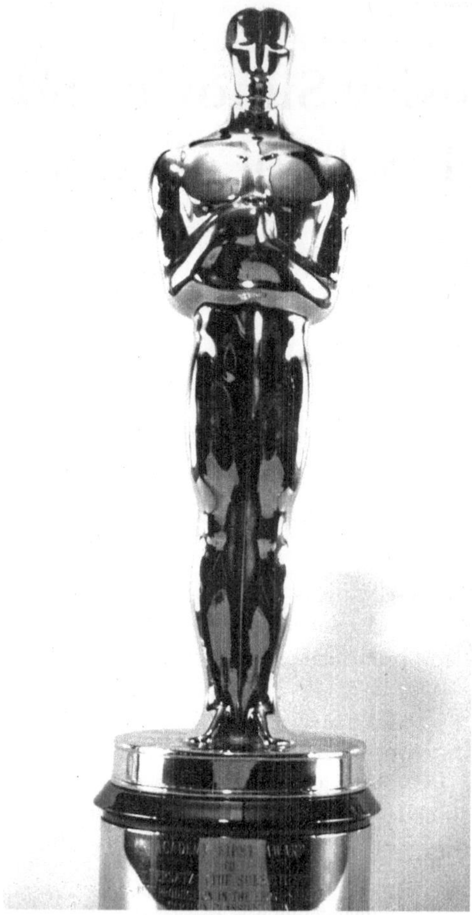

FIGURE 11.1 The Substitute's *Oscar for Best Short Subject (Cartoon). Photographer unknown. Courtesy of Croatian State Archive/Zagreb Film.*

Ante Zaninović, Vladimir Jutriša, Pavao Štalter, Zdenko Gašparović and Joško Marušić. They worked as freelancers (none of them was employed in Zagreb Film) and each of them preserved his own approach (Majcen Marinić 2014: 14).

brought numerous awards to their authors including an Oscar for *The Substitute* (*Surogat/Der Ersatz*), made in 1961 by Dušan Vukotić.[2]

Also, stylistic, aesthetic and narrative solutions of the Zagreb school of animation were adopted by the international animation scene during the 1960s and 1970s. Majcen Marinić concludes that the Zagreb school may be considered the best articulated 'modernist movement' in animated film of the era (2014: 9–10).

With regards to music, this meant the usage of modern means of expression: short motives instead of long themes, unusual chords instead of consonant ones, merging with other sounds (i.e. Foleys), accentuated rhythms, using unusual 'live' and synthetic instruments separately or altogether, using unusual techniques of playing, sometimes in conjunction with electronica and tape music. Beyond the merging of sounds, animated films from the Zagreb school allowed for the merging of different musical styles and different musical genres, enabling the usage of modern classical music, together with folk music, jazz, different types of dance music, rock, pop, etc.

It is interesting that this kind of musical writing is attributed only to one man: Tomislav Simović, often listed as Tomica Simović (1931–2014). Just like some other 'sound people' who occasionally worked in Zagreb Film (such as the creator of artificial sounds, i.e. 'Foley genius', Miljenko Dörr, and music supervisor and music editor Tea Brunšmid), Simović was considered a part of the Zagreb school team (Majcen Marinić, ibid: 11–12). Even so, some people think of Simović as the author and equal member of the Zagreb school of animation, not only because of the enormous quantity of scores he produced (175 of them just for animated films, altogether 300 film scores) but because of his careful re-thinking of animated material.[3]

Simović's music education was elementary (he went to music school where he learned to play double-bass and piano),[4] but in terms of composition, especially the composition for animated films, he was self-taught. For example, he passionately followed news about jazz, buying magazines and listening to American radio shows, notably 'World of Jazz', which was apparently recorded and sent to him by friends from the United

---

[2] *The Substitute* was the first non-US animated short to win this award.

[3] Other composers also made their contribution to animation in Zagreb. Before the school started, Duga film, the very first studio for animation in socialist Yugoslavia, hired Eduard Gloz (*The Big Meeting/Veliki miting*, 1951; *Merry Adventure/Veseli doživljaj*, 1951), Vladimir Kraus-Rajterić (*How Kićo was Born/Kako se rodio Kićo*, 1951; *The Enchanted Castle in Dudinci/Začarani dvorac u Dudincima*, 1952), Ivo Tijardović (*Revue in a Courtyard/Revija na dvorištu*, 1952) and Milutin Vandekar (*Gool!*, 1952). When Zagreb Film came to prominence, the composers were also Anđelko Klobučar, Vladimir Kraus-Rajterić and Živan Cvitković, all of whom previously worked for Dubrava film, but also Aleksandar Bubanović, Miljenko Prohaska, Igor Savin and Ozren Depolo.

[4] The Vatroslav Lisinski music school in Zagreb.

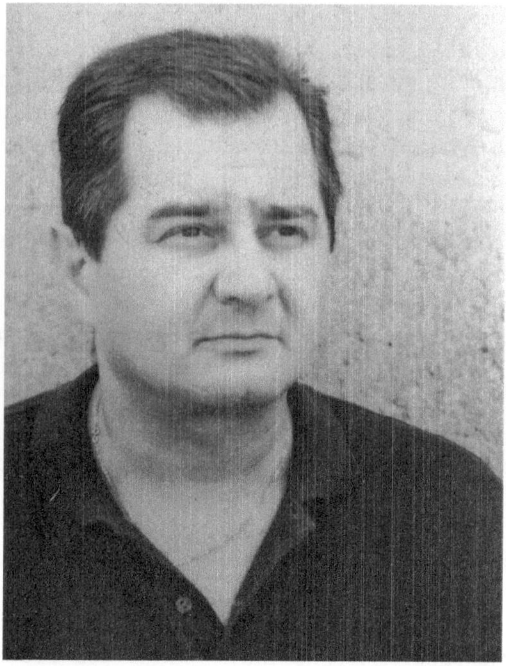

FIGURE 11.2 *Tomislav Simović. Photographer unknown. Courtesy of Jučer Danas Sutra.*

States (Paulus 2016). As a composer, he showed a considerable amount of imagination and creativity: his musical approach to films was never the same. By accommodating the style of the visuals and the story (if there was one), Simović developed his own philosophy:

> The image of animated film needs its own imaginary space that, as opposed to the music which is surrounded by silence, has its determined structure within which fluctuate variations, variability of colour, free perspectives, concentration that swiftly jumps from object to object and creates an impression of fantasy. . . Looking for similarities in visual and auditory is not the rule, and that is where, for me, writing the music for animated film starts.
>
> PAULUS 2011: 41

Musical modernism of *Diary*

Simović's description of Zagreb Film's animated visuals, which he sees as inseparable from the music, may be a description of any animated film from the Zagreb school, but is particularly close to the perception of Nedeljko

Dragić's *Diary* (*Dnevnik*, 1974). As the 'suppression of believability' and the 'creation of a continuously moving and mocking universe' (Bendazzi 2016: 265), and as extremely subjective, but also extremely vivid description of the author's impressions of his visit to the United States, Dragić's highly praised *Diary* brings music solutions that reflect the stylization and fragmentation of the visuals. It can be said that the style of music is highly modern, but it escapes any categorization. The score combines several contemporary music styles – such are serialism, pointillism and bruitism – which were, at the time, accepted by many composers, scholars and intellectuals.[5] But contemporary classical music with combined modernistic styles is not the only layer of the score. Rather, it is 'one of the many' since it merges with jazz, popular music, old medieval music, musical folklore, etc. Moreover, the perception of some parts of the score changes if listened to *with* the movie than if listened to without it – one example is a short transition with a red car and symbols of traffic where a sound, like the buzz of bees, could be interpreted as a pop melody when heard without images.

The simultaneity of musical styles and genres goes even further: at times, the sound of musical instruments becomes unrecognizable and many times we are not sure if we are listening to a sound effect, speech, or music. For example, in a middle section of *Diary*, a cat appears in a highly stylized, almost antique apartment – here, a kind of plucked, maybe string, maybe electrical, instrument is heard. This instrument sounds like a harpsichord, but could be anything else. Earlier in the film, a head turns into an egg, and there is a sound which could be identified as a wooden percussive instrument, but it has the semblance of a voice. A roughly sketched bird comes out of the egg, and it sounds like a jumping ball. At the first sight of a sketched party of business people, music babbles like human beings and acts like speech, even a quarrel, although we are aware these sounds come from blown instruments, perhaps trumpets.

Structurally, although fragmented, the film shows a tendency towards closure. In the last scene, there is a subtle music allusion: the man wears a cowboy hat and that is enough to evoke the feeling of Ennio Morricone's music from the spaghetti westerns, played on an instrument, what could be a saxophone. But, when we hear a flute again, and another flute which resonates with the technique of *flutter-tonguing*,[6] and a specific jazzy rhythm, we know that this *is* the end of the movie. We do not need to see repeated visual elements; we know because these are the musical motives that we recognize from the beginning of the film.

---

[5] The association brings forth a thought of the Zagreb Music Biennale, the International Festival of Contemporary Music, founded in 1961. Simović's composition 'Lady Frankenstein', subtitled 'Monstrumonium for mezzosoprano, 4 clarinets and piano', was performed at the Biennale in 1983.

[6] *Flutter-tonguing* or *Flatterzunge* is technique of playing wind instruments in which the performer flutters his/her tongue to make the characteristic 'Frrr-Frrr' sound.

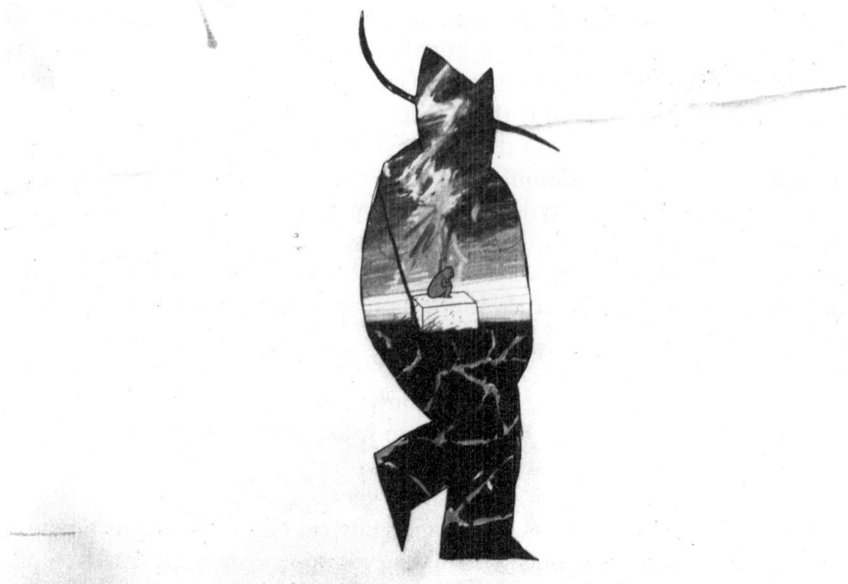

FIGURE 11.3 *A man with a cowboy hat in Dragić's* Diary. *Courtesy of Croatian State Archive/Zagreb Film.*

For the end credits of *Diary*, there are only two cards representing the crew. The first one shows two names: Nedeljko Dragić, who did the script, drawings, animation and direction; and Tomica Simović, who was the composer of the music. These two are thus perceived as the most important contributors. The second card registers other people who worked on the film, the animators, trick camera operator, and other collaborators, among them two important names related to technical handling of the music: the music supervisor Tea Brunšmid, and the sound editor Mladen Prebil.

According to the critic Željko Luketić, who profoundly studied Simović's personal material related to his film score composition – audio tapes, scores, notes, receipts, bills, etc., Simović created *Diary*'s soundtrack by recording each element of the score separately.[7] Elements of separate sounds (like acoustic drums or string instruments which were hit like drums) were layered one above the other, or were put in succession of one after the other, creating specific, harsh sounds. Moreover, Luketić emphasized that Simović approached the scoring of *Diary* as a tape music, which was considered very modern at the time. Composer manipulated sounds with the tape by using

[7] Simović recorded no less than three hours of music material, which he used to cover a mere eight minutes of the film (Paulus 2016).

montage, cut-ups, scratching, and other techniques, as well as lugging, which can be easily heard by an experienced ear. The process of composing matched the process of creating visuals: Dragić and Simović, each one within his own art, started from abstractions and impressions, and continued through to improvisations, letting them lead somewhere 'out of the box' (Paulus 2016).[8]

Professor Balthazar and Maestro Koko: scientific dance-music for an elephant

Diary fascinates with its creative visuals and musical avant-garde, which reflects not only Dragić's (negative and unpleasant) perception of the United States but different experiments and new creative approaches in contemporary classical music. Unfortunately, artistic recognition of *Diary* was mostly confined to circles of connoisseurs and animation scholars. So, if Dragić's film was highly praised,[9] what Simović did with music stayed mostly unrecognized. Nevertheless, the composer reached the broad public with another project – music for twenty-five episodes (from the total of fifty-nine) of the animated series *Professor Balthazar* (*Profesor Baltazar*).[10] Three authors of *Professor Balthazar*, Zlatko Grgić, Ante Zaninović and Boris Kolar, invited Simović only after composer Aleksandar Bubanović wrote music for the first episode, *Inventor of Shoes (Izumitelj cipela*, 1967, Zlatko Grgić). Bubanović wrote a quite neutral, jazzy musical background mostly concentrated on establishing the moderate tempo, continuity and atmosphere; Simović's task was to develop themes and to make the sound of the episodes more recognizable. He joined the crew from the second and the third episode, both made in 1969: *Flying Fabian (Leteći Fabijan*) and *Windy Tale* (*Vjetrovita priča*).[11]

---

[8] Luketić mentions an illegal bootleg edition of Simović's music for *Diary* in Mexico (published by Dolor Del Estamago – MISA under the name: 'Nedeliko Drajéc/Tomica Simović: Animation Soundtrack'). This is amusing, Luketić said, since the music for *Diary* was labelled as 'vex sound background' (Ajanović-Ajan 2008: 268) and the film itself as 'weird', 'very strange and disconcerting-and not altogether pleasant' (O n.d: *Dnevnik* (1974)). Of course, concludes Luketić, it is nice that some people in Mexico like this music, but Simović deserves better, and legal editions (Paulus 2016).

[9] In 1975 *Diary* was awarded with the Grand Prix of Animafest Zagreb, The City of Zagreb Award, Gold Medal in Chicago and Will Wehling Award in Oberhausen.

[10] The Zagreb school mostly concentrated on artistic films, but the authors were aware of the lack of animation for children. *Professor Balthazar* was their first attempt to fill the gap.

[11] *Komisija za predikatizaciju* (Committee for predicates), in charge of labelling films to decide which were going to get additional state financial support, corresponding to the committee's grade, characterized *Flying Fabian* as a 'likeable children's movie and one in a genre which was domestically quite neglected. Considering that it has some pedagogic and coloristic values, it deserves to be stimulated'. It was graded with the lowest mark C–2 (Munitić 1978: 235).

To represent Simović's musical mastery in *Professor Balthazar*, I take as an example its fourth episode, *Maestro Koko* (1969). It was the first in the series to be co-produced by the German studio Windrose-Dumont Time,[12] and also the first among many *Balthazars* (and other films of the Zagreb school) to use music as the subject of its story.

Maestro Koko is an elephant who is an appreciated musician of Balthazar-town. Every day, he plays his trunk in front of the big audience and every time he gets standing ovations. He also plays at home, to his best friend Filip (who is a human). As a reward, Filip always brings Koko his favourite meal: ice-cream. One day, Koko falls ill from eating too much ice-cream. He is cared for by his best friend, and after two weeks, gets well. But following the illness, Koko discovers that his trunk is of no use for playing any more. Completely shattered, Koko disappears. Filip is terribly worried and must ask Professor Balthazar for help. The professor invents a car and joins Filip on a journey in search of Koko. Finally, the two find him in the North Pole. Koko is happy: his newly found friends, the penguins, dance while he showers them with his trunk.

Maestro Koko is created within the already established scheme of the series: it presents the characters, develops a story and introduces the problem. The problem seems unsolvable, so the character(s) must go to Balthazar to find a solution. Parallel to the story-scheme, Simović established recognizable musical material for the main elements of the film's structure. These are: 'Music for credits', 'Music for the narrator's introduction' and 'Invention music'. Each of these musical ideas contains several smaller musical statements. 'Music for credits' contains the Zagreb Film logo (trumpet fanfare), the introduction to the theme song (made of parts of the 'Invention music') and the 'Balthazar song'.

The 'Balthazar song' is a prime example of Simović's mastery: he used the simplest musical means, i.e. a catchy melody put against the world's simplest text made of the main protagonist's name ('Bal-Bal-Balthazar'). The repetition is key here, so after a short instrumental bridge used to prepare a modulation, the melody is repeated in a new tonality that marks a second, concluding strophe. The song is simple but melodious and it became one of the most beloved children's songs in Yugoslavia. To establish the musical theme of the song, Simović used a short instrumental variant of it once again in the 'Narrator's introduction' section (the melody is played on a mouth harmonica now). This part introduces the story by using a voice-over, the voice of an invisible narrator over visuals that show Balthazar-town.

The voice-over in *Professor Balthazar* was an exception for the Zagreb school's treatment of sound, and the authors were very careful with it. They

---

[12] Winrose-Dumont Studios signed the contract with Zagreb Film after seeing *Flying Fabian* and *Windy Tale*. *Maestro Koko* was credited with the Silver Hugo Award as the most amusing film of the Chicago Festival in November of 1969 (ibid: 239).

did not use it in other projects, but felt that animation for children must have a voice-over to help the understanding of the story. Despite the possibility of jeopardizing the autonomy of the visuals, colours and animation, the result showed that these fears were needless (Munitić 1978: 229). The voice-over was used sparingly, summarizing the main points of the story, alternating its explaining function with the visuals and the music.[13]

Simović was also very careful when it came to voice-overs or using voices; he cleverly composed music around the voice-over or the dialogue. For example, he seized a musical phrase on the dominant to give space to the narrated words ('His best friend was Filip'), but at the same time he used the same dominant for an introduction of new musical material (as Koko walks to his friend's house, a steady strings passage comes at the place of background variation of Koko's theatrical musical number from the previous scene). Also, the same interval is repeated (literally or with variations) to give way to the 'dialogue',[14] or to create tension (as during a scene of Balthazar thinking about how to solve a problem).

Enjoying the story, the viewer is a little (or not at all) aware of the smallest bits of time given to the composer to express himself. But Simović was quite confident: his trick was to use the simplest musical means in the most effective ways. Repetition is one of them, the other one is the use of variations (for example in the scene were Filip searches for Koko).[15] With variations, the composer sometimes develops a musical form (theme and variations), which is often used to give a sense of, at first glance, only nonsensical musical material. Besides the theme and variations, a bipartite and tripartite form is also frequently used. For example, the form of three parts is given to the scene of Koko eating an ice-cream; and the 'Balthazar song' has two parts (two strophes conjunct by the musical bridge).

The 'Invention music' on the other hand, consists of at least four different, but recognizable components. The beginning of Invention is Balthazar thinking about a problem and searching for a solution. He walks up and down, and strings accompany him by 'jumping' up and down, by repeating and changing only one rhythmically presented interval. The goal of such a musical solution is not a mickey-mousing of Balthazar's walking, but building association with the ticking of the clock, that is, the passage of

[13] For example, in the sequence of Koko's illness, voice-over and visuals literally supplement each other. The voice-over says: 'He was ill one day. . .' and visuals show Koko in bed with Filip pouring him a cup of tea; 'second day. . .' voice-over continues and visuals show Koko still in bed with Filip bringing him medicine; 'third day. . .' and we see Filip measuring Koko's temperature, and so on.

[14] Characters in *Professor Balthazar* communicate with non-articulated sounds. Nevertheless, with the help of music and visuals, the viewer does not have a problem understanding them.

[15] Luketić claims that Simović kept tape with seventy minutes of recorded variations of 'Invention music', which lasts only a few minutes in each episode (Paulus 2016).

time. When Balthazar rethinks the problem, the 'ticking' stops shortly by reaching one tone, and then, as Balthazar runs to his 'invention machine', the downward sequence in triplets, this time played by wind instruments, bridges towards the beginning of new musical material.

Balthazar's invention machine is a strange engine composed from unusual objects (the viewer recognizes an ear, an umbrella, bulbs, buttons, some circles, laboratory instruments, etc.) and the music accordingly sounds messy and chaotic. It again associates with the ticking of the clock, and gives the feeling of a busy tempo. The musical 'mess' clears up with the sounds of a melody victoriously played by strings, associated both with Balthazar's good thinking and the invention itself.[16] A drop of 'wizardry' liquid turning into an invention (in this case, a car) is accompanied by the sound of a vibraphone, which gives it a 'magical' sound.[17]

As the merging of different types of music with different textures played in different tempi shapes the 'Invention music', its interesting sounding owes much to the instrumentation. Simović uses a small, but varied ensemble of acoustic instruments,[18] which become very important in the process of shaping and 'enlivening' the characters. Balthazar is associated with string instruments, and the elephant Koko with a bassoon. Also, Koko's trunk naturally sounds like a trumpet – so, when Koko plays his musical piece in front of the big audience it sounds like a serious, virtuoso piece of classical music composed for a trumpet solo. The piece could be comic, but Simović's understanding of animated humour goes further than that: many times, he avoided the direct illustration or literal repetition of the visuals in his sounds, considering the music an autonomous entity, approaching the story in its own way.

On the other hand, Koko's music for Filip is more entertaining and less serious, showing the warmth of the home's atmosphere. Both pieces are dance-like, the one for the big audience is played in the ternary metre of a waltz, and the one for Filip is played in the binary metre of a joyful 'domestic' dance. In Simović's mind, dance and choreography were akin to animation and animated sound. Even so, he thought of the *Professor Balthazar* series as an 'animated ballet' and treated its characters as 'figures who dance'

[16] Strings are easily associated with Balthazar because, subconsciously, they have the same positive value as Prokofiev's string melody for Peter in his orchestral illustration of children's story *Peter and the Wolf*.

[17] Simović called 'Invention music' simply 'Formula' (*Zvukopis* 2017), which partly puts into question my interpretation of this music as 'magical'.

[18] We do not know which musicians performed Simović's music. Željko Luketić shows that Simović had an orchestra called Tomica Simović's Orchestra or Tomica Simović's Ensemble. He used it to record some of his pop music (songs), jazz music and unconventional classics. On the other hand, Simović himself mentioned the existence of the Symphonic Film Orchestra of eighty members that recorded for Vukotić's feature *The Seventh Continent* (*Sedmi kontinent*, 1966; cf. Pata 2007: 28). From an informal conversation with Luketić (2016).

(Paulus 2016). Does this not ally with the thesis that 'with its incessant and lively motion, the cartoon really represents a kind of dance' (Prendergast 1992: 184) stated long ago by the composer Ingolf Dahl and restated later by the music editor Roy Prendergast?

Annoyance and overlapping in *The Man Who Had to Sing*

Another animated short of the Zagreb school, which had music as its subject, was *The Man Who Had to Sing* (*Čovjek koji je morao pjevati*, 1970). The film was directed by Milan Blažeković, Nedeljko Dragić wrote the script and Simović composed the music. Unlike the two previous films, this one needed the participation of the Foley artist, Miljenko Dörr.[19]

The Man Who Had to Sing is a tragicomic story about a man who devoted his life to singing the same melody. 'The melody is not ugly, the voice is not unpleasant, but everything is constantly the same' (O n.d: *Čovjek koji je morao pjevati*). Singing the same melody brings the hero into trouble: he is kicked out from his parents' home, from other people's homes, from his wife's home, from a madhouse, from the military, from a hotel, etc. The melody annoys everybody and, at the end, the man is killed and buried – but he doesn't stop singing, even in his grave.

The film was structured around the melody, which was cleverly forged in a classical manner: by repeating and developing the main motive (according to Midhat Ajanović-Ajan, a tune was borrowed from Frank Sinatra's repertoire).[20] Singing without words put the melody in the foreground, its triviality came more from the repetition of the same syllable 'ye' than from the melody itself.

On the other hand, the trick was to develop an overlapping of the musical materials: the foreground music (which is always the melody of the Man) and the background music (which is, actually, never in the background); or, what is in the feature film more distinct, diegetic music and non-diegetic music. For example, the Man sings his little melody simultaneously or successively with other people. He sings with children who, led by their teacher, sing their 'school' music represented with the musical major scale – do re mi fa so la ti

[19] In all the three films discussed, the sound engineer was Mladen Prebil, who often recorded sound for the Zagreb school. The tasks of the 'sound and music people' were constant in different films, but their roles were still frequently changed. Majcen Marinić (2014: 14) and Dovniković (1998: 6) emphasize that functions of director, cartoonist, animator and scriptwriter were not strictly separate in Zagreb Film. This was the key element for the emergence of auteurs, who did most of the work by themselves (directing, drawing, animating, scriptwriting).
[20] From unofficial conversation with Midhat Ajanović-Ajan in autumn 2016.

do. Two pieces – a 'ye' melody and solfege melody – contradict each other; so, the teacher tries to 'correct' the Man's singing, but does not succeed. The Man is persistent, and gets kicked out of the school.

The overlap of two different melodies, or the singing and playing of different tunes, is not uncommon in life. It happens here and there, and the tunes sometimes do not match: the result is a cacophony. Overlapping non-diegetic and diegetic music in film – which, especially in a feature film, have different qualities and different roles – can be disturbing. Diegetic/non-diegetic overlapping is common in *The Man Who Had to Sing*. The Man's singing comes simultaneously with the nursery music, with the military trumpet, with the musical background for a man who tries to adopt him as a baby, with the policeman's music, etc. This is a procedure that filmmakers of features try to avoid. But used in an animated short, it is perceived differently. Here, the Man's tune is the film's subject, and diegetic/diegetic and diegetic/non-diegetic overlapping is quite acceptable in the service of the story.

Moreover, Simović employs music and musical fragments because of their associations. There are two Croatian, well-known drinking songs – *Samoborci, piju vino z lonci* (People from Samobor drink wine from jugs), sung by a policeman with the neutral syllable '*lai*, *lai*, *lai*' (which is the way of singing the refrain of this song), and *Još ni jedan Zagorec* (Not a single man from Zagorje), which appears as an instrumental version, accompanying a group of drinkers who will later on join the overall chase of the Man. Tango as the music of love-and-jealousy in the scenes with the Man's wife, the trumpet as a signature of an army and several dramatic drum beats as an announcement of the death penalty are also recognizable musical signatures. However, besides the Man's song, there is only one genuine leitmotiv, and that is a nursery instrumental, which is played every time when the Man's Father reappears with a family picture, trying to bring the Man back home.

It seems that Simović had less work with composing the new material than with the clever assembling of well-known musical signs. Still, his music, again inspired by the film's visual solutions (such as the treatment of the mental institution as a factory) follow the main idea of the film; that is, a repetition as the main device of artistic expression.

Different faces of musical 'tapestry' in *The Substitute*

As mentioned before, Tomica Simović's creative work marked animated shorts of different authors. The most fruitful collaboration he had was with the director Dušan Vukotić who was the first to invite him into the world of animated film. Vukotić chose a composer for his animated short *Abrakadabra*

(1957) by listening to recordings of radio-shows in the record library of (today's) national Croatian Radio (Hrvatski radio). At that time Simović quite often composed for radio, and his music was very suggestive. The collaboration with Vukotić marked Simović's first experience in the field of animation and of film in general.

The composer quickly adapted to the genre, and although he composed for other genres as well (thirteen feature films, fifty-one documentaries and eleven commercials) he became irreplaceable in Zagreb Film's production of animated films.[21] He felt the pulse of each film, and his music 'behaved' and changed swiftly and promptly. At one point, it could be a quotation, at another it became a sound effect, in the third it turned into the sounds of a circus hurdy-gurdy, and in the fourth it transformed to jazz. Simović did not use only instruments, but human voice as well, either sung in an unrecognizable language, murmured or hummed.

Humming became synonymous with the famous Zagreb Film short, Dušan Vukotić's Oscar winning *The Substitute* (*Surogat*).[22] The humming was performed by Ozren Depolo, a composer and multi-instrumentalist, but the composer was Simović. The importance of the voice became vivid in the very opening credits, which was musically based on a repetition of the word *Surogat*. It is a little unintelligible, but we recognize the procedure as it is repeated in the opening of the animated serial *Professor Balthazar* as well. The only difference is that Balthazar had a melodic tune, which became famous and well-known among small and grown-up children, and *The Substitute* remained with its unintelligibility. It had only one instantly recognizable musical element – rhythm.

Rhythm becomes the latent driving force of the musical accompaniment for Vukotić's famous film. There is a rhythm of steps of the figure that 'metamorphically' changes its appearance and its form in Dragić's *Diary*. Ajanović-Ajan noted that this rhythm stays with us constantly, until the end of the film (2008: 266). The same thing happens in *The Substitute*. The rhythm binds Ozren Depolo's humming, the sound effects of pumping, digging, laughing, screaming etc, with the background musical 'tapestry'. When the tempo changes, with the banal evocation of the love-on-the-beach music, we still feel the rhythm. It becomes the basis of bonding different musical elements. It also bonds the music with the visuals in the unifying

[21] Simović also composed classical music – orchestral works, chamber works, piano pieces, songs and a ballet. His chamber music piece *Professor Balthazar's Adventures and Misadventures (Zgode i nezgode profesora Baltazara)* for wind quintet, is clearly inspired by his music for the animated series.

[22] Besides an Academy Award, *The Substitute* was awarded with First Prizes in San Francisco (1961) and in Belgrade (1962), The City of Zagreb Award (1962), Special Jury Award in Oberhausen (1962), First Prize and Audience Award in Prague (1963), Special Merit Award in Philadelphia (1971).

whole, which makes it clear that this and other films of the Zagreb school are created as the result of team work, and creative and imaginative brainstorming, not only of the author of the visuals, but also of the composer.

The merging of the voice, music and sound of bursting balloons in the opening credits announces the film's theme. By rhythmically repeating the word of the title ('Su-rro-gat-s-s-s-su-rro-gat') it takes away the verbal quality of the word, inviting the viewer into the fantastic world of animation and sound where everything is possible. The quality of the voice is clearly changed or transformed – it sounds unreal, as if the singer inhaled helium: the voice sounds as if it were a child, not an adult who is singing. All this, combined with the sounds of numerous balloons, which occasionally burst, announces the playful story about reality/fantasy in which everything, even the main character, is fragile and artificial. In this playing with different layers of the film's meaning, the voice becomes extremely important.[23]

It is interesting to remember how careful Zagreb Film animators were when it came to voice-over in *Professor Balthazar*. In *The Substitute*, the voice of the Man from the beach equals his leisure. Words are not important, even a melody is not important. But the atmosphere is. When the story is becoming complicated, with the sexy Girl who rejects the Man to be with a more handsome Surfer, the Man's humming disappears. He is angry and must act, for humming does not have a place in this part of the story. When things clear up, when the Surfer and the Girl are 'dead' (deflated, that is), he continues to hum as if nothing has happened.[24]

Humming is part of the musical composition. So, at times, it is replaced by a musical instrument (for example, when the Man hides the Shark behind his back, his humming is replaced by whistling, which is performed by a flute). Part of the composition has sound effects, too. For example, music seizes or stops for a moment for the sound of pumping up objects to be heard. Music also replaces sound effects by imitating them (for example, the sound of throwing things out of the bag is done by orchestral instruments). This makes the merging of all the sounds complete; they are all equally important in realization and in function.

At first, the music sounds neutral, with only the task of creating atmosphere. But a closer listening reveals numerous details that participate

[23] Animated films often reverse the sound hierarchy of a feature film. Instead of the hierarchy (1) dialogue/monologue (i.e. voice), (2) sounds and effects, (3) music, they put the music, which acts for and substitutes other components, in the foreground. So it becomes: (1) music, (2) effects, (3) voice. *The Substitute* has its own hierarchy: (1) music, (2) unintelligible humming (i.e. Voice), (3) effects. In this hierarchy, music and voice are almost of equal importance.

[24] Girl sounds like a small animal (by transformation of human voice). This draws attention to the treatment of female characters in Vukotić's films (the female android in SF feature *Visitors from the Arkana Galaxy/Gosti iz galaksije*, 1981 vacuums and prepares food, outshining The Writer's girlfriend).

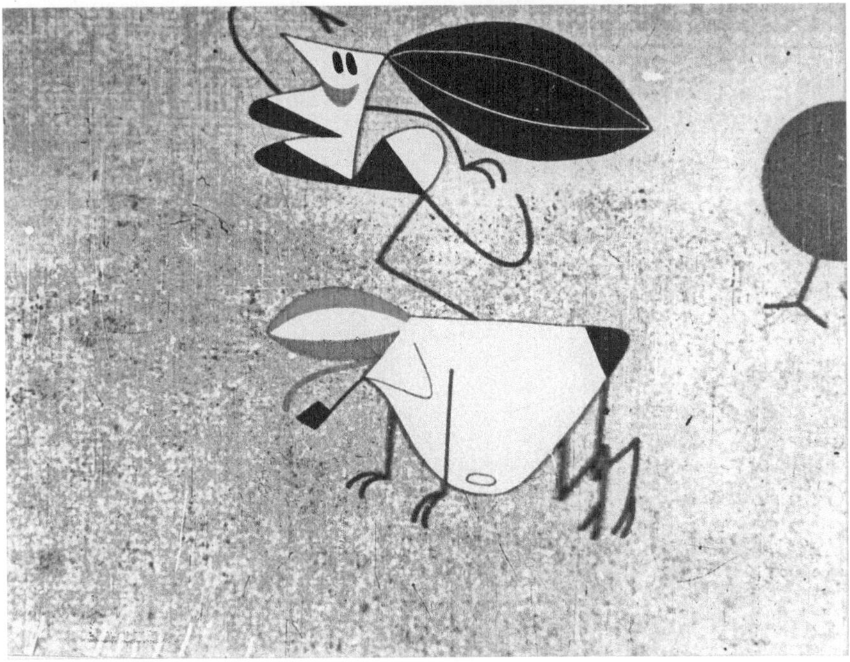

FIGURE 11.4 *The Girl and the Man in* The Substitute. *Courtesy of Croatian State Archive/Zagreb Film.*

in 'catching' the movement, following and subtly commenting on the story. The 'jazzy background' or musical 'tapestry' turns out to be very active in using a small ensemble of instruments (there are lots of *pizzicatos*, *tenutos*, the sudden movements of a bow, *staccatos* and short notes of a trumpet and other instruments) in colouring the story, creating its tempo and even its thematic characterization.

Some motives and short themes are used as leitmotivs (for example, the 'sexy' saxophone melody signals the Girl; a short theme from the opening credits signals the Man). To be sure in his musical comments, on the verge of parody, Simović deliberately used clichés: low tones for the Shark, increasing the volume of the music in a rhythmically accentuated scene of the Man walking in anger; a 'Hollywood' melody on trumpet to show how the Surfer fell in love with the Girl; dramatic *tremolo* to increase suspense when the Surfer decides to commit suicide by pulling out a cork (an amusing gag here is combing his hair first, so he can die handsome). We also receive an appropriate musical commentary of the scene, that is, a variation of the Third movement of Chopin's Piano Sonata No. 2 in B flat minor, better known as the Funeral March.

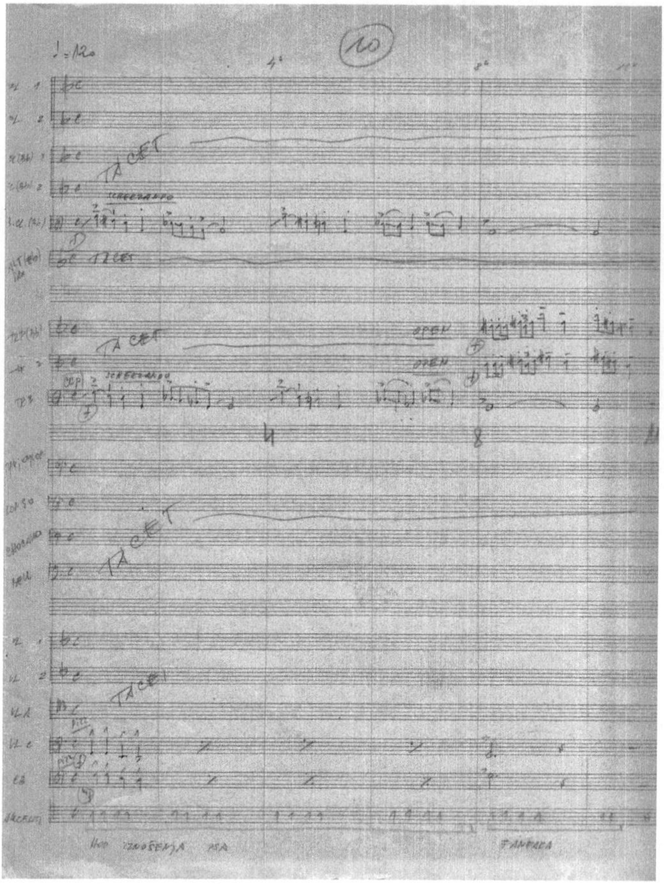

FIGURE 11.5 *A page from* The Substitute's *score. Composer's manuscript. Courtesy of Jučer Danas Sutra.*

Music of great diversity

The role of music in feature and animated films – at least at first glance – is similar: it sets a mood, it 'fills' gaps, helps the narrative and creates the continuity of the story. But – 'the genre's debt to music as both a dynamic and illustrative device went far deeper' (Cooke 2008: 287). Firstly, music reinforces the movement and makes animation believable. Secondly, music participates in the characterization of animated beings, which could be humans (such as an old and smart professor-scientist), but also plants (like flowers), animals (like an elephant), different objects (such as balloons) and other non-living things. Music uses its emotional suggestiveness to humanize the artificially created imagery. According to Cooke, 'cartoons were often distinguished by a satisfying symbiosis of music and image as mutually supportive dynamic entities, each contributing equally to a compelling choreography of sound and movement' (ibid.).

Cooke learned these characteristics of the music of animated films by studying music written by Carl Stalling of Warner Brothers, Scott Bradley of MGM and Frank Churchill, Paul Smith and Leigh Harline of Walt Disney Studio. The same could be said for the music of Tomislav Simović, the 'good spirit' of Zagreb Film, who gained his musical education only partly through official institutions.[25] He stayed true to his love of music and, after involving himself with the Studio for animated films in Zagreb Film, displayed extremely wide interests, musical curiosity and openness to all artistic possibilities. He shared a life with the authors of the Zagreb school; only they knew that the 'secret' and obligatory 'ingredient' of their animated shorts was Simović's music.

In light of contemporary thinking about music and animation, Simović, who discovered this world on his own, started from a standpoint that all music genres are of equal value. 'The layman asks if the music is merry or sad, the educated musician asks if it is good or bad,' he wrote (1989: 49). Simović did not like the separation of music genres, and that was an attitude of great importance for his compositions, especially for his music for animated films.[26]

The composer understood well that film music 'doesn't act independently but always as an applied complement to the image' (1985: 27) and he felt within his heart that music for an animated movie can do much more. Finding the need to explore both mediums and possibilities of their conjunction, Simović worked out his scores to the smallest detail. The result wasn't, however, fragmented (as one might think), but he always managed to put logic in the otherwise strangely chaotic score of diverse music materials. By doing so, he composed (with ease, one might say, considering the number of his scores) in the manner of Scott Bradley who also succeeded in conjuncting different musical styles and genres in the logical and likeable scores for the *Tom & Jerry* serial.

The 'fragmented' approach opened to all musical genres, swift changes and rapid thinking marked both Bradley's and Simović's music. It is not known if Simović knew the music of Scott Bradley but, considering the eagerness with which he followed musical events of all types (especially in contemporary classical music and jazz), it is possible that he was well acquainted with Bradley's style. He was encouraged to develop his own

---

[25] Eventually, Simović studied History of Fine Arts.

[26] Simović's only long-play record published during his lifetime, *Zagrebačke impresije* (*Impressions of Zagreb*, Jugoton LSY–66081 1979), was not accepted well, because of its unusual mixture of genres – jazz, film music, electronica and easy listening music (Paulus 2016).

approach, although the parallels of the two composers go as far as entering the world of – in a feature film widely avoided – twelve-tone technique.[27]

With its visuals, which were highly innovative and different even in terms of the Zagreb school of animation, Dragić's *Diary* could be approached with a dodecaphonic score as well. But Simović decided to go with something different, so he applied the notion that any sound can be music, and that any technique, even non-musical ones, could be used as a composing tool. *Diary*'s musical score becomes an example of musical montage, a technique that Simović occasionally used in other, less modernistic films, even in the children's series *Professor Balthazar*.[28]

In *Professor Balthazar*, Simović's most popular score, the composer's diversity comes to the foreground. Namely, he was not only the composer of 'highbrow' classical music, but he composed, arranged and orchestrated popular songs for the most prominent music performers in former Yugoslavia.[29] To compose a catchy song for a children's animated movie was not a problem at all, but he was smart enough to make it simple and accessible to all of the public. On the other hand, Simović's most famous film in terms of awards was *The Substitute*.[30] This animated short not only uses numerous musical details but also successfully hides them within threads of highly profound and diverse musical textures.

We can discuss Simović's use of themes and hidden use of leitmotivs, we can say much about clichés and musical quotations, and their usage as recognizable archetypes (as in *The Man Who Had to Sing* and other shorts as well) or pay attention to the relationship of the film's narration and

---

[27] Bradley occasionally used twelve-tone technique in *Tom & Jerry* shorts (for example, *Puttin' on the Dog*, 1944 and *The Cat that Hated People*, 1948). Simović partly used the technique in Marušić's *Fisheye* (*Riblje oko*, 1980), which he described in the magazine of new music, *Ear* (1985: 27) and *Filmska kultura* (Film Culture, p. 52) in detail. Simović used an unusual ensemble of seven cellos and divided the score into two parts. The first part (for the idyllic landscape of a fishing village) is tonal and played *arco* exclusively – the composer used variations of a popular old song *To My Green Pine Tree (Boru moj zeleni)* as a main theme. The second part, which shows a massacre, is atonal, and Simović used twelve-tone technique. Cellos play only *pizzicato* in this segment.

[28] 'The cutting desk can also be an "instrument for composing" if we record, having analysed the image and using any technique, several differently designed musical elements, intervals, melodies, rhythms, moods without getting outside the meaningful framework of the image. Parallel editing of these independent "passages" produces very interesting and rich layers which often have a more active effect within the rational sphere of the image than the pre-planned content of the score' (Simović 1985).

[29] Arsen Dedić, Tereza Kesovija, Višnja Korbar, vocal group 4M and other Yugoslav popular music stars owe much to Simović's arranging and orchestrating skills (Paulus 2016).

[30] For *The Substitute* Simović was credited with an Honorary Award for music at the Festival in Belgrade. During his life, he received many awards, including the Award at the International Festival of Animated Films in Ottawa (1980) and the ASIFA's Life-achievement Award (2011) presented to him in Zagreb.

musical form, or call forth incredibly imaginative orchestration. . . Instead, I decide to follow Simović. Still aiming to show how great (and neglected) a composer he was, I quote his words:

> The film image provides an inexhaustible source of material, but the composer knows only of the measurable tone and arranged tonal system, melody and harmony and their rhythmic manifestations. . . . There is no objective approach to the experience of music, for only that which has been objectivised – the work itself – is important. The extent to which music and the moving image become an artistic unity depends on the artists themselves.
>
> SUDOVIĆ 1985: 27

References

Ajanović-Ajan, M. (2008). *Karikatura i pokret*. Zagreb: Hrvatski filmski savez.

Bendazzi, G. (2016). *Animation – A World History 2: The Birth of A Style – The Three Markets*. Boca Raton: CRC Press, Taylor & Francis Group.

Cooke, M. (2008). *A History of Film Music*. Cambridge, New York: Cambridge University Press.

Dovniković, B. (1998). 'Jedna velika karijera – Dušan Vukotić Vud'. *Hrvatski filmski ljetopis*, 4 (15): 3–14.

Goldmark, D. and Y. Taylor, eds (2002). *The Cartoon Music Book*, Chicago: A Cappella Books.

Majcen Marinić, M. (2014). *Prema novoj animaciji*. Zagreb: Meandarmedia.

Munitić, R. (1978). 'Zagreb film 1956–1972', in Zlatko Sudović (ed.), *Zagrebački krug crtanog filma*, 1, 129–266. Zagreb: Zavod za kulturu Hrvatske, Zagreb film.

O: 'Čovjek koji je morao pjevati', *Zagreb film katalog*. Available online: http://www.zagrebfilm.hr/katalog_film_detail.asp?sif=99 (accessed 1 May 2016)

O: 'Dnevnik (1974)', *Internet Movie Database*. Available online: http://www.imdb.com/title/tt0475949/ (accessed 21 March 2017).

Pata, N., ed. (2007). *Dušan Vukotić Vud*. Zagreb: Korpus, Zagreb film.

Paulus, I. (2002). *Glazba s ekrana*. Zagreb: Hrvatsko muzikološko društvo, Hrvatski filmski savez.

Paulus, I. (2011). 'Disney kao uzor?/Disney as a Role Model?', in Marta Kiš and Karla Pudar, (eds), trans. Z. Šaškin, *Surogat stvarnosti/Surrogat of Reality*, 38–49. Zagreb: Hrvatsko društvo likovnih umjetnika.

Paulus, I. (2016). Interview with Željko Luketić, raw material recorded for the purposes of the radio show *Zvukopis*.

Prendergast, R. M. (1992). *Film Music – a Neglected Art*. New York, London: W. W. Norton & Company.

Simović, T. (1985). 'Animation and Auditory Surrealism'. *Ear*, 9 (5)/10 (1): 27.

Simović, T. (1989). 'Kompozitor i "živa" slika'. *Filmska kultura*, 178: 48–53.

Zvukopis (2017). Croatian National Radio 3, 15 February 2017, 10.30 pm.

mentalism, are all forth incredibly ... with significance. Instead, I decided to follow a movie. Still unique to show how great a neglected a composer he was. I quote his words:

> The film music provides are merely the source of material, but the composer knows only of the melody, tone and treated tonal system—melody and harmony and their rhythmic manifestations. ... There is no objective approach to the experience of music for only that which has been objectivised—the work itself—is important. The extent to which music and the moving image become an artistic unity depends on the artists themselves.
>
> [illegible]

References

12

The Puppet as Not-Puppet

The Notion of Puppet as 'Human in Theatrical Performance' in the Works of Barry Purves (the Case of *Screen Play*)

Fatemeh Hosseini-Shakib

A puppet is a puppet is a puppet. Wrong! Puppets subjugated to the purposes of animation are distinctly different from all other figurative forms and figurations that are generally subsumed under this term. Animation puppets are not hand puppets or marionettes – although they are to be looked at, they are not decorative . . . Their life expectancy is usually quite brief because they are commodities . . . It is not the puppet that counts, but its cinematic image.

BASGIER 2003: 97

The puppet animations of Barry Purves show his continued passion and fascination with theatre, opera and other forms of live performance. Purves's puppets in films such as *Next* (1989), *Screen Play* (1992), *Rigolletto* (1993),

Achilles (1995), *Gilbert and Sullivan: The Very Models* (1998) and *Tchaikovsky* (2011) take the place of human actors in acting out different methods of live performances. Most prominently, puppets are used in place of actors in theatre and opera performances, and go beyond any straightforward notion of puppet films as represented and experienced by Purves' predecessors. This approach to puppets is also dissimilar to the great amount of puppet animation series Purves has made for children as an animator or director, and to the animal characters in his film *Hamilton Mattress* (2001).

Purves as a master puppet animator has worked for animation companies since 1978. However, in his independent films, he emerges as an *auteur* of a canon of films with certain themes and iconographic elements that give a central weight and significance to his puppets to the point of 'blurring the line between actors and puppets' (Purves 2008: 20).

This chapter explores the very diverse and innovative notion of puppets in Purves's films, epitomized in his *Screen Play*, as the main case study in relation to the idea of 'puppet realism'. The terms 'realism' and 'puppet realism' should be used with caution as in this chapter I do not take them to mean the precise copying of life, or a filmic record of it, which is often understood as 'realistic-ness' or 'lifelikeness'. Purves himself is not at all inclined to understand realism in the sense of simulating physical reality point by point. Reminiscing about his childhood memories of Snow White in *Snow White and the Seven Dwarfs* (1937), he compares the exaggerated stretched and squashed movement of the dwarves with those of Snow White's 'realistic timing and movements', and concludes that the illusion created by the dwarves' exaggerated actions were much more truthful and credible than Snow White's rotoscoped performance based on 'real' action. Her movements to his judgement had 'an unsettling effect' that he would rather not watch (ibid.).

As for Purves, the animator must be a performer *per se*, and thus his puppets, whatever role they play, must be credible:

> There are moments in my films when the animation becomes invisible. I'm pleased that the audience doesn't always notice my black figures in *Screen Play*, nor do they assume that the lifeless characters in *Next* or *Achilles* are actually animated. These characters seem to fall with appropriate weight and react naturally to being picked up . . . I like the irony of putting as much effort into making something look lifeless as it does to make it look full of life.
>
> PURVES 2008: 251

Yet, Purves's puppets hardly fit into traditional definitions. A closer examination of Purves's independent works shows that, for Purves, the concept of puppet is neither heir to how it is understood in puppet theatre or 'a cartoonish character' that has made its way into the three-dimensional realm; these are rather 'humans in a theatrical performance'. From the very realistically rendered and animated puppets in *Next*, *Screen Play*, *Achilles* and *Tchaikovsky* to more stylized ones in *Rigolletto* and *Gilbert and Sullivan: The Very Models*, all of Purves's puppets represent human 'actors/actresses' rather than cartoon characters or anthropomorphized animals, and they 'perform' as if on a live 'theatrical' stage, 'filmed' by a camera of sorts. It is as if all that is possible in the stop-motion technique serves Purves to simulate and create his own version of theatre, albeit in animation. This is Purves's imagined, rather extravagant theatre, made possible by stop-motion technique and his elaborate skill of animating and performing with detail and precision.

By concentrating on the works mentioned, and *Screen Play* as the key exemplar of such an unconventional and rather unusual approach to puppet realism in animation, this chapter theorizes on the question of realism in 3D puppet animation. The approach to realism in these films, it is argued, makes the question of realism peculiar to a disparate notion of realism rather than what is generally understood as realism – or 'hyper realism' as termed by Wells (1998) – in commercial and mainstream works of companies such as Disney, Pixar, DreamWorks, Aardman and Laika.[1]

The scarcity of studies on non-CG 3D animation and puppet animation as an immensely varied form with a historical cannon of endless styles, techniques and approaches, makes any discussion of 3D animation hard to launch. The puppet films of Barry Purves, especially his *Screen Play* made in 1992, provide a rich site to study a type of realism that may contribute to the debates surrounding realism in puppet animation. Furthermore, the centrality of the notion of the puppet as a non-puppet or as 'human beings in performance' in Purves's work creates a space to discuss a typology of puppets in puppet animation in general.

The problem of realism

Historically, it seems that the question of realism in animation was raised, and mostly rejected, even in the early days of cinema theory, by the few cinema theorists who bothered to discuss animation at all. The 2D 'animated cartoon' was the dominant form of animation emerging from the United States in the early decades of animation history, therefore animation was considered to be synonymous with this technique. Based on the now infamous thesis of 'medium specificity', early theories considered animation (2D cartoons) as belonging to the realm of fantasy and imagination, as opposed

---

[1] In fact, this is part of a much bigger query researched in my PhD thesis on realism in stop-motion animation (Hosseini-Shakib 2009).

to live-action cinema, which was vastly believed to be the 'right' and 'appropriate' field for physical reality and its image. Hence, debates over realism, if any, rotate solely around the legitimacy or otherwise of animation to represent physical reality the way live-action cinema does. In this, the whole argument is reduced and reshaped as prescribing certain missions for animation, in contrast to the missions prescribed to live-action cinema.

Yet, realism as an essential style of imaging, drawing or painting has not been as much of a problem for animation as it has when compared with the use of live-action cinema's narrative tools and cinematic language. Thus, the problem with realism in animation may be epitomized in Disney features, beginning with *Snow White and the Seven Dwarfs* (David Hand, 1937).[2] Other films in one way or another follow their recipe in adopting the codes and conventions of mainstream cinematic narrative. Siegfried Kracauer, an important theorist of realism in cinema, expresses his belief in the unsuitability of animation to represent what he called 'camera reality', and offers a fundamental definition of animation as 'life reproduced in drawings' (Kracauer 1960: 90). He criticizes the realist tendencies that ultimately dominated Disney's aesthetics: 'There is a growing tendency towards camera-reality in his [Disney's] later full-length films. Peopled with the counterparts of real landscape and real human beings, they are not so much "drawings brought to life as life reproduced in drawings"' (Ibid).

In *Understanding Animation* (1998) Paul Wells asserts that in contrast to all Disney's attempts at realism, animation is a medium that inherently 'resists' realism, and instead creates several styles that are 'about realism'. Wells, himself deeply dissatisfied with the prevalence of Disney's style causing other forms to be overshadowed, still suggests Disney realism to be the 'yardstick' to measure other types of realism in animation (Wells 1998: 25). What Wells means by hyper-realism is the particular manner by which a somehow exaggerated account of physical reality is mixed with cartoon conventions and cinematic language to shape a form that does not exactly resemble reality, although it is not far from it, and at times goes beyond the possibilities of physical reality using the cartoon's unique vocabulary of exaggeration and fantasy.

The anti-realist stances towards animation can be summarized as the problematic relationship between live-action and animation, specifically, the copying of 'cinematic-realism' of live-action by animated feature films of Disney and the like.[3] Elsewhere I have tried to demonstrate how 3D animation, like many non-mainstream or non-cartoon forms of

---

[2] Hand was the supervising director of the film.

[3] In comparison, the many forms and styles of 3D animation have suffered a total lack of attention and theorizing by scholars. Thus, Wells's and other studies of realism in animation, while seminal in the study of 2D Disneyesque realism, may not always assist in understanding 3D and puppet animation.

animation, has been subject to two types of discrimination. First, in defining animation, only the most common form of animation is taken into consideration (the 2D, drawn cartoon). Thus, most of the issues and debates surrounding the aesthetics of animation, including realism, disregard the specific properties of other forms of animation. Second, a historically medium-specific perspective, based on such a generic definition of animation, prescribes missions for all types of animation, even if the basic specific traits of the common form are absent. It has been suggested that these 'generic' definitions of animation create more problems than they solve. Thus, I would argue that any discussion of realism in animation should take into account the associated technique and medium, as each raises specific issues and has different relationships with the representation of reality (cf. Hosseini-Shakib 2009: 8–16).

On the other hand, while 2D animation, especially in its cartoon form, has suffered hostilities and controversial disputes in relation to realism (Wells 1998; Rowley 2005; Moritz 1988; John Hallas and Joy Bachelor cited in Hoffer 1981: 3), 3D and stop-motion animation have enjoyed a much easier relationship with it. From inception, the form not only existed along with 2D 'animated drawings' and later cartoons,[4] but was also widely used for special effects integrated into live-action footage to represent imaginary creatures, worlds and events without much difficulty (Frierson 1994: 98). Historically, however, it is possible to distinguish the beginning of early forms of 2D and 3D animation; whereas Emil Reynaud's *Théâtre optique* was developed in 1888, and thus technically 2D animation was possible before the invention of the cinematographic camera, it seems 3D and puppet animation could not have existed without the availability of such a registering mechanism. Interestingly enough, in his short, but thought-provoking essay, 'In the Puppets' Universe', Thomas Basgier stresses the historical bond between cinema and puppet animation, and its distinction from the generic rules of 'animation': 'in all pre-cinematographic techniques, such as the optical theatre, which often must be simultaneously categorised as the forerunners of the animation technique, puppets rarely play a role' (Basgier 2003: 99).

Donald Crafton goes even further to emphasize the centrality of the stop-motion technique in the process of the maturation of animation from its very early forms. Believing that the stop-motion, 'trick film' genre initiated by George Méliès was the main source that created more developed forms of animation in the first place, he proposes that 'the iconography and primitive narrative structure of animation' developed from those films that began to use the stop-motion substitution technique (Crafton 1993: 9). Here I would like to stress again that theorizing 3D animation (including

[4] In *Dreams of Toyland* (Arthur Melbourne Cooper, 1908), officially considered the first puppet film, toys come to life in a boy's dream (Bendazzi 1994: 40).

realism) requires one to go deeper than generic definitions of animation and realism, and pay attention to the ontological differences it has with that of 2D animation. Basgier is among the few who draw attention to the affinities between puppet animation and film, and seek definitions for 3D animation outside 'the two-dimensional primacy'[5] (ibid.).

Apart from that, perhaps Michael Frierson's influential study of American clay animation is amongst the very few works so far dedicated to studying the form. The question of realism is explicitly raised here, in a chapter examining the works of Will Vinton and his realistic approach to the clay puppets. There are also a few other books that have recently emerged, most prominently Barry Purves's *Stop Motion: Passion, Process and Performance* (2008), in which he shares a broad range of experience, insights, observations and more, regarding his masterful expertise in puppet animation. Yet, on the side of theorizing and critically thinking about animation, the works dealing with 3D animation remain few, and the literature meagre.

In *Clay Animation: American Highlights 1908 to the Present* (1994), Michael Frierson proposes that, compared with 2D drawn animation, the nature of 3D animation, including clay, is more real. He thinks that 'clay metamorphoses – and at some level, any dimensionally animated action – benefit from the fundamental realism of cinema by being an objective recording of raw, three-dimensional reality' (Frierson 1994: 24). He believes that three aspects of cinematic realism, as shown by Bazin, can be found in 3D animation: 'objectivity', meaning that the images are photographs of tangible objects in the real world; 'rawness', meaning that the medium is transparent or 'effaced', much as in live-action where the viewer is unaware of the medium involved; and 'three-dimensionality', meaning that the real and three-dimensional space is shown as it is, using the same process as live-action cinematography (ibid.).

Thus, this somewhat 'relaxed' attitude to the adoption of cinematic realism by puppet, and most 3D animation may be a result of the medium's cinematic ontology. The cinematographic shots in puppet animation are, after all, real instead of drawn. The *innate* cinematographic quality of puppet, and in fact all 3D animation, elevates the camera's status from a simple inscription tool, as in 2D drawn animation, to a vehicle with narrative ability. Summarizing the previous discussion, it may be suggested that the question of realism in the world of puppet and clay animation falls into three major areas:

I. *Ontological*: spatial realism (realism of spaces, objects, textures and the material world).

---

[5] 'It was film itself – through representation of moving objects in space and later through camera movements in space – that was able to create a perceptual experience that suddenly became a perceptual need' (Crafton 1993: 99).

II. *Technical*: cinematic realism (the use of cinematographic techniques of inscribing and constituting shots as well as established codes of narration peculiar to conventional narrative cinema).[6]

III. *Character*: puppet realism (specific to puppet animation).

While it is easy to imagine the realism of spaces and objects and how a cinematic recording of them would be comparable to a cinematic recording of real spaces and objects in live-action film, the 'puppet realism' is not that apparent or, for that matter, considered as 'inherent' in the form. As Wells has argued with regard to 2D animation, the animation generally 'resists realism', which in the case of puppets means the realistic movement and action of puppets is not so 'natural' or expected from them, and is thus the main challenge in achieving a realistic animation. Perhaps that is why all traditional theoreticians of puppet animation regard realistic puppets as unacceptable or, in their medium specific polemics, not suitable to the medium.

The multifarious concept of 'puppet' in puppet animation, being part of the grand neglect, has also hardly been studied or taken seriously except for a few scattered references and general discussions. One of the few scholarly discussions of puppets in puppet animation comes from Bruce Holman's (1975) rather old book, where, putting Kracauer's medium-specificity hat on, he asserts: 'a work should be in keeping with the medium in which it is executed' (Holman 1975: 75), stressing the 'puppet-ness' of puppets in animation. In this, he suggests that the characteristics, parameters and limitations of the medium should be defined in order to achieve a form that coheres with its medium. His position is evidently based on a definition of puppet animation as heir to puppet theatre and thus distinct from both live-action and cartoon characters. Praising the puppets of Jiří Trnka, the Czechoslovakian master of puppet animation as the highest point ever achieved in this form (by that time), Holman emphasizes the centrality of puppets in the medium:

> a puppet is a puppet. He is neither a live actor nor a cartoon film character, he is unique and in a medium of his own. To force puppet animation beyond its point of efficiency by over-elaboration, or to waste carelessly the potentials which puppets possess, are violations of the principle of poetic economy . . . The integrity of the medium, however, should be respected. Style and presentation, and much of the form itself may change, but there should not be conscious attempt to imitate other media, nor should puppet animation be forced into a configuration to which it does not lend itself.
>
> HOLMAN 1975: 76

---

[6] The terms *ontological* and *technical* are borrowed from Kracauer's categorization of 'cinematic properties' (Kracauer 1960: 41).

In a similar line of argument, Bendazzi's pro-Trnka stance sees puppet animation, especially in the former Czechoslovakia, as the 'natural' continuation of the country's grand tradition of the puppet theatre.[7]

Bendazzi opposed 'non-Trnka' puppet animation, in which puppets were engineered to resemble real human beings with lip-synch and non-theatrical performances. Trnka puppets have solid painted faces, with unblinking eyes and fixed mouths. Bendazzi regarded them as 'true' puppets that did not try to look human (Bendazzi 1994: 170). He sees in Trnka's method a notion of puppet faces as theatrical masks 'to be fixed and sacred as masks' (ibid.). Bendazzi, thus, regards these puppets, 'characterised by contained expressions and almost stately movements' as superior to those of artists who 'loosened' their puppets' joints, making them look like 'animated drawings' (ibid. stresses are mine). In this, importantly, he implies that lip-synch and facial expression are attributes of 2D drawn cartoon.

Thomas Basgier's account of puppets, too, draws attention to the two poles of live-action and 2D cartoon characters, and places puppets somewhere in between, in a hybrid universe and a 'medium of reconciliation between two diverging worlds, that of the great cinema of people and the no less moving cinema of puppets' (Basgier 2003: 102).

Indeed, the history of animation to the current day shows that so many anti-realist theories have not stopped 2D cartoon animation from becoming increasingly and madly obsessed with cinematic realism, they have not succeeded in persuading animation puppets to stay in their 'puppet-ness' realm. In reality, puppets in puppet animation, pre- and post Trnka, have certainly represented different approaches to animation and the puppet itself. Sometimes the puppets are closer to 2D cartoon characters, from George Pal's wooden puppets, to Tim Burton's puppet animations (e.g. *The Nightmare before Christmas*; Henry Selick, 1993 and *Corpse Bride*, Tim Burton, Mike Johnson, 2005), or Nick Park's Wallace and Gromit films. Sometimes they remind us of live-action actors, such as clay puppets in Derek Hayes and Stanislav Sokolov's *Miracle Maker* (2000), or more recently the most live-action-esque puppet animation *Anomalisa* by Charlie Kaufman (co-directed with Duke Johnson, 2015).

There are also puppets that may represent 'real' people in everyday situations, closer to observational documentaries, films such as *Going Equipped* (Peter Lord, 1989) and many others made in the earlier phases of Aardman Studio's works. From storybook puppets in Soviet and East European puppet animations, to Will Vinton's clay puppets in *Rip Van Winkle* (1978) and *The Adventures of Mark Twain* (1985), towards the

[7] 'There is no visible hiatus between puppet theatre and animated puppet cinema. The transition occurred smoothly, with those minimal changes required by the new means of communication but with the same acting and scene design' (Bendazzi 1994: 168).

novel use of puppets in surreal works such as Jiří Barta's *The Vanished World of Gloves* (1982) and *Toys in the Attic* (2012), to the original experiments such as *Madame Tutli-Putli* (2007) by Chris Lavis and Maciek Szczerbowski, there is a broad range of animation puppets, none of them adhering to the old-fashioned puppet-ness dominion. As technical advancements have allowed for more experiments and explorations into the possibilities of puppet animation, a rather exciting range of approaches to puppet animation has been erupting onto the scene, from Aardman's *The Pirates! Band of Misfits* (Peter Lord, Jeff Newitt, 2012) to Laika's uses of optical printers in *Boxtrolls* (Graham Annable, Anthony Stacchi, 2014) and *Kubo and the Two Strings* (Travis Knight, 2016), in which Laika created the most precise shape, texture and movement on their ground-breaking puppets, mixing very different sets of capabilities and features, although still remaining in the realm of cartoon characters. Hence, there is a range of imaginable approaches and styles of puppet animation and puppets that all fall outside the narrow lines of traditional puppets pertaining to puppet theatre.

In contrast, for instance, in Trnka's grand work *A Midsummer's Night Dream* (1959) taken from the Shakespeare play, he used the codes and conventions of cinematic narrative of his time without any prejudice or problem in order to narrate his story (in a feature length running time); yet his puppets were obviously 'puppety' both in appearance and action. His world consists of puppets with static faces with the obviously doll-like clothes and hair, animated by the innocently, uncomplicated movements of puppets (instead of mocking elegant human-like theatre performances) and surrounded by simple storybook settings instead of accomplished realistic ones.

Cataloguing animation puppets

To the witness of the history of the medium, puppets in puppet animation are typically 'cinematic or cartoon characters' of various sorts rather than limited puppet-puppets, and in many instances, they may be a 'hybrid'. The idea of the puppet in animation as a means of copying or simulating different sorts of characters, or importantly 'create a filmic image' of it, makes them go far and beyond what puppets stand for in traditional or even modern puppet theatre. As indicated earlier, a stop-motion puppet may be animated to look like and move as freely as a real human, or as limited as any type of puppet in puppet theatre (string puppets, glove puppets, *bunraku* puppets), as they may be animated to look like lifeless 'dolls'. The list is endless, including whatever can be termed and named as a puppet in animation, such as shapeless objects or non-human things that may play the role of their own object-ness (a fork being a fork) or put on the symbolic mask of humans, such as anthropomorphized vegetables representing the main characters in *Oedipus* (Jason Wishnow, 2004). Last, but not least, we have a long history of the anthropomorphism of animal puppets, which was common as early as the works of Starevich in the *Tale of the Fox* (co-directed with Irene Starevich, 1939) or more recently in Anderson's *Fantastic Mr Fox* (2009).

From reviewing all these, I come to a general conclusion that the puppets, as important parts of the stop-motion animation technique, may be regarded as 'means of simulating effects' of different sorts, including real or fictional characters. After all, the whole history of special effects in live-action cinema is full of diverse uses of stop-motion as 'real' or fantasy creatures and events, disguised and integrated into the fictional world of the film.

Thus, for the sake of clarification and based on the very distinction Holman and Bendazzi have made, I have 'artificially' categorized puppets in three groups, each representing a central point within an imagined 'spectrum' with 'puppets as puppets' at the mid-point, and cartoon puppets and human-like puppets at the polar extremes.[8] Puppets as puppets stand somewhere between a resemblance to human beings, with different degrees of abstraction and restrictions of movement, and some symbolic behaviour taken from reality; their representation is based on an imaginary account of characters from fairy-tales, epic stories, children's stories and so on. Cartoon puppets are copies of 2D cartoon characters; as such they are mainly comic and exaggerated renditions of puppets in cartoon contexts, but they are also parodic copies of live-action actors. Puppets as human beings are neutral 'simulations' of real human beings, with no exaggeration and minimum abstraction; as such, they may be copies of an imaginary live-action reference (fictional or otherwise).

Obviously, puppets may be hybrids that fall into more than one category, and different types of puppet may coexist in a single film, so this is only a general method of locating puppets in different films.[9] The categories are shown in Table 12.1.

In my study of Aardman animated documentaries I had concentrated on puppets as human beings in real-life situations, in films that were mainly simulations of observational live-action documentaries or interviews. In the case of Barry Purves's works and especially his *Screen Play*, I am going to concentrate on the concept of 'puppets as humans in performance'.

---

[8] The last two may be seen as hybrid forms that draw their formal properties from both reality and fantasy.

[9] The categories are not comprehensive: the possibility of imagining or creating other kinds of puppet cannot be dismissed. In object animation, for example, objects may represent people in an abstract or surreal way.

TABLE 12.1 Puppet Categories

Puppet as cartoon character	Puppet as puppet	Puppet as human being
Puppets in 3D cartoon animations and anthropomorphized puppets, e.g. *The Nightmare Before Christmas*, *Wallace and Gromit, Boxtrolls*, *Corpse Bride* . . .	Traditional puppets in puppet animation such as in many Trnka films or Russian/German/ British puppet animation. Puppets as a continuation of puppet theatre in fairy tales, children's stories, so on.	Many Aardman early shorts, including *On Probation*, *Down and Out*, *Confessions* . . ., *Going Equipped* . . . Purves's puppets in films such as *Screen Play*, *Tchaikovsky* and *Rigoletto.* The Puppets in *Anomalisa.*

Barry Purves's puppets: the puppet as a human being in theatrical performance

The works of Barry Purves under question, especially his *Screen Play*, compared with those of Trnka's are useful examples to demonstrate the two very distinct approaches to puppets. It is possible to generally claim that Barry Purves is obsessed, not with the puppet theatre, but with many diverse forms of live theatre performances for adults, which he borrows from and re-enacts with animated puppets. Performance, then, for Purves seems to be a central theme and preoccupation and puppets are not puppets, but humans who are performing theatrical roles. The notion of theatrical performance and a camera (Purves's eyes) to capture it seems to be all that Purves has attempted to do in these films.

In *Screen Play* a still camera is apparently 'filming' objectively, and without intruding, a Japanese Kabuki theatre on a rotating stage in which all the codes and conventions of such a theatre performance are observed – this is of course until the end of the faked 'happy ending' when another story unfolds, something I will come to later. In *Rigolletto*, on the other hand, an elegant and sophisticated opera is performed by very life-like, opera-esque puppet/singers and a moving camera, as a sophisticatedly directed televisual recording 'presents' the performance to the viewer. In *Next*, Shakespeare himself is auditioning, for Peter Hall, performing and interacting with a life-sized ragdoll and much more. In *Gilbert and Sullivan*, a very much naturalistic puppet of Richard D'Oyly Carte interacts with two stylized, almost caricature-like, puppets of Gilbert and Sullivan with huge paper heads. Yet, all three are regarded as human actors performing on a stage with a dark background, while lip-synched, with dances and performances similar to such actors in real-life operas, though with a very complicated *mise-en-scène* that may not be easily performed in live opera. In *Achilles*, again an imaginary theatre is performed by very realistic, nude puppets in an empty dark background, and a half-circle stage.[10] *Screen Play* uses no conspicuous cinematic device for its narration as the camera stays motionless during the main Kabuki theatre segment, but in the three other films the camera and a cinematic language is used to add to the variety and possibilities of narration. Yet in all these films the puppets are animated to resemble real human actors and actresses that are sometimes going far beyond their human abilities by the magical tricks of animation.

The film *Screen Play* importantly consists of two sections. The first, longer one is the Kabuki theatre in which the love story between Takako and Nayoki is told and seen from a non-moving camera in which all that moves is within a non-moving, non-changing frame. No cuts, no zooms in or out, or any camera movements are used here. The story is narrated by the codes and conventions of an imaginary Kabuki theatre and a Japanese traditional tale (of course accompanied by Purves's use of specific animation tricks that are not normally possible in a live theatre such as morphing the puppets' heads repeatedly). The second part, however, when the traditional happy ending arrives and the spectator expects to see the final credits, is where a 'cinematic' (to be read as: alternative) account of the story begins, ending in disaster. Instead of living happily ever after, the two lovers are killed in a bloody battle with the jealous, revenging Samurai, their bodies and love nest destroyed in fire.

I will initially concentrate and analyse the first theatrical part, investigating the concept of the puppet in it. Later I will come to the second part, the real end of the film and the way the notion of puppet, as opposed to the first part and in line with the rest of the narrative style, changes to provide a completely different world of puppet film.

The Kabuki theatre section

In this section, which comprises most of the film's running time and may be considered the main story, and a finished work in its own right, what we may call puppets includes a host of different things. The narrator who uses sign language and stands in front of the scene, the puppets of the main

---

[10] It is worth mentioning that complex camera work is at play in all these films except *Screen Play* in its main part, which needs specific attention. Purves exploits an eclectic, unconventional operation of camera shots and movements to create a narrative that is not similar to any conventional cinematic narrative.

characters (Takako, Nayoki, Takako's father and her old maid), and the all-black-clad puppeteers/actors. On one level all these puppets stand for human beings who play different roles; the narrator and the rest of the main characters play human roles in a conventional stylized manner as expected in a Kabuki theatre, while the black-clad 'actors/actresses' are 'invisible' humans who move and play 'puppets' such as the suitors' masks – which are in fact bunraku puppets – butterflies, and hold or play objects that are shown to represent certain things symbolically or directly in the play according to the story's requirements. At times these all-black humans/puppets are seen to sit idle and motionless to 'wait for their turn' to start, next to the colourful setting and 'acting' puppets. They also change the setting by moving the sliding wooden screens or doors; hold, open up and close umbrellas and paper fans to form shapes and patterns; and move strips of blue cloth to suggest the ocean, or shoot red-coloured strips to imply blood and killing, and so forth.

The human characters, on the other hand, move and act according to the codes of action in this kind of play. They all wear a kind of heavy make-up or rigid masks, without any motion, facial expression or change in their faces. All the changes in the mood and body expressions are achieved either by change in the style and methods of lighting or setting, or by the symbolic acts and movements of their body. The occasional change of the narrator's face to Takako's father or her old maid, and vice versa, although achieved by tricks of stop-motion replacement, are acted out and visible in front of the camera/audience. As such, there is always an act or move that resembles a change of facial mask to change a character in the play. The body language and movements of the narrator, while playing the narrator role and standing outside the story space, is much more 'realistic' and expressive in natural ways compared with those human characters 'inside' the story.

All the real events, human feelings and natural phenomena have a symbolic equivalent in the vocabulary of the Kabuki theatre. Things such as blood, ocean water, shooting, strapping, escape, distress, anger, love-making and so forth are demonstrated by objects and symbols, and symbolic moves such as colours and coloured cloth (the drowning of the father), round screens or paper fans on which a 'shadow play' shows part of the story (such as the lovebirds escaping). Some narration, especially in relation to change of scenes, space and time, is also made by the use of traditional paintings on narrow screens (suggesting a garden, an island, a boat), or the rotating stage itself that brings a new location/time to the story. Thus, the spatio-temporal narration is a non-realist, non-linear one in which time lapses and places merge (e.g. showing the nightmares of Takako in the same space as she is sitting and thinking).

Such is the role and place of puppets in the first part, humans directly or invisibly acting out their roles in a supposedly 'live' theatre performance. Nothing in the settings and design of the puppets reminds us of puppets and their puppetness. Even the overtly self-reflexive method of representation in which all scene changes happen 'in front of the viewer' – which is of course only a simulation of such a thing – does not stop the 'real viewer' (us) accepting that these animation characters are there to represent and be understood as human actors and actresses, and not puppets.

These three species of human beings in the performance (the narrator, main human characters and black-clad players) serve different functions within the play as if it were a real live performance, and as for the animated version, they serve different functions all accomplished by a generic term: 'puppet'. A similar argument applies to *Rigolletto* in which all 'puppets' stand for professional opera singers, in an impressively luxurious high-brow opera setting and a breath taking complex 'filming' of the event with complicated camera movements, the use of various cameras and a masterful combination of each in representing the opera, which is assumed to be going on on the stage. This is the essence of a kind of approach to puppets that has never been so fully developed or consciously exploited to simulate a bottom up, imaginary performance as if it were happening in real life. Such conventionality of any representation of puppet and puppet animation can only be fully understood if we begin to compare and contrast the first/main section with the second in which an alternative ending is suggested.

The cinematic ending section

Motivated by revenge and robbed of his bride, the raging Samurai, who was only referred to as a painting on the paper screen so far, tears away the painting and emerges from behind, beginning a new story.

Stylistically, the 'puppet' of the Samurai does not resemble any of the previous puppets we have seen before. He is a furious evil warrior whose mask resembles more of a monster than a human. From this scene onwards, the cinematic editing, change of shot angles and framing, along with the uses of close-ups, fast editing, and action style begins. The narrator, whose 'real' identity as the old wise man we know by now – turns back with surprise at the scene of the raging Samurai; almost as fast, he is beheaded by Samurai's sword, his head rolls on the ground, gushing 'real' liquid blood and smearing the scene. In all that follows a fast editing of close shots shows us the event, the Samurai opens the door of the lovers' bedroom where the two are resting together, follows them as they escape, and Nayouki is hit by the sword. Then we see the backyard of a 'real' traditional Japanese house in which the Samurai and Takaki fight, as he is also killed by his own sword in a 'heroic' act from Takaki. Later she kills herself (we don't see her suicide as the camera moves upwards showing the house in flames and the two lovers 'dead' bodies resting next to each other). In this part of the film, of course, there is no narration.

The linear time, the conventions of spatio-temporal continuity editing, the uses of certain editing styles, the use of a suspense element and the final scene (the superimposition of the house in flames, Takako's bloody head resting next to Nayuki's, the finalizing music as the camera moves upwards towards blue sky and a branch of a Japanese cherry tree) may be seen as that in a Samurai genre film. Unlike the theatre version, here puppets are seen from a much closer distance and from different camera angles and sizes where the details of red liquid (blood) and the synthetic doll-like hair and clothes can be seen, and the settings are realistic. Stressing the 'reality' of the three-dimensional space with a roaming camera, and more importantly a visible change in the 'acting' of puppets as now they are human beings, as film characters, divides the two worlds totally apart. The puppets still have no facial expressions or lip-synching, yet the codes of action and narration makes them totally different puppets, moving them even farther from any notion of being puppets.

Purves cleverly plays with our knowledge of the conventions of performance, of cinema, theatre and television, and shows us two different stories with apparently the same puppets. Barry Purves takes his puppets and us wherever he wants as his puppets can play Kabuki theatre, sing and play in opera, and play in films. He gets what he gets from his puppets, as his puppets can allude to all or some of the listed functions. The last scene, when, with a gradual zoom out we are taken to see 'behind the scene', the setting and a photo of Purves in a newspaper among the rest of the stuff, and the filmmaker's hand ticking a box and closing the file of yet another successful film, once again refers to the old notion of the creator and the creation, a notion much loved by Purves, the master of puppets.

References

Basgier, Th. (2003). 'In the Puppet's Universe', in *Fantoche Catalogue*, Baden: The Fantoche International Animation Film Festival: 96–103.

Bendazzi, G. (1994). *Cartoons: One Hundred Years of Cinema Animation*. London: John Libbey & Company Ltd.

Crafton, D. (1993). *Before Mickey: The Animated Film*. Chicago; London: University of Chicago Press.

Frierson, M. (1994). *Clay Animation: American Highlights 1908 to the Present*. New York; Toronto: Twayne; Maxwell Macmillan International; Maxwell Macmillan Canada.

Hoffer, Th. (1981). *Animation: A Reference Guide*. Westport, Connecticut: Greenwood Press.

Holman, B. (1975). *Puppet Animation in the Cinema: History and Technique*. South Brunswick; New York; London: Barnes; Tantivy Press.

Hosseini-Shakib, F. (2009). *The Hybrid Nature of Realism in the Aardman Studio's Early Animated Shorts*, PhD Thesis, Farnham: University for The Creative Arts@Farnham, UK.

Kracauer, S. (1960). *Theory of Film: The Redemption of the Physical Reality*. London: Oxford University Press (reprinted in 1976).

Moritz, W. (1988). 'Some Observations on Non-Objective and Non-Linear Animation', in John Canemaker (ed.) *Storytelling in Animation: The Art of the Animated Image, Volume* 2, 21–32. Los Angeles: American Film Institute.

Purves, B. (2008). *Stop Motion: Passion, Process and Performance*. Oxford; Burlington: Elsevier (Focal Press).

Rowley, S. (2005). 'Life Reproduced in Drawings: Preliminary Comments upon Realism in Animation', *Animation Journal*, 13: 65–85.

Wells, P. (1998). *Understanding Animation*. London: Routledge.

13

Subversive Machinery

DIY Method in the Work of Julian Antonisz

Michał Bobrowski

In 1984, *The Polish Film Chronicles* (*Polska Kronika Filmowa*, PKF, 1944–1994), a weekly propaganda newsreel used by the Communist government for communicating with Polish moviegoers, dedicated two-and-a-half minutes to an extravagant filmmaker and inventor, Julian Józef 'Antonisz' Antoniszczak. Antonisz was known to a significant number of Polish viewers mostly as the author of oddball 'non-camera' films, drawn, painted, scratched, burned or woodcut-printed directly on 35 mm tape. For a film historian, this piece of archive footage may prove interesting or even inspiring, for it provides a peculiar example of dialogue between two antithetical discourses functioning within a very specific public debate that remained strictly controlled and regulated, but at the same time constantly renegotiated, dynamized by inner tensions and polemics. By the time the issue PKF 84/27[1] was released, Antonisz had completed six episodes of his

[1] 'The issue featuring the material on Antonisz is built upon a model structure of *The Polish Film Chronicles*. It contained six items: two mandatory propaganda news pieces focused on successes of Polish industry (a segment praising brimstone mine in Tarnobrzeg) and friendship between socialist countries (meeting of Polish and East German youth); two critical items which are meant to create an impression of objectivity (insufficient production of socks in Aleksandrów Łódzki, and a case of bad management in the town of Pińczów); two entertaining items (a clip from Opole pop music festival and a segment devoted to Antonisz titled *An Unconventional Artist/Artysta niekonwencjonalny*). Such formula ensured the newsreels a genuine popularity among viewers who usually approached them with a mixture of true fondness and distrustful 'we all know it's just a game' attitude' (Cieślinski 2006).

parody of *The Polish Film Chronicles*. This subversive and surprisingly independent 'do it yourself' project, titled boldly *Polish Non-Camera Chronicles* (*Polska Kronika Non-camerowa*; twelve episodes, produced between 1981 and 1987), twisted the audiovisual language of the political apparatus into an aleatoric carnival with the use of the limited means of expression of hand-made animation.

Let us try to put ourselves in the situation of an average citizen in 1984, post-martial law People's Republic of Poland who occasionally visits cinema theatres and therefore is well acquainted with the poetics of the official newsreels, who may have recently watched one of Antonisz's offbeat mockeries of the late socialist realism and who is suddenly presented with the two coupled together in an imposed coexistence[2] (the newsreel PKF 84/27 contains excerpts from Antonisz's films). The characteristically pulsating opening credits of *Non-Camera Chronicles*, which are accompanied by an insanely joyful musical theme deriding the hyper-optimism of the socialist propaganda, are recaptured by the Big Brother's eyes and ears embodied by the camera lens and microphone of *The Polish Film Chronicles*. There is something perverse about this specific case of a 'film within a film' situation. Together with the 1984 viewer, we have a chance to observe how the official channel, representing the voice of the dominant ideology, transmits its own distorted reflection in order to lighten its image with the use of the familiarizing quality of self-irony. We witness the process of the seizure of the discourse – an attempt to tame, takeover and assimilate the subversive content. But quickly we are happy to realize that Antonisz is ready to take up the game. The artist willingly employs the strategy of a court jester in order to disarm the omnipotent ideology infusing every semantic layer of the transmission.

After the short introduction read by one of the most recognizable speakers of *The Chronicles*, Jerzy Rosołowski (the *Non-Camera Chronicles* are cordially referred to as 'the competition'), the voice is granted to the artist himself. Hidden behind his misleading reputation of a harmless eccentric, Antonisz seems to feel quite comfortable in this ambiguous situation. With a sarcastically pleasant tone of voice he expresses a sort of a gratitude for the economic insufficiency of the socialist system, which he describes as an artistically stimulating factor. 'Difficult conditions temper and allow for the new techniques to appear,' he claims, 'I couldn't live in the West, I'd just die out of lack of possibilities for creative fulfillment. Out there everything can be bought in shops, there's no need for self-constructed cars or tractors.' Antonisz's voice-over commentary is illustrated by shots taken in his studio. Surrounded by numerous technical inventions constructed by the artist

[2] A full cinema screening included an obligatory issue of *The Polish Film Chronicles*, a short film (often animated) and a feature film. Antonisz's work was distributed mostly in bigger cities.

himself, he resembles a clichéd 'bonkers' professor from a science-fiction B movie.

Described by Marcin Giżycki as the most colourful figure among filmmakers gathered around the Animated Film Studio in Krakow (Giżycki and Zmudziński 2008: 64), Antonisz was a multi-talented creator, an experimental filmmaker, musician, visual artist and a skilled innovator who did not differentiate between art and technology, and who nonchalantly rejected everything that constituted commonly understood professionalism in filmmaking. His vivid artistic personality by far exceeded the grey and gloomy reality of Communist Poland and yet his work epitomizes certain features of this particular era. The economics of shortage, to use the widespread term coined by János Kornai (1980), compelled people living in the territories of the Warsaw Pact to act like the two popular characters from the Czechoslovak puppet series *Pat and Mat* (started under the title . . . *A je to!*), who exercise technical creativity in reusing, recycling or substituting rationed products. Developing know-how accordingly to the DIY principle was not a lifestyle choice, but a matter of a practical necessity. These hard circumstances made Antonisz's art flourish. His witty comment in the *Chronicles* was essentially honest – the director was perfectly aware that his work undeniably benefited from the situation of constant deficit, and as an artist he remained intrinsically connected with the reality of the authoritarian country just as the *Non-Camera Newsreels* were inseparably coupled with *The Polish Film Chronicles*.

Bakhtinian inspirations

When writing about Antonisz for the international readers one has to take into account a colossal disproportion in the reception of his work in Poland and abroad. Although in his lifetime Antonisz's films had gained significant success at European festivals (especially in Oberhausen[3]), nowadays they are rarely screened outside Poland. Regretfully, Antonisz's output is known almost exclusively to the small group of experts on the niche genre of direct on tape animation and remains virtually forgotten by the international

[3] Antonisz had a special relationship with the Oberhausen Festival, where his films were frequently awarded. The Grand Prix in 1984 was granted for the sixth issue of the *Non-Camera Chronicles*, which included a segment titled *Weg zum Nachbarn*, dedicated to the festival itself. The festival in Oberhausen appears also in Antonisz's animated reportage from his trip to West Germany, titled *Oberhausen, Duisburg, Düsseldorf, Dortmund, Hannover, a Non-camera Report on the Federal Republic of Germany* (*Oberhausen, Duisburg, Düsseldorf, Dortmund, Hannover, Hamburg, czyli non-camerowy reportaż po Republice Federalnej Niemiec*, 1985).

circuits of animation aficionados.[4] On the other hand, in Poland Antonisz's artistic persona was surrounded by an aura of a legendary *enfant terrible* of the Polish School of Animation, and he was well appreciated for his ability to reconcile the experimental approach to film with the absurd mockery of socialist reality, appealing primitivism and insane burlesque. Highly praised in his lifetime, also after the artist's premature death in 1987, his films have never lost their acclaim. Antonisz's artistic method based on radical dedication to a DIY philosophy, his anarchistic sense of humour, as well as his natural distrust of authorities and mainstream doctrines earned him high esteem among young people identifying themselves with the punk movement, which in Poland was especially vital in the 1980s.

In the next decade Antonisz's status as a cult classic was cemented. His films circulated on blurry VHS copies and were frequently presented on underground 'unofficial' night screenings in bars and clubs. In the new millennium, the interest in Antonisz has even increased and his animations, especially *How a Sausage Dog Works* (*Jak działa jamniczek*, 1971) became hits of online video channels.

The spontaneous popularity of Antonisz's shorts among film buffs has been skilfully accelerated by professional curators and film culture promoters. Especially in recent years the director's name has appeared on posters advertising a whole range of events, from large undertakings like the retrospective of all his thirty-six films presented in 2007 by one of Poland's major film festivals Era Nowe Horyzonty, to local, intimate screenings in squats like the ones organized by the independent distributor, Animation Across Borders. It is necessary to mention the dedication of the artist's daughters, Malwina and Sabina Antoniszczak, in preserving the memory of their father's work among Polish cinephiles and art enthusiasts. Thanks to their efforts, most of Antonisz's films were digitized and the large collection of his inventions and notes was scrupulously catalogued. In 2013 the collection became a basis for a major exhibition 'Antonisz: Technology for Me Is a Form of Art', curated by Joanna Kordjak-Piotrowska, held in Zachęta National Gallery of Art in Warsaw and the National Museum in Krakow. The event was complemented by the publication of a beautifully printed catalogue, as well as a volume of Antonisz's comic strips and graphic novels containing such treasures as his childhood story, *The Adventures of Hitler* (*Przygody Hitlera*), where the Führer, like Wile E. Coyote, finds himself in one painful mishap after another, or a storyboard for the never completed film *Thunders* (*Pieruny*) about Silesian miners who drill a tunnel through the centre of the earth straight to Australia.

[4] One of the few exceptions was the retrospective 'Rebel Without a Camera – Films by Julian "Antonisz" Antoniszczak' presented as a part of 'Animarchy Retrospective' at 26th Animafest Zagreb (6–11 June 2016).

The disproportion between the domestic and international reception of Antonisz's work is equally visible in the critical and academic literature. Authors of English language books on the history of animation certainly do not consider Antonisz films as a part of the core canon of the Polish animation, which itself has gained a significant recognition among international critics and scholars. It strikes one as symptomatic that in the second volume of Giannalberto Bendazzi's *Animation: A World History*, in a twenty-four-page chapter devoted to Polish animation in the period 1960–1991, Antonisz's name appears only in a short text in a footnote provided with an annotation: 'A disambiguation note necessary for the archivists' (Bendazzi 2016: 245). The only substantial English language publication on the subject is a translation of the catalogue *Antonisz: Technology for Me Is a Form of Art* (Kordjak-Piotrowska and Homely 2013), which is valuable not only as an art-book filled with big scale reproductions of the artefacts presented on the exhibition (mainly Antonisz's inventions and handwritten notes) annotated with detailed descriptions, but also as a relevant academic source.

Contributors to this collective volume, all of them acknowledged Polish film critics and art theorists, ponder over various aspects of Antonisz's output. Especially compelling are the new perspectives on the artist's work that can be found in Joanna Kordjak-Piotrowska's thorough analysis of the so-called 'Ideabooks' (numerous folders and notebooks filled with Antonisz's notes, sketches and cut-out collages) as well as Łukasz Wojtyszko's remarks on the linguistic level of the director's films. Regretfully a small number of the book's copies was printed and currently it is practically impossible to obtain one.

Another valuable academic publication on the subject is Ewa Borysiewicz's (2013) monograph focused on political aspects of Antonisz's films. Analysing the strategies through which the director undermined the authoritarian power reflected in the dominant discourse, Borysiewicz puts an emphasis on Antonisz's conscious rejection of a classically narrative approach to cinema in favour of the impression-oriented understanding of the medium. 'The cinema based on impression is by far more resistant to actions aiming at upholding the hegemonic relations' (Borysiewicz 2013: 73). Both in the book and in her article in the above-described collective work, Borysiewicz frequently refers to the concept of a carnival as understood by Mikhail Bakhtin. The Bakhtinian context is by all means adequate, for in his artistic undertakings Antonisz released the counter-cultural creativity of the unreduced, ambiguous laughter that breaks down the established hierarchies and their oppressive, homophonic narrations.

The atmosphere of a preposterous carnival that fills Antonisz's non-camera animations seems to be a spontaneous response of a disobedient individual confronted with the symbolic violence of the official doctrine. The author's strategy of carnivalistic diversion is distinctly visible in his *Non-Camera Chronicles*. Protected by the bulletproof shield of pure nonsense, the artist broke into the very core of the dominant discourse and replaced the required idealization, smoothness and pathos with a cacophony of noise, pop-music and shreds of psychedelic voice-over commentaries loosely corresponding with the kinetic anarchy of vibrating shapes and colours.

In his frequently cited quote, which incidentally might serve as an accurate description of the relationship between *The Polish Film Chronicles* and Antonisz's parody, Bakhtin states:

> We have already spoken of the structural characteristics of the carnival image: it strives to encompass and unite within itself both poles of becoming or both members of an antithesis: birth-death, youth-old age, top-bottom, face-backside, praise-abuse, affirmation-repudiation, tragic-comic, and so forth, while the upper pole of a two-in-one image is reflected in the lower, after the manner of the figures on playing cards. It could be expressed this way: opposites come together, look at one another, are reflected in one another, know and understand one another.
>
> BAKHTIN 1984: 176

Certainly, in the case of Antonisz's complex and multidimensional artistic output, the wide intellectual perspective open for the *coincidentia oppositorum* principle should prove far more efficient than the classical, Aristotelian binarism.

As Kordjak-Piotrowska points out, Antonisz's films and drawings are populated by essentially ambivalent, hybrid creatures that belong to 'the repertoire of the language of grotesque explored by Mikhail Bakhtin where the body is presented in a state of transition, the phase "in-between" the animal, the plant, the machine and the human' (Kordjak-Piotrowska 2013: 16). This insightful observation may be extended to other, non-diegetic aspects of Antonisz's oeuvre, where the line separating the usually dichotomous categories of original and replica are as blurry as the division between a tool for the creation of art and the artefact itself, or the borders between inanimate technology and biological life. In the following parts of this chapter I shortly reflect upon these three pairs of antithetical playing card figures (original-copy, technology-art, technology-life). The text concludes with some more remarks on the political inclinations of Julian Antoniszczak's work.

Original-copy or the curse of the reproduction

Antonisz's artistic career visibly divides into two major chapters. The turning point came with the proclamation of the *Non-Camera Manifesto* in 1977, when the filmmaker declared the artistic programme of the ultimate rejection of photography from the filmmaking process in favour of direct on tape animation. In the first decade of his career the artist experimented with various techniques, treating direct on tape animation as one of various means of expression. His well-deserved status of an outsider among the Polish School of Animation's authors does not mean that he was not influenced by some of his more experienced colleagues. The technical experiments of Antonisz's early films follow the footsteps of artists who in the late 1950s explored the territories situated between cinema and visual art. Among Antonisz's predecessors it is necessary to recall Andrzej Pawłowski, the author of *Cineforms* (*Kineformy*, 1957), a live-action recording of an abstract ballet of elusive shapes and colours achieved thanks to the projector designed especially for this purpose. Adriana Prodeus mentions in this context the experiments undertaken by Mieczysław Waśkowski whose short film was inspired by the art informal, titled *Somnambulists* (*Somnambulicy*; 1958, made in collaboration with Tadeusz Kantor). This film is composed of colourful, amorphous patches of liquid paint spilled on a glass surface (Prodeus 2013: 43).

Undoubtedly the strongest and most direct impact on Antonisz's early work was made by Kazimierz Urbański, his teacher and advisor, who himself was an influential, experimental filmmaker, founder and a long-time head of the Film Drawing Workshop (Pracownia Filmu Rysunkowego, established in 1957) at the Fine Arts Academy in Krakow. This was the first Polish academic unit specialized in animation and the first European film department at an artistic academy (see Margolis 2016: 217). Forced to deal with a low-budget and low-supply working conditions, Urbański motivated his students to exercise the DIY method. Due to a very limited access to film stock, first year students did not get to shoot films. Instead the professor encouraged them to exploit the possibilities generated by direct contact with the film material. Textures achieved by the students' direct interventions on short fragments of reused film stock were complemented with abstract shapes and strong colours, achieved during the projection through live manual manipulations with different oils and fluids as well as chemical and thermal processing of the stock itself. In a statement given by Urbański in an interview from 2013[5] he claims that the entirety of Antonisz's artistic career was in fact an extension of what he learned during the first year of this animation course.

Besides being an artist and a pedagogue, Urbański was a skilful organizer and activist, pursuing creative independence in times of political control. Thanks to his efforts in 1966 a branch of the Warsaw Studio of Film

[5] Video interview available at the Mediateka website, an online media archive under the auspices of the Ministry of Culture and the National Heritage and National Museum in Krakow: http://www.mediatekamnk.pl/obiekt.php?id=1526 (accessed 12 May 2016).

Miniatures was opened in Krakow. In 1974 the studio gained legal autonomy and functioned as the Animated Film Studio until 2003 when it was eventually shut down. The studio gathered the most talented filmmakers of the Krakow animation scene, artists such as Antonisz and his younger brother, Ryszard Antoniszczak, Ryszard Czekała, Jerzy Kucia or Krzysztof Kiwerski. In her interesting article on Urbański Hanna Margolis argues that in his diverse endeavours the artist negotiated with the authoritarian, centralized structure of state institutions in order to create within its framework a space for an artistic movement resembling American and West European underground film scenes (Margolis 2016: 217). Antonisz, who was an integral part of the Animated Film Studio community, was deeply inspired by its creative atmosphere, which influenced his way of thinking about films, not only regarding their content but also their production and distribution.

On a purely technical level Antonisz's early works bear certain similarities to Urbański's 1960s films such as *Playthings* (*Igraszki*, 1962) and *The Lament of the Thug* (*Tren zbója*, 1967) in which liquid, non-geometric abstraction was used for backgrounds. However, from the very beginning his work was marked by the unique, individual touch manifested in the bizarre aesthetics, as well as the reappearing set of themes and authorial obsessions. For instance, the author's debut, *Phobia* (*Fobia*, 1967), at certain moments (particularly in the opening sequence) may bring to mind Urbański's *Moto-gas* (*Moto-gaz*, 1963), yet youthful flippancy of Antonisz's film makes the work of the doyen of the Krakow circle look rather old-fashioned and academic. Cheerfully exploring the photogeny concealed in decomposition, ugliness and dirt, the director tells a surprisingly coherent, utterly enjoyable story of a pretentious, egocentric painter searching for inspiration in the countryside and his painful journey into his own subconscious hiding the shocking truth about his talent and his wife's fidelity. The film is a wild, explosive mixture of direct on tape techniques and various tricks and optical effects learned by the author in Urbański's classes.

It is worth mentioning that originally *Phobia* functioned as a live picture show, resembling performances of proto-cinematic magic theatres. Antonisz entertained audiences of cultural centres with the effects achieved through the mechanical manipulation of the stock, but also by burning it with corrosive substances or a too-strong projector bulb, as well as drowning it in colourful liquids. For the purpose of the film, the live tricks were projected on the screen and recaptured by a camera (set either on live-action or frame by frame mode). Although Antonisz's aesthetic convictions were yet to be crystallized in his future non-camera programme, we may assume that the director must have been aware of a certain, cryptic sadness of this technique. Even if the film feels overfilled with the spontaneous spirit of improvisation and acceptance of chaos, the uniqueness of the original performance has been irretrievably lost. Antonisz, who treated the techniques of reproduction as a necessary evil and who was always happy to run special screenings of his hand-made films from the original tapes, greatly valued the artistic energy of a singular occurrence, a quality he missed in the mainstream cinema, understood as a tool of mass communication.

In this respect Antonisz's views were convergent with the ideas developed by the Frankfurt School's theoreticians who claimed that the individual aura of an artwork cannot be reproduced by the means of industrial technology, which itself always remains influenced by political forces. In his classic essay, Walter Banjamin writes:

> The aura surrounding Macbeth on the stage cannot be divorced from the aura which, for the living spectators, surrounds the actor who plays him. What distinguishes the shot in the film studio, however, is that the camera is substituted for the audience. As a result, the aura surrounding the actor is dispelled – and, with it, the aura of the figure he portrays.
>
> BENJAMIN 2003: 260

Even if in the case of *Phobia* the photography was still an unavoidable part of the process, the film, along with other animations made by Antonisz in the early 1970s such as *How a Sausage Dog Works* or two amusing educational films for children explaining the secrets of paper production (*How Science Made it Out of the Woods/Jak nauka wyszła z lasu*, 1970) and television transmission (*Agnisia Asks How It Is That We See a Teddy Bear on the Screen/Jak to się dzieje pyta Agnisia że na ekranie widzimy misia*, 1970), to a significant extent anticipates the style of Antonisz's later non-camera films.

The other current in his work is the usage of live-action footage, usually mixed with animated sequences. In many cases the movement recorded in real time is purely automatic. For instance, in films like *A Thousand and One Trivia* (*Tysiąc jeden drobiazgów*, 1972) and *Film about (Office) Art* (*Film o sztuce . . . (biurowej)*, 1975) instead of actors we are presented with Dadaist mechanical objects carrying out some obscure, seemingly pointless, tasks assigned to them by their constructor. Occasionally the author employed living actors and staged some more conventionally narrative scenes, often marked by a distinctive flair for the vintage atmosphere of early cinema visible in the grainy textures of usually black and white photography, but also in over-expressive acting techniques from insane slapstick (the sequence *At The Dentist* in *Horror Film/Film grozy*, 1976) to campy burlesque (*In the Grips of Sex/W szponach sexu*, 1969; *A Few Practical Ways to Prolong One's Life/Kilka praktycznych sposobów na przedłużenie sobie życia*, 1974).

In the Grips of Sex is arguably Antonisz's most successful live-action film. This witty satire, somewhat resembling the mood of French and Czechoslovak new wave cinema, tells the story of an attractive single lady with an apartment who wishes to find love through a matrimonial ad. The film is rather daring (considering the moral standards guarded by the censors) in its depiction of contemporary erotic life. Even though we do not see sex and we do not hear it being mentioned in the dialogue, the whole film is filled with easily readable hints suggesting sexual intercourse (repetitive bouncing on beds, animistic screams and yells, etc.). One by one the heroine rejects her lovers who have failed to satisfy her physical and emotional needs (each split-up scene begins with the actress dropping artificial tears into her eyes). Finally, there comes a good-hearted champ that may remind audiences of the male protagonist of John Cassavetes' *Minnie and Moskowitz* (1971) who wins her heart with a line: 'Perhaps what you need is a little warmth, it seems that the central heating is broken.' Due to direct on tape colouring, their faces transform into a kitschy wedding photo, the immortal token of marital happiness.

The stylistic strength of *In the Grips of Sex* lies in the dazzling combination of the film's techniques. Again, it is possible to point out one of Urbański's films that seems to have inspired Antonisz. The way the latter artist approached the live-action footage is analogous to the method employed by his older colleague in *Sweet Rhythms* (*Słodkie rytmy* 1965) – an elusive collage of the real-time recording of beehives and vibrating shapes, and patterns burned or stamped directly on the film stock. Using essentially the same idea of applying the direct techniques onto the developed tape containing live-action footage, Antonisz in a certain way confounded the abuse of the mechanical copy and restored the aura of originality. This burning need to escape the curse of reproduction (quite an unusual urge for a filmmaker), visible already in Antonisz's earliest films, eventually led him to the radical anti-photographic turn. As he argued in one of his interviews,

> The weakness of animated film derives from the advantage of technology over art. An author, usually a visual artist, supported by a group of animators draws the original piece of art on paper or celluloid. And then they make a diminished and visually reduced copy. The original graphic compositions, the very essence of art, are being disposed. It's as though Picasso would take a picture of his Guernica, throw away the original painting and exhibit the photograph in a museum.
>
> ANTONISZ and ZAREMBA 1977: 14–15

In order to transcend what he considered the limitations of frame by frame photography, Antonisz reached out to the technique that enabled him to realize his profoundly paradoxical desire to project on the cinema screen the original creation, instead of its mere reproduction. As Ülo Pikkov puts it, 'direct animation gives the author a chance to create the visual universe of the film without relying on cameras [. . .]. While other animation techniques are essentially recordings or reproductions, direct animation is, by definition, a direct presentation. Both the achieved illusion (of motion, space etc.) and the film stock (or material) itself become objects of film' (Pikkov 2010: 122).

Technology-art or the soul of an instrument

From his early years Antonisz revealed an extraordinary talent for technical work, and throughout his entire artistic career his carnivalesque visual imagination was supported, complemented and inspired by his true passion for various kinds of machines and automata. The director enjoyed observing and analysing their mechanisms, reading about them in the professional press, but above all, constructing them. Antonisz's fondness for the DIY method became a subject of countless anecdotes. For instance, Ryszard Antoniszczak reminisces about assisting his brother in constructing a muscle-engined car built indoors out of two bicycles and then lowered down from the window. A Krakow-based critic, Jerzy Armata recalls how he once complained to the artist that due to short supplies of glass he had not been able to find a glazier willing to fix his broken window. In response, he heard: 'screw the glazier, just take some sand, some tap-water and make your own glass!' (Armata 1996). Symbiotically adjusted to the hard circumstances he frequently visited junkyards, digging for potentially useful materials. 'Antoniszczak seems to perfectly fit the model of a 20th-century avant-garde junk-artist – whose practice uses all manner of litter, leftovers, used-up, useless and discarded objects whose status was reduced to that of garbage' (Kordjak-Piotrowska 2013: 20).

In his apartment, the director constructed several advanced technical devices designed to make the animation process simpler, faster and more precise. In time, the collection accumulated into a private, self-sufficient manufacture of direct on tape films. Antonisz's first film made without using any photographic technologies was *The Sun* (*Słońce*, 1977). The film is not one of his most artistically successful accomplishments, yet it is worth mentioning for its historical value (the premiere was accompanied by the publication of the *Non-Camera Manifesto*) and technical innovativeness. It was made with the use of a 35-mm film-printer, a device inspired by the traditional graphic printmaking techniques, which impressed a template image on following film frames (the illusion of a vibrant movement was achieved due to the small differences between individual prints). It appears that the relatively limited narrative potential of this method made Antonisz turn his attention to another old technique, which has been used in architecture and the visual arts since the seventeenth century.

The basis of the large number of machines constructed by the filmmaker was the instrument known as the pantograph, a duplication drawing tool allowing one to automatically enlarge or minify an image with the use of mechanical linkage (based on the principle of parallelograms) that transmits the movement of a pen to another pen, which draws a proportionally scaled copy of the original image. With his 'Pantograph Animagraph' ('*Pantograf animograf*'), the artist was able to draw a picture on an A4 sheet of paper, while the arm attached with a needle simultaneously copied the drawing onto the stock (scratched contours were later coloured manually). The machine was equipped with an optical projection system (based on the idea of an epidioscope, or the opaque projector), making it possible to preview the animated frames. Over the years, the artist built several versions of this device constantly modifying and improving it. His famous 'Antonisz's Piano', or 'Pantograph 24 Frame Phasing Animagraph' ('*Pantograf-animograf fazujący 24-kadrowy*'), which is perhaps his most incredible invention, used basically the same idea, but multiplied by twenty-four. Although it is hard to believe, thanks to his 'piano' it was enough for Antonisz to draw the first and the last frame of the twenty-four-frame sequence as the remaining in-between images were automatically generated.[6] The only difficulty was that he had to draw with two hands at the same time.

It was due to these and many other, equally amazing inventions that it became possible for Antonisz to develop his own recognizable style, distinctly observable, especially in his work after 1977 when he was focused exclusively on his non-camera projects. Paradoxically, his anti-photographic turn, motivated by the need to escape the limitations of reproduction, was possible due to a complex machinery creating a distance between the author and the material. As a matter of fact, Antonisz's non-camera films were not drawn directly on tape. Although the advanced technology of non-camera remained completely parallel to the one predominating in the mainstream culture, it was based on the essential principles of mechanical reproduction, not only duplication (simple pantograph), but also automatization (phasing animagraph, 35 mm printer). This paradox appears even more striking once we realize how his major innovations, based on the most fundamentally

[6] The mechanism of 'Antonisz's Piano' is best described in the catalogue *Antonisz: Technology for Me Is a Form of Art*: 'An elaborate pantograph was equipped with two arms, used for drawing on A6-sized paper, connected by a mechanical linkage with 24 needles that scratched film. Owing to the establishment of correct points of support and the placement of the needles in relation to the pantograph's arms, the device was able to produce the intermediate phases of movement in a film shot. The use of a "phasing pantograph" made it possible to work on 24 frames at a single time, which corresponds to one second of film. The artist drew using both hands simultaneously: drawing the first phase of a given shot with his left hand, and the last with his right hand. The images of the intermediate phases of movement were drawn automatically on the film' (Kordjak-Piotrowska and Homely 2013: 194).

old-school technology, which in most cases did not even need any electric power, have anticipated the simplicity and efficiency of flash animation.

'Constructing the machines is strictly connected with artistic activities. Machines inspired the films, films influenced the machines' (Fejkiel 1981: 46). Indeed, in the case of Antonisz's work it is impossible to set a border between the tool and the artistic creation. First of all, the technology itself belongs to major themes of his films. Antonisz's unmistakable iconography consists of all kinds of mechanical parts, toothed wheels, gears, cranks, levers, irrational devices designed for ridiculous tasks, and bio-mechanical hybrids. Moreover, Antonisz's inventions themselves certainly deserve to be treated as works of art. In some ways, they are a more complete realization of the creator's vision than the films, for the machines do not bear the 'original sin' of reproduction. Fascinated with the era of early pioneers, the prehistory of cinema when technological inventiveness and the artistic process were inseparable as two sides of a coin, Antonisz once provocatively stated that the cinema died with the advent of Lumière brothers (Fejkiel 1980). Indeed, his approach to cinema was in many respects outdated, rooted in the times from before motion pictures became an industry. In his work, Antonisz tried to evoke the original spirit of the magical illusion, hence his esteem for the physical materiality of the film tape itself, as well as the machinery that allows the creation and recreation of the streams of moving images (Fejkiel 1980).

Naturally, Antonisz was not the only filmmaker developing the direct on tape technique. His strong inclination towards visual experiment makes his work akin to internationally acclaimed artists such as Norman McLaren, Stan Brakhage and Len Lye, but also authors of the next generations like Steven Woloshen, Boris Kazakov and Mitja MančRek. However, in comparison with all these artists, Antonisz's output appears less hermetic and exclusive. Another blurred border in Antonisz's case is the one separating the realms of avant-garde and pop-culture. The distinctive feature of his output is the combination of radical visual experiment and tawdry playfulness of the proto-cinematic picture shows. In the majority of Antonisz's films this ludic quality assumes the form of the humorist voice-over commentary that structures the seemingly random streams of animated images and helps to maintain the viewer's attention. If devoid of the literary text the director's films would be far more difficult to 'digest' and most likely would have never reached the wider audience. In order to verify that last remark one should see his films *People Wither Away Like Leaves* (*Ludzie więdną jak liście*, 1978) and *A Light in the Tunnel* (*Światło w tunelu*, 1986). On the visual level neither of the two films differs significantly from Antonisz's other non-camera works. However, the replacement of the usual voice-over with more abstract sound design containing noises and hums scratched on the tape with a razor (naturally, Antonisz used one of his own inventions, a device called 'The Unique Razor Blade Sound Machine'/'*Dźwiękownica unikalna żyletkowa*') greatly affected the general atmosphere of both films, which are darker and more tiresome than other Antonisz shorts, closer to the kind of experimental films we are used to watching in half-empty art-house theatres.

Antonisz's films were meant to be audience-friendly and the great majority of them are comedies, even if the humour is not always bright, varying from bitter satire to existential irony. One of the main reasons for his films' success is his unconditional anti-professionalism. The director emphasized hand-made and home-made qualities of his films. The animation in his non-camera films looks harsh and clumsy, just like the live-action footage in his early works is often blurry or underexposed. The editing of both sound and image seems rapid and chaotic. The maniacally cheerful music, usually written and performed by the director himself, is poorly recorded, full of discords and mistakes. But, above all, the voice-over narration – Antonisz's trademark – is in many cases read by non-professional actors (most famously Aniela Jaskólska, a janitor at the Krakow Animated Studio), who frequently stammer or mispronounce the difficult lines, filled with neologisms and pseudo-scientific jargon. According to the director's method, they were supposed to read the text, which they had not seen before, from a piece of paper covered with Antonisz's unclear, handwritten notes. Such longing for imperfection seems to be a logical consequence of his essential aesthetic beliefs. In order to preserve the aura of the singular occurrence, the author constantly pushed for broadening the space for blind chance and artistic disarray.

Biology-technology or the DIY organisms

'Two themes seem especially important in this extraordinary imagery: the human body and technology, closely bound together and full of – as the artist proves – analogies' (Kordjak-Piotrowska 2013: 16). Searching for ideas, Antonisz used to rummage among scientific books and journals. On his shelves, books on modern technology, chemistry and physics shared space with anatomy albums and academic textbooks in subjects like zoology, botany and medicine. In his art, he frequently tested the possibilities of combining these two sources of inspiration. The most vivid and explicit evidence of Antonisz's fascination with organic machinery is his famous *How a Sausage Dog Works*, a film that might be described as a psychedelic reinterpretation of the Cartesian concept of an animal as a biological automaton. The animation begins with a one-minute long sequence presenting miscellaneous examples of imaginary, surrealist mechanisms with ridiculous names such as 'cherry lemondripper', 'diffusion sawcuterling' and 'electrosauerkraut'. The introduction concludes with the narrator stating the question that became the film's title. What follows is a Dada anatomy lesson 'explaining' the complex machinery of the animal organism. The sausage dog appears on a screen in a spinning zoom and the first thing he does is crow like a rooster at dawn. In accordance to the principles of educational genres, we are presented with the creature's longitudinal section – among pulsating veins and organic looking intestines we may observe Antonisz's characteristic toothed wheels, foreign mechanical elements actually added on the celluloid tissue of the film by means of a method akin to Tadeusz Kantor's assemblage technique.

The intentional inconsistency of the presented reality is manifested in the film's composition, characterized by the jazzy levity of Antonisz's best films. Watching it feels like the author's ideas pop out, like it was an improvised process, an animated stream of consciousness. The lecture on the sausage dog is brutally interrupted by the character named Ewaryst (one of the reoccurring strange names in Antonisz's films, hilarious for Polish ears) crushing the dog with his heavy foot. The poor creature dismantles into a pile of bio-mechanic waste. 'Let us not destroy the sausage dog, for it is a complicated machine that makes a computer look silly!' – exhorts the narrator (the voice-over is read by an older lady with the characteristic accent from eastern Poland), 'Let us not destroy a kitty! Let us not destroy a pickerel! Let us not destroy a butterfly,' she continues. This way the Cartesian vision of an animal as a soulless machine (suggested by the use of the word 'destroy' instead of 'kill') becomes a point of departure for an unexpected humanitarian, environmental argument, involving a backbreaking method of estimating the economic value of a butterfly. We learn that an eye of a butterfly comprises thousands of biological photodiodes, and since the price of one photodiode in a shop is 75 zloty, by eradicating a single specimen, one destroys a biological equipment worth roughly 30 million.

In Antonisz's universe the DIY principle does not have to be limited to the domain of inanimate technology, but can also be applied to living organisms. Moreover, in the crude reality of the People's Republic of Poland, the science of genetics must not be restricted to advanced laboratories, but should be available to enthusiastic amateurs, such as the protagonist of *Magister Kiziołł's Additional Digestive Goitre* (*Dodatkowe wole trawienne magistra Kiziołła*, 1984), a courageous inventor who finds an indefectible solution to a potential economic crisis (the narrator assures the viewer that currently the economy is booming). In order to be able to digest cellulose Magister Kiziołł undertakes a biotechnological experiment on himself. At first, he uses a mechanical implant that pre-digests the grass and leaves, but soon his body develops its own additional organic goiter, which looks like a pair of gigantic testicles hanging from the character's proud phallic neck. An equally bizarre example of biological DIY may be found in the tenth episode of the *Non-Camera Chronicles*, which includes a segment presenting the brave new method of revitalizing the seniors, which should turn out to be the solution to the lack of supply on the labour market. Like used cars, the pensioners are being dismantled into parts that are later reused to construct Frankensteinian creatures capable of performing their working duties. The narrator praises the glory of the socialist science and explains the secrets of the technology while the viewer watches gruesome figures like the three-headed steel mill worker or the three-legged blacksmith with a gigantic hammer instead of a penis.

Antonisz's carnivalesque imaginary, exploiting the comical potential of breaching universally accepted taboos, was in some strange way linked with his true love of nature. An emblematic example of this curious combination is the fourth episode of the *Chronicles*, which contains a segment exposing the treacherous conspiracy of plants.[7] The viewer is informed that people are nothing but tools in the hands of plants – lifeforms that are far more intelligent and technologically advanced than we are. They function within an ecological matrix and communicate with the use of some mysterious green network of data transmissions. The civilization of plants is to blame for all global conflicts. They manipulate the world leaders with the use of the aggression enzyme, for their goal is the nuclear annihilation of mankind, and overtaking the planet fertilized by the carcass of the dead soldiers.

This strange and hilariously misanthropic sci-fi tale reworks the global anxieties of the late Cold War era, but at the same time reveals Antonisz's own intimate obsessions. Both his films and his private notes are overfilled with motifs of illness, entropy, corrosion and passing of time usually approached with morbid humour that scarcely conceals the author's profound fear of death. His preoccupation with the bio-machinery was strongly connected to the ultimate existential absurdity of the human condition. In *A Few Practical Ways to Prolong One's Life*, one of Antonisz's underrated outstanding achievements, comparable to David Cronenberg's auto-thematic short *Camera* (2000), the author put forward a theory of the 'biological relativity of time' that explains why it is that with age time seems to run faster and faster. The premonition of his early death, articulated more or less directly in many of his films and notes, seems to be the reason for the incredible tempo of his work, as well as his gradually growing concern for his own health. In one of his notebooks Antonisz wrote: 'Remember that you are a robot . . . a human biological machine (take care of your parameters' (Catalogue 2013: 18).

[7] The ecological messages, reappearing in Antonisz's films since *How a Sausage Dog Works*, are not always mixed with such transgressive grotesque elements. Sometimes, as in the cases of the segments about the pollution of the Vistula river and the decreasing number of bees (both appear in the second episode of *Non-Camera Chronicles*) or the segment about plans for building a steel mill on the top of one of Poland's highest mountains (the ninth episode of the *Non-Camera Chronicles*), the environmental content is relatively obvious and straightforward, albeit embellished with characteristic elements of parody and linguistic humour.

Antonisz: art, politics, laughter

In his films, especially the ones made in the 1980s, an extremely unstable decade in Polish history, Antonisz frequently tested the limits of both the audience's and the censors' endurance. Already his second short, *In the Grips of Sex*, had caused major problems. The censor's office expressed reservations in regard to the film's depiction of contemporary sexual customs, but the biggest issue was the fact that the film referred to the difficult housing situation – a serious concern of the government, which was not supposed to be openly discussed. After many complications, the film was finally accepted for limited distribution and caused an outrage among Catholic morality defenders accusing Antonisz of youth deprivation (there was even a plan to collect and destroy all copies of the film, see Armata 2005). The artist directly addressed the subject of censorship in one of his most remembered non-camera shorts, ironically titled *Sharp Engaged Film* (*Ostry Film Zaangażowany*, 1979). The double meaning of this ludicrous story of a greedy kiosk keeper was accurately discerned by the jury of the 1980 Krakow Film Festival (former Polish Short Film Festival) whose unusual decision to give the prize for the best Polish film to an animated film was intended to be read as a political statement (a critique of the state's censorship, which banned quality documentaries from the selection; see Janicka 1980, Giżycki 1997–1998).

Watching some episodes of *Non-Camera Chronicles* one may ask the question, 'how on earth did it pass the office?' It is a well-known fact (see Bendazzi 2016, Giżycki 2016, Sitkiewicz 2011) that in Communist Poland animated film served as a medium allowing many authors to smuggle their 'artistic contraband' – elements of the forbidden political critique hidden behind allegories. However, unlike artists such as Daniel Szczechura and Mirosław Kijowicz who use the Aesopian language of hints and suggestions, in Antonisz's work the critical content is openly exposed. Let us take a brief look at the sixth episode of the *Chronicles*, a very representative example of Antonisz's late period. The whole piece is simply sated with carnivalistic anti-propaganda. It opens with a segment *The Pumped-out Nation*, explaining that the reason for the country's economic insufficiency lies in the bad quality of state-produced rubber that makes the Poles lose all their energy on pumping up bladders and tyres ('No wonder that in the Federal Republic of Germany the economy is blooming,' says the narrator, 'while we were pumping, they were building their prosperity'). In the next sequence the viewers are encouraged to try the new specialty of Polish cuisine known as 'pizza crisisiana'. Furthermore, the episode contains two characteristic DIY segments (how to make a car out of a horse and how to make shoes out of a mink coat). It concludes with an exquisite piece dedicated to the Oberhausen festival openly referring to the Cold War arms race paranoia.

As we can see, the political comments and jokes are rather blunt and direct. It seems that thanks to the oddball style of his generically unclassifiable films, equally extravagant as his artistic persona, Antonisz created for himself a special negotiating position in the framework of his compelling relationship with the authorities. But this certainly could not satisfy his hunger for unconstrained artistic expression. Antonisz wished to liberate the art of film from the studio system that was strictly controlled by the authoritarian state. All his non-camera inventions served one major goal – to enable him to limit the studio to his own room and thus to escape from the official circuit of production. In his passion for developing technological alternatives to the mainstream models of film production he postulated a general change both in the accustomed approach to storytelling and in the distribution process. Antonisz dreamed of recreating the unique magic of the times from before cinema was dubbed the most important art form, giving the medium of film 'back to the people', making the communication between author and viewer as direct as possible, devoid of institutional go-betweens. He believed in the great potential for a grass-roots cinema movement and heralded a Renaissance of small cinemas accompanied by an explosion of self-produced and direct animations, manufactured by amateur craftsmen in their attics or garages and screened in local cinemas.

Antonisz's utopian dream of a non-camera, audiovisual revolution has not come true. Nonetheless, his own prolific oeuvre became a significant part of the motley landscape of Polish dissident art in the last two decades of the socialist regime. Similar to the activists of the Orange Alternative, who proclaimed the artistic programme of socialist surrealism and exposed the absurdity of the dominant ideology through outdoor events and street-art, the punk rock bands playing illegal concerts and encouraging their audience to spread their bootlegs on audio cassettes, or the publishers of underground press and photocopied fanzines, Antonisz employed guerrilla methods for establishing unrestrained channels of communication and distribution of art and ideas.

References

Antonisz, J. and B. Zaremba (1977). 'Film bez kamery, albo twarzą w twarz z Julianem Antoniszem. Julian Antonisz w rozmowie z Bogdanem Zarembą' ['A Film without a Camera, or Face to Face with Julian Antonisz. Bogdan Zagroba Interviews Julian Antonisz'], *Film*, 32: 14–15.

Antoniszczak, J. (2013). *Opowieści graficzne* [*Graphic Stories*]. Kraków/ Wydawnictwo: Ha!art.

Armata, J. (1996). 'Urwany film Antoniszczaka' ['Antoniszczak's Broken Tape'], *Gazeta w Krakowie*, 28.

Armata, J. (2005). '18. rocznica śmierci Juliana Józefa Antonisza' ['18th Anniversary of Julian Józef Antonisz's Death'], *Gazeta Wyborcza Kraków*, 28

January. Available online: http://krakow.wyborcza.pl/krakow/1,35796,2517791.html?disableRedirects=true (accessed 15 August 2017).
Bakhtin, M. (1984). *Problems of Dostoevsky's Poetics*, trans. C. Emerson. Minneapolis, London: Minnesota University Press.
Bendazzi, G. (2016). *Animation: A World History: Volume II: The Birth of a Style – The Three Markets, vol. 2*. Boca Raton: CRC Press.
Benjamin, W. (2003 [1935]). 'The Work of Art in the Age of ItsTechnological Reproducibility', in (his) *Selected Writings: Volume 4: 1938–1940*. Cambridge, Massachusetts, London: The Belknap Press of Harvard University Press.
Borysiewicz, E. (2013). *Rausz kinetyczny. Animacja bezkamerowa Antonisza jako projekt polityczny* [*Kinetic exhilaration. Antonisz's Non Camera Animation as a Political Project*]. Warszawa: Ha!Art.
Cieśliński, M. (2006). *Piękniej niż w życiu. Polska Kronika Filmowa 1944–1994* [*Better Than Life. The Polish Film Chronicles*]. Warszawa: Wydawnictwo Trio.
Fejkiel, J. (1980). 'Film skończył się z nadejściem braci Lumiere . . . Rozmowa z Julianem Antoniszem ['Cinema Has Died with the Advent of Lumière Brothers . . . In conversation with Julian Antonisz'], *Kultura*, 27.
Fejkiel, J. (1981). 'To Paint a Film' ['Namalować film'], *Sztuka*, 4: 46.
Giżycki, M. (1997–1998). 'Diariusz polskiego filmu animowanego 1917–1981' ['Polish Animated Film Timeline 1917–1981'], *Kwartalnik Filmowy*, 19/20: 21–44.
Giżycki, M. and B. Zmudziński eds (2008). *Polski film animowany* [*Polish Animated Film*]. Warszawa: PWA.
Giżycki, M. (2016). 'Why Has Polish Animation Stopped Biting?', in M. Bobrowski and O. Bobrowska (eds), *Obsession, Pereversion, Rebellion: Twisted Dreams of Central European Animation*, 17–25. Bielsko-Biała, Kraków: Galeria Bielska BWA.
Interview with Kazimierz Urbański (2013). [Video Interview] Mediateka, 27 May. Available online: http://www.mediatekamnk.pl/obiekt.php?id=1526 (accessed 12 May 2016).
Janicka, B. (1980). 'Kraków 80. Dopóki się kręci' ['Kraków 80. As Long As It Rolls'], *Film*, 23: 4–5.
Kordjak-Piotrowska, J. and J. Homely, eds (2013). *Antonisz: Technology for Me Is a Form of Art*, Catalogue, Kraków, Warsaw: Zachęta – National Gallery of Art, National Museum.
Kordjak-Piotrowska, J. (2013). 'Technology for Me Is a Form of Art and "Handymanish"', in J. Kordjak-Piotrowska and J. Homely (eds), *Antonisz: Technology for Me Is a Form of Art*, 11–34. Kraków, Warszawa: Zachęta – National Gallery of Art, National Museum.
Kornai, J. 1980. *Economics of Shortage*. Amsterdam: North-Holland Publishing Company.
Margolis, H. (2016). '"Wszędzie byłem obcy" Kazimierz Urbański i underground w PRL ['"I Was Always A Stranger" Kazimierz Urbański and the Underground in the People's Republic of Poland'], in M. Giżycki and A. Trwoga (eds), *Magia animacji. Z archiwum Animatora* [*Magic of Animation. From the Animator's Archvies*]. Warszawa: Wydawnictwo PJATK.
Pikkov, Ü. (2010). *Animasophy: Theoretical Writings on Animated Film*, Tallinn: Estonian Academy of Arts.

Prodeus, A. (2013). 'Man without a Movie Camera: Non-camera by Julian Antonisz', in J. Kordjak-Piotrowska and J. Homely (eds), *Antonisz: Technology for Me Is a Form of Art*. Kraków, Warszawa: Zachęta – National Gallery of Art, National Museum.

Sitkiewicz, P. (2011). *Polska szkoła animacji* [*Polish School of Animation*]. Gdańsk: słowo/obraz terytoria.

Wojtyszko, Ł. (2013). 'All This Seems Quite Serious', in J. Kordjak-Piotrowska and J. Homely (eds), *Antonisz: Technology for Me Is a Form of Art*, 75–90. Kraków, Warszawa: Zachęta – National Gallery of Art, National Museum.

14

Lynsey Martin

A Case Study of 1970s Australian Experimental Animation

Dirk de Bruyn

Introduction

> I like to think of much of my work as being finely crafted with great attention given over to editing where each frame is important and the film is as short or as long as it needs to be.
>
> MARTIN 2015

The history of experimental animation in Australia remains largely unknown outside its borders. Although Norman McLaren and Len Lye's films are recognized internationally within animation practice such experimental hand-made cinema generally sits less comfortably under a traditional animation umbrella. Such work occupies its creative and innovative margins. Australian experimental animation's obscurity can be further explained by this activity being embedded in and framed by the avant-garde, non-narrative experimental film cultures present in Sydney and Melbourne in the 1960s and 1970s rather than being presented publically under an animation banner.

Understandably, such local activity can fly under the radar even within a broad historical sweep of national animation cinemas, like Giannalberto

Bendazzi's *Animation: A World History, Volumes I, II, III*. Bendazzi recognizes the deserved international reputations of Australian animators Dennis Tupicoff and Adam Elliot and the innovation of Bruce Currie, Ann Shenfield and numerous others (Bendazzi 2016). The experimentation of Corinne and Arthur Cantrill, Sabrina Schmid and Neil Taylor is evident but not the abstract and graphic experimentation of Lynsey Martin, Michael Lee, Jonas Balsaitis and Hugh McSpedden, all so much part of the local Melbourne activity focused on here.

The emergence and amenity of digital technologies and the resultant new image manipulation strategies have impacted animation's definition. This shift invites a re-calibration and re-evaluation of such 1970s Melbourne experimentation in terms of animation strategies and techniques. We can locate rudimentary forms of those image manipulation strategies that now populate the filter menus of digital editing software within such work. In the networked-society the impact of the tyranny of distance on Australian culture's visibility and accessibility also dissipates to some extent. As a result, the generation of Australian experimental animation to which Lynsey Martin belongs and within which he plays a critical role can be made visible. This discussion examines Martin's practice and its position in relation to other local Melbourne experimental animation activity.

The situation into which Martin's work emerged was enabled by the earlier experimentation of Arthur and Corinne Cantrill in Melbourne and the Ubu Collective in Sydney. In Melbourne, the Cantrills promoted hand-made experimental animation through their magazine and workshops. This advocacy was influenced by the Ubu Collective's earlier activity in Sydney in the late 1960s and early 1970s. The Ubu Collective[1] included artists Albie Thoms, Aggie Read and David Perry, and the experimental animation *Bluto* (Thoms 1967) is representative of the Ubu Collective's multiple outputs in this area. The Cantrills foregrounded hand-made and abstract film, including this Ubu work, in their film culture magazine. *Cantrills Filmnotes* was first published in roneoed form in 1971. Despite this magazine's international presence, it is interesting and ironic that many of the films by the artists populating its pages remain obscure. Lynsey Martin's neglected output is representative of this state of affairs.

[1] This group further participated in Sydney's alternative artist collective The Yellow House from 1970 to 1973 through multimedia events, light-shows, workshops and screenings. The Yellow House was initiated by Martin Sharp on his return to Australia from London. His notoriety rested on his involvement with *OZ* magazine. Sharp's psychedelia also created Cream's Desreali Gears record cover. Sharp is considered an influence and antecedent to the artists behind the irreverent Mambo Graphics clothing label. In 2000 the Mambo style was showcased in the Sydney Olympics opening ceremony, through Reg Mombassa's cartoon-like sculptures that are also reminiscent of Robert Crumb's cartoon style.

In step with Ubu's *Bluto* Martin's films use hand-painting and direct on film techniques applied to the film's surface. These films further relate back to abstraction, the diary film and found footage cinema. They use collage and design elements to test and explore the act of looking in both public and private space. Though incorporating, like the Cantrills, formalist elements, Martin's films relate back to the suppressed and invisible traces of everyday life, expressed though technical strategies that lie outside normal viewing habits.

Martin's experimentation first came to public view in 1972 through a Cantrills filmmaking workshop documented in *Cantrills Filmnotes*. Martin describes his animation work as a self-funded artisanal practice: 'My films are essentially self-made, self-produced in the sense that as an artist, I aim to exercise control over as many aspects of the medium that I possibly can. That is production direction, photography editing, sound etc.' (Martin 2013). Martin's experimental 16mm cinema remains largely forgotten in Australia today despite a portion of his innovative thinking available in *Cantrills Filmnotes* (Nos 9, 12, 16, 17/18, 23/24, 29 and 30) and a solid public screening programme through the 1970s and 1990s, before such 16mm experimentation was replaced in public screenings by Super 8, video art and new media. Film curator and artist Jim Knox has described Martin's short innovative films as 'some of the most extraordinary cinema ever made in this country, and still largely unknown' (Knox 2009: 49).

Background

Born in 1951, Lynsey Martin was introduced to photography through his father's Minolta Rangefinder 35mm camera. In the late 1960s and early 1970s, he studied photography, film and graphic design at Preston Institute of Technology and Victoria State College in Melbourne. This was a time when these institutions' curriculum was loosely structured, allowing the freedom to follow your own intuitions (Martin 2015a). Beginning with the use of his father's camera Martin started to collect the still and moving image run-ins, which are part of the normal practice of loading still and moving image cameras. When loading these cameras Martin advanced the film to avoid the fogged area. Without looking through the camera's viewfinder he would routinely shoot the window of his room. These short redundant strips of film were saved, compiled and re-animated through the 1970s for the still incomplete work-in-progress, *Frames*. Such collected ongoing gestures mark Martin's preoccupation with the mundane and everyday events at the core of his film work. Similar habitual material appeared in the 3-screen version of *Parts 1–6* in 1973.

After his tertiary training Martin worked in graphic design and educational film and television production and later for more than 20 years as a Secondary school teacher. Martin taught subjects such as Visual

Communication and Design, Art and Art History. He has identified Laszlo Moholy-Nagy, Piet Mondrian, Kasimer Malevich's *House Under Construction* (1914) and El Lissitzky's *Beat the Whites with the Red Wedge* (1919) as influences in his teaching and moving image practice. Lissitzky's painting especially manages a strong narrative through its graphics. 'As an Art teacher at Lakeside Secondary College in Reservoir, much of the work that I taught was heavily design based with a high emphasis placed on attention to detail, accuracy and fluency in the communication of ideas' (Martin 2015).

Expanded cinema

While still at secondary school Martin began experimenting with multimedia projection using, this time, his father's 35mm slide projector.

> In the late 60s, I was fascinated by photographs that I saw in magazines of 'psychedelic light shows' that formed the background to rock concerts in America where artists such as Jimi Hendrix, The Cream, Janis Joplin etc. performed. All music that I was heavily into and the images were mostly abstract. I was already painting abstract pictures in acrylics on canvas.
>
> MARTIN 2015

Using inks, enamel and acrylic paints on coloured acetate and combining these techniques with found or discarded sections of 35mm film, Martin created similar light show images to the ones found in the rock magazines. These images were further informed by the works of abstract expressionist painters such as Jackson Pollock, Willem de Kooning and Franz Kline. 'Some of these images were very delicate, detailed and like mini works of art in their own right' (Martin 2015). Using as many as seven slide projectors, 'It wasn't long before I was doing light shows myself at High School social functions with as many school projectors that I could commandeer' (Martin 2015).

Such light shows were pursuits undertaken by a number of Melbourne contemporaries. James Clayden's and Hugh McSpedden's early performances incorporated projected slide material. Clayden's John Cage-influenced three-screen film and slide event, *Black Dog* (1971), incorporated half-tone positives and negative slides cut out of discarded sheets that were projected onto other images (Clayden 1971: 20).

Commencing in the late 1960s Hugh McSpedden, as the Edison Light Company,[2] continually expanded his light show techniques. These strategies

[2] McSpedden was the Edison Light Show, although he also enlisted other artists, like Michael Lee, to manipulate his hand-built contraptions during performances.

also found their way into his 16mm abstract animated films. McSpedden constructed hundreds of transparencies of hand-painted images and crystalline structures. To this archive McSpedden added moving and rotating filters and prisms to transition from slide to slide. These performances became known as the 'Giant Edison Screw' and were notorious fixtures at alternative music events like the TF (Too Fucking) Much Ballroom in Fitzroy, Melbourne. This music venue was organized by John Pinder and McSpedden's brother, Bani, and could accommodate up to 1,500 patrons. Mike Rudd, lead singer of the celebrated Australian innovative rock band, *Spectrum*, recalls 'We also had the Edison Light Show, which was Hugh McSpedden's thing, which was projected over the stage and made it a very heady, acidy thing' (McIntyre 2006: 181). McSpedden's arsenal creatively emerged out of poverty and scarcity. 'I had something like two ultraviolet tubes and a flicker wheel and a few chunks of mirror and my 8mm projector' (McSpedden 1971: 14).

Influences

Martin's filmmaking is uniquely intertwined with the Cantrills' practice. He contributed to *Cantrills Filmnotes* from its 1970s beginnings and emerged out of their workshop activity. *Billabong* (Will Hindle 1969) and *Sirius Remembered* (Stan Brakhage 1959) were films that the Cantrills had lobbied the national library to purchase and they featured them in the first issues of the magazine (Cantrill and Cantrill 1971a). 'Billabong & The Great Blondino are the first in a group of films with which the national library has begun to rejuvenate its study collection' (A. Cantrill 2008: 140). The other films in this initiating acquisition were *Sirius Remembered*, *Breathdeath* (Stan Vanderbeek 1963) and *Watts Towers* (Gerard Varney 1967).

During the 1970s and 1980s Corinne and Arthur Cantrill screened such 16mm experimental films to a group of artists and colleagues in their home on Sunday evenings. These were both local films and films from the Film Study Collection held at the National Library in Canberra at this time. Martin attended these informal screenings along with other Melbourne artists such as myself, Michael Lee, James Clayden, Hugh McSpedden, Jonas Balsaitis, Chris Knowles and Maggie Fooke. This was our de facto initiation into experimental and abstract film. The induction ranged through viewings of formalist work, personal cinema, avant-garde animations, artist film and video and innovative documentary. Such events included animated works by Robert Breer, Pat O'Neill, Oskar Fischinger, Malcolm Le Grice, Kurt Kren, Peter Kubelka, Lotte Reiniger, Jeff Keen, Berthold Bartosch, Bruce Conner and Stan Brakhage. 'Saw Billabong and Sirius Remembered, read Gene Youngblood's Expanded Cinema (3 times, McLuhan, Buckminster Fuller, and John Cage)' (Martin 1972: 11).

Over the next twenty years Australian experimentation was incorporated into this Library resource, eventually including Martin's *Approximately Water* (1972), *Whitewash* (1973), *Inter-View* (1973), *Leading Ladies* (1975–1979) and *Automatic Single Continuous* (1982). This availability enables this analysis. This work was here placed next to work that had influenced Martin, the earlier hand-made Ubu Collective films and work by Corinne and Arthur Cantrill.

The Cantrills incorporated films like Albie Thoms' *Bluto* (1967) into their workshop presentations and re-published the Ubu Collective 'Handmade Film Manifesto' in their magazine. In Thoms' *Bluto* images were incised with pins, razor blades, styli, sandpaper, steel wool and coloured with texta pens. Ben Goldsmith and Geoffrey Lealand remark that *Bluto* 'reflected artist Paul Klee's concept of taking a line for a walk' (Goldsmith and Lealand 2015: 80). The Cantrills noted hand-made film's marginal cultural position: 'Hand Made film "painting and scratching on film", is the touchstone of contempt expressed by the commercial/professional critics and film industry technicians' (Cantrill and Cantrill 1971a: 4). When noting that hand-made film can sharpen perception, 'to nuance the movement quality and subtlety of calligraphic forms' (Cantrill and Cantrill 1971a: 4), they identify the unique movement and flow that Martin demonstrates in *Approximately Water*.

Despite its current invisibility, in 1980 Sam Rohdie sought out and highlighted Martin's work in a survey of Australian avant-garde film. Rohdie linked it into the self-reflexive structural work emanating out of the London Filmmaker's Co-Op. He also referred to the 1967 Ubu Manifesto on the Handmade Film, penned in Sydney by the Ubu Collective. 'The means of image production coincides with the image produced-the films are "about" scratch, incising paint and dye' (Rohdie 1980: 183). For Rohdie, Martin's 'carefully controlled system and structure' (Rohdie 1980: 207) sets it apart from the more anarchic Ubu work.

Even with this difference Martin does share with Thoms and others a political edge, discussed in the examination *Inter-View* and *Leading Ladies* in particular. For Thoms Godard's idea of making films politically rather than about politics was critical. Though abstract the Ubu films like *Bluto* participated in Australia's anti-war movement, screening at anti-war events. For Thoms these films reflected 'the anxiety of the times, created by Australia's involvement in the Vietnam War and the conservative government's resistance to change' (quoted in Cox 2010: 234).

Martin echoes similar sentiments in the thought bubbles of a political cartoon published in *Cantrills Filmnotes*. 'Smash down the doors of repression, liberate film stocks and equipment and discourage the current trend of regressive nostalgia' (Martin 1972a: 1). Martin's films performs what the Ubu Collective laid out in their manifesto for hand-made film: 'Let no media be denied to hand-made films – they can be scratched, scraped, drawn, inked, coloured, dyed, painted, pissed on, black and white, or coloured, bitten, chewed, filed, rasped. Punctured, ripped, burned, burred, bloodied, with any technique imaginable' (Mudie 1997: 77).

It's worth noting that in 1967 Thoms participated in the 4th International Experimental Film Competition at Knokke-le Zout in Belgium. Thom's film *Bolero* (1967), made with a grant from the Royal Belgian Film Archive, was a finalist, sitting next to films by Michael Snow, Steve Dwoskin and Werner Nekes. *Bluto* was also screened during this festival at an information screening. Thoms' participation in this influential international film event suggests that it is really this next generation of Australian experimentation that followed the Cantrills and Ubu that is unavailable internationally.

Apart from these aesthetic and political considerations, Martin's work colleague, film editor Tony Paterson, has provided sustained technical advice and influence. Tony Paterson was already an experienced film editor when he began working with Martin producing educational films. Paterson was renowned for cutting episodes of the television cop shows, *Homicide* and *Division 4* at Crawford Productions. Upon completing his tertiary studies Martin worked with Paterson as a graphic designer and assistant director making educational films and television, exhibition design and publications. This relationship across film art and the commercial sector began during the Australian film industry's resurrection, in which Paterson played a key role. Paterson edited the first legendary *Mad Max* (George Miller, 1979) for which he won the AACTA (Australian Academy Cinema Television Arts) editing award. The frantic editing tempo of the action sequences of *Mad Max* were at a pace not previously realized. Paterson encouraged Martin's experimentation with technical advice on films like *Leading Ladies* and *Automatic Single Continuous* and by providing sound editing and equipment support for these films.

Formalism

Everything is visual information which either communicates something about itself (A STATEMENT) OR about someone or something else.

MARTIN 1972: 15

Despite the formal bent identified by Rohdie, Martin's own assessment of the structural work emanating from the London's Filmmaker's Co-Op (LFMC) was mixed. On a visit to London for 'a self-imposed exile for four and a half months' (Martin 2014: 27), he reported in correspondence back to *Cantrills Filmnotes*. 'It seems to me that the structural film movement in general, is attempting to aim for the same degree of purity that painting and conceptual art have achieved' (Martin 1976: 33). The discussions around structuralist film he witnessed in London were both "stimulating and depressing" (Martin 1976: 9) and 'seem to totally disregard perceptual experience and any sort of aesthetic appreciation and enjoyment. The approach is one of cold and clinical intellectualizing. Everything is reasoned and artisanal. The intuitive has no place' (Martin 1976: 9). Martin responded similarly to semiology, its signs and signifiers: 'I felt that theory and dissection were important but their approach was somehow divorced from reality. A kind of almost clinical, scientific approach to an inherently humanistic, expressive endeavor' (Martin 2014).

These personal reactions to LFMC's structuralist project in particular suggest that the formalist approach Martin developed may have embraced formalism and explored the nature of perceptual processes but retained a place for the personal and the impact of everyday life he adduced as lost to the work he encountered in London. Similar hybrid approaches are evident in the Melbourne based graphic cinema[3] explorations of this period that emerged out of painting. Jonas Balsaitis explored a dynamic mesh of content and form, Bill Anderson built a meta-narrative of abstract form and performance, Michael Lee explored a dynamic recreation of form inspired by Henri Bergson's thinking on the nature of time while the Cantrills' experimentation emanated out of a personal and intimate laboratory in which their interpersonal dialogues played a key role. The technical and the formal were evident in these approaches but the personal and the intuitive remain in place.

Painter Jonas Balsaitis describes his hour-long film *Processed Process* (1976) as 'completely romantic in concept, symbolic content and decorative in quality' (Balsaitis 1976: 49) in his manifesto-like script. The organized layering of iconic and graphic elements are: 'Geometric structures in continuous transformation through space and time. The code contains the information' (Balsaitis 1976: 50). Bill Anderson's feature-length film *Cross-Sections* (1977) is similarly positioned to *Processed Process* as a mixture of formal strategies further framed with more performative material. It is described in the NFSA database as: 'An experimental film including negative footage, animation and collage images to produce a cross-section of different film techniques'. *Cross-Sections* contains hand-drawn graphic sequences, cut-out animation of an automobile manual, kaleidoscopic effects and rear projections: 'The implicit content then is recent art phenomena and history and this of course includes art movements like impressionism, post-impressionism, expressionism, cubism, futurism, dada, surrealism, abstract-expressionism, minimal, pop and so on. You might call it a cartoon and a parody of this relatively recent art phenomena' (Anderson 1978: 68).

The kaleidoscopic effect deployed in Michael Lee's short film *National Geographic* (1972) is also reflexively informed by the technical considerations of film projection. Images are faded in and out in series, so that each image

[3] Such painting and moving image work by Jonas Balsaitis and Bill Anderson was showcased at Bruce Pollard's Pinecoteca Art Gallery in the early 1970s. The gallery's screenings also included films by James Clayden and Michael Lee.

overlaps and fades into the next. This metamorphosis has the perceptual effect of focusing the viewer's attention not so much on the image itself but on subtle changes in focus and framing. Essentially this technique softens the hard edge of the implicit flicker at the base of projected film and the foundation perceptual phenomenon of persistence of vision at cinema's base. Lee's technique was informed by Henri Bergson's critical thinking around duration and the nature of time. 'His idea was that things continually recreate themselves. It's not a linear structure, it's a continual recreation. And I visualized this as something out of focus and coming into focus' (Lee 1972: 6).

Critic and artist Vikki Riley has also remarked on such a mixture of the technical and the aesthetic in the Cantrill's three-colour separation works: 'This illusion of condensed time, synthetically produced by the three-colour separation technique of shooting three apparently similar scenes and printing them together, for me secures a Romantic ideal of Cinema as a laboratory, a factory where experimentation is lovingly practised and celebrated' (Riley 1985).

The films

Apart from the ephemeral expanded cinema work and often with a multi-year gap Lynsey Martin has completed fourteen single channel self-funded films between 1969 and 2017. As stated, his early work, *Approximately Water* (1972), *Whitewash* (1973), *Inter-View* (1973), *Leading Ladies* (1975–1979) and *Automatic Single Continuous* (1982), is available from the NFSA Non-Theatrical Lending Collection, which was previously housed at the National Library in Canberra. These films, with *Light and Dark* (2006), form the body of the following analysis and are discussed in order of completion.

Approximately Water (1972, four minutes)

This film emerged out of a two-week film workshop organized by Corinne and Arthur Cantrill while Martin was a second-year student at Phillip Institute of Technology:

> We wanted to give the workshop an orientation towards new cinema concepts-film as a means of personal communication, rather than a general filmmaking course imitating film industry procedures. The idea was not only to make film, but for the participants to see as much new work as possible, to meet other filmmakers, and to be aware of the relationship of film ideas/concepts to style and technique.
>
> CANTRILL and CANTRILL 1972: 4

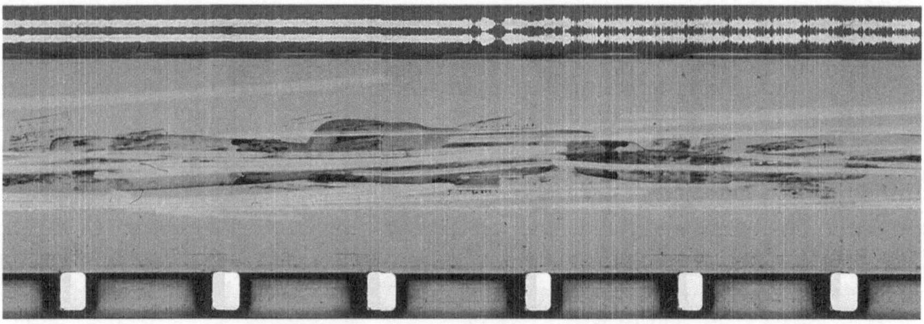

FIGURE 14.1 *Filmstrip:* Approximately Water *(1972) by Lynsey Martin.*

Approximately Water is a conceptual work, focusing on the filmstrip's materiality of film and the mechanics of film projection. It is a straightforward recording of a stream of running tap water. The image-stream is one long continuous shot on a stationary camera. Over the duration of the film different direct-on-film techniques are layered over the running tap-water. The soundtrack is also of running water.

What Martin 'was interested in was the old thing of abstraction vs. reality and the use of the mundane, day to day phenomena as a vehicle of expression' (Martin 1972: 6). The film's content reiterates the medium's mechanics, a strand of film streaming through a film projector or camera gate. The mechanics of the film projector and the film strip are the subject of the film. It is a time slice of running water. When you scroll through the film over a light table every drop of water that passed by the camera lies before you in sculptural form. *Approximately Water* both de-familiarizes and reduces the commonplace to a perceptual exercise in pattern recognition.

This dialogic flow between water, time and film introduces in rudimentary form what Corinne and Arthur Cantrill later explored in their three-colour separation landscape film, *Waterfall* (1985). The same rhythm is also present in their silent *Floterian – Hand Printing from a Film History* (1981). This film was produced by contact printing strips of 35mm, 16mm and 8mm onto discarded 35mm negative film. 'The selection of material was done rather arbitrarily. Four-foot lengths of 16mm, standard 8mm and Super 8 film were hand-contact-printed onto 35mm Eastmancolor negative, using room. The light source was a low-level flood of light and also a beam from a pencil torch, moved along the film' (Cantrill and Cantrill 1988).

The politics of these films differ. In *Waterfall* the Cantrills transport Martin's mundane view of urban everyday existence into a picturesque Australian landscape and in *Floterian* they frame the privilege of history. Martin's *Approximately Water* remains steadfastly stationed in the commonplace, at a routine water fixture servicing the suburban garden.

Whitewash (1973, four minutes)

Whitewash was conceived as a piece of 'pure' hand-made film: 'its realization as a piece of pure hand-made film is that it is created purely with incising and sanding instruments on perfectly transparent, colourless film' (Martin 1973: 14). As with a number of other short films this work was completed over an extended period of time, 'conceived as a piece of handmade film in 1969 it wasn't until a 3-day week-end early in 1973 that I finally got down to realizing the piece' (Martin 1973: 14).

This film's soundtrack is appropriated from Pink Floyd's *The Narrow Way*, from the 1969 *Ummagumma* album and part of band member David Gilmour's creative output. Gilmour uses multiple overdubs to combine the instruments played, a pre-digital practice opened up by magnetic multi-track recording devices that became a standard strategy in the 1960s. Such sonic overdubbing is a similar technical strategy to the visual layering Martin employs in both *Approximately Water* and *Whitewash*.

Martin describes *Whitewash* as not having a beginning, middle or end. The scratches on clear film stock, produced by incising and sanding instruments, communicates a constructed invisibility that resonates with Martin's stuttering public profile. These are ephemeral and fleeting incisions that are difficult to identify. Its first inscriptions are vertical lines, which then shift to horizontal movements and other effects like hole punches and the pulsing effect of scratching intensely on one frame and then leaving the next frame blank to create a soft flicker effect. There is also the subtle rhythm of watermarks created by leaving sprayed water to dry on the film after being over-sprayed with a fixative.

The images of the film documented on the pages and cover of *Cantrills Filmnotes* in 1973 were produced from the original scratched material and highlight the scratches in a way not available in a viewing of a print of the film. These stills were shot with light from the side of the frame as well as from behind the image to produce a three-dimensional quality. The incision's cavity and its removed residue are visible. This original *Whitewash* is materially different from its fogged-like copies. Essentially this film, through its reproduction, white-washes itself. Every new generational copy made of it is whiter than the original. The mutilations disappear. Such erasure stresses an essential characteristic of analogue film that sets it apart from the digital moving image where each copy is a perfect clone. Analogue decay is progressive where digital decay tends to crash a file completely. *Whitewash*'s content is the progressive material process of whitewashing.

The title *Whitewash* invites multiple meanings. Whitewash originally described a low-cost lime and chalk based paint used on farms to aid in equipment sanitation. During World War II in winter 'whitewash' camouflaged military equipment. In the laundry boiling white cloth with a whitewash additive brightened these textiles. Such uses have been transformed into metaphors utilized in public and political debate. Whitewash came to describe one-sided sporting contests, or the act of cleaning up of one's political profile, to neutralize any negative implications. Whitewash can be a metaphor for censorship; 'to gloss over or cover up vices, crimes or scandals or to exonerate by means of a perfunctory investigation or through biased presentation of data' (Merriam-Webster Dictionary n.d.).

Today 'whitewash' can also be a derogatory term describing a racial minority that has successfully assimilated into western society. In Australia 'whitewash' can indicate a racist event or agenda. There is a powerful scene at the beginning of Phil Noyce's *Rabbit Proof Fence* (2002) that demonstrates the White Australia policy's originating fervour in relation to indigenous Australians. Neville, Protector of Western Australian Aborigines in 1931, in a slide slow presentation demonstrates how half-caste aborigines will be 'bred out' through the whiter offspring of succeeding generations. This is Neville's demonstrated definition of the government's assimilation policy. Martin's use of the title *Whitewash* is read here as an ethical yet inarticulate revulsion against such racist views. The skin of the film is a metaphor for the skin of the Australian body as performed by Neville and Martin's self-mutilation of it.

Whitewash sets in train a serial self-mutilation. When we inscribe our own bodies in this way, it is considered a form of traumatic self-harm. As a psychological term, self-injury is the act of deliberately harming the surface of your own body, such as cutting or burning yourself. It's typically not meant as a suicide attempt. Rather, this type of self-mutilation is an unhealthy way to cope with emotional pain, intense anger and frustration. 'Self-injury is defined as the intentional destruction of body tissue without suicidal intent and for purposes not socially sanctioned' (Klonsky 2007: 1039). Whitewash also brings to mind acts of obsessive cleaning. Again, within clinical psychology this is a well-known form of obsessive compulsive disorder and it is characterized by the presence of recurring repeating intrusive and unwanted thoughts, images and impulses. Inside Martin's formalism, the personal and the political return as a material mutilation that discounts itself.

Inter-View (1973, twenty-five minutes)

Certainly, the revulsion, self-harm and censorship at the heart of *Whitewash* takes clearer form in Martin's next film *Inter-View*. Here, related erasure strategies are directed at newsreel footage connected to the Vietnam War and the numbing effects experienced by Martin of propaganda and censorship identified in the nightly television news.

Inter-View has two parts, the first is of news connected to the Vietnam War shot directly off the television screen with a Bolex 16mm camera. The television monitor's signature rolling bars are intermittently visible. The second part is composed of original 16mm television broadcast material, discarded black and white out-takes of interviews. Martin did not scratch the original broadcast footage, which had a magnetic stripe soundtrack, but had a print made, which was then systematically mutilated. The film is silent despite the importance of the voice to convey the original meaning. Like the partial erasure of the image, sound has been totally muted. This film's duration and silence imposes a different way of looking on the viewer. Martin enlists a Zen saying to make his point: 'If something is boring for 2 minutes, try it for 4, if still boring after 4 try it for 8 and if still boring try it for 16 and so on. Soon one discovers it is not really boring at all' (Martin 1973: 15).

Once this boredom subsides another way of looking opens up. As we watch *Inter-View* our interest in deciphering what faces say falls away. We search for other clues. Instead we focus on gestures, eye movements and pauses. Incidental features such as the microphone, a hand or a mouth become our focus as increasing amounts of the image are erased by razor blade. The dance of this erased texture and its abstracted terrain become the subject. This image removal as an angry response to the Vietnam War. Martin understands his incisions are an attack on the manipulative nature of the originating newsreel material.

For Martin's generation, the Vietnam War left a lifetime impact. Eighteen-year-old friends were conscripted and sent to war. You were conscripted by chance, by a roll of the dice, announced on the radio like a macabre TattsLotto result. How do you respond to this possibility from inside the safe suburban sprawl that has cocooned your childhood? Martin's response both enlists and creates a critical visual language that talked to this situation's visceral impact on his body and senses. Although abstracted such experimentation is implicitly political but of a different register from that provided by any explicit documentary form. Such a language's syntax and address stand in contrast to the master's house, the language of the dominant culture.

There are four versions of *Inter-View* in existence. The first version is the 16mm original with its degenerating magnetic soundtrack containing the conversations that are denied the viewer. This version has never been available for public viewing and sits undisturbed in Martin's shed. Second, there is the systematically mutilated and fragile copy, with its grooves, residue and uneven surface with no soundtrack. Third, there is the projection copy, which has been printed from this second mutilated roll of film. Its surface is smooth and clean. The earlier incisions are now only a photographic record. The fourth copy is a digital transfer from this projection copy, now eternally reproducible with no progressive decay. Further, the digital is prone to instant decay. Any degeneration would render this file unplayable. It is one or the other with nothing in between.

Leading Ladies (1975–1979, five minutes)

> Collingwood Technical School was considering setting up a 16mm projectionists' licence training facility in opposition to RMIT, and procured a large box of discarded film leaders from the State Film Centre. When the school decided to scrap the idea of running the course, the leaders were to be thrown out. Having made films using 'found' footage, I recognised the leaders as having the potential to become a film and asked if I could have them. Thus, *Leading Ladies* was born.
>
> MARTIN 2015b

Leading Ladies assembles those images placed at a film's head and tail by laboratory technicians for quality control. It also uses countdown leader and other physical marks made by technicians to quality control the projected film. Images of women's faces, countdown leader, other laboratory reference strips, lettering and printer sync marks. The countdown numbers enabled projectionists to focus the film before the real action began. The women's faces, referred to as 'Kodak Ladies' or 'China Girls' are colour images spliced into the films to check the colour balance and exposure of the prints, to ensure that the film processing is operating within industry standards. These are not the leading ladies chosen by the casting department or hired on the director's couch, but nameless women accessible to the production line's proletariat. This hidden material becomes the film's subject.

These strips are designed to be inspected over a light table and so only need to span a handful of frames. Their speed produces a subliminal trace when screened. These 'China Girls' regularly held a colour bar, to further aid in colour grading. These faces are consistently easy on the eye, likely the residue of male dominated workplaces. The women's white skin can remind us that exposure and colour in cinema has been calibrated for white skin, not black or brown. Such hidden consequences of racism can be the most

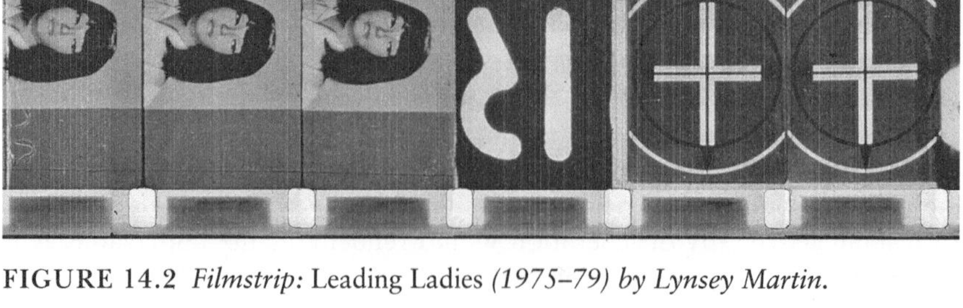

FIGURE 14.2 *Filmstrip:* Leading Ladies *(1975–79) by Lynsey Martin.*

coercive, as they are woven seamlessly into the fabric of daily life and consequently 'forgotten'.

The soundtrack is similarly compiled from the clicks and buzz sounds of the laboratory's printing and processing operations. The soundtrack was constructed with the assistance of Tony Paterson using an EMS synthesizer and other studio equipment. Martin had been able to use Tony Paterson's flat-bed editing table to assemble *Leading Ladies*. In the title Martin dedicates the film to Bruce Conner's *Cosmic Ray* (1961), although he had only seen that film after he had nearly finished *Leading Ladies*. Placed at the start of the film Martin's text states: 'I have dedicated *Leading Ladies* to Bruce Connors [sic] *Cosmic Ray* (b & w 1961), the two films are similar in some respects, although I had not seen *Cosmic Ray* until 1976, when my film was nearly finished' (Martin 1979: 32).

This is an ambiguous and equivocal gesture. Clearly Martin recognized an affinity with Conner's work but he had undoubtedly come to it through his own creativity. This dedication turns Martin's film into an even more denied practice than Conner's. Through this dedication Martin erases his own originality and reasserts a subsidiary role for Australian experimental film in the 1970s.

Automatic Single Continuous (1982, nine minutes)

A film largely misunderstood although its aims are quite straight forward. An understated materialistic depiction of the same scene that emphasizes the role of the camera, the element of chance and the lyricism of the constantly moving camera.

MARTIN 2015

Automatic Single Continuous records the traffic and crowd movement at Melbourne's busy Flinders and Swanson Streets intersection from the elevated square opposite Flinders Street Railway Station. The title refers to the automatic exposure function of the Super 8 camera on which the film was shot, the three single takes from which the film is constructed and the continuous recording this entails. Two takes were shot in daylight and one was shot at night. The sounds of traffic, co-edited with Tony Paterson, make up the soundtrack.

It is a summer's day with even and clear light. The camera moves effortlessly over moving bodies, faces and the intersection's architecture, tram lines, light poles and cars and wiring, all abstracted elements connected through movement and space. The section ends with the camera panning upwards to the sky. Although not strictly animation, the quick camera movements, particularly in the night scene, approach the kind of visual artifacts normally provided by single frame transitions and movement. At night, the moving camera paints with the lights of the moving cars and the traffic lights. This effect is reminiscent of the kind of hand-drawn gestures and visual artifacts Martin constructs in *Whitewash* and *Approximately Water*.

This material was originally shot on Super 8 and blown up to 16mm on the Melbourne State College JK Optical Printer, where Arthur Cantrill taught film. Because of its age the film has acquired a red tint. This is due to the breakdown of dyes in the film's emulsion. Dyes fail over time, decomposing through temperature and light fluctuations and through chemical reactions to materials within the dyes themselves. In the 1980s cyan dye has proved to be particularly unstable.

The viewer's scanning eye becomes the subject of the film. We are mapping public space subjectively from the perspective of the performing body. Martin's camera movement suggests the same saccadic rhythms, scans and double takes that the eye performs effortlessly in negotiating three-dimensional space. This film documents a fragmented mode of looking that has evolved through the requirements of inner city living. In this post-industrial space movement in and out of crowds, taxis, cars and public transport creates a complex layering of faces, movement, reflected light and screens. This is the perceptual impact of city life that Martin's *Automatic Single Continuous* constructs into a cohesive whole.

Light and Dark (2006, twelve minutes)

> An ambitious film that pushes photochemical representation to its limits, is almost a complete summary of what the hand made film can do (and all in black and white) and is my first film in which 'the music and sound' is completely of my own doing.
>
> MARTIN 2015

The black and white *Light and Dark* was started in 1973 and completed in 2006. Martin emerged out of a deep depression to complete *Light and Dark*, decades after it was shot. The film was started when Martin moved out of his parents' home to house-sit the Cantrill's Brunswick residence while they lived in Oklahoma. *Light and Dark* was shot on inexpensive black and white film but printed onto colour print stock, giving the screening copy a brownish tinge, approaching sepia. It examines the intimate recesses of a private living space. *Light and Dark* is a dark and foreboding work that appears largely shot at night.

It was shot towards and out of the window of the room from which Martin was house-minding the Cantrill's home. A scratch film reminiscent of *Whitewash* is projected onto the wall and onto the window's blinds. Scratches on the film mimic, are in dialogue with, similar incisions on the projected film inside the film. Similarly, there are layers of design on the film's surface and inside the photographed image. It is as if Martin has transformed this living space into a large Camera Obscura.

The window onto which these moving images are projected faces west. There are three takes of the window and in the last the blinds roll up and the film projects through into the darkness onto the brick wall next door. These shots are framed like a still life, with ferns visible, a book about Dada and an image from a Robert Crumb cartoon.

Light and Dark showcases a library of effects. It is a mixture of stanzas of animation mixed with real-time imagery. These effects include sections of countdown leader, flicker and pieces of Letratone attached to the film. Slowly scrolling through these sections the hand drawn fades and strips of Letratone are visible as balanced stanzas of graphic design. Inspection over a light table reveals their intricate, detailed and considered patterns. Clearly the film was assembled in consideration of this dormant sculptural state.

Martin's sequences of dormant design codes have a precise and determined function in relation to cinema yet deliver a very different language when viewed as scrolls. These are artifacts from, and traces of, Martin's design teaching. As a visual communication and design teacher Martin delivered an emphasis on technical drawings, finely crafted and accurate design, the clear and uncluttered presentation of information. The found image, so much part of *Inter-View* and *Leading Ladies* was also part of the curriculum he communicated to his students through Duchamp's ready-mades or Warhol's pop images. This is all locatable here in *Light and Dark* as a scrolled-through musical score. In Martin's visual communication teaching practice such imagery is not only about aesthetics and form. As my analysis argues about Martin's own films, it is also about content and the message that each particular form delivers.

A belated historic bridging

That *Light and Dark* was initiated in 1973 and completed twenty-five years later defines and overwhelms this film. This timespan transforms its content into a forgotten memory, as time itself transforms the film's meaning. All forgetting that has taken place over previous decades becomes unwittingly incorporated as content. The film folds in on itself, embracing all that frustration and darkness resident in the lost open-ended incomplete works.

During these three decades, there was a shift from analogue to digital moving image practices. The opportunities to screen film as film have diminished and the accessibility of digital cameras and editing software has brought about a marked increase in short film production. Consequently, the way 16mm films are now received by an audience has changed, moving from participation in an underground artist community to the slippery realm of the unique inaccessible artifact or performative event.

Martin's filmic language is grounded in the technical and the micro level of the frame and its image clusters rather than the filmed sequence of photographable events and its inherent truths. When the photographed image is available in his work it is acted upon, de-stabilized, mutilated and blurred. Having familiarized himself with this abstract language's rhythms and effects in *Approximately Water* and *Whitewash* Martin has indexed these rhythms in relation to the impact of mass media (*Inter-View*) to the architecture of public space (*Automatic Single Continuous*) and then personal space and memory (*Light and Dark*).

Martin's project fits neatly into a disappeared community of Australian abstract experimental filmmaking activity from the 1970s in Melbourne. Despite its documentation within *Cantrills Filmnotes* these films are largely unknown and inaccessible internationally. Where Corinne and Arthur Cantrill achieved and retain an international profile for their experiments, which included animation, artists such as Martin did not. Framed by its appearance in *Cantrills Filmnotes* this community of animation activity included the work of Jonas Balsaitis, Bill Anderson, Hugh McSpedden, Michael Lee and the Cantrills themselves. These film artists although clearly concerned with form retained a commitment to content. This shared project partially took on the formalisms that emerged internationally in the 1960s and 1970s in film art under the banner of structuralist film. The closer reading of Martin's work undertaken here suggests that its distinction and difference from a purely formalist abstract cinema is apparent in a continued engagement with the personal and political impact of daily life and lived experience.

References

Anderson, B. (1978). 'Cross-Sections', *Cantrills Filmnotes*, 27/28 (March): 64–68.

Balsaitis, J. (1976). 'Processed Process: Script of the Film by Jonas Balsaitis', *Cantrills Filmnotes*, 23/24 (July): 44–50.

Bendazzi, G. (2016). *Animation: A World History. Volumes I, II, III*. Boca Raton: CRC Press.

Cantrill, A. (2008). 'Right Back to the Billabong (1970)', in S. MacDonald (ed.) *Canyon Cinema: The Life and Times of an Independent Film Distributor*, 140. Oakland: UC Press.

Cantrill, C. and A. Cantrill (1971). 'New American Cinema in the National Library of Australia Film Collection', *Cantrills Filmnotes*, 2 (April): 17–19.

Cantrill, C. and A. Cantrill (1971a). 'The Hand Made Film: A Survey of Work by Len Lye, Albie Thoms, Aggy Read, Harry Smith, Stan Brakhage, Terry Turney, Andrew Pike, Fred Harden', *Cantrills Filmnotes*, 2 (April): 4–10.

Cantrill, C. and A. Cantrill (1972). 'How Do You Arrange a 14 Day Film Workshop', *Cantrills Filmnotes*, 9 (August): 4.
Cantrill, C. and A. Cantrill (1988). 'San Francisco Cinematheque Program Notes'. San Francisco Cinematheque.
Clayden, J. (1971). 'Interview with James Clayden', *Cantrills Filmnotes*, 6 (October): 15–20.
Cox, D. (2010). *Sign Wars: The Culture Jammers Strike Back!* San Francisco: Ledatape.
Goldsmith, B. and G. Lealand (2015). *Directory of World Cinema Australia and New Zealand*. Bristol: Intellect Books.
Klonsky, D. E. (2007). 'Non-Suicidal Self-Injury: An Introduction', *Journal of Clinical Psychology: In Session*, 63 (11): 1039–1043.
Knox, J. (2008). 'On, Off, Into and Across the Record', *RealTime Arts*, 83 (Feb/Mar): 49. Available online: http://www.realtimearts.net/article/issue83/8908 (accessed 1 September 2017).
Lee, M. (1972). 'An Interview with Michael Lee on his film National Geographic Magazine', *Cantrills Filmnotes*, 6 (December): 6–7.
Martin, L. (1972). 'Short Films', *Cantrills Filmnotes*, 9 (August): 6.
Martin, L. (1972a). 'Violence and the Destruction of the Anaemic Cinema', *Cantrills Filmnotes*, 12 (December): 1.
Martin, L. (1973). 'Notes and Notations', *Cantrills Filmnotes*, 16 (December): 13–22.
Martin, L. (1976). 'Letters from Lynsey Martin and Jeff Keen', *Cantrills Filmnotes*, 23/24 (July): 9, 13, 33.
Martin, L. (1979). 'Leading Ladies', *Cantrills Filmnotes*, 29/30 (February): 32.
Martin, L. (2013). 'Program Notes provided for Screening Belgrade', Serbia (Melbourne, Self-Published Notes 2013) (accessed 1 September 2017).
Martin, L. (2014). *Frames: The Casual and The Considered and Beyond*, Melbourne: Self-Published Notebook: 1–49.
Martin, L. (2015). Email Correspondence Monday, 13 April 2015, 7.32 pm.
Martin, L. (2015a). Email Correspondence Sunday, 12 April 2015, 5.06 pm.
Martin, L. (2015b). 'Notes for Abstract Cinema Screening'. Handout Melbourne International Animation Festival.
Merriam-Webster Dictionary. Available online: https://www.merriam-webster.com/dictionary/whitewash (accessed 1 September 2017).
McIntyre, I. (2006). *Tomorrow Is Today: Australia in the Psychedelic Era 1966–1970*. Kent Town, South Australia: Wakefield Press.
McSpedden, H. (1971). 'Alternative Cinema: Interview with Hugh McSpedden', *Cantrills Filmnotes*, 4 (July): 10–15.
Mudie, P. (1997). *Ubu Films: Sydney Underground Movies 1965–1970*. Sydney: UNSW Press.
Riley, V. (1985). 'The Film Work of A. & C. Cantrill', *Scratch* #6, Paris. Available online: http://www.arthurandcorinnecantrill.com/Vikki%20Riley.doc.htm (accessed 1 September 2017).
Rohdie, S. (1980). 'Avant-garde', in S. Murray (ed.), *The New Australian Cinema*, 183–199. Melbourne: Nelson.

CONTRIBUTORS

Midhat Ajanović-Ajan is a writer, film scholar, cartoonist and filmmaker born in Sarajevo in 1959. He studied journalism in Sarajevo and practised animation in Zagreb Film Studio of Animation. Since 1994 he has lived in Gothenburg where he obtained a PhD in Film Studies. He teaches theories of visual communications as well as film and animation history at University West in Trollhättan and has published a number of literary and scholarly books. Some of his most prominent books on animation are *The Man & the Line* (2014, Croatian and English), *Life in a Cartoon* (2010; Croatian and English), *Den rörliga skämtteckningen* (2009; Swedish), *Caricature and Movement* (2008, Croatian) and *Animation and Realism* (2004, Croatian and English). He worked as the organizer and artistic director on several festivals, and was a member of a number of international juries. At the 20th World Festival of Animated Film, Animafest Zagreb 2010, he received the Award for Outstanding Contribution to Animation Studies.

Giannalberto Bendazzi, currently an independent scholar, is a former Visiting Professor of History of Animation at the Nanyang Technological University in Singapore and a former professor at the Università degli Studi di Milano. Bendazzi started his career as a journalist and an independent, self-funded scholar. He turned to full-time academic teaching in the late 1990s and has lectured extensively in all continents. An Italian by birth, Bendazzi's best efforts are devoted to international projects. An acclaimed author in his sphere, his best-known book is *Cartoons: 100 Years of Cinema Animation*, a world history of the medium published in Italian, English, French, Spanish and Persian. In 2016, he continued this research with the three-volume work *Animation: A World History*. He was the recipient of the Animafest Zagreb Award for Outstanding Contribution to Animation Studies in 2002.

Olga Bobrowska (1987) is a PhD candidate in Film Studies at Jagiellonian University, Kraków and an author of academic articles on the subjects of Polish and Chinese animation. She is the director and co-founder of StopTrik International Film Festival (Maribor, Slovenia; Łódź, Poland), a festival dedicated to stop motion animation. She frequently collaborates with other festivals, among them Animateka (Ljubljana), Etiuda&Anima (Kraków) and Krakow Film Festival. Film programmes she curated have been presented at various festivals and events in Poland, Slovenia, Croatia, The Netherlands, Finland and China. Her reviews and critiques have been published in the Polish magazine *Kino* and international animation magazine *Zippy Frames*. In 2016, she co-edited the monograph *Obsession. Perversion. Rebellion. Twisted Dreams of Central European Animation.*

Michał Bobrowski (1981). In 2010, he obtained a PhD in Film Studies at the Jagiellonian University in Kraków. He is the author of the book, *Akira Kurosawa: The Artist of the Borderlands*. Currently he teaches in the Faculty of Philosophy at Jagiellonian University in Kraków. He is the Programme Director of the StopTrik International Film Festival, an event dedicated to stop motion animation, held in Slovenia and Poland. He is a curator, a cultural activist and an author of over thirty articles devoted to classic Japanese and American cinema as well as animation. In 2016, he co-edited a monograph *Obsession. Perversion. Rebellion. Twisted Dreams of Central European Animation.*

Franziska Bruckner (1981, Salzburg, Austria) studied theatre, film and media studies at the University of Vienna as well as painting and animation at the University of Applied Arts Vienna. From 2009 to 2013 she was a university assistant at the department of Theater, Film and Media Studies in Vienna and on the editorial board of the e-journal *rezens.tfm*. From 2013 to 2017 she worked as a lecturer for animation theory and practice at the University of Vienna, University of Tübingen and University of Applied Sciences Upper Austria. Since 2017 she has been Head of the Research Group Media Creation at the St. Poelten University of Applied Sciences. She is co-coordinator of the AG Animation within the German-speaking Society of Media Studies and board member of ASIFA-Austria.

Dirk de Bruyn is Associate Professor of Screen and Design at Deakin University, Melbourne, Australia. As well as sustaining his own creative experimental animation and multi-screen performance practice for over 40 years he has written about this area in *Cantrills Filmnotes* and *Senses of Cinema*. His book *The Performance of Trauma in Moving Image Art* was published in 2014. He is committed to documenting, promoting and presenting Australian animation in his teaching practice and at national and international forums.

Edwin Carels is a teacher and researcher in the arts at the School of Arts KASK/HoGent. He holds a PhD in the arts, for which he wrote the dissertation *Animation beyond Animation – a Media-archeological Approach to the Use of Animation in Contemporary Art*. He is currently working on a post-doctoral project under the title 'Counter-archives'. Edwin

Carels is also active as a film programmer and curator for the International Film Festival of Rotterdam. As a writer, he publishes essays on media-archeology, visual arts, film and animation. His most recent publication is a monography on the Quay Brothers (*The Black Drawings*, Ludion publishers, 2018). Recent exhibitions have involved collaborations with Chris Marker, The Quay Brothers, Robert Breer, Jan Švankmajer, Zoe Beloff and Ken Jacobs, among many others.

Nikica Gilić (1973, Split, Croatia) Film theorist (PhD) and historian, works as associate professor and Chair of Film Studies at the Department for Comparative Literature, Faculty of Humanities and Social Sciences in Zagreb. He also teaches at the Academy of Drama Art in Zagreb. Member of the Council of Animafest Zagreb, he is also an Associate Research Fellow at Graduate School for East and Southeast European Studies in Regensburg and Münich. Editor-in-chief of the film journal *Hrvatski filmski ljetopis/Croatian Cinema Chronicle*, he is a member of editorial board of Germany-based online journal *Apparatus*. He has published three books in cinema studies and numerous articles in journals and books. He was editor of *Filmski leksikon* (Film Lexicon, 2003, with Bruno Kragić), which also deals with animation.

Marcin Giżycki is an art and film historian, critic and filmmaker. Professor at Polish-Japanese Academy of Information Technology in Warsaw, Poland. Artistic Director of 'Animator' International Animated Film Festival in Poznan, Poland. Senior Lecturer at Rhode Island School of Design, former Editor-in-Chief of *Animafilm* magazine (1979–81). He is the author of seven books and over 300 articles on film and art, including *Avant-Garde and Cinema: Film in Polish Avant-Garde Circles Between the Wars* (1996), *Disney Was Not the Only One* (2000), *The End and What Next? Essays on Postmodernism, Contemporary Art, and the End of the Century* (2001) and *Wenders Go Home!* (2006). His interests range from history of Avant-Garde movements in the twentieth century to history of animated, experimental and documentary film to the theory of Postmodernism. He has made a number of documentary, experimental and animated films, among them *The Island of Jan Lenica* (1998), *Travels of Daniel Szczechura* (2005), *Panta Rhei* (2008), *Aquatura* (2010), *A Magic-Lantern Life* (2014) and *Monument* (2016). He received the Animafest Zagreb Award for Outstanding Contribution to Animation Studies in 2016.

Chunning Guo (Maggie) teaches at Art School at Renmin University of China. She was a visiting artist at Central Saint Martins of UAL and she was also a resident artist at Centre Intermondes in France. Recently she gained her PhD with a paper about Independent Animation. She has presented papers at Animafest Scanner II and III in Zagreb, Twisted Dreams of History

Forum I and II in Poland, and 2015 BFX Conference and APES 2015 in the UK. She worked as a visiting scholar at the Vancouver Film School. She received a Jury Award at the 11th Chinese Independent Film Festival, the NETPAC Award at the Busan Short Film Festival. Her collaborative work *Ketchup* was selected by the Stuttgart Animation Festival, FANTOCHE Animation Festival, Animafest Zagreb etc. Recently she has worked as a visiting scholar in Radboud University in the Netherlands for a year.

Mikhail Gurevich, independent scholar and critic, was born in Moscow, Russia. He writes on literature, theatre and film, with special interest in animation, puppetry and experimental theatre and cinema. From the late 1970s he was contributing to major cultural publications in Russia and later edited independent periodicals. He worked as a consultant for professional associations in theatre and cinema and served as a board member and an adviser at Soiuzmultfilm and Pilot animation studios. From 1992 he has lived in the USA. He has written on animation for *ASIFA* magazine, and festival and academic publications. He has recently contributed extensively to the history of world animation by Giannalberto Bendazzi. He was a guest lecturer in a number of universities internationally and participated in many festivals as curator, juror and discussant. Lately, he has been in charge of animation selection and the jury at the Blow-up Film Festival (Chicago). He is also a documentary filmmaker, interpreter and translator.

Fatemeh Hosseini-Shakib is currently Head of Animation Department and a lecturer of animation theory/aesthetics as well as cinema/media theory in the departments of Animation and Cinema of the Faculty of Cinema and Theatre, Tehran Art University, Iran. She has formerly been a lecturer/research student in animation studies in the UK (UCA, Farnham) until 2009. Her current research interests include the question of representation and realism and its hybrid nature in traditional 3D/puppet animation (as well as in CGI and digital animation), Iranian Animation and its emerging forms and discourses, and finally animation as a tangible element of modernity in the non-western countries.

Holger Lang (1964, Nürnberg, Germany) is an Austrian artist, filmmaker and producer, living and working in Vienna. Since 2007 he has worked as a researcher in media arts at Webster University in Vienna, where he has also taught – both in the United States and Austria – since 1995. In addition to his academic and artistic practice, he runs an art gallery in Vienna, curating exhibitions and also programmes of selected European and Austrian animation and experimental films for various international venues. For several years he has been a board member of ASIFA Austria. Currently he also serves as an ambassador for Austria at the European Animation Award. In collaboration with various associations and institutions, he is organizing and/or participateing in the coordination of academic, artistic and media-based projects and events.

Irena Paulus (1970, Zagreb, Croatia) graduated in Musicology at the Music Academy of the University of Zagreb; specialized in Film Music at the European Film College, Denmark; and earned her MA and PhD degrees in film studies at University of Zagreb. Paulus is a tenured teacher at the Franjo Lučić Art School in Velika Gorica, Croatia. She also teaches film music at the Academy of Dramatic Art and the Faculty of Humanities and Social Sciences and, occasionally, at the Music academy in Zagreb. She is a long-time collaborator of the Croatian National Radio (Hrvatski radio). Paulus has written four books on film music in Croatian: *Music from the Screen: Croatian Film Music Between 1942 and 1990*, *Brainstorming: Notes on Film Music*, *Kubrick's Musical Odyssey* and *Theory of Film Music through Theory of Film Sound*.

Andrijana Ružić (Belgrade, 1972) graduated in History and Criticism of Art at the Università degli Studi in Milan, Italy. She specialized in History of animated film under professor Giannalberto Bendazzi. The subject of her thesis was the opus of John and Faith Hubley. For the last six years, she has been a curator of programmes dedicated to independent animated film on the International Comics Festival in Belgrade. Based in Milan, Italy she continues to write articles and essays regarding the independent authors of animated film.

Mareike Sera studied 'Visual Theories' (BA Hons.) and 'Film History and Criticism' (MA) at the University of East London and recently completed her doctoral degree on the grotesque in the work of Jan Švankmajer at Humboldt University Berlin. Her research focuses on intermediality: where do different media intersect and how are they experienced and understood in this interrelation? The approach that she pursues is inspired by thinkers such as Franco 'Bifo' Berardi, Gilles Deleuze and Paul Ricoeur. Ms Sera publishes in international book collaborations and journals, such as *Intermediality in Contemporary Eastern European and Russian Cinema* (Ágnes Pethő, ed.), *Critical Studies: An Interdisciplinary Journal* and *Im Wandel: Metamorphosen der Animation* (Julia Eckel, Erwin Feyersinger und Meike Uhrig, eds).

Daniel Šuljić (1971, Zagreb, Croatia) is a filmmaker and musician. He graduated at the University of Applied Arts Vienna in 1997. In his film making he employs different animation techniques, from oil on glass, sand animation to cutouts and pencil drawings. His awarded films include: *Transparency* (2015), *Evening Star* (1993), *Leckdonalds* (1995), *The Cake* (1997), *Sun, Salt and Sea* (1997), *Film with a Girl* (2000), *Short Life* (2007),

I Can Imagine It Very Well (2004) among others. He was an associate lecturer at the Department of Animation and New Media at the Academy of Fine Arts in Zagreb and at the Art University in Linz. Since 2011 he has been artistic director of the World Festival of Animated Film, Animafest Zagreb.

Hrvoje Turković (1943, Zagreb, Croatia). Film theorist and critic, he worked at the Academy of Drama Art, University of Zagreb, lecturing mostly film theory (theory of film editing and film discourse) from 1977 until retirement in 2009 as a full professor; he is still teaching as an external professor. He was the editor-in-chief and is now a member of the editorial board of the film journal *Hrvatski filmski ljetopis/Croatian Cinema Chronicle*, and the chief editor of the *Filmski enciklopedijski rjecnik/Film Encyclopedic Dictionary* (in progress, LZ Miroslav Krleža). He has published numerous articles and fourteen books on film and TV, one of them on animation (*Život izmišljotina/Life of Fabrications*, 2012). He received major Croatian life-achievement awards for outstanding contribution to cinema scholarship and cinema cultures.

Paul Wells is Director of the Animation Academy, Loughborough University, UK, and has published widely in Animation Studies, including *Understanding Animation*, *Re-Imagining Animation*, *The Animated Bestiary* and the forthcoming *Animation, Sport and Culture*. Paul is also an established writer and director for film, TV, radio and theatre, and conducts workshops and consultancies worldwide based on his book, *Scriptwriting*. His latest documentary is *Mackinnon & Saunders: A Model Studio*, featuring Tim Burton, and recent scripts include 'The Oil Kid', 'Trios' and a feature animation currently in development. Paul is also the Chair of the Association. He is the recipient of Animafest Zagreb Award for Outstanding Contribution to Animation Studies in 2018.

INDEX

A Da 71, 75–80
AARON computer program 7
Abductees (Vester) 104
Academy Leaders Variations 78–9
'Adventures in Success' (Allen) 60
advertising/commercials 89, 106
Åhlin, Per 107
Albala, Hans 89, 90
Alice (Švankmajer) 30, 38, 40, 42–5
Alice in Wonderland (Carroll) 42–3, 45–6
Allen, Rebecca 60
analogy 29–31, 46–7
  Czech Surrealism 32–5, 45
  and dialectics 32–5
  examples 35–46
  missing premise 31–2
Anderson, Bill 240
Animafest see World Festival of Animated Film/*Animafest*, Zagreb
Animafilm 3, 4
animasophy 61–2, 63
animation, ASIFA definition 3–4
animation festivals 3–5
'Animation Spectrum' 14–18, 20–1
'animification' 19–22, 23, 24, 25, 26
Anstey, E. and Elton, A. 103
Antonisz: Technology for Me Is a Form of Art 217
Antonisz, J. and Zaremba, B. 222
Antonisz, Julian: DIY method 213–15
  art, politics, laughter 229–30
  Bakhtinian inspirations 215–18
  biology-technology or DIY organisms 226–8
  original copy or curse of the reproduction 218–23
  technology-art or soul of an instrument 223–6
Anwar, Roshihan 70
Apollinaire, Guillaume 138
Approved for Adoption (Jung) 102
Approximately Water (Martin) 241–2, 250
Arnulf Rainer (Kubelka) 90
ART I computer program 57
Asian-African Film Festival 70
ASIFA 3–4, 24, 95, 96, 97, 163–4
aspiration, phenomenology of 42–4
Association of the Austrian Cinematic Industries 87
Australian experimental animation *see* Martin, Lynsey
Austria: small production environment 83–5, 97–8
  opening world – exponential expansion 94–7
  origins and backgrounds 85–7
  slow ascent to progressive thinking 87–91
  women artists 91–4, 96
Austriaco, Padiglione 14
Automatic Single Continuous (Martin) 247–8, 250

Bachelard, Gaston 43–4
Bakhtin, Mikhail 217, 218
Balsaitis, John 240
Barthes, Roland 36–7
Basgier, Thomas 197, 201, 202, 203
Bataille, George: *Story of the Eye* 35–7, 40
Bendazzi, Giannalberto ix–x, 66, 143–4, 178, 181, 204, 217, 233–4
Benjamin, Walter 138, 221

Berardi, Franco 'Bifo' 31, 40–2, 45
Bergdahl, Victor 105–6
Billeter, Fritz 93
biographies, visual 102–3
biology-technology 226–8
Blossoming No 3369 (Kovásznai) 24–5
Blu-Karma-Tiger (Hulterstan and Actis) 111
Bluto (Thoms) 234–5, 238, 239
Borysiewicz, Ewa 217
Breer, Robert: flipbooks 117–18
  animated archives 130–1
  back and forth 139–40
  doodle or spaghetti 122–4
  frame by frame 120–2
  hand and eyeglasses 125–6
  loops and mutations 126–30
  multiple firsts 135–7
  pivotal moments 118–20
  semantic cinema 133–5
  subverting the aura 137–9
  synaptic cinema 131–3
Broken – The Women's Prison at Hohemeck (Schlecht and Lahl) 102
Bruckner, Franziska 93
Bubble Bath: A Musical Special Effects Film to the Rhythm of a Heartbeat (Kovásznai) 25–6
Burford, Jennifer 122, 128, 132
Burson, Nancy 59

Ça-ira: Song of the French Revolution (Kovásznai) 25
Cantrill, A. and Cantrill, C./*Cantrills Filmnotes* 234, 235, 237, 238, 239, 240, 241, 242, 243, 248–9, 250
Carroll, Lewis: *Alice in Wonderland* 42–3, 45–6
Castoriadis, Cornelius 30
censorship 229, 244
Chinese animation 61–2, 79–81
  and cultural nationalism: origin of *minzu* style 62–9
  how the canon was tempered 69–79
Chisaan, Choirotun 70
The City Through My Eyes (Kovásznai) 25
Clarke, Joan 53
clay animation 202–3
Clayden, James 236
Cohen, Harold 7
Cold war era 14, 19, 20, 21–6, 228, 229
commercials/advertising 89, 106
Communism *see* Chinese animation; Czech Surrealism; Hungarian Cold War; Poland; Soviet Russia; *Tale of Tales* (Norstein)
computers *see* feminism and digital art; digital technology
A Conversation with Haris (Sofian) 104
Cooke, M. 192–3
Copy Shop (Widrich) 96
Crafton, Donald 16, 201
Creature Comforts (Park) 104
critical documentaries 108–10
critical perspective *see* Munitic, Ranko: Zagreb School of Animation
Cross-Sections (Anderson) 240
Crulic: The Path to Beyond (Damian) 102
cultural nationalism, China 62–9
Cummings, P. 129, 131, 138
Czech Surrealism 32–5, 45

Damian, Anca 102
Dassnovsky, Robert von 89–90
de Valck, M. and Loist, S. 69–70
Deleuze, Gilles 42–3, 45
Denise René gallery (*Le Mouvement* exhibition), Paris 118, 119–20, 121, 122, 123–4, 135, 136–7, 140
dialectics and analogy 32–5
Diary (Dragić) 171–2, 180–3, 194
digital technology 5–8
  Australia 234, 249–50
  Austria 96, 97
  Sweden 110, 111, 113
  see also feminism and digital art; 3D

Disney studio 12–13, 14, 26, 87
Snow White and the Seven Dwarfs 198, 200
DIY method *see* Antonisz, Julian
documentaries
interviews 103–5
non-photographic 100–2
visual biographies 102–3
see also Sweden: animated documentaries
Dragić, Nedeljko 171–2, 180–3, 187, 194
'drawings for projection' 18
Drawn from Memory (Ferlinger) 102
Dreyfuss, Lawrence 13, 14, 20–1
Dryje, František 46
Duan Xiaoxuan 68
Duchamp, Marcel 136–8

Edera, Bruno 6, 71, 74
Edison Light Show, Australia 236–7
educational films 101, 221
sex 111
Effenberger, Vratislav: 'The Platform of Prague Twenty Years On' 32–3, 34
Ehrlich, David 75, 77, 79
and Jin Tianyi 66, 72*n*
'Eighth Art': 'Twelve Principles' 12–13
Eisenstein, Sergei 60
Embryo (Thorsander) 111
Esping, Ingrid 110
Etkind, Alexander 156
European and American animation 13–14
experimental and popular animation 13–14
Export, Valie 92, 93

'Face Codes' (Müller-Pohle) 59–60
Fast Film (Widrich) 96
Fejkiel, J. 225
feminism and digital art
chorus of 'The Second Wave' 58–60
computer as artistic medium: absence of women artists 54–5
computer development and Father Power 52–3
images of Father Power and voices of women artists 51–2
'Manifesto' of women artists 56–8
Ferlinger, Paul 102
A Few Practical Ways to Prolong One's Life (Antonisz) 228
Fijalkowski, K. and Richardson, M. 32
Film Festival Studies 62, 69–79
flipbooks *see* Breer, Robert: flipbooks
Floterian - Hand Printing from a Film History (Cantrill and Cantrill) 242
folioscopes and mutoscopes 126–8
Folman, Ari 105
Form Phases (Breer) 118, 122, 125
formalism 239–41
48 Heads from the Szondi-Test (Kren) 91
The Fox and the Hunter (Hu Xionghua) 74
Frierson, Michael 202

'gamification' 17
Gandini, Erik 109
The Gang of Lidingo (Lindström) 111
gestalt
'Animation Spectrum' 14–18, 20–1
'animification' 19–22, 23, 24, 25, 26
Giesen, Rolf 72–3
Ginzberg, Lidiya 148, 149
Gizycki, Marcin 3–9
Glad, Teresa 111
Goddard, Michael 45–6
Goldmark, D. and Taylor, Y. 177
The Great Adventure (Sucksdorf) 109

Halas, John 23–4, 74–5, 170–1
Hamlet (Kovásznai) 24
Hand, David 200
Havoc in Heaven 71, 72
Heilborn, H. and Aronowitsch, D. 111
Helman, Alicja 73
Herzog, Werner 79–80
Hidden (Heilborn and Aronowitsch) 111

historical bridging 249–50
historical events, reconstructed 101–2
historiography *see* Chinese animation; Munitić, Ranko: Zagreb School of Animation
Holiday Home (Jansson) 107–8
Holman, Bruce 203
Honess Roe, Annabelle 100
Housing Problems (Anstey and Elton) 103
How a Sausage Dog Works (Antonisz) 216, 221, 226–7
Hu Jinqing 76
Hu Xionghua 74
Hultén, Pontus 119–20, 122
Hulterstan, M. and Actis, C. 111
Humanic Varese (Albala) 89
Hungarian Cold War: Kovásznai 11–12, 14, 17, 18–26
hyper-realism 199, 200

I Was a Winner (Odell) 113
Ideal Filmmaking 86
Image par Images/Image by Images (Breer) 121, 122–3, 125–6, 136, 140
imagination and remembering, phenomenology of 36, 37–40
Imitation of Life (Poledna) 14
The Imitation Game 53, 54
In the Grips of Sex (Antonisz) 221–2, 229
In the Head of an Old Man (Åhlin) 107
index cards 130–3, 138–9, 140
Inter-View (Martin) 244–5, 250
interviews 103–5
Iran 102–3
'inverse imagination' *see* analogy
Irzykowski, Karol 8
Iványi-Bitter, B. 11, 20–1, 24

Jabberwocky (Švankmajer) 37–40
Jansson, Birgitta 107–8
Jarl, Stefan 109–10
Jasmine (Ughetto) 102–3
Jin Xi 67, 72, 74, 75
Jung, Henin 102

Kabuki theatre 208–10
Kael, Frederick 21
Kentridge, William 11–12, 14, 17–19, 23
Khoo, Eric 102
Kitson, Clare 144–5, 146, 155
Klahr, Lewis 12, 16
Klüver, Billy 121, 122, 129
Kordjak-Piotrowska, Joanna 216, 217, 218, 223, 226
Kostelac, Nikola 167–8
Kovásznai, György 11–12, 14, 17, 18–26
Kovásznai Research Centre Foundation 18–19, 20
Kracauer, Siegfried 200
Krakow 215, 216, 219–20, 229
Krauss, R. 12, 18, 19
Kren, Kurt 90–1
Kubelka, Peter 89, 90, 120, 135
Kuo, M. 131, 134

Landreth, Chris 104–5
Lassnig, Maria 92–4, 95, 96
Leading Ladies (Martin) 246–7
Lee, Michael 240–1
Legrand, Gérard 32
Lent, J.A. and Xu Ying 66, 71
'Leo/Lisa' (Schwartz) 58–9
Li Dazhao 65
Libertson, J. 35
Lies (Odell) 112
Light and Dark (Martin) 248–9, 250
A Light at the End of the Tunnel (Antonisz) 225–6
light shows 236–7
Lindström, Maja 111
London
  exhibitions 13, 17–18, 21–2
  film festivals 71, 72
Lopes, Dominic McIver 7
The Lunar Eclipse of the Krona (Olsson) 106

M5 gun director 55
McCay, Winsor 101, 105
Macdonald, Sean 63, 66, 67, 71–2, 121, 129

McSpedden, Hugh 236–7
Maestro Koko 183–7
The Magic Brush (Jin Xi) 67, 72
The Magic Mountain (Damian) 102
Magister Kiziołł's Additional Digestive Goitre (Antonisz) 227–8
A Man and his Dog out for Air (Breer) 139
The Man Who Had to Sing 187–8
Marey, Étienne-Jules 134
Martin, Lynsey: Australian experimental animation 233–5
  background 235–6
  expanded cinema 236–7
  films 241–9
  formalism 239–41
  historical bridging 249–50
  influences 237–9
Memory of the Summer of '74 (Kovásznai) 25
Metamorphosis (Kovásznai) 23–4
A Midsummer's Night Dream (Trnka) 205
minzu style, origin of 62–9
Modernism 14, 21, 22, 23
  China 73
  New York and Paris 118–19
  visual and musical 177–83
Molnár, Vera 57
Monologue (Kovásznai) 22–3
morphing faces 59–60
morphological approach 168–70
Moritz, William 154
Le Mouvement exhibition (Denise René gallery), Paris 118, 119–20, 121, 122, 123–4, 135, 136–7, 140
Müller-Pohle, Andreas 59–60
Munitić, Ranko: Zagreb School of Animation 163–5, 172–4
  critical reviews and theory of critics 170–2
  genesis of an almanac 166–8
  theory and aesthetics 168–70
music *see* Simović, Tomislav
mutoscopes and folioscopes 126–8
Nash, Katherine 52, 55, 56, 57, 58, 60
National Geographic (Lee) 240–1
Never Like the First Time! (Odell) 111, 112
New York 93, 118–19, 127, 135, 137
Nezha Conquers the Dragon the King 71–2
Nights in the Boulevard (Kovásznai) 25
Non-Camera Chronicles (Antonisz) 214–15, 217–18, 227–8, 229
Non-Camera Manifesto (Antonisz) 218–19, 223
non-camera projects 213–14, 224–6, 230
non-photographic documentaries 100–2
Norstein, Yuri *see Tale of Tales* (Norstein)

Odell, Jonas 111–13
Olsson, Arvid 106
One Night in an Art Gallery 71–2
original copy and reproduction 218–23

pantograph animation 223–4
Paris
  Le Mouvement exhibition (Denise René gallery) 118, 119–20, 121, 122, 123–4, 135, 136–7, 140
  and New York 118–19
Park, Nick 104, 146
Paterson, Tony 239, 247
Paulus, 180, 183
People Wither Away Like Leaves (Antonisz) 225–6
People's Home and critical documentaries, Sweden 108–10
Persepolis (Strapi and Paronnaud) 102
phenomenology 40–2
  of aspiration 42–4
  of imagination and remembering 36, 37–40
Phobia (Antonisz) 220–1
Pikkov, Ülo 61–2, 222–3
Poland 3, 4–5
  Julian Antonisz: DIY method 213–32

Poledna, Mathias 14
The Polish Film Chronicles 213–15, 218
political animation 8–9
  Australia 238–9, 243–5
  Hungary (Kovásznai) and South Africa (Kentridge) 11–26
  Iran 102–3
  Poland 229–30
  Sweden 108–10
  see also Chinese animation; Czech Surrealism; Soviet Russia; *Tale of Tales* (Norstein)
Processed Process (Balsaitis) 240
Professor Balthazar 183–7, 189–90, 194
propaganda films 8
Purves, Barry: puppet animation 197–9
  cataloguing puppets 205–7
  a problem with realism 199–205
  puppet as human being in theatrical performance 207–8
    cinematic ending 210–11
    Kabuki theatre 208–10
Pushkin, Alexander 155, 159–60

Radio Alice 44–6
Rainer, Arnulf 90, 92–3
Recreation (Breer) 125, 126, 133, 136, 137, 138
remembering and imagination, phenomenology of 36, 37–40
reproduction and original copy 218–23
Revolver (Odell) 112
Reynoldner, Thomas 85–6, 87, 88, 89, 96
Riley, Vikki 241
Rotary Demisphere (Duchamp) 136–7
Rotating Broom Stick (Breer) 129
Rushton, Richard 29–30
Russett, R. and Starr, C. 135
Ryan (Landreth) 104–5

Scheugl, Hans 91
Schlecht, V. and Lahl, A. 102
Schmidt Jr., Ernst 94
Schwartz, Lillian 52, 55, 56–7, 58–9, 60
Schwechater (Kubelka) 89
Screen Play (Purves) 198, 199, 207, 208–11
'self-figurative' animation 16
semantic cinema 133–5
Seuphor, Michel 131–2
Sex on the Map (Glad) 111
Shanghai Animation Film Studio (SAFS) 62–3, 67–8, 71, 74–6
Sharp Engaged Film (Antonisz) 229
Siegert, Michael 91
Sielecki, Hubert 95
Simović, Tomislav: music and Zagreb School of Animation
  Diary 180–3
  diversity 192–5
  The Man Who Had to Sing 187–8
  Professor Balthazar and *Maestro Koko* 183–7
  The Substitute 188–92
  visual modernism 177–80
The Sinking of the Lusitania (McCay) 101
Sito, Tom 5–6
Slaves (Heilborn and Aronowitsch) 111
Snipe-Clam Grapple (Hu Jinqing) 76
Snow White and the Seven Dwarfs (Disney) 198, 200
Sofian, Sheila M. 104
South African apartheid 19
Soviet Russia 9, 19, 70, 100
  see also Czech Surrealism; Hungarian Cold War; *Tale of Tales* (Norstein)
Stampfer, Simon von 85–6
Story of the Eye (Bataille) 35–7, 40
Strapi, M. and Paronnaud, V. 102
Strukov, Vald 9
'Studio for Experimental Animation', Vienna 93–4
The Substitute 188–92
Sucksdorf, Arne 109
Sudović, Zlatko 166, 167, 171, 172
The Sun (Antonisz) 223
Švankmajer, Jan 35
  Alice 42–5
  Jabberwocky 37–40

Sweden: animated documentaries 99
developments 110–13
fact-based animation 105–8
People's Home and critical documentaries 108–10
The Swedish Theory of Love (Gandini) 109
Sweet Rhythms (Urbański) 222
Symphony of the City (Sucksdorf) 109
synaptic cinema 131–3

Tale of Tales (Norstein) 143–4
of dreams and visions 149–51
of eras and escapes 154–5
of expectations and frustrations 144–6
of gaps and subtexts 156–7
of the plane and the amalgamated 157–8
of plot and verse 146–9
of times and spaces 151–4
of wolves and incarnations 158–60
Tatsumi (Khoo) 102
Te Wei 63–4, 66–7, 69*n*
technology-art *see* Antonisz, Julian: DIY method
Teige, K. 35
theoretical perspective *see* Munitić, Ranko: Zagreb School of Animation
They Call Us Misfits (Jarl) 110
36 Characters (A Da) 76, 78
Thoms, Albi 234–5, 238, 239
Thorsander, Emma 111
Three Monkeys (A Da) 75, 76
3D
and 2D forms 200–3
CGI 101–2, 111, 113
Trnka, Jiří 67, 154, 203–5, 207
Tscherkassky, Peter 89, 90
Turing machine 53, 54
Tusilago (Odell) 112

Ubu Collective, Melbourne 234–5, 238–9
Ughetto, Alain 102–3
Ugly Feelings (Glad) 111
Urbański, Kazimietz 219–20, 222

Venice Biennale 14, 93
Venice International Film Festival 67
Vertigo 54–5
Vester, Paul 104
Vienna 85, 86, 87
film festivals 72, 96, 97
University of Applied Arts 93, 94–5, 97
University of Applied Sciences 96
Viennese Actionism 90–1, 92
visual biographies 102–3
Vinton, Will 123, 218, 220
Vukotić, Dušan 167, 169, 179, 188–9

Waltz with Bashir (Folman) 105
Wan brothers 62–3
Waterfall (Cantrill and Cantrill) 242
Weitzenfeld, Julian S. 31
Wells, Paul 12, 21, 199, 200, 201
Where Is Mama? (Te Wei) 66–7, 68–9
Whitewash (Martin) 243–4, 250
Whitney, John 54–5
Why Is the Crow Black? 67, 72
Widrich, Virgil 96
Williams, Richard H. 57
Wolf, Dave 6
women animators 91–4, 96, 102, 107, 111
see also feminism and digital art
World Festival of Animated Film/*Animafest*, Zagreb 3–4, 163–4
Austria 83, 96
China 71, 75–9, 80
Tale of Tales 144–5
Wu Weihua 66, 67, 80

Young Man Playing the Old Masters' Gallery (Kovásznai) 23

Zagreb *see* Munitić, Ranko: Zagreb School of Animation; Simović, Tomislav: music and Zagreb School of Animation; World Festival of Animated Film/*Animafest*, Zagreb